Ordinary Workers, Vichy and the Holocaust

Should French railwaymen during the Second World War be viewed as great resisters or collaborators in genocide? Ludivine Broch revisits histories of resistance, collaboration and deportation in Vichy France through the prism of the French railwaymen – the cheminots. De-sanctifying the idea of railwaymen as heroic saboteurs, Broch reveals the daily life of these workers who accommodated with the Vichy regime, cohabitated with the Germans and stole from their employer. Moreover, by intertwining the history of the working classes with Holocaust history, she highlights unexpected histories under Vichy and sensitive memories of the postwar period. Ultimately, this book busts the myths of cheminot resistance and collaboration in the Holocaust, and reveals that there is more to their story than this. The cheminots fed both the French nation and the German military apparatus, exemplifying the complexities of personal, professional and political life under Occupation.

LUDIVINE BROCH is a lecturer in History at the University of Westminster. She is the co-editor of *France in an Era of Global Wars, 1914–1945: Occupation, Politics, Empire and Entanglements* (2014).

Studies in the Social and Cultural History of Modern Warfare

General editor
Jay Winter, *Yale University*

Advisory editors
David Blight, *Yale University*
Richard Bosworth, *University of Western Australia*
Peter Fritzsche, *University of Illinois, Urbana-Champaign*
Carol Gluck, *Columbia University*
Benedict Kiernan, *Yale University*
Antoine Prost, *Université de Paris-Sorbonne*
Robert Wohl, *University of California, Los Angeles*

In recent years the field of modern history has been enriched by the exploration of two parallel histories. These are the social and cultural history of armed conflict, and the impact of military events on social and cultural history.

Studies in the Social and Cultural History of Modern Warfare presents the fruits of this growing area of research, reflecting both the colonisation of military history by cultural historians and the reciprocal interest of military historians in social and cultural history, to the benefit of both. The series offers the latest scholarship in European and non-European events from the 1850s to the present day.

This is book 44 in the series, and a full list of titles in the series can be found at: www.cambridge.org/modernwarfare

Ordinary Workers, Vichy and the Holocaust

French Railwaymen and the Second World War

Ludivine Broch

University of Westminster

CAMBRIDGE
UNIVERSITY PRESS

CAMBRIDGE
UNIVERSITY PRESS

University Printing House, Cambridge CB2 8BS, United Kingdom

Cambridge University Press is part of the University of Cambridge.

It furthers the University's mission by disseminating knowledge in the pursuit of education, learning and research at the highest international levels of excellence.

www.cambridge.org
Information on this title: www.cambridge.org/9781107039568

© Ludivine Broch 2016

First published 2016

Printed in the United Kingdom by Clays, St Ives plc

A catalogue record for this publication is available from the British Library

Library of Congress Cataloguing in Publication Data
Names: Broch, Ludivine M. E. (Ludivine Marie Elisabeth), 1983- author
Title: Ordinary workers, Vichy, and the Holocaust : French railwaymen and the Second World War / Ludivine Broch.
Description: Cambridge : Cambridge University Press, [2016] | ©2016 | Series: Studies in the social and cultural history of modern warfare ; 44 | Includes bibliographical references and index.
Identifiers: LCCN 2015040827 | ISBN 9781107039568 (Hardback)
Subjects: LCSH: Société nationale des chemins de fer français. | Railroads–France–Employees. | World War, 1939-1945–Deportations from France. | World War, 1939-1945–Transportation. | World War, 1939-1945–France. | France–History–German occupation, 1940-1945. | Holocaust, Jewish (1939-1945)–France.
Classification: LCC HE3070.S65 B76 2016 | DDC 940.53/1813–dc23 LC record available at http://lccn.loc.gov/2015040827

ISBN 978-1-107-03956-8 Hardback

*This book is dedicated to my parents
for having loaned me their car for a whirlwind archive trip
in August 2011,
and for absolutely everything else.*

Contents

Figures

Maps

Table

Acknowledgements

Over the years I have been indebted to far too many people and institutions, and whilst I cannot thank everyone the names on this page give some indication of how grateful I am for all the support I have received. First, there are a number of institutions who have given me both the financial and intellectual support to carry out my research. I would like to thank the Arts and Humanities Research Council, Brasenose College and the History Department at the University of Oxford; the Society for the Study of French History; the Pears Institute for the study of Antisemitism; the history departments at Birkbeck College, the University of Bristol and the European University Institute; the Max Weber Programme at the European University Institute and finally the History Department at the University of Westminster. Second, I am very grateful for the welcome I received in the archives, not least in Le Mans and Béziers when archivists went above and beyond to help me meet tight deadlines. Encounters with Marie-Noëlle Polino (*Association pour l'Histoire des Chemins de fer Français*) and Hélène Luisin (*Musée de la Résistance et de la Déportation en Picardie*) were vital to this research.

No book is written alone, and I have been lucky to have a number of scholars take the time to read and discuss my work over the years. I would like to start by thanking my doctoral supervisor, Ruth Harris, whose unwavering support and scrupulous editing has helped me in countless ways. She continues to inspire me. I am hugely indebted to Tom Beaumont, Martin Conway, Jean-Marc Dreyfus, Robert Gildea, Julian Jackson and Josie Mclellan who have carefully read my work at various stages – from PhD to book proposal to final manuscript – and whose intellectual support and friendship over the years have been invaluable. All errors which remain in this monograph are entirely my own. I have also been lucky to have rich discussions with Matthew Cobb, Hanna Diamond, Laura Downs, David Feldman, Michael Marrus and Dan Stone which have helped shape my thinking and writing over the years. Not only that, but being invited to give papers at

Birkbeck, Birmingham, Bordeaux, Brunel, EUI, Huddersfield, the Imperial War Museum, the Institute of Historical Research, the Institut Historique Allemand, Oxford, Paris I, Swansea and Westminster has allowed me to air my ideas and get amazing feedback which has significantly enhanced this book. Although they may not realise it, discussions with Herrick Chapman, Thomas Fontaine, Sarah Gensburger, Renée Poznanski, Georges Ribeill, Henry Rousso, Anne Simonin, Annette Wieviorka and Olivier Wieviorka have also been very influential. Finally, I am very grateful to the editors at Cambridge University Press – Michael Watson and Rosalyn Scott in particular have been extremely helpful throughout this process.

There is no way one can survive almost a decade of research and writing without the incredible support of academic and non-academic friends alike. I would first like to thank Alison Carrol, Eleanor Davey, Lucy Eddowes, Mike Finch, Erika Hanna, Melanie Janning, Tamson Pietsch, Rob Priest, Jonathan Saha, Andrew Smith, James Thompson, Tom Williams and Grace Vesom. These brilliant academics have provided much-needed inspiration and humour (and drinks) over the years. Grazie Mille to the wonderful Max Webers – Phillip Ayoub, Franziska Exeler, Eirini Karamouzi, Valerie McGuire and Akis Psykgas – for their enthusiasm and reflections in these final stages. This book is peppered with their support and insights. Many thanks also to dear friends in Paris, London and Oxford who have listened to me talk about the cheminots for a decade: Juliette Eschalier, Hannah Harvey, Nora Khayi, Claire Lemoalle, Richard Mailey and Virginie Toulemonde. And a big thank you in particular to Daniel Lee, who has pushed and inspired me since the first days of my doctorate, and who remains one of my greatest allies and trusted friends.

My family has been a constant source of support over the years. My grandparents, Joséphine and Hubert Marchal, lived through the war and witnessed the first years of this project. They continue to influence my life in so many ways. The Hinks family welcomed me (and my academic projects) into their lives. Phil Hinks, whom I met on the first week of my PhD at Brasenose, is now my husband. You put up with my commuting, my travelling, my monologues about cheminots and far too many things to list here. Inspite of this, you have shown me support, guidance and love at every turn. Thank you. Your passion and determination for your own career are still my biggest inspiration. I would also like to thank our wonderful son, Elliott Huxley, for waiting until the day after I submitted this manuscript for production to come into the world. Excellent timing on his part. And finally my parents,

Michèle and François Broch, who have come to know far more about the cheminots, Vichy France and the Holocaust than they probably would have ever thought. There have been no limit to your love and support over all these years. It is an understatement to say I could never have done this without you. This book is dedicated to you.

Abbreviations

AHICF	*Association pour l'Histoire des Chemins de fer Français*
AN	*Archives Nationales*
BCRA	*Bureau Central de Renseignements Alliés*
BNF	*Bibliothèque Nationale de France*
CAS	*Comité d'Action Syndicaliste des Cheminots*
CDJC	*Centre de Documentation Juive Contemporaine*
CDLL	*Ceux de la Libération*
CFTC	*Confédération Française des Travailleurs Chrétiens*
CGQJ	*Commissariat Général aux Questions Juives*
CGT	*Confédération Générale du Travail*
CGTU	*Confédération Générale du Travail Unitaire*
CLCF	*Comité de Libération du Cinéma Français*
CNR	*Conseil National de la Résistance*
DB	*Deutsche Bahn*
EBD	*Eisenbahnbetriebsdirektionen*
FTP	*Francs-tireurs Partisans*
FMD	*Fondation pour la Mémoire de la Déportation*
HVD	*Haupt Verkehrsdirektion*
LVF	*Légion des volontaires français contre le Bolchévisme*
MRP	*Mouvement Républicain Populaire*
MUR	*Mouvements Unis de la Résistance*
NAP	*Noyautage des Administrations Publiques*
OCM	*Organisation Civile et Militaire*
PCF	*Partie Communiste Français*
PTT	*Postes, télégraphe et téléphone*
RB	*Deutsche Reichsbahn*
Res-Fer	*Résistance-Fer*
RNP	*Rassemblement National Populaire*
SCAP	*Service du contrôle des administrations provisoires*
SNCF	*Société Nationale des Chemins de fer Français*

SOE	*Special Operations Executive*
TGV	*Train à Grande Vitesse*
TK	*Transportkommandanturen*
UNSA	*Union nationales des syndicats autonomes*
WVD	*Wehrmacht Verkehrsdirektion*

Maps

Map of France (1940–44)

Villeneuve-d'Ascq,
Lille
Arras
**Zone attached
to the German
Command in Brusses**
Amiens
Brest
Caen
**Forbidden
Zone**
Laon
Tergnier
Rennes
Le Mans
PARIS
Reims
Novéant
Metz
Occupied Zone
St-Dizier
Bar-le-Duc
Nantes
Tours
**Reserved
Zone**
Strasbourg
Orléans
**ATLANTIC
OCEAN**
Poitiers
Châteauroux
Dijon
**Annexed
Zone**
Angoulème
Limoges
Chalon-sur-Saône
Vichy
Nantua
Bordeaux
Lyons
Vienne
Grenoble
**Italian Zone
(June 1940-
Nov. 1942)**
Valence
**Free Zone
(after Nov. 1942)**
**Italian Zone
(after
Nov. 1942)**
Toulouse
Montauban
Avingnon
Montpellier
Aix
Menton
Marseilles
Toulon
Nice
SPAIN

1 Map of Vichy France (1940–44).

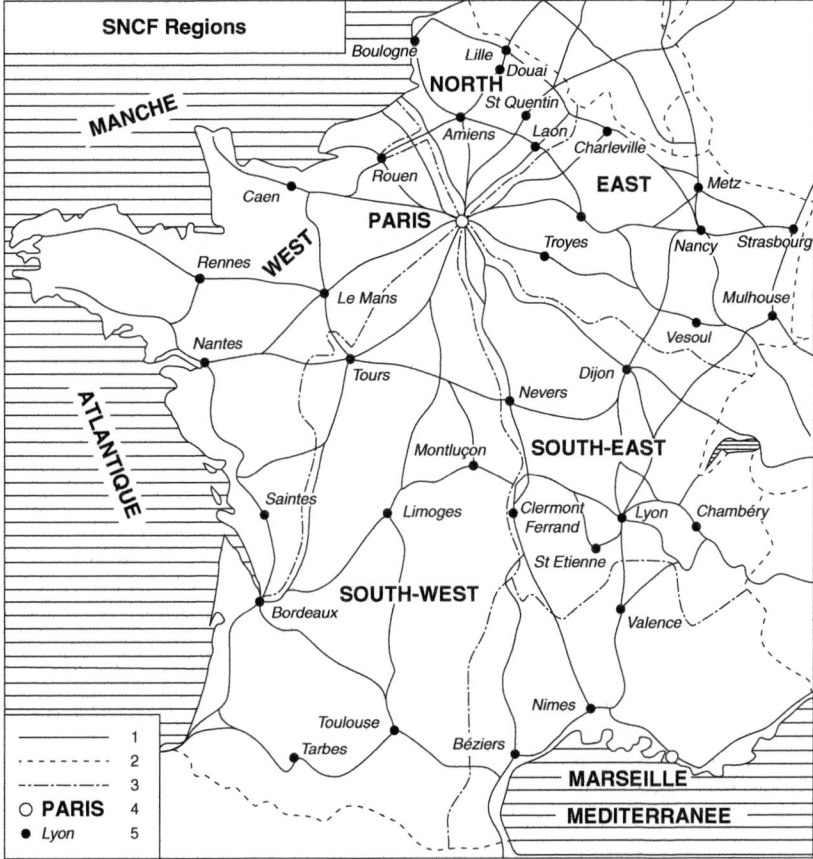

2 Map of French Railways.

3 Map of SNCF depot sabotages between April–July 1944.

Introduction

On 8 December 2014, the French state signed a contract with the American government to pay sixty million dollars to victims of the Holocaust in the United States. The money was to be distributed to the non-French Jews deported from France between 1942 and 1944 and who had not yet received reparations from the French state. The French would pay this lump sum which would subsequently be divided up by Washington and distributed to the recipients, 'hundreds of survivors, spouses, children and heirs'. Each survivor would receive approximately 100,000 dollars.[1]

This highly mediatised agreement between the French and American governments was the result of many years of debate around the role of the French National Railway Company, the *Société Nationale des Chemins de fer Français* (SNCF), in the Holocaust. Since the late 1990s, the SNCF had been repeatedly accused by American lawyers and plaintiffs for its role in the deportation of 76,000 Jews from France. This was not an isolated phenomenon, however, since similar procedures were being carried out in France itself: Kurt Werner Schaechter and the Lipietz family had brought claims against the SNCF in the late 1990s and mid-2000s. But the repeated attempts to bring the SNCF to trial in America had escalated over the past decade, and by 2014 the SNCF was facing serious economic sanctions as well as legal pursuits. Indeed, when Americans decided to build new high-speed railway trains in certain states in the late 2000s, the SNCF saw itself actively excluded from all potential economic activity. Legislators in California, Florida, Maryland and New York were vocally criticising the SNCF, claiming that it was 'an affront' to Holocaust survivors for this company 'to bid on projects funded by tax revenues from some of the very victims it

---

[1] 'La France va verser 60 millions de dollars aux victimes américaines de la Shoah', *Le Figaro*, 5 Dec. 2014, www.lefigaro.fr/societes/2014/12/05/20005-20141205ARTFIG00353-la-france-va-verser-60-millions-d-euros-aux-victimes-americaines-de-la-shoah.php.

deported'.[2] Guillaume Pepy, the Chairman of the SNCF, tried to appease these tensions in 2010 and 2011 by issuing formal regrets in both America and France in regards to the SNCF's actions during the war.[3] However, the pressure from American lawyers, legislators and victims continued. In 2013, a bill – the Holocaust Rail Justice Act – was submitted to the United States Congress to make it legally possible to sue the SNCF in American courts for its actions during the Second World War.[4] Until then, all legal claims against the SNCF had been rebuffed in American courts due to issues of national sovereignty. Although this bill did not pass, it added to the on-going tensions between Americans, the French and the SNCF over Holocaust reparations.

By paying sixty million dollars in reparations, the French government was putting an end to over fifteen years of relentless attacks against the SNCF for its role in the Holocaust. Indeed, part of the agreement behind this payment was that all attempts to either bring the SNCF to trial in America or to prevent the SNCF from bidding for high-speed rail contracts – which could potentially amount to billions of dollars for the French company – would cease. Yet this settlement also acknowledged an important fact which for years had been disputed by the American lawyers, legislators and victims involved in the affair: that the SNCF was not responsible for the deportations of Jews from France, that it had been a company acting on behalf of the French government at the time. The fact that it was the French government who paid the sixty million dollars, and not the SNCF, thus confirmed that the responsibility for the deportations lay not with the railway company itself, but with the French state.

This recent agreement fits into a longer story of what I will now refer to as the SNCF affair. The affair goes beyond these American disputes and resonates strongly with France's own memory problems.[5] After the Liberation of France in 1944, the history of the cheminots (French railway workers) was discussed through the lens of postwar myths and ideological struggles. In René Clément's film La Bataille du Rail (1945), the story of French railway workers sabotaging German railroads was framed in a broader discourse of French resistance and martyrdom. This threw the cheminots at the heart of the Resistance myth, and they were often

---

[2] 'High Speed Rail Interests & Legislative Hurdles', Coalition for Holocaust Rail Justice, http://holocaustrailvictims.org/learn-the-issues/high-speed-rail-interests/.

[3] Hugo Schofield, 'SNCF apologises for role in WWII deportations', BBC News, 13 Nov. 2010, www.bbc.co.uk/news/world-europe-11751246; Maïa de la Baume, 'French Railway Formally Apologizes to Holocaust Victims', New York Times, 25 Jan. 2011, www.nytimes.com/2011/01/26/world/europe/26france.html?_r=0.

[4] Holocaust Rail Justice Act, H. R. 1505, www.govtrack.us/congress/bills/113/hr1505/text.

[5] The affair will be discussed in greater detail in the Epilogue of this book.

mentioned in passing as great saboteurs in accounts of this period.[6] The brilliant historians Rod Kedward, Jean-Louis Crémieux-Brilhac and M. R. D. Foot all commented on the cheminots' usefulness in the fight against the Germans, but a lack of in-depth analysis only further upheld this heroic image.[7] Only two works, both authored by ex-cheminot resisters, Paul Durand (1968) and Maurice Choury (1970), examined the 1939–45 period specifically. But while Durand and Choury made valuable points, their sweeping statements about the heroic and patriotic nature of cheminot identity and activity was seriously tainted by postwar Resistance myths. Durand, a Gaullist corporatist, argued that the SNCF as a whole had resisted the Germans, whilst Choury, a fervent communist who had authored other works on communist resistance under Vichy, argued that only the communists had actually resisted within the SNCF.

By the late-twentieth century, however, the heroic image of the cheminot resister was being actively challenged. In the early 1980s, a few scholars began to ask some uncomfortable questions over the role of French railway workers in the Jewish deportations: if cheminots had been so involved in sabotaging German transports, why had they never sabotaged the Jewish deportation trains?[8] The question was never really picked up beyond the works of Michael Marrus, Robert Paxton and Annie Kriegel, although two little-known films released in 1984 and 1998 told the story of a cheminot suffering from an internal, moral crisis as he remembered his involvement in the Jewish deportations.[9] The pivotal moment came in the 1990s when the SNCF was charged for crimes against humanity first in France and then in the United States. Since then, the SNCF has seen a wave of criticism and accusation, not least in non-academic studies often written by journalists which have reinforced Manichean interpretations of its role in the Holocaust.[10]

[6] Coralie Immelé discusses this in detail in 'Le regard des historiens de la Résistance sur l'engagement des cheminots (1944–1997)', in *Les cheminots dans la Résistance, une histoire en évolution, Revue d'Histoire des Chemins de Fer*, n°34 (Spring, 2006) 39–49.
[7] H. R. Kedward, *In Search of the Maquis rural resistance in Southern France, 1942–1944* (Oxford: Clarendon Press, 2003, c1993) 61–70. See also Jean-Louis Crémieux-Brilhac, *Les Français de l'an 40*, vol. 2 (Paris: Gallimard, 1990) 326–9; Michael R. D. Foot, *SOE in France: An Account of the Work of the British Special Operations Executive in France 1940–1944* (London: Frank Cass, 2004) 158.
[8] Michael Marrus and Robert Paxton, *Vichy France and the Jews* (New York: Basic Books, c1981) 331; Annie Kriegel, *Réflexion sur les questions juives* (Paris: Hachette, 1984).
[9] *Gare de la Douleur* (1984), dir. Henri Jouf; *Je suis vivante et je vous aime* (1998), dir. Roger Kahane. Michel Ionascu, *Cheminots et cinéma: le représentation d'un groupe social dans le cinéma et l'audiovisuel français* (Paris: L'Harmattan, c2001) 65–6.
[10] Raphaël Delpard, *Les convois de la honte: enquête sur la SNCF et la déportation (1941–1945)* (Neuilly-sur-Seine: Michel Lafon, c2005); Françoise Laborde, *Ca va mieux en le disant* (Paris: J'ai lu, 2008) 95–6; Françoise Laborde, *Une histoire qui fait du*

The SNCF and the *Association pour l'Histoire des Chemins de Fer Fran-çais* (AHICF) soon realised the urgent need for a historical re-evaluation of its role in 1940–44, and Christian Bachelier, a discreet and thorough Vichy historian from the *Institut d'Histoire du Temps Présent*, was commis-sioned to write a new history of the SNCF during the Second World War. Bachelier spent four years sifting through the historical documents, and in 1996 he released the Bachelier Report, which is almost one thousand pages long, and is available on the internet. Despite being an invaluable source, the report is extremely difficult to read: it is less of a coherent narrative, and more of a collection of notes separated into neatly divided topics and sub-topics. The online version of the report also has a clunky format which is not at all user-friendly.

The railway community has responded to this new line of enquiry that casts a dark shadow over their previously glowing historical image. Following Guillaume Pepy's regrets (for the SNCF's involvement in the Holocaust) at the Bobigny memorial in France on 25 January 2011, cheminot trade unions were especially quick to recall the widespread cheminot resistance during the Occupation. The cheminot branch of the *Confédération Générale du Travail* (CGT), France's biggest trade union, declared that it was necessary to 'understand the difference between the level of German presence within the SNCF, the collabor-ation of certain cheminots and the fact that a large part of the company resisted'. The railway section of the *Union nationales des syndicats auton-omes* (UNSA-cheminots), which is the other big trade union presence within the railway milieu, stated that 'the necessary historical inquiry unto the company's role in the war must not lead us to forget the cheminots' courageous involvement in the fight against the Nazis'.[11]

Only a year earlier, when I was invited to give a talk at the *Musée de la Résistance et de la Déportation de Picardie* in Tergnier in 2010 to discuss the history of resistance and deportation in the SNCF, I was greeted by a mixture of applause and criticism. Tergnier was an old railway town, and many cheminots and/or their children were present in the audience of about one hundred people. Whilst some were grateful that I was opening up such a sensitive topic, others were less impressed. Recalling the experiences of their fathers and/or grandfathers, they accused me of ignoring the obvious fact that cheminots had been resisters of the first

---

bruit (Paris: Fayard, 2011); Alain Lipietz, *La SNCF et la Shoah: le procès G. Lipietz contre État et SNCF* (Paris: les Petits Matins, 2011); Jean-Pierre Richardot, *SNCF. Héros et salauds pendant l'Occupation* (Cherche Midi, 2012).

[11] 'SNCF/Shoah: ne pas oublier 'l'héroisme des cheminots', selon les syndicats', *L'Humanité*, 26 Jan. 2011. www.humanite.fr/26_01_2011-sncfshoah-ne-pas-oublier-lh %C3%A9ro%C3%AFsme-des-cheminots-selon-les-syndicats-463307.

hour. The letter I received a few days later – signed by several members of the community – further confirmed their reluctance to hear anything aside from a glowing review of cheminot resistance.[12]

An important, if small, literature has emerged around the cheminots, readjusting to some extent the Manichean approaches to cheminot history in the Second World War. Articles by several French historians –including Georges Ribeill and Christian Chevandier, leading experts on French railway history – have concentrated on cheminots' resistance experiences, giving new insights into their methods of protest and disobedience.[13] Another area of focus has been cheminots' involvement in the Forced Labour Service, the *Service du Travail Obligatoire* (STO),[14] whilst the AHICF has been particularly active in tracing railway history between 1939 and 1945. It has published a series of journals on cheminots during the Second World War, as well as conducting a series of interviews with ex-cheminots.[15] In 2000 it organised an international colloquium on the SNCF in 1939–45, presided by Henry Rousso. From the perspecive of the deportations, Holocaust historians have also added to existing literature and presented new approaches to cheminot history.[16]

---

[12] I discussed this event in a conference paper in Chicago. Accepted for publication, Ludivine Broch, 'The SNCF Affair: Trains, the Holocaust and Divided Memories of Vichy France', in *Lessons and Legacies XII* (Northwestern Univerity Press, expected Nov. 2016).

[13] Jean-Yves Boursier, *La Résistance dans le Jovinien et le groupe Bayard: mémoire et engagement* (Joigny: Groupement Jovinien Bayard, 1993); Christian Chevandier, 'La résistance des cheminots: primat de la fonctionnalité plus qu'une réelle spécificité', *Le Mouvement social*, 180 (Jul.–Sept., 1997) 147–58; Georges Ribeill, 'Les Cheminots face à la lutte armée: les différenciations sociologiques de l'engagement résistant' in François Marcot, ed., *La Résistance et les Français, lutte armée et maquis* (Annales littéraires de l'Université de Franche-Comté, 1996) 71–81; Serge Wolikow, 'Syndicalistes cheminots et images de la Résistance' in *Une entreprise pendant la guerre: la SNCF 1939–1945* (Paris, Assemblée Nationale, 21–22 Jun. 2000); Laurent Douzou, 'La résistance des cheminots, un champ ouvert à la recherche' in *Une entreprise pendant la guerre: la SNCF 1939–1945* (Paris, Assemblée Nationale, 21–22 Jun. 2000).

[14] Laurence Bour, 'La réquisition des cheminots pour le travail en Allemagne. L'apport des archives de la SNCF' in Christian Chevandier and Jean-Claude Dumas, eds., *Travailler dans les entreprises françaises sous l'Occupation* (Besançon: Presses universitaires de Franche-Comté, 2008) 131–5; Marie-Noëlle Polino, 'La réquisition des cheminots pour le travail en Allemagne. Une étude de cas' in Chevandier and Dumas, eds., *Les entreprises françaises sous l'occupation* (2007) 155–74.

[15] A full list of the publications by the Association pour l'Histoires des Chemins de fer Français is available on their website: www.ahicf.com/les-publications-de-l-ahicf.html.

[16] Jochen Guckes, 'Le rôle des chemins de fer dans la déportation des Juifs de France' in *Revue d'histoire de la Shoah, Le Monde Juif*, 165 (Jan.–Apr. 1999) 29–110; Denis Peschanski, *La France des camps: L'internement, 1938–1946* (Paris: Gallimard, 2002) 332–4; Annette Wieviorka, 'La Shoah, la SNCF et le juge', *L'Histoire*, 316 (Jan. 2007); Georges Ribeill, 'SNCF et Déportations', *Historail*, 4 (2008); Jean-Marc Dreyfus and Sarah Gensburger, *Nazi Labour Camps in Paris: Austerlitz, Lévitan, Bassano, Jul. 1943–Aug. 1944* (New York: Berghahn Books, 2011).

When the research for this book began in 2006, it aimed to better understand these divided memories over cheminot history which seemed to mirror France's own 'Vichy syndrome' in the late-twentieth century. Why had the SNCF's role in the Holocaust been silenced for so long? How had cheminot sabotage been mythologised over the years, and how much truth lay behind this myth? What archives were now available to allow us to understand the role of railways and railway workers in the deportation of 76,000 Jews? As Marrus and Paxton asked in 1981: why had cheminots not sabotaged the Jewish convoys? Whilst doing research in archives, however, I became aware of a growing need to look beyond these commemorative barriers and really understand the community of railway workers itself. A new set of questions thus emerged: What kind of pressures had the SNCF come under during the Occupation? What did everyday life look like for the cheminots? To what extent was their experience during this period tied to class struggle? This book, the final product of years of research and writing, is a combination of both approaches. Indeed, one cannot do away completely with the familiar categories of collaboration, resistance and deportation which had initially shaped my enquiry – these are far too entwined in the history of the cheminots/Vichy France to be completely discarded, and they remain useful tools of analysis. Rather, these categories need to be revisited and expanded. In doing so, one uncovers a more textured history of the Occupation that has to do not only with resistance and deportation, but also with theft, class struggle and wartime economic pressures.

The railway and working-class archives were particularly rich in material. First, there were the SNCF archives in Le Mans, where a very large quantity of railway archives had been centralised over the years. Held in one of the warehouses near the Le Mans railway centre, it contains vast amounts of boxes detailing the history of the Central and Regional Services, as well as SNCF Personnel. The archives there mostly offer a top-down perspective, allowing us to understand the personnel and material concerns of the Direction. Yet some collections – the reports on cheminots' impressions of working in Germany, the South-West disciplinary records, the collection of anti-national tracts – offer valuable insight into the everyday lives of the cheminots. Moreover, the archives in Le Mans contain every issue of *Notre Métier* and *Renseignements Hebdomadaires*, the SNCF's official paper before and during the Occupation. The SNCF archives in Béziers hold individual personnel files, and these are particularly useful when looking for specific names. The pension reports filed in these dossiers are often very revealing. Aside from containing a fantastic library of works on the French railways, the AHICF in Paris has a unique collection of cheminot memoirs and interviews.

Meanwhile, the *Archives nationales du monde du travail* (ANMT) in Roubaix contain a wealth of material on working-class communities in France, not least on railways before 1939 and the creation of working-class and railway cities – the *cités ouvrières* and *cités cheminotes*. There was also some fascinating files relating to the pre-1938 disciplinary cases in the era of private railway companies, but also to the strikes and purges in the postwar period.

A lot of the research for this book also took place in Paris itself. The Second World War collection in the National Archives (AN) is well known, and it contains a plethora of materials on railways and railway workers during this period. Some of the most interesting include Paul Durand's collection of over one hundred cheminot postwar testimonies which were all examined thoroughly for this research. There is also an abundance of material on resistance networks and sabotage during this period, not least on *Résistance-Fer*, the controversial railway resistance 'network'. The AN also had an almost complete collection of the monthly meetings between the Ministry of Transports and the SNCF for much of the period of the Occupation, as well as valuable sources on the deportation and transfer of Jews and non-Jews during the Occupation. The *Bibliothèque Nationale de France* (BNF) contains a collection of a cheminot right-winged review from the 1930s which certainly merits further exploration. In order to gain better insight into the deportations, the *Centre de Documentation Juive Contemporaine* (CDJC) contains many documents in German about the organisation of transports from the Occupied Zone to the camps, and is a necessary source when attempting to trace the Jewish personnel in the SNCF. The *Fondation pour la Mémoire de la Déportation* (FMD) also contains dozens of unpublished memoirs of non-Jewish but also some Jewish deportees who recorded their experiences, almost all of which mention their experience during the railway deportations themselves, even if briefly, giving great insight into the diversity of experiences.

Going to departmental and municipal archives helped to supplement a lot of the material I had already gathered at this stage. The archives in Aix-en-Provence, Marseille, Toulouse and Foix allowed me to collect some very diverse material, not least on local attitudes and behaviour, sometimes beyond the railway community. Local incidents including strikes, shortages and non-Jewish deportation trains showed the diversity of life under the Occupation. Looking at the archives of the internment camps in South-West France did not, however, really reveal anything new about the role of the SNCF in the transfer and deportation of Jews. Finally, carrying out a dozen interviews myself with ex-cheminots all across France allowed me to hear the voices of these men. This was fundamental for two reasons: first, I needed to become better acquainted with this community, and seeing them in their homes, first hand, allowed me to truly appreciate the uniqueness of the railway milieu. Second, their memories and their stories help to distinguish the individual from the collective in this study. The personnel at the *Musée de la Résistance et de la Déportation en Picardie* in Tergnier was especially helpful in helping me locate and interview ex-cheminots.

Based on these sources, *Ordinary Workers* busts the myths of cheminot resistance and collaboration in the Holocaust. This is not to say that cheminots did not resist, nor that they were not facilitators in the Final Solution. However, their history is more complicated than that. And in the dawn of the twenty-first century, as the heated and passionate debates around Vichy memory are beginning to die down, it is becoming possible to revisit the history of this period without getting completely entangled into the politics of the past. This book thus tells the story of the cheminots during the German Occupation of France between 1940 and 1944 in eight chapters and one epilogue. It takes an overarching chronological approach, starting with a history of the cheminots pre-1939 and ending with an epilogue which explores the rise (and fall) of cheminot memory. The seven chapters in between are slightly more thematic, exploring topics of accommodation, resistance and deportation as well as everyday life, cheminot professionalism and class struggle.

This book is based on three major arguments that aim to contribute not only to existing scholarship, but also to a more public discussion of the role of cheminots in the Second World War. First, cheminots were not all resisters. Railway historians Chevandier and Ribeill have given a more nuanced picture of cheminot resistance since the late 1990s, showing that it was more scattered, circumstantial and individual than it was organised or violent.[17] However, by intertwining national and corporate archives with oral histories and memoirs, and by looking back at nineteenth-century professional traditions and identities, my research fully re-writes the history of cheminot resistance. It explains that *Résistance-Fer*, still considered the official cheminot resistance organisation under Vichy, was only created after the war in 1945, and that there was never a real, uniform cheminot resistance organisation. As for sabotage, cheminots had refused to partake in industrial sabotage since the late-nineteenth century because it destroyed their beloved railway machines and risked the lives of colleagues and travellers alike. These feelings were still very much alive under the Occupation, and few cheminots engaged in sabotage as a result

---

[17] Christian Chevandier, 'La résistance des cheminots' (1997); Georges Ribeill, 'Les Cheminots face à la lutte armée' (1996) 71–81.

of this. Finally, as I explore hitherto unknown archives about employee theft and re-examine cheminot clandestine press, my book argues that cheminot resistance was not just about fighting the Germans, Vichy or the fascist authorities: it was also about fighting the SNCF. Cheminot resistance cannot, therefore, be explained by politics, corporatism or patriotism alone: cheminots' professional frustration was central to all forms of defiance and protest. This points to a much longer class struggle between workers and bosses, and to a shift in mentalities in the early 1940s. These new approaches fit into a rich literature on resistance by French and English-speaking historians alike.[18] Their works are a strong reminder that there is no longer a need to either embrace or reject a Resistance myth – rather, it is possible to approach the topic of resistance from a historical and more nuanced lens. Resistance studies are far from dead, and can in fact offer new and exciting revelations about this period.

Second, the book argues that cheminots accommodated and collaborated with Vichy. Until now, discussions of collaboration had focused on the SNCF management. Yet sources in departmental, national and company archives actually show that many blue-collar cheminots were quick to accommodate to – and even eager to collaborate with – the Germans and Vichy. This is largely because cheminots are far more conservative than is often assumed. Under Vichy, ex-trade union leaders joined the Vichy regime; small groups of right-wing cheminots hailed the rise of Pétain; cheminots bonded with the German railwaymen over their common professional interests. The list of purged cheminots from all hierarchical levels further exemplifies their hitherto unknown 'collaboration'. German historians had previously shown how German workers cooperated with the Nazi party and ideology[19]; in France, it is only in the past few years that studies have examined working-class conservatism and collaboration in the 1930s and 1940s.[20] This study of the cheminots is thus part of a new field of investigation.

[18] Kedward, *In Search of the Maquis* (1993); Julien Blanc, *Au commencement de la Résistance: du côté du Musée de l'Homme 1940–1941* (Paris: Seuil, 2010); Sébatsien Albertelli, *Les services secrets du général de Gaulle: le BCRA, 1940–1944* (Paris: Perrin, 2009); Robert Gildea, *Fighters in the Shadows: A New History of the French Resistance* (Harvard University Press, 2015).

[19] Detlev Peukert, *Inside Nazi Germany: Conformity and Opposition in Everyday Life* (London: Batsford, 1987); Tim Mason, *Nazism, Fascism and the Working Class* (Cambridge: Cambridge University Press, 1995).

[20] Joe Starkey, 'The Silent Minority: Working class Conservatism in Interwar France' in Ludivine Broch and Alison Carrol, eds., *France in the Era Global Wars, 1914–1945: Occupation, Politics, Empire and Entanglements* (London: Palgrave Macmillan, 2014) 111–32; Jean-Pierre Le Crom, *Syndicats, nous voilà!: Vichy et le corporatisme* (Paris: Editions de l'Atelier, 1995).

Finally, *Ordinary Workers* highlights that the relationship between Jews and cheminots, between the SNCF and the Final Solution, is far from straightforward, and it argues that the SNCF was not only a cog in the wheel of the Final Solution, but also that cheminots and SNCF directors were not indifferent to the fate of the Jews. This book engages with Holocaust history in three different ways. First, it outlines the SNCF's role in the Final Solution. Aside from the archival documents, it relied on major works by railway as well as Holocaust historians.[21] In doing so, it clearly explains how the deportation convoys were organised and financed in both the Free and Occupied Zones. This book also steps away from the deportations to examine the question of the Jews who worked for the SNCF. Indeed, recent studies have shown the value of looking beyond camps and deportation, not least those by Claire Zalc and Nicolas Marcot, which examines Jews in Lens, and by Jean-Marc Dreyfus and Sarah Gensburger, which examines Jewish work camps in Paris.[22] By going through the SNCF's personnel archives, I thus uncovered a fascinating story of networks of survival, of Jewish accommodation with the Vichy regime, and of the possibilities but especially limitations of bureaucratic 'rescue' and assistance. This approach offers a different view of Jewish experiences under Vichy, inspired not least by Daniel Lee's recent work on Jewish youth which re-evaluates Jewish life (and accommodation) under Vichy.[23] Finally, the issue of Holocaust memory looms large over this book. The memory of Vichy France is also still a sensitive – if not burning – topic, and beyond Henry Rousso's *Vichy Syndrome* the recent works by Sarah Gensburger and Marc Olivier Baruch show the fascinating tensions between history, memory and politics in contemporary French society.[24] Michael Marrus has in fact

[21] Alfred Mierzejeski, *The Most Valuable Asset of the Reich: A History of the German National Railway, vol. 2, 1933–1945* (Chapel Hill: University of North Carolina Press, 2000); Ribeill, 'SNCF et Déportations' (2008); Christian Bachelier, *La SNCF sous l'occupation allemande, 1940–1944, rapport documentaire*, 4 vols. (Paris: IHTP-CNRS, 1996); Raul Hilberg, *The Destruction of the European Jews*, vol. 2. (London: Yale University Press, 2003, c1961); Renée Poznanski, *Les Juifs en France pendant la Seconde Guerre mondiale* (Paris: Hachette Littératures, 1997, c1994); Tal Bruttmann, *Au bureau des affaires juives: l'administration française et l'application de la législation antisémite, 1940–1944* (Paris: La Découverte, 2006); Serge Klarsfeld, *Vichy-Auschwitz: La 'solution finale' de la question juive en France* (Paris: Fayard, 2001, c1993).

[22] Claire Zalc and Nicolas Mariot, *Face à la persecution: 991 Juifs dans la guerre* (Paris: Odile Jacob: Fondation pour la mémoire de la Shoah, 2010); Dreyfus and Gensburger, *Nazi Labour Camps* (2011).

[23] Daniel Lee, *Pétain's Jewish Children: French Jewish Youth and the Vichy Regime, 1940–1942* (Oxford: Oxford University Press, 2014).

[24] Henry Rousso, *The Vichy Syndrome, History and Memory in France since 1944* (Cambridge, MA: Harvard University Press, 1991, c1987); Sarah Gensburger, *Les Justes de France: politiques publiques de a mémoire* (Paris: Presses de la Fondation

carried out a rare study of the French trials against the SNCF, and the epilogue contributes to a further understanding of these memory studies.[25] Moreover, if studies[26] have previously shown the transnational effects of Vichy memory on society, politics and culture, the recent demonisation of the SNCF in France and America reveals the economic repercussions of Holocaust memory, placing France at the centre of a global memory culture.

Yet this book also contributes to a new literature on working-class communities. There have been studies exploring the significance of the backgrounds of workers in Vichy France, reminding us how individuals are affected by socio-professional communities and identities.[27] Historians have recently examined the men and women involved in French industry – from workers to bureaucrats – in the Vichy period[28], whilst others have given insight into French industry and production before and after the 'dark years'.[29] The study of daily life in Vichy France has also changed the way we understand the Occupation, and offers nuanced accounts of life in wartime Europe.[30] These works tell a different story of the Second World War, one that cannot be reduced to victims or

nationale des sciences politiques, 2010); Marc Olivier Baruch, *Des lois indignes? les historiens, la politique et le droit* (Paris: Tallandier, 2013).

[25] Michael Marrus, 'The Case of the French Railways and the Deportation of Jews in 1944', eds., David Bankier and Dan Michman, *Holocaust and Justice: Representation and Historiography of the Holocaust in Post-War Trials* (Jerusalem, 2010), 245–64.

[26] See epilogue in Tony Judt, *Postwar: A History of Europe since 1945* (London: William Heinemann, 2005); Peter Carrier, *Holocaust Monuments and National Memory Cultures in France and Germany Since 1989: The Origins and Political Functions of the Vel d'Hiv in Paris and the Holocaust Monument in Berlin* (New York; Oxford: Berghahn, 2005); Rebecca Clifford, *Commemorating the Holocaust: The Dilemmas of Remembrance in France and Italy* (Oxford: Oxford University Press, 2013).

[27] Marcot, *La Résistance et les Français* (1996); Antoine Prost, ed., *La Résistance, une histoire sociale* (Paris: les Editions de l'Atelier-Edition ouvrières, 1997).

[28] Michel Margairaz, *L'État, les finances et l'économie: histoire d'une conversion 1932–1952* (Paris: Comité pour l'histoire économique et financière, 1991); Xavier Vigna, *Histoire des ouvriers en France au XXe siècle* (Paris: Perrin, 2012); Marc Olivier Baruch, *Servir l'Etat français: l'administration en France de 1940 à 1944* (Paris: Fayard, 1997);

[29] Jackie Clarke, *France in the Age of Organization: Factory, Home and the Nation from the 1920s to Vichy* (New York: Berghan Books, 2011); Talbot Imlay, *The Politics of Industrial Collaboration during World War II: Ford France, Vichy and Nazi Germany* (Cambridge: Cambridge University Press, 2014); Philip Nord, *France's New Deal: from the thirties to the postwar era* (Princeton, Woodstock: Princeton University Press, 2010).

[30] John F. Sweets, *Choices in Vichy France: The French under Nazi Occupation* (Oxford: Oxford University Press, 1986); Shannon Fogg, *The Politics of Everyday Life in Vichy France: Foreigners, Undesirables and Strangers* (Cambridge: Cambridge University Press, 2009); Robert Gildea, *Marianne in Chains: In Search of the German Occupation of France 1940–1945* (London: Pan Books Macmillan, 2003, c2002); Pierre Laborie, *L'opinion Française sous Vichy* (Paris: Seuil, 1990); Lynne Taylor, *Between Resistance and Collaboration: Popular Protest in Northern France, 1940–1945* (Basingstoke: Macmillan, 2000).

perpetrators, but instead places workers and industry at the centre of this conflict. This book aims to do just that – and ultimately, if cheminots were in many ways a 'distinct' community of workers throughout modern history, their experiences under Vichy remind us that, like most French men and women, their attitudes and behaviour were those of ordinary workers looking to survive the war and the Occupation.

Indeed, beyond the three major arguments outlined here, the study of the cheminots under Vichy makes a significant contribution to working-class history. Traditional working-class histories examined political structures and organisations.[31] However, the data I located and analysed on employee theft between 1939 and 1942 shows the importance of studying subaltern activities and everyday forms of defiance. Moreover, the topic of class struggle is intertwined all throughout the book, from the emergence of class-consciousness in the nineteenth century to the post-war strikes of 1947. Cheminots were major actors in these postwar strikes, but this actually contrasts sharply with their absence from the general strikes in 1936, and their historic attitude towards political activism. Did Vichy change cheminots' attitudes towards political protest? This question requires much careful consideration, not least in regards to how political protest overlapped with resistance activities. After exploring the many facets of this question throughout the book, I come to conclude that Vichy was a turning point in cheminots' political but also socio-cultural identity, although the continuity of attitudes and behaviour should not be dismissed completely.

Of course, in a study of this kind – which focuses on a group of almost half a million men – there is an on-going tension between the individual and the collective. Is it possible to write a history of the cheminots? Does the term 'cheminots' not obliterate the significance of individual experiences, and thereby prevent any real understanding of the years of Occupation? Does it not reduce the individual to his/her collective identity? In many ways it does, and this is an almost inevitable outcome of writing the social history of a community. However, this book repeatedly relies on individual experiences and memories to show the complexity of attitudes, behaviour and experiences during the German Occupation. The cheminots are far from being a single uniform body, and if their community values and identity set them apart from other social groups in France, their diversity within their own community is nonetheless visible throughout their history.

---

[31] E.P. Thompson, *The Making of the English Working Class* (London: Gollancz, 1980); Eric Hobsbawm, *Labouring Men: Studies in the History of Labour* (London: Weidenfeld and Nicolson, 1986).

1   Cheminots

The centrality of the railways to the story of modern France is best understood by looking at a map. A bird's-eye view of the French railway network gives the impression of a nervous system, with the tracks as veins steadily pumping blood into the nation. (See Map 2) The heart is Paris, the central point which not only ties all lines together, but all departments, all regions, all people. The axes of communication which emanate from this focal point stretch out across the country, nourishing it with the flow of goods and materials. In the body of France, railways provided the blood flow of the nation; without it, the heart and the body of the nation would collapse.

And so in late June 1940, as the country had crumbled under the swift and humiliating German offensive, the French railway was one of the only things still maintaining the nation together. But of course, the railway was nothing without its workers: 470,733 men sat on the edge of France's greatest asset. They came from all corners of France and from all socio-economic backgrounds. Many had familial ties with the railways, following in the professional footsteps of their fathers or grandfathers. Most were blue-collar, skilled (or unskilled) workers, whilst 1,276 worked in regional directorial positions, 2,309 in Central Services and 3,236 in Financial Services.[1] The overwhelming majority were male, and the atmosphere was predominantly masculine and patriarchal. Very few women worked in the railway industry, which was considered to be extremely dangerous and thereby reserved for strong, skilled workers. A very small percentage of women were thus confined to less labour-intensive roles, such as level-crossing keepers, or more generally to social roles in welfare and medical services.[2] This group of workers – largely male, white and skilled – are known as the cheminots, and their story lies at the very heart of this book.

---

[1] SNCF/25/LM/1123: Situation des Effectifs du Personnel au 30 juin 1939.
[2] Georges Ribeill, *Les Cheminots* (Paris: Editions La Découverte, 1984) 95–6.

Now that France had just been defeated by the German army in a mere six weeks, what would become of these men? Until then their role had been clear: by working for the railways, cheminots had inherently been one of the main pillars upholding the national economy. But now the nation as such had changed: as of 25 June 1940, France was separated into different zones, and the majority of their territory was under German control. The war was still raging in the East, there was a looming conflict with Britain, and France had been de-militarised. Moreover, the SNCF was put at the disposal of the Germans as of 25 June, meaning that the cheminots thus worked for both France and Germany. How would they react to these changes? How would they face working for the Germans? To what extent did they manage to continue to uphold the national economy, and was this effectively showing support for Vichy?

By working for both Hitler and Pétain, cheminots were placed in a completely unique and conflicting position, and the only way to understand the sequence of events which followed between 1940 and 1944 is to familiarise ourselves with the history of the cheminot community since its birth in the nineteenth century. Indeed, the only way to discuss cheminot behaviour under Vichy is to first and foremost understand the roots of this community. By identifying the historical values which shaped it over time and distinguished it from other working-class groups, the complexities and contradictions of cheminot history during the Second World War not only come into sharper focus, but they are also easier to understand. Why did cheminots support the war in 1939–40? Why did they steal so much from their employer during the war? Why did they hesitate to engage in active resistance? Why did they not stop the deportation trains? Why did they rise in a national insurrection in August 1944?

The answers to these burning questions about cheminots under Vichy are rooted in the long history of this community from the mid-nineteenth century to 1938. There are four main issues to consider. First, how this community was built from the ground up in the mid-to-late nineteenth century, turning *travailleurs du rail* (men working the railways), into *cheminots* (railwaymen). Second, how this community distanced itself from active political protest in 1898–1920, and thereby distinguished itself from other working-class groups. Third, how it embraced, to an extent, the paternalistic, militaristic and hierarchical professional culture upheld by the railway barons and directors. Finally, the absence of the cheminots from the 1936 strikes and the subsequent nationalisation of the French railways (1937). These different insights into cheminots' history paint a more traditional and conservative picture of the cheminots than is generally assumed. Far from being hot-headed strikers, the cheminots were a largely conservative community, especially before the Second World War.

This did not mean they were not politicised or involved in defending workers' rights – but more so than other working-class groups, cheminots were tied to the conservative professional values which dominated the railway milieu, and incidentally which shaped their lives both in and outside of work.

1   From *travailleurs du rail* to cheminots

In 1814, the engineer Pierre Michel Moisson-Desroches from the prestigious *École des Mines* approached Napoleon with an idea to revolutionise the Empire: he would build seven large railways, which would all emanate from Paris and then spread across the whole of Europe. Territorial distances would be considerably reduced, and the French capital would become the centre of Europe.[3] Napoleon was immediately intrigued. Not only would it benefit his empire, but France could catch up with its historic enemy, Britain, who was leading an industrial revolution. Napoleon would doodle railway tracks or machines, dreaming of future expansion, centralisation and domination. But behind this great man and his drawings lay the real forces for railway construction: financial investors and engineers.[4]

And thus began one of the greatest modern adventures: the development of a nation-wide railway system. The first railway track opened in 1827. It linked Saint-Etienne to Andrézieux, was 22 kilometres long and used animal traction to carry coal in the Loire valley – this hardly resembled the grandiose ideas of imperial domination that Moisson-Desroches had painted. The line was founded by the engineer Louis de Gallois and the *École des Mines* graduate Louis-Arnaud Beaunier, who had both been fascinated by British railways, and financed largely by the Séguin brothers, Camille and Marc.[5] This initial success inspired many other projects, and work started on the first passenger line from Paris to Saint-Germain-en-Laye in 1837.[6] Yet the French elite was torn by 'the railway question'. Some were passionate supporters of railway expansion: in 1832, a Parisian play was based around the story of a father who refused to give his daughter's hand in marriage

---

[3] Pierre Michel Moisson-Desroches, 'Mémoire sur la possibilité d'abréger les distances en sillonnant l'Empire de sept grandes voies ferrées' (1814).

[4] Archives Nationales du Monde du Travail (ANMT), Roubaix.

[5] ANMT/12/AQ/25: Louis de Gallois, 'Des chemins de fer en Angleterre, notamment à Newcastle dans le Northumberland' (1818); Michel Cotte, *Le choix de la révolution industrielle: Les entreprises de Marc Séguin et ses frères (1815–1835)* (Rennes: Presse Universitaires de Rennes, 2007).

[6] Roger Hutter, 'Les ingénieurs, anciens élèves des Mines de Paris, créateurs de chemins de fer en France et en Europe (à partir de 1824)', *Bulletin de l'association des anciens élèves de l'Ecole des mines de Paris* (1964).

unless her beau invested in the Paris–Saint-Germain line.[7] Others warned against the social and financial dangers of the railway. François Arago, an esteemed scientist and influential politician, was strongly opposed to the construction of the Paris–Saint Germain tunnel,[8] whilst Marc Séguin himself admitted that his railway investments – counted in millions – were not fully reliable.[9]

Despite these mixed feelings, a law was passed in 1842 committing the French to building a widespread rail network.[10] Six major private railway companies emerged in the nineteenth century: the *Compagnie du Nord, de l'Est, du Paris-Lyon-Marseille* (PLM), *de l'Ouest, du Paris-Orléans* (PO) and *du Midi*. Jewish families were at the heart of many of these enterprises, with the Rothschilds being big investors in the North and PLM Companies, and the Péreire brothers at the head of the Midi Company, which soon merged with the PO Company.[11] Each time a new line was opened, the Companies organised lavish celebrations, inviting everyone from ministers to intellectuals to religious figures. Also known as the *barons du rail*, – the railway barons – these wealthy investors hosted extravagant inaugurations: red carpets, sumptuous banquets, anything for their guests of honour.[12] Reports on the 1843 Paris-Rouen inauguration ceremony described it as 'a meal (...) resembling the feasts of heroes in Homer'.[13] For the opening of the Paris-Lille line in 1845, James de Rothschild invited 1,700 guests including Hector Berlioz and Victor Hugo, and hired sixty cooks to prepare the banquet.[14]

But if railways were made on dreams of imperialism and engineering, they were physically built by men. The first railway workers were not

[7] François Caron, *Histoire des chemins de fer en France*, vol.1, 1740–1883 (Paris: Fayard, 1997) 84.
[8] James Lequeux, *François Arago, un savant généreux: physique et astronomie au XIXè siècle* (Paris: Observatoire de Paris, 2008) 407.
[9] Séguin pointed out that if the Manchester–Liverpool line had been successful for eight years, there was still no conclusive evidence that it was a perfectly infallible financial investment. Marc Séguin, *De l'influence des chemins de fer et de l'art de les tracer et de les construire* (Lyon: Imprimerie Pitrat aîné, 1887) 25.
[10] André Martel, 'Armées et chemins de fer en France de 1830 à 1918: pensée stratégique et emploi des forces armées' in *Armées et chemins de fer en France, Revue d'Histoire des Chemins de Fer*, 15 (Automne 1996) 216.
[11] See Pierre Birnbaum, 'Le rôle limité des juifs dans l'industrialisation de la société française', in Chantal Menoyoun, Alain Medam et Pierre-Jacques, eds., Rotjman *Les Juifs et l'économique: miroirs et mirages* (Toulouse: Presses universitaires du Mirail, 1992) 174.
[12] ANMT/2002/026/087: Inauguration du Chemin de Fer d'Orléans à Bordeaux, Section d'Orléans à Tours.
[13] Cited in Terry Coleman, *The Railway Navvies: A History of the men Who Made the Railways* (London: Penguin, c1968, 1981) 208.
[14] Caron, *Histoire*, vol. 1 (1997) 620.

French: British navvies laid down the first tracks in Saint-Etienne. It was not that France was short of workers, but rather that none of these workers had ever seen a steam engine or a passenger car. In the early-nineteenth century, only the elite travelling to Britain knew what a train looked like. So the railway barons brought in a skilled foreign workforce to start building the railways and train a French workforce.[15] This created tensions between the British and French workers, the latter resenting the fact that the former were better paid. But by the mid-nineteenth century, once hundreds of French workers had been trained, (most of) the British returned home.

The departure of British navvies in the 1850s created a sudden gap in the workforce, which the private Companies filled by hiring inexperienced French workers en masse. They came from all over France, most of them agricultural labourers looking for temporary work which would keep them busy during the dead seasons.[16] Skilled workers were later integrated from other industries: builders were recruited to lay down tracks, metal workers were sent to the workshops.[17] Such a mixture of professional trades, cultural backgrounds and regional origins prevented the formation of a unified corporate body. It also meant that bad habits were transferred from the industrial to the railway community, one of the main being drinking. This was a familiar stereotype of nineteenth-century industrial workers who often went to the *brasserie* after work. Working with a hangover – or worst, drinking on the job – was a serious detriment to security and productivity, and bosses resented these drinking habits. Measures were regularly put into place to curb these 'immoral' activities, but they failed to put an end to drinking. The railway milieu, made up of industrial workers and farm-hands, was no exception. On 26 March 1856, a train driver got so drunk that he walked onto the railroad tracks, impersonated a chief engineer, yelled random orders to those in earshot and then shouted some obscenities at a lady travelling on her own.[18] Of course, not all men working on the railways behaved like this, but there are many similar reported cases. Those who were caught drinking on the job were immediately fired, no questions asked, but even those identified as having a 'drinking habit' also risked losing their jobs.[19] Railway workers'

---

[15] See Coleman, *The Railway Navvies* (1968).   [16] Ribeill, *Les Cheminots* (1984) 91–5.
[17] Pol-Jean Lefevre and Georges Cerbelaud, *Les Chemins de fer des origines à 1890* (Paris: Europe Editions, 1969) 297.
[18] Caron, *Histoire*, vol.1 (1997) 275.
[19] SNCF/243/LM/10: Registres des punitions et gratifications du Service Materiel et Traction dans la Compagnie du Sud-Ouest, 1857–1911.

tendency to drink even inspired the liquor company Ricard for their advertisement campaign in 1900.[20]

The first railway workers were thus regarded as disobedient, unreliable and immoral by their bosses. Log books regularly mention how they ignored the strict rules of hierarchy, and allowed their friends to drive the locomotive.[21] They insulted their chiefs, or threatened them with language and physical violence. Sometimes they did not bother turning up for work, or refused to carry out orders. Amongst all these worries, theft was a particularly big concern. The railways were an ideal location to pinch some of the goods transported all over France, and railway workers were occasionally accomplices who received a little bonus if they helped robbers get access to materials. More frequently, they were themselves guilty of stealing wheat, coal, wood or wine. The railway barons were extremely frustrated by these men whom they considered to be untrustworthy and lazy, and they were always adding new rules and regulations to discipline their workers. Moreover, railway workers had such a public-facing role that they were under the constant scrutiny of the general public.

But from a worker's point of view, why should he invest himself in a profession which exploited him on a daily basis? The men working on the railways did long shifts of nine to fourteen hours on a meagre salary which was barely enough to provide for one man, let alone an entire family.[22] Not to mention the terrible conditions they were working in: night shift dorms were filthy, cold, dark and 'infested with vermin'.[23] Railwaymen also ran huge risks working with such treacherous machinery, and in their minds, injury was synonymous with death. If you were severely injured and lost the ability to work, you became unemployable. Little to no compensation was given to families in those days, so descent into desperate poverty was almost inevitable. Aside from this, postal agents affiliated to the railways suffered from a number of symptoms such as rheumatisms, loss of hearing and some even adopted a specific

---

[20] See figure 6 in Georges Ribeill, 'Les cheminots reflétés aux miroirs de la pub', Actes du séminaire, 'Les cheminots, images et représentations croisées' (2002–2005) available at http://rhcf.revues.org/109#ftn11.

[21] SNCF/243/LM/10: Registres des punitions et gratifications, opt. cit.

[22] Working hours varied from year to year, depending on which Compagnie they worked for, and what type of job they had. But over all, railwaymen throughout Europe suffered from excessive hours. See Peter Jenkins, ed., Railway Workers' Wages and Hours of Duty on the Prussian State Railways, 1890 (Pulborough: Dragonwheel, 1994). See also Martine Courbin, 'Les cheminots et leur famille dans le quartier de la gare Saint-Jean 1856–1905', Les Chemins de fer, l'Espace et la Société en France, Actes du Colloque, 18–19 mai 1988, (Paris: AHICF, 1988) 249.

[23] Camille Warion, 'Quelques considérations sur l'hygiène des chemins de fer', doctoral thesis at the Faculté de Médecine de Paris, (Paris: Imprimeur de la Faculté de Médecine, 1872) 24.

swagger due to the straining positions they held when standing up for long railway journeys.[24] Long periods of separation from their families also left railwaymen emotionally isolated. In the early days of railway building many workers lived nomadic lives, going from site to site, travelling wherever work was available.[25] Later, those working on running trains spent many nights away from the family home. Even for those working in fixed locations such as depots and stations, the hours remained completely asocial – machines were running around the clock, covered by three shifts – making it difficult, if not impossible, for a railway worker to maintain a traditional family lifestyle.

Cramped housing, excessive hours and limited intellectual stimulation were common working-class complaints during the Industrial Revolution. The condition of railway workers is in fact reminiscent of miners or sailors. According to nineteenth-century statistics, miners were the first victims of job-related accidents and/or deaths (railway workers came in second). As for sailors, their emotional isolation was far more prolonged than that of railwaymen, and they had to endure the additional dangers of the open sea. Because they worked in such difficult conditions, these groups of skilled male professionals were subject to specific medical research and statistical studies. Still, the railway workers believed they had it worse than other workers. Albert Schillings, the departmental head of the Orléans-Bordeaux railways, described it as the 'hardest, most subjugating profession that exists'.[26] Indeed, railway workers' jobs were more risky and physically straining. One second of inattention could see a hand crushed, a leg amputated, a body burnt to third degree. One train manager was so frustrated by the situation that he quit his job: 'if I resigned from my post, it is only because as a father of two my life is too precious. Every day I was exposed to a thousand dangers, and for what? A miserable salary of eight hundred francs a year from which they still deduct social security and uniform costs!'[27]

Some railway barons agreed that these conditions were unbearable. M. de l'Angle Beaumanoir, from the West Company, believed that they were exploited just like black slaves, whilst the Baron de Janzé accused

---

[24] *Ibid.* See also Prosper de Piétra-Santa, 'Etude médico-hygiénique sur l'influence qu'exercent les chemins de fer sur la santé publique', *Annales d'hygiène publique et de médecine légale*, series 2, n°12 (Paris: Jean-Baptiste Baillière, 1859); Edouard-Adolphe Duchesne, *Des chemins de fer et de leur influence sur la santé des mécaniciens et des chauffeurs* (Paris: Mallet-Bachelier, 1857).

[25] Ribeill, *Les Cheminots* (1984) 91–3.

[26] Albert Schillings, *Traité pratique du service de l'exploitation des chemins de fer* (Paris: Carilian-Goeury et Vor Dalmont, 1848) 4.

[27] *Les Inconvénients de voyages sur les chemins de fer, par un ex-Chef de train (X***)* (Paris: Amyot Librairie-Editeur, 1862) 13.

Company directors of abusing their privileges and maltreating their workers.[28] Other railway barons were influenced by contemporary theories linking professional satisfaction to output: that a happier worker would make a better worker. Small concessions would therefore hopefully distract the workers from revolting against the management. And so the Company carried out some small gestures: they built *économats*, these local shops destined to sell goods and materials at reduced prices, or hired private doctors to give workers specialised medical care.

But the meagre efforts of the railway barons were not enough to truly change the situation, and the appalling working conditions of railwaymen in the nineteenth century ultimately played a central role in the emergence of a more unified community. In a first instance, only the railway 'elite' unified: locomotive drivers (*mécaniciens*) joined together in 1848 to combine funds for pension and health insurance, forming one of the first small associations of its kind, the *Société fraternelle des mécaniciens français*.[29] Other workers, however, were not able to join this *Société* because they were not part of the 'elite' who worked on locomotives. Indeed, the locomotive was the most powerful element of the railway world, and those who worked on it were not only highly skilled and respected, but they were also better paid. Since many workers could not afford the membership fees for the *Société*, some created their own local and regional associations, notably in the Saint-Germain–Versailles (1853), the North Company (1865) and the West Company (1868).

In 1871, a group of railwaymen drew up the first large petition to make demands regarding salary, work hours and paid leave. The petition was rejected, however, since railway barons knew that requests made by such a small, disparate group of signatories could be easily swept aside. Indeed, each Company had different rules and there was no way of making widespread claims. Other petitions were regularly rejected, but railway workers persevered at local level: in the Northern villages of La Bassée and Haisnes, the townspeople and local railway workers sent a petition to the Minister of Public Works requesting the transfer of the despised station master, Mr Tomasi.[30] Whether these petitions were successful or not, what mattered was the visible emergence of small clusters of railway workers coming together to make demands.

---

[28] Guy Thuillier, 'La pétition des mécaniciens et des chauffeurs des chemins de fer en 1871' in *Le Mouvement Social*, 66 (Jan.–Mar. 1969) 85–6.

[29] Annie Kriegel, *La grève des cheminots, 1920* (Paris: Armand Colin, 1988) 30.

[30] ANMT/202/AQ/1224: Pétition des habitants de la Bassée et du Faubourg d'Haisnes tendant au déplacement de Mr Tomasi, chef de la station à la Bassée.

Figure 1.1 Cheminot apprentices in front of their first locomotive, *Renseignements Hebdomadaires*, 76 (12 Mar. 1943). SNCF – Centre National des Archives Historiques.

This sudden engagement with political action in the late 1860s and early 1870s also reflected a changing political climate. At the time France was experiencing a great turmoil within its borders, with the threat of German invasion and political collapse looming over the hexagon. The 1868–70 strikes signalled increasing industrial agitation which threatened the live-lihood of the elite, and although attempts to unify workers in a single, powerful national socialist body failed, socialist political ideas were spreading nonetheless.[31] By the 1890s, the rise of anarchism and direct industrial action was threatening the fabric of society, and socialists began to realise the need for more unified action.

The working classes eventually unified in the 1890s, when local unions – also known as the *Bourses du Travail*, or labour exchanges – merged into the first national trade union, the *Fédération des Bourses de Travail*. Yet the *Fédération*, led by Fernand Pelloutier, was considered by some as too radical and idealistic. A more 'tempered' national union emerged in 1895: the *Confédération Générale du Travail* (CGT).[32] Rail-way activists – who were beginning to realise that their battle for better working conditions could not be done alone – were inspired. In 1895, Eugène Guérard, a well-loved railway chief who had become head of the

---

[31] See Theodor Zeldin, *France 1848–1945: Politics and Anger* (Oxford: Oxford University Press, 1979) 367–9.
[32] Although the radicalism of the CGT should not be completely dismissed. As Tom Beaumont has pointed out, the CGT always had strong anarchist leanings within its ranks, and these would continue right through the twentieth century. See Thomas Beaumont, 'Communists and Cheminots: Industrial Relations and Ideological Conflict in the French Railway Industry, 1919–1939', doctoral thesis at the University of Exeter (University of Exeter, 2011).

Chambre Syndicale des ouvriers et employés du chemin de fer français[33]
merged his Trade Association with the CGT. He subsequently became
the political voice of the railway workers.[34]

From a disparate group of workers, the men working the railway were
slowly becoming a powerful force in industry, economics, politics and
society. Indeed, it was during the political turmoil of the late-nineteenth
century that the word *chemineau* was coined.[35] Originally, it was a pejorative play on the word *cheminer*, which means to walk along, or to wend
one's way through. The original word then developed into *cheminot*,
when it was added to the *Petit Larousse* Dictionary. The word now
signified rigour, obedience, punctuality, patriotism, quasi-militaristic
values. The cheminot was proud and responsible, and his notion of duty
knew no bounds. On a collective level, he was part of a community which
extended beyond geographical and hierarchical limits. From the company director to the most lowly employee, everyone was a cheminot.
Internally, workers still disputed who was a 'real' cheminot, and who was
not; but a sense of community identity had nonetheless emerged from
this sense of shared grievances and activism.

2   Protest, unions and strikes in the railway milieu

If the cheminot community was largely built on a shared sense of injustice
and a growing political consciousness, one should not overestimate the
radical nature of this phenomenon. The cheminots wanted to improve
their working conditions, but they were not spearheading the radical
working-class movements of the turn of the century. This is most evident
in the study of strikes in the late-nineteenth and early-twentieth centuries.
Strikes had long preceded the emergence of trade unions, mainly driven
by artisans engaged in 'craft specific' strikes and protests.[36] Since the
fifteenth century there were strikes of baker boys, of tailors in Paris, of

---

[33] Larry S. Ceplair, 'La théorie de la grève générale et du syndicalisme: Eugène Guérard et
les cheminots français dans les années 1890', *Le Mouvement Social*, 116 (Jul.–Sep. 1981)
21–46.

[34] Guérard could have chosen to align himself to Pelloutier, but the *Fédération* was
considered too radical it was 'to the CGT what the Knights of Labour were to the
AFL [American Federation of Labour]: A first draft, more radical, more idealistic, more
romantic than the big syndical organisation'. Jacques Julliard, *Fernand Pelloutier et les
origines du syndicalisme d'action directe* (Paris: Editions du Seuil, 1971) 102.

[35] Christian Chevandier, *Cheminots en grève, ou la construction d'une identité (1848–2001)*,
(Paris: Maisonneive & Larose, 2002) 8.

[36] Patrick Fridenson, 'Le Conflit Social' in Ebdré Burguière and Jacques Revel, eds.,
Histoire de la France: les conflits (Paris: Seuil, 1990) 386; Roger Gould, *Insurgent
Identities: Class, Community and Protest in Paris from 1848 to the Commune* (Chicago;
London: University of Chicago Press, 1995) 195.

milliners in the North and in Marseille, of cloth merchants in Normandy, of stationers in Avignon and even in Lyon 1539, a printers' strike lasted three years.[37] These strikers were initially described as 'groups of unruly, misguided (and usually drunk) workers under the sway of subversive middle-class hotheads', but scholars now acknowledge that they not only had 'self-defined interests', but also 'the capacity to elaborate and articulate those interests'.[38] As the number of skilled and unskilled workers grew, and as urban planning took on new forms in the nineteenth century, location and neighbourhoods became significant factors in organising active protests, not least in 1871.[39] The creation of the *Fédération* and the CGT twenty years later would truly propel systematic, organised and violent action at the heart of working-class protest.

Not everyone agreed on what tactics should be used to protest for better working conditions. When the CGT called for the first general strike in October 1898 and encouraged workers to sabotage their professional machinery, the leaders of the railway workers' movement bolted. Unlike the activists Emile Pouget and Fernand Pelloutier who encouraged violent action, Guérard warned against the use of industrial sabotage during the strikes. The strikes had to be carried out '[without] excess or violence towards chiefs or material'.[40] Some cheminots ignored his request, and the press related several harmless incidents: electric lines had been cut in the Paris suburbs, and switches had been blocked in the provinces.[41] Most, however, abided by this view. The very disciplinarian nature of their profession, their 'absolute submission to orders from above' and 'the fear of losing their work-related advantages make the large majority of workers oblivious to revolutionary discourse'.

The 1898 strike turned out to be a 'complete failure', especially for the railway workers. Hundreds of flyers had been going around depots, workshops and stations to rally the railway workers to the idea of a general strike. The story leaked, and on Friday, 14 October, the police and the military were stationed along tracks, workshops and train stations, preventing any kind of protest. Still, 135 men went on strike, 36 of whom were subsequently made redundant. Redundancy sparked great panic in the heart of railway workers, not least because they were often the sole breadwinners of their families.[42] And after 1898, the workers' unions became seriously divided: revolutionaries felt that direct action – which involved

---

[37] Henri Castel, *Histoire Ouvrière* (Vichy: Mouvement GLE, 1944) 9.
[38] Gould, *Insurgent Identities* (1995) 195.   [39] *Ibid.*, 197.
[40] Chevandier, *Cheminots en Grève* (2002) 66.   [41] *Ibid.*
[42] *Ibid.*, 60–3. See also Marie-Louise Goergen, ed., *Cheminots et militants: un siècle de syndicalisme ferroviaire* (Paris: Editions de l'Atelier, 2003) 231.

general strikes, boycottage and sabotage – was necessary, whilst reformists criticised 'direct action' for being too violent and encouraging unnecessary redundancies.

The wounds of 1898 ushered in a period largely defined by the major division between reformists and revolutionaries. Guérard resigned months after being elected head of the CGT in 1901, claiming he was exhausted by the constant pressures from the revolutionaries. It is likely that his resignation further alienated the railway workers from the general working-class mouvements of that decade. When the death of 1,100 miners on 10 March in the Courrières mines triggered a wave of protest throughout the country – 60,000 miners immediately went on strike in the Nord-Pas-de-Calais, and postmen, automobile factory workers, typesetters and artisans all followed suit – yet railwaymen were absent from the strikes.[43]

It was only in 1910, when two colleagues were made redundant, that the cheminots attempted another general strike; but the strike was another debacle which further dampened enthusiasm for syndicalism and active protest.[44] The strike spread on 12–14 October, but by the following week everyone had returned to work. First, there were ongoing internal divisions which prevented a strong, unified action, with locomotive engineers (*conducteurs*) and drivers (*mécaniciens*) on one side, and the rest of the cheminots on the other. Second, neither the Companies nor the state would bend to their demands. Finally, 3,000 employees were laid off.[45] The trauma of these redundancies combined with the absence of concrete results saw the number of unionised cheminots in Marseille drop from 1,008 in 1910 to 150 in 1911.[46]

The period of 1884–1910 saw the beginning of working-class unification, but the concept of the general strike was still new and not entirely successful. Furthermore, cheminots refrained from industrial sabotage. That being said, they had many grievances, their conditions were still deplorable and their profession was characterised by low salaries, increasing living costs and ineffective retirement schemes. Railway workers shared the same fate all through Europe, and a British railway clerk in 1911 wrote that railway horses received better treatment than the workers.[47] For many, collective action seemed the only way to change things.

---

[43] Fridenson, 'Le Conflit Social' (1990) 389.

[44] Chevandier, *Cheminots en Grève* (2002) 388.   [45] Kriegel, *La grève* (1988) 33.

[46] Héloïse Rouge, 'Gares et dépôts marseillais: histoire d'un syndicalisme cheminot 1890–1937', Masters thesis at the Université de Provence, Aix-Marseilles I (Jun. 1999) 97.

[47] *The Life of a Railway Clerk. A brief description of the main conditions of employment in the offices of British Railway Companies, and a statement of the case for higher scales of salary for all grades of railway clerical workers. Prepared by three experience railwaymen, etc.* (London: Railway Clerks' Association, 1911) 22.

The declaration of war in 1914 had, if anything, dampened the cheminots' enthusiasm from the trade union cause. Retirees were immediately re-integrated into the railway Companies, men were sent to the front, and the railway workers, unlike other workers, responded positively to this call to arms.[48] But by 1917, people were wary and tired of war, and their own personal grievances resurfaced.[49] In Marseille, most of their grievances revolved around salaries, but there were other issues like working hours or the suppression of women amongst rolling personnel.[50] The cheminots were also growing wary of their barracks, which had bad ventilation and which were often hijacked by soldiers passing through.[51] But Héloïse Rouge is careful to point out that the resurgence of trade unionism was not explained by wartime circumstances alone: 1917 also marked the birth of the *Fédération Nationale des Travaillerus des Chemins de fer de France, des Colonies et pays de Protectorat*, a project which aimed to unify engine and train drivers with other cheminots. This unification had been planned for the past ten years, and now finally came to fruition.[52]

The events of 1917–19 set the wheels in motion for a strengthening of trade union action and a growing confidence in strikes. By 1919, workers were demanding an increase in salary and an eight-hour workday; by 1920, they were out on the streets. On a cold day in January 1920, the cheminots in the Périgueux workshops came to work to see that the lavatory sinks which they had repeatedly requested were still not installed despite promises from management. This is technically how the famous 1920 strike started, although the battle cry for sinks was soon replaced by a much more burning issue: the reintegration of the *révoqués* from the 1910 strike. Gradually, the strike spread more or less evenly to other workshops. In Marseille, for instance, it did not start immediately. Even if trade unionism had recently flared up in the region, the debates about whether or not to go on strike were still on-going. Indeed, joining a strike was not a natural or immediate decision – but given the right circumstances, things could flare up instantly. By the end of February, 85% of the cheminots in Marseille were on strike.[53]

Similarly to 1910, the 1920 strike would have long-lasting consequences on the cheminot community, not least on their trade union activity. After the strikes died down in early March, they again exploded in May before collapsing completely, with 133 cheminots fired, others

[48] Rouge, 'Gares et dépôts Marseillais' (1999) 102–3.   [49] *Ibid.*, 107–8.
[50] *Ibid.*, 114.
[51] ANMT/202/AQ/1224: Revendications du personnel des chemins de fer, 1914.
[52] Rouge, 'Gares et dépôts Marseillais' (1999) 105–7.   [53] *Ibid.*, 125.

arrested and even tried.[54] The consequences were terrible for the trade unions: the CGT separated into those who wanted direct action (the *unitaires*), the CGTU, and those who did not, the CGT.[55]

And yet, we should not be too quick to view these first attempts at strikes and grievances as failures. Despite divisions and disinterest which came in waves, the strikes were important in shifting the power relations between the chiefs and their subordinates, and there were even concrete results like 'being paid on strike'. What emerged, more importantly, was that strikes encouraged the state to intervene in the affairs of the workers, usually to the benefit of the latter. This, Rouge argues, made it clear to workers that only through state intervention could they actually bring about change. The 1920s and 1930s would thus be spent with one main goal in mind: the nationalisation of the railways.[56]

3   A pro-militaristic, hierarchical and patriarchal community

Before discussing the project of railway nationalisation which culminated in 1937, it is important to take stock of the cheminot community's defining characteristics beyond their political activities. Indeed, the cheminots distinguished themselves from other working-class groups in more ways than one: not only did their attitudes towards strikes and sabotage show a hesitation and even disdain for violent action, but their socio-cultural and professional values were also separate from general working-class norms.

First, cheminots were not anti-military or anti-war; in fact, it was war itself which had elevated their status within the nation in 1870. Two years prior, in 1868, train drivers had been exempt from military service due to the strategic importance of the railways. Yet when war broke out in 1870, those in government realised that even this was not enough: the trains were vital for both the front line and the home front, and no one could be spared. Thus a law enforced in 1870 allowed all railwaymen to request exemption from military service, which Ministers unofficially encouraged the Companies to take advantage of.[57] This new link to the nation, and this added patriotic responsibility, put the railway workers in an interesting position: they were now at the peak of their bargaining power. Indeed, the 1870–1 war was the first 'modern' war where all men and

---

[54] See Kriegel, *La grève* (1988); Chevandier, *Cheminots en Grève* (2002).

[55] Christian Chevandier, 'La Répression des Syndicats en France, avant, pendant et après les "*années noires*"', Congreso Historia Ferroviara, Palma (14–16 Oct. 2009) 5.

[56] For more information about the relationship between the cheminots and the state, see Conclusion in Rouge, 'Gares et dépôts Marseillais' (1999) and Kriegel, *La grève* (1988).

[57] See Caron, *Histoire*, vol.1 (1997).

material were moved by rail. The role of railway workers had thus become paramount to military success.

The outbreak of the First World War confirmed the centrality of the cheminots to France's national security in wartime. Immediately after the Franco-Prussian war, military strategists and railway engineers combined their efforts to plan the mobilisation of the railway system in future wars. Between 1880 and 1913, seventeen different plans were erected to facilitate the total mobilisation of the railway in wartime. To maximise efficiency, for example, the average train speed increased from 25–30 to 30–35km/h, and the average weight of convoys went from 480 to 550 tons.[58] The latest plan was put to use in 1914, and 'mobilisation went beautifully'.[59] However, a number of unexpected situations arose thereafter.[60] Indeed, tragedies such as the Verdun and the Somme contributed to a crisis in the transport system: no new material was being produced, and existing material was worn out. The role of railway workers became more important than ever as only a cheminot could rectify the flow of machines. The relationship between railway workers and the military was subsequently strengthened, but much to the horror of cheminots, many ordinary people were outraged that cheminots were not fighting actively on the front line. They called them the *planqués*, or those who hid, stashed away, during the war. Soldiers on leave would often banter and even taunt cheminots, and by 1916 they made it a habit of humiliating cheminots, not least in songs.[61] Despite these social tensions, the material contribution of the cheminots to the war was evident.

Not only were cheminots being mobilised for unique purposes in wartime, but they were also 'soldiers' in peacetime. Indeed, industry was like warfare, with its casualties and risks, its patriotic and physical sacrifice: 'like a war, modern industry has its dead and its wounded'; 'industry, and modern industry in particular, is a real battlefield'. In particular, railway workers were constantly battling against bad conditions, fatigue and danger for the good of the nation.[62] And so, if many working-class men took an anti-military stand, railwaymen felt a part of

---

[58] A. Marchand, *Les chemins de fer de l'Est et la guerre de 1914–1918*, (Paris: Berger-Levrault, 1924) 9.
[59] Chevandier, *Cheminots en grève* (2002) 88–9.
[60] Marchand dates one of these 'unexpected' situations as early as 26 Jul. 1914. See Marchand, *Les chemins de fer* (1924) 39–40.
[61] Emmanuelle Cronier, 'Les permissionnaires du front face aux cheminots pendant la Première Guerre Mondiale', *Images de Cheminots, Entre représentations et Identités*, Revue d'histoire des chemins de fer (Paris: AHICF, 2007) 91–105.
[62] For links between war and industry, see ANMT/2002/026/119: Congrès International des accidents du travail (9–14 Sep. 1889). See in particular sections 4 and 5 on 'Physiologie Expérimentale' and 'Organisation et Assurance'. Mines and railways were

this body of soldiers who fought for their nation in *both* war and peace. This would distinguish them from certain sections of the working class, not least in the Second World War. In the meantime, it is important to underline that this transformation of their role meant that railway workers began to see themselves as an extension of military power.

There are resemblances between the military and the railway milieus, not least in the strict hierarchical divisions which run through both sectors. There was a clearly defined structural division within the railways, with every worker fitting neatly into a vast, highly organised and completely inflexible system.[63] Each private Company was divided into three major Departments, the first being the *Service d'Exploitation*, or Department of Exploitation. This Department was generally the largest one, hiring the most cheminots, and overlooking the formation and circulation of trains, the train stations and all commercial issues. It included sedentary personnel, like those working in the stations, the signalmen and those in the triage centre, but also some of the 'rolling' personnel, like the controllers, brakemen and yardmen. The second was the *Service du Matériel et de la Traction*, or Department of Material and Traction, which was made up of workshops, where workers built the rolling stock and carried out large-scale reparations; the depots, where they did smaller repair jobs; and delivery, which was in charge of delivering all this material to the necessary sites. The workers in this Department were either agents working on the locomotives (locomotive engineers and train driver, otherwise known as the 'elite') or the ordinary workers in charge of general maintenance and upkeep. Finally, there was the *Service des Voies et Bâtiments*, or Department of Tracks and Buildings, which was in charge of supervising, repairing, building the fixed material, rather than the rolling stock: rail tracks, buildings or level crossings. This universe was divided by regions, districts and cantons.[64]

These strict structures meant that railwaymen were neatly categorised and that, despite an overarching word which defined them – the *cheminots* – they all had different roles, skills, duties. As previously noted, this meant there was a certain sectarianism within the railways. Those who drove the locomotives were part of an undeniable elite which was probably as respected as it was despised by other workers. But tensions existed at all levels, and bitter disputes emerged. A depot chief was teased and taunted by his nickname, *gratte-cul* (rose-hip), the wild flower which can poke you. The older cheminots refused to show younger recruits how to work the

considered the riskiest professions, although it was generally acknowledged that miners were worse off than cheminots.
[63] Ribeill, *Les Cheminots* (1984) 21–32.
[64] See organigram in Rouge, 'Gares et dépôts marseillais' (1999) 30.

machines, or hid the tools around the depot.[65] Colleagues spied on each other and denounced any errors in anonymous letters to their chiefs. And of course, there were the tensions between the railway directors and the ordinary workers. Some cheminots despised the fact that these technocrats who managed the railways knew nothing about the reality of cheminot work: 'Although they disagree amongst themselves, technocrats are all bound together by solidarity. Like all chiefs, they are completely full of themselves. (...) Yet a machine cannot be run by a man's pride, nor by his authority. The machine only obeys those who understand it, and those who have taken the time to know it'.[66] Rather than showing the disintegration of the railway hierarchical organisation, these tensions showed the efficiency of a system which was never questioned let alone overturned.

Running the trains on time and in a safe manner required an unconditional respect for the hierarchical system and a strict division of labour, and cheminots were only too aware of this. In fact, the emphasis on obedience, discipline and rigour permeated everywhere in the railway milieu. Part of this was imposed from above: from their watches to their uniforms, everything went under strict inspection, and a breach of the (endless) rules was considered a serious infraction. This was not a purely French phenomenon: between 1849 and 1905, the rule book for the railway in Leeds had more than doubled in size, with the first rule reading that 'All persons employed by the Company must devote themselves exclusively to the Company's service; they must reside at whatever places may be required, par prompt obedience to all persons placed in authority over them, and conform to all the Rules and Regulations of the Company'.[67] But the cheminots themselves also embraced these rules, not least because a strict discipline ensured the safety of the cheminots themselves. Railway accidents were a European phenomenon in the nineteenth century, and France (along with Great Britain) repeatedly featured quite high in the international statistics. In terms of passengers alone there were approximately 140 victims a year between 1869 and 1878, and one must of course recall that workers themselves were often the first victims of any accident.[68] Moreover, rules and hierarchical

---

[65] Interview Gabriel Bonnin (22 Mar. 2008).
[66] Jean Alcide Paroche, *Un Cheminot face aux technocrates à la SNCF* (Paris: La Pensée Universelle, 1976) 8–9.
[67] Great Western & Midland Joint Railways, *Rules and Regulations for the Guidance of the Officers and Men in the Service of the Great Western and Midland Railway Companies on their Joint Railways and at their Joint Stations*, (1 Jan. 1905) 33.
[68] 'Tableaux statistiques des accidents arrivés de 1869 à 1878 sur les divers chemins de fer d'Europe et leur rapport avec le nombre de voyageurs transportés' in Léon Malo, *La Sécurité dans les chemins de fer* (Paris: Dunod, 1882).

structures ensured that in case of an error or an accident, responsibilities could be laid at the feet of individual workers, thereby ensuring the protection of numerous others. But more importantly, the very risky nature of their job required the need for a collective consciousness centred around principles of solidarity: by following the rules, cheminots were protecting not only themselves, but also their colleagues. As Ribeill underlines, this professional solidarity was noticeable to all, not least those living outside of the railway milieu.[69]

The example of Raoul Dautry's *cités cheminotes* – or railway towns – is particularly pertinent in showing the imposition of a strong sense of discipline from above, and also reveals the patriarchal nature of this community. Born into an unpretentious family with working-class roots, Dautry was one of a handful of men within the railway elite in the early-twentieth century who were concerned with the plight of railway workers. He had joined the railways in 1888 and become a director in the North Company by 1902. In the interwar period Raoul Dautry was a rising star of French technocracy as he continued to run the North Company until the nationalisation of the railways in 1937 when he stepped more firmly into French government duties. In the Phoney War he was in charge of armaments and eventually he was put in charge of postwar reconstruction.[70]

Dautry dreamed that cheminots could become moral and fulfilled workers: not only would this benefit them as individuals, he argued, but it would develop their sense of duty and professional pride, thereby increasing their loyalty to the Companies. If the Companies had devoted workers, the risk of social upheaval would be significantly reduced, whilst productivity and customer satisfaction would increase. Dautry's claims initially fell on deaf ears: the 1910 strike had been successfully repressed, and the railway workers posed no real threat. Moreover, why should railway barons listen to Dautry? But during the war, Dautry had distinguished himself: his organisation of railway transports helped win the Battle of the Marne. From then on, his reputation would precede him, and railway barons became more interested in his ideas.

After the First World War, Dautry went hard to work trying to resolve the housing crisis. Until then, cheminots had been unable to 'completely integrate themselves' into existing workers' cities. 'They are a world

---

[69] Ribeill, *Les Cheminots* (1984) 21–6, 34–5; François Caron, *Histoire eds chemins de fer en France, 1883–1937*, vol. 2 (Paris: Librarie Arthème Fayard, 2005) 432–4.

[70] Dautry was accused of going into hiding during the German Occupation, when he retrieved himself from public and political life and stayed, with his wife in their country home. See Rémi Baudouï, *Raoul Dautry: 1880–1951: la technocratie de la République* (Paris: Balland, 1992).

apart', Martine Courbin states.[71] In contrast, Dautry's *cités* aimed to educate and transform the working classes, to give them a sense of community, loyalty and unity, and to reconnect industrial workers with nature.[72] Over thirty cheminot garden-cities were created in Northern France between 1920 and 1928.[73] The most spectacular was Tergnier, built to fit perfect ideals of architecture and social living:[74] 'The idea of a railway world materialises, and is no longer a distant image, when flying over a city such as Tergnier, with its depots and triage centres, its 26 kilometres of street which separate tidy homes over 110 hectares'.[75] The cities provided affordable housing and moral benefits for its residents. They were run by a Board which, aside from its traditional administrative duties, was in charge of making sure that 'everyone participated in the collective well-being'.[76] Indeed, the aim was to create living, not lethargic, spaces. A number of cultural activities were thus organised, from children's Summer Camps, to film showings, to sports games.[77] Cheminots' wives and daughters could perfect their skills at home-economic classes organised in the *cités*, and they became so popular in some areas that the Councils asked to build extra communal spaces.[78] Moreover, Dautry hoped to turn your average cheminot into a worker-gardener (*ouvrier-jardinier*), an idea he got whilst admiring the First Great Western Railway's impeccable flowerbeds in Great Britain.[79] By cultivating their own flowerbeds in garden-cities and on railway sites, he hoped to offer cheminots an outlet for their individual creativity – and an alternative to the local bars. Award ceremonies were even organised for the nicest gardens.[80]

Dautry's mantra was that 'Man works well only if he is healthy and happy. His domestic happiness will dictate his professional output. (...) Physical health, moral health and social health all go hand in hand'.[81] Behind this corporate paternalism lay a desire to transform the skilled

---

[71] See Courbin, 'Les cheminots et leur famille' (1988) 245.
[72] Christian Chevandier, 'Les Cités PLM dans l'agglomération lyonnaise au cours des années 1930: les cas de Vanissieux et d'Oullins', *Les Chemins de fer, l'Espace et la Société en France*, Actes du Colloque, 18–19 May 1988 (Paris: AHICF, 1988) 256–7.
[73] For more on these cités, see AN/307/AP/60: Le Réseau du Nord devant la Crise (1936), Ermont et Moulin-Neuf, Chemin de Fer du Nord, L'Atelier de la Voie.
[74] Chevandier, 'Les Cités PLM' (1988) 253–63.
[75] Jean Falaize and Henri Girod-Eymery, *A travers les Chemins de Fer, de l'origine à nos jours* (Paris: Denoël, 1948) 358.
[76] AN/307/AP/60: Le Réseau du Nord devant la Crise (1936) 79.   [77] *Ibid.*, 84.
[78] ANMT/202/AQ/1191: Letter (17 Feb. 1928) from Tettlin to Javary.
[79] C. E. R. Sherrington, *Raoul Dautry: An Appreciation* (Belmont, Surrey: The Author, 1950).
[80] ANMT/202/AQ/1192: Rapport du Comité (19 Dec. 1925) signed by Javary.
[81] *Ibid.*, Bulletin du Ministre du Travail (dated c. Jun. 1923) 176.

worker into a moral, apolitical being. 'I wish', Dautry said, 'for religious and political fervours to be buried at the bottom of the hearts of railway workers as long as they are in the city. Indeed, such fervours only serve to divide people and should therefore be expressed outside of the city. I find it necessary to rid the city of all divisive elements. (...) I can only accept things that unify cheminots'.[82] Of course, this was not completely successful. In 1921, a communist-led railway workers' union (*Fondation Nationale des Cheminots Unitaires*) was created. Although it was not a mass movement, it had between 700 and 2,500 cheminot members from each Company. Moreover, religious sentiment could not be squelched: residents continued to ask for the erection of local churches, although the Company directors repeatedly refused to finance such projects.

Politicised acts of defiance in the 1920s and 1930s confirm Dautry's inability to unite the workforce around purely professional ideals. In 1926, fourteen depots in the broader Paris region were suspected of concealing around '7,000 firearms from Belgium or Germany, financed with Moscow's money'. According to Beaumont, 'plans for a general strike and widespread sabotage of the rail arteries were thought to be afoot'. Later, in April 1929 and May–June 1930, two strikes occurred in a repair centre north of Grenoble, 'demonstrating for the authorities, the often troubling mix of labour militancy, Communist agitation and the presence of migrant workers in an important industrial centre'. Indeed, the government feared that the rise of communism amongst railwaymen would jeopardise the railways, so central to France's survival.[83]

The cheminot community was not perfectly uniform, and there were tensions, fractures and problems; nonetheless, a cheminot spirit, or '*esprit cheminot*', rooted in disciplinary, militaristic and hierarchical values shaped not only the policies of the railway companies and the professional environment of their workers, but also the personal, familial, everyday lives of the cheminots. The cheminot profession was in fact a family affair: as a woman you were a *femme de ch'minot* (wife) or a *fille de ch'minot* (daughter). Sons, *fils de ch'minots*, were expected to follow in their fathers' footsteps. As Huckendubler commented in his interview: 'You recognised the cheminot milieu, it was often made up of the sons of humble people, humble railwaymen (...) Parents were very proud when their sons entered the railways. As a result of this, I immediately found

---

[82] Rémi Baudouï, 'La cité-jardin de Tergnier de la Compagnie du Nord, 1921–1950: Eléments d'analyse d'un modèle de société cheminote', *Les Chemins de fer, l'Espace et la Société en France*, Actes du Colloque, 18–19 May 1988 (Paris: AHICF, 1988) 268.

[83] Beaumont, 'Communists and Cheminots' (2011) 84, 88–9.

myself immersed in this cheminot atmosphere'.[84] Professional solidarity
and respect were founding principles, and the shared quasi-militaristic
values of punctuality, obedience, security and unionism cemented this
railway community in many ways. As the shadow of Nazism loomed over
Europe, and the country stepped into total war for the second time in
thirty years, these traditions would be embraced more strongly than ever
before.

4   The 1936 strike and the birth of the SCNF

To what extent does this conservatism – professional, political, cultural –
explain the cheminots' absence from the general strike in 1936? Indeed, by
the end of the 1930s workers united in the strike of 1936, a landmark
protest in French history, to improve their working conditions. The cheminots, however, were visibly absent. How to explain this? What does this
say about their commitment to political activism? Were they simply disin-
terested? Not at all, and it is important to understand how cheminots'
unique circumstances shaped their attitudes towards this general strike.

First, one must understand that the 1936 strikes were not inevitable.
The 1920s and 1930s had been mostly marked by divisions within the
left, not least after the birth of the French Communist Party (PCF) in
1920.[85] Those who did not believe in communism left trade unions
altogether; others believed they should continue negotiation; and others
still wanted to look to Moscow for directives. By 1922, trade union
activity was mainly divided between the CGT (who were anti-
revolutionary), the CGTU (the *unitaires*, or radicals, who looked towards
the Communist International) and the *Confédération Française des Travailleurs Chrétiens* (CFTC, the Christian union born in 1919).

But internal tensions died down in the mid-thirties as international
and national politics threatened the workers. First, there was the rise of
fascism in Europe. Following the riots of 6 February 1934, the CGT
declared a general strike in objection to fascism on 12 February in which
100,000 workers took part. Second, the Laval government passed crippling decrees in 1935: after forcibly lowering bonuses, indemnities and
family allocations, the government reduced the budget of public works
by 10%.[86] But the 'fratricidal struggle between CGT and CGTU' was

---

[84] AHICF: Interview transcript, Jean-Claude Huckendubler (19 Oct. 1999) 3.
[85] For a history of the Popular Front, see Julian Jackson, *The Popular Front in France:
Defending Democracy, 1934–1938* (Cambridge: Cambridge University Press, 1988).
[86] Projects of unification were being planned since 1924. Vigna, *Histoire des ouvriers* (2012) 121.
See also Julian Jackson, *France: The Dark Years 1940–1944* (Oxford: Oxford University Press,
2002) 65–80.

Figure 1.2 'What does a cheminot think about? ... Being on time!'
Renseignements Hebdomadaires, 57 (23 Oct. 1942). SNCF – Centre
National des Archives Historiques.

coming to an end: in January 1936, the Communists, Socialists and Radicals signed a Popular Front programme to confront these growing problems.[87]

The Popular Front won a landslide victory in May 1936, propelling the socialist Léon Blum to the head of the government. But winning an election was not enough – workers wanted to be heard. The boiling of working-class dissatisfaction – and also of local power struggles over who had control of the unions and the workers – erupted that year, and 'close to two million workers were involved in over 12,000 strikes' between May and July. Employers and the government succumbed to many demands, but 'much to the surprise of both [the] CGT and government' they did not return to work. On 11 June Maurice Thorez, the leader of the PCF, felt obliged to intervene as he explained to the workers that they 'should know how to end a strike'.[88] The strikes eventually ended, and these events ultimately inspired a new generation. CGT subscriptions went from 785,000 in 1935 to 4.1 million in 1937[89], and workers had won considerable battles, not least the forty-hour working week.[90] Even the popular image of ordinary workers was improving in films such as *La Belle Équipe* (1936), *La Bête Humaine* (1938), the CGT-sponsored *Grèves d'occupation* (1936) or the trilogy *Sur les routes d'acier, Les Bâtisseurs, Les Metallos* (1938).[91]

The cheminots were not isolated from these events. In 1932, the cheminot Pierre Semard, an *unitaire* trade union leader, viciously denounced the socialists and all those who associated with them in his pamphlet entitled *Brochette of Renegades*.[92] But the fears of the mid-1930s inspired some cheminots to join ranks with other workers. Although there is no way of telling how many cheminots participated in the 1934 anti-fascist riots, a group of them in Marseille wrote to the prefect to justify their involvement in the strikes: they 'had not acted out of lack of professional duty, but in adherence with their syndicalist and republican values'.[93] In December 1935, Semard and Jean Jarrigion (moderate) became the leaders of the railway trade union which officially adhered to the CGT in March 1936.[94]

Yet cheminots were noticeably absent from the 1936 strikes, and this for two main reasons. First, the ramifications of the 1898, 1910 and 1920

---

[87] Jackson, *Popular Front* (1988) 92.
[88] H. R. Kedward, *La Vie en Bleu: France and the French since 1900* (London: Penguin, 2006) 186–7.
[89] Vigna, *Histoire des ouvriers* (2012) 129.
[90] SNCF/25/LM/1123: Extract from the *Journal Officiel* of 28 Aug. 1937 (Application of the law of 21 Jun. 1936).
[91] Vigna, *Histoire des ouvriers* (2012) 132.
[92] ADBR/28/J/273: Pierre Semard, *Brochette de Rénégats* (Paris: Publication du Parti Communiste Français, 1932).
[93] Rouge, 'Gares et dépôts Marseillais' (1999) 179.   [94] *Ibid.*, 180.

strikes, especially in terms of redundancies, still traumatised the cheminot community who were not inclined to risk their livelihood for meagre – if any – results. Second, and most importantly, cheminots were on the verge of winning a long political battle: the nationalisation of the railways. The nationalisation of the railways had been on the cards since the nineteenth century, and the state had always been partially involved in the railways.[95] The French government funded the tracks, while the companies were in charge of running the trains. In 1908–9, the *Réseau de l'État* (State Network) which owned a few private railway companies bought out the *Réseau de l'Ouest* (West Network). In wartime, the state also had total control over the railways.

After the First World War, cheminots became more and more convinced that a state-led railway would allow for true, radical change: only through nationalisation could they ensure long-term professional security, and the way to obtain this was not through strikes, but negotiation. This falls in line with Michael Seidman's argument that the urge to nationalise industries was greater than ever before during the interwar period, and that revolutionary fervour was side-lined from the trade unions. 'The reformism of Albert Thomas, questioning revolutionary syndicalism before World War I, had come to dominate thinking concerning workers' control', he stated.[96] It is important to underline that trade union members did not all support nationalisation, however, precisely because nationalisation was perceived as an abandonment of revolutionary principle.[97] Moreover, nationalisation was not just the result of trade unions and workers' mobilisation. The interwar period had seen an acute crisis amongst the private rail companies which were running huge deficits, and the only way out seemed to be to get the state involved.

A law was passed on 31 August 1937 to create a national railway, and the SNCF was officially born on 1 January 1938. The SNCF was defined as a semi-public limited company, with the state owning 51% and the other 49% resting in the hands of private owners, not least the Rothschilds. Nationalisation did not signal a serious shuffle of the railway system, and the structure of the newly erected SNCF remained largely the same. The old structure flowed almost imperceptibly into the new one.[98] The five

[95] Zeldin, *France 1848–1945* (1979) 189.
[96] Michael Seidman, *Workers Against Work: Labor in Paris and Barcelona during the Popular Fronts* (Oxford: University of California Press, 1991) 195.
[97] Cheminots' ambivalence towards nationalisation is discussed in Serge Wolikow, ed., *Pierre Semard: Engagements, Discipline et Fidélité* (Paris: Cherche Midi, 2007).
[98] For more information on how each service worked, see AN/F/7/14913: Notice sur l'Organisation Général des Services de la SNCF et les Relations à Etablir avec ces

main private Companies were essentially transformed into five Regional Departments – North, East, South-East, South-West, West – whilst the inner structure of these Departments, which contained 97% of the personnel, remained intact.[99] Like the Companies before them, each region had three different technical departments: the Department of Exploitation (EX), Department of Material and Traction (MT) and the Department of Tracks and Buildings (VB). Only a few adaptations were made to facilitate the centralisation of the complex administrative structure, such as creating seven Central Services which overlooked the Regional Services. Otherwise, things stayed largely the same. The majority of cheminots remained in their current posts, and the same men who had run the private Companies were assigned to run the SNCF.[100]

At the top of the SNCF pyramid (1938) sat three men: Robert Le Besnerais, the Managing Director; Frédéric Surleau, the Assisting Managing Director; and the Chairman, Pierre Guinand. Despite their status, they wanted to blur the lines of hierarchy in order to create a familial atmosphere. 'Seeing as you all practice the same profession', said Guinand, 'I know we agree when saying that you are all part of the same family. Although I have only recently joined you, I would like to say, with your permission: *we* are all part of the same family'.[101] In fact, there was a world of difference between the ordinary cheminot and those men who sat at the top of the SNCF. Marc Olivier Baruch has underlined 'the role that the men who went through the SNCF, breeding ground for technocrats since Dautry, eventually played in Vichy'.[102] Jean Berthelot became a Minister under Vichy; Pierre-Eugène Fournier, who would replace Guinand in 1940 as Chairman, would simultaneously head the economic aryanisation programme in 1940–1; Filippi who became a

Services, par le personnel de la garde des communications. See also Lartilleux, *Le Réseau National* (1948) 33–41.

[99] According to Lartilleux, out of 500,000 people working for the French railway, 15,000 worked for management and the central services. *Ibid.*, 42.

[100] For example, the Director of the North Network, Robert Le Besnerais, became the Managing Director of the SNCF. Likewise, the Director of the Alsace-Lorraine Network, Frédéric Surleau, was made Assisting Managing Director. For more information on Surleau, see *Mémoires d'ingénieurs, destins ferroviaires. Autobiographies professionnelles de Frédéric Surleau (1884–1972) et Robert Lévi (1895–1981)*, RHCF, Hors Série, n°8 (Mar. 2007).

[101] *Notre Métier* (15 May 1938) 2. Before he was appointed to this role, Pierre Guinand was the First President of France's Court of Auditors (*Cours des Comptes*) in 1936–1937. There, he showed his intolerance for indiscipline amongst the workforce, taking harsh measures against workers who had 'committed infractions'. (See Seidman, *Workers Against Work* (1991) 28.) Guinand was released by Vichy and replaced by Pierre-Eugène Fournier in September 1940.

[102] Baruch, *Servir l'Etat français* (1997) 74.

general secretary; and finally Surleau, 'the last delegate of national equipment'.[103]

Unfortunately, not much is known about most of these technocrats. Those with more illustrious careers under Vichy or who have written memoirs, such as Jean Berthelot, are more familiar. Born in 1897, Berthelot worked his way through the railway hierarchy before officially entering a government post under Anatole de Monzie in 1938. He maintained this post whilst he was promoted to the SNCF as Assisting Managing Director. Under Vichy, he was appointed Minister of Communication and Transports. Others who held important posts under Vichy such as Fournier frequently appear in history books; that being said, aside from their official functions, there are few details of their personal lives. For example, the Managing Director, Robert Le Besnerais, remains enigmatic, there is almost nothing written on him. Only the sources in the SNCF archives provide an image of a rigid and professionally conscious man.

Conclusion

The railway world had gone from being a dream of the French elite in the early-eighteenth century to a massive semi-public company upholding the French nation on the eve of the Second World War. The few thousand seasonal workers initially employed to build and run the first railways had also, by 1938, transformed into a homogenous group of 515,000 workers with a unique identity. Over the course of a century, a relatively homogenous cheminot community emerged, defined not least by a set of conservative socio-cultural and professional values. The emergence of an *esprit cheminot* – which had to do with professional devotion, obedience and pride, as well as a strong sense of quasi-familial bond – further distinguished them from other working-class groups. This *esprit cheminot* was not only a bottom-up phenomenon, but was also imposed from the upper echelons whose strong belief in hierarchy and patriarchy only strengthened over time.

But this unique railway milieu was about to face its greatest challenge yet. Although nationalisation seemed to be the culmination of decades of working-class political struggle, the imminent collapse of the Popular Front and the dissolution of the Communist Party – from both outside and in – were strong reminders that the class war was far from won. Moreover, the military defeat of France in May–June 1940 and the

---

[103] The book by Marc Olivier Baruch offers many sporadic insights into these technocrats whose lives remain nonetheless mysterious. See, amongst many other passages, Baruch, *Servir l'Etat français* (1997) 25, 74.

subsequent occupation of France would be another huge blow. How would the cheminots react to these new obstacles? How would they adapt – or not – to Vichy and the German Occupation of 1940–4?

Studying the origins of the cheminot community and the SNCF has allowed us to gain considerable insight into this community. The number of unionised cheminots is impossible to know for sure, or even of those who went on strike. But this history of the cheminot community shows that, far from being a radical working-class group, cheminots were generally professionally conscious and politically moderate. Indeed, their absence from the 1936 strikes is particularly telling. With this in mind, it will be possible to better understand the attitudes and behaviour which would unfold in the upcoming war, defeat and occupation.

2   Vichy

Before the declaration of the Second World War and the defeat of June 1940, French workers had already suffered two major blows. The first was the collapse of Léon Blum's government. In Spring 1938, Edouard Daladier took the reins of the Popular Front government and began dissolving recent advancements made in favour of ordinary French workers. A strike was called in November 1938, but it did not take off, not least amongst the railway milieu.[1] The second blow was when Stalin signed a non-aggression pact with Hitler in August 1939: whilst some agreed that preserving the peace was more important than anything, others felt betrayed that Stalin would ally himself to the fascist dictator. Indeed, the trade union leader Pierre Semard was convinced that Stalin's decision should be welcomed, and he insisted that 'the outcome of the non-aggression pact between the Soviet Union and Germany can only contribute to the establishment of a long-lasting peace in Europe and the World.'[2] But many communists did not agree, and the CGT officially condemned the pact on 24 August 1939.[3] The divisions in the political left were resurfacing.

These serious political disruptions were followed by two of the biggest military events in twentieth-century European history: the declaration of the Second World War in September 1939, and the capitulation of France in June 1940. The subsequent erection of a Franco-German collaboration supported by a government in Vichy would become a definitive moment in modern French history. How would French workers – and cheminots in particular – respond to this new crisis? Whereas postwar myths would suggest that the French – and cheminots in particular – resisted from the first days of the German Occupation, this chapter reveals much more controversial responses to Vichy. Indeed, a study of war and defeat, national reconstruction, moral regeneration and

---

[1] Beaumont, 'Communists and Cheminots' (2011); Bachelier Report, 3.7.2. Le communisme isolé et anti-national, 1938–1941.
[2] Chevandier, *Cheminots en grève* (2002) 159.   [3] Vigna, *Histoire des ouvriers* (2012) 143.

the *Charte du Travail* (the Labour Charter) shows that cheminots were not immediately dismissing Vichy. Indeed, the political blows of 1938 and 1939 had created a real sense of disillusion amongst many working class communities, and the despair only got worst after the defeat. Could it be argued that Vichy was also a chance for new opportunities for many cheminots?

1   War and defeat

Once war was declared on 3 September 1939, everything swung into motion – or almost. Cheminots had started to be mobilised in June 1939, although at this stage it concerned mostly lowly employees or apprentices.[4] By August, the SNCF had begun transporting material and several hundred thousand conscripted men to the front.[5] Mass mobilisation truly started on 1 September, and by the 3rd, stations were 'swarming with people'. The number of trains destined to certain stations such as Lille and Valenciennes doubled, or even tripled, and troop transports were prioritised over traveller trains. 'One million three hundred thousand men had left in the previous days, and in addition to that over a million and a half men in 48 hours used the 3 185 trains put to their disposal by the Republic'.[6]

After the initial surge of activity – which had been well-planned and smoothly executed – the initial hype died down. The Phoney War was largely a waiting game. Industries were busy switching to wartime production under the Minister of Armement, Raoul Dautry, but soldiers on the front were extremely bored. 'The Germans are in Warsaw and my husband sits in the Maginot Line and gets boils', said one dairywoman.[7] Cheminots tried to alleviate the boredom of their fellow workers who had volunteered for the front by sending them books to distract themselves, but this did not dispel a growing sense of uselessness.

The efforts of the SNCF managers and personnel were immediately praised: 'With the impulsive energy of its Managing Director, Monsieur Le Besnerais (...) and thanks to a meticulous preparation and the feeling of duty which always animated its personnel, [the SNCF] completed every transport required by the military command'.[8] In November 1940,

---

[4] SNCF/206/LM/1: Liste des agents ayant été détachés en usine (Dépôt de Belfort).
[5] François Cochet, *Les soldats de la drôle de guerre: septembre 1939–mai 1940* (Paris: Hachette, 2004) 42–4.
[6] Pierre Thomas, *Des trains contre les Panzers: septembre 1939–mai 1940* (La Voix du nord, 1999) 28.
[7] Arthur Koestler, *Scum of the Earth* (London: Elan, 1991, c1941) 59.
[8] Cited in Georges Ribeill, 'L'accommodation sociale de la SNCF avec ses tutelles vichyssoise et allemande: résistance et/ou compromissions?' in Marie-Noëlle

the SNCF received the commendation of the *ordre de l'Armée* for its efforts and devotion during the war.[9] The achievement was all the more remarkable because a fifth of the SNCF's workforce had been drafted for the war.[10] In fact, the first measures that the SNCF took during the Phoney War were focussed on solving their personnel shortage problems. They did away with the recent Popular Front decrees which had introduced the forty-hour week, and cheminots were now supposed to work between 54 and 72 hours.[11] Recent retirees were encouraged to return to their posts, while a number of women were taken on. The introduction of women had already been used in 1914–18, but it had caused some problems back then. These new recruits (which also included unskilled immigrants) stood out amongst a workforce which had established itself as male, white and skilled. Eventually, women became somewhat accepted in the community – after all, they were often the wives or daughters of cheminots, and in 1917, they swelled the ranks of the trade unions. But this time around, the SNCF was careful to release positive propaganda from the onset: a woman doing heavy-duty work made the front cover of the April 1940 issue of *Notre Métier*, the SNCF's official newspaper, and the women were praised for their diligence and adaptability.[12] Another factor behind the SNCF's efficiency was technology, for the burden of military transport was not carried by the railways alone anymore, but was spread out in trucks and air transports.[13]

Meanwhile, other workers were accused of sabotaging the war effort. Communists were hunted down for allegedly hindering the French war effort by skipping work, working slowly or badly, or, worse still, sabotaging military material. In 1946, Daladier publicly condemned workers of the Phoney War: 'there are terrible cases of men sabotaging plane motors in the Farman factory at Boulogne-Billancourt'.[14] The most famous case of sabotage during the war was the Rambaud Affair. It concerned a small group of men who sabotaged a tank which exploded, killing the Frenchman inside it. After a merciless witch-hunt, the saboteurs were eventually executed in June 1940.[15] Industrial sabotage was, in fact, a rarity during the Phoney War. According to the historian and ex-Free French fighter Jean-Louis Crémieux-Brilhac, sabotage statistics have been significantly exaggerated. After re-examining 50 alleged 'sabotages', he revealed that

---

Polino, ed., *Une entreprise pendant la guerre: la SNCF 1939–1945* (Paris: Presses Universitaires Françaises, 2001).
[9] *Ibid.*   [10] AN/72/AJ/478: Rapport Moral 1939.
[11] Chevandier, *Cheminots en grève* (2002) 157.   [12] *Notre Métier* (15 Apr. 1940).
[13] *Un Siècle en Train* (Paris: Editions La Vie du rail, 2000) 131.
[14] Cited in Crémieux-Brilhac *Les Français*, 2 (1990) 290.   [15] *Ibid.*, 299–302.

over 50% of these incidents were not caused by deliberate acts of destruction, but by human errors on a production line.[16]

Only two professional groups emerged unscathed from the prevailing criticism against the working classes: the miners and the cheminots.[17] They were praised for their hard work, and the archival research mentioned above certainly confirms this. Moreover, the cheminots were beginning to show a clearer distance from pro-Stalin communist sentiments. The *Bureau Fédéral des Cheminots* had initially abstained from a formal decision in regards to the Nazi-Soviet pact, but the declaration of war put things in sharp relief, and they now voted to condemn it.[18] Indeed, the pro-military nationalism which had always distinguished the cheminots came into full swing, seeing many turn their backs to the Communist Party. The government officially dissolved the PCF on 26 September, and two days later the *Bureau* voted to exclude communists from the federation thirteen votes to three: Pierre Semard was expelled from the cheminot trade union, with Jean Jarrigion now at its head. Four cheminots tried to start a clandestine communist union on 30 November 1939, but they were identified on 19 February 1940 and their union immediately dissolved.[19]

However, the immaculate image of railwaymen in the Phoney War – as hardworking, devoted, united and never obstructive – is slightly misleading. A comic strip published in the SNCF's newspaper, *Notre Métier*, referred to the vice of the cheminots – alcohol – which continued even during the Phoney War.[20] The two cartoon cheminots, Bogy and Tampon, thought that they had just come under enemy attack. However, the loud noise they heard was not a gas bomb, but a group of cheminots popping open a bottle of champagne and drinking merrily. In fact, they were drinking the station master's champagne which they had probably stolen, a further indicator of the internal tensions within this body of workers. The text in this comic strip undoubtedly had a nationalist and victorious overtone, but it also implied that cheminots were not as saintly as it was often suggested.

The author of this comic strip would have had numerous stories to inspire him. One Saturday afternoon in January 1940, Marcel Rejaud, a lowly employee in the South-West Region, was drinking on his shift. His superior spotted him giving the machine repairmen some hassle while

[16] *Ibid.*, 294.   [17] *Ibid.*, 326–8.   [18] Chevandier, *Cheminots en grève* (2002) 160.
[19] The archives do not give details about what would happen to them subsequently. SNCF/201/LM/1: Letter (26 Mar. 1940) from Chef d'Arrondissement Exploitation (Nantes) to Chef de l'Exploitation (West Region).
[20] 'Bogy et Tampon. … Il y a erreur', *Notre Métier* (15 Mar. 1940).

they were trying to fix a machine which Rejaud was supposed to use later that day. At this point Rejaud, who had spotted his superior in a drunken haze, and probably expected reprisals, started shouting abuse 'to all those who were against him, and especially to the *boches*'.[21] When he was finally dragged into his chief's office and confronted with a questionnaire which he had to fill in and sign to justify his behaviour, Rejaud scribbled *non* on the sheet of paper and continued cursing everyone around him. The confusion of enemies – his superior, all those 'after him' and the Germans – suggests that the 'professional' enemy was not being completely disassociated from the 'national' enemy.

There are countless more examples of disruptive behaviour in the archives. One cheminot in Arras was denounced in June 1939 for possessing a large number of pro-Hitler tracts.[22] In August 1939, several cheminots were arrested and suspended for detaining a vast quantity of anti-militarist, communist propaganda.[23] When the war erupted, the SNCF took part in the nation-wide hunt for foreign-influenced, anti-militarist, anti-national, pro-communist individuals. All cheminots were given a severe warning in January 1940 after some of them were suspected of falsifying papers and information regarding the soldiers on leave.[24] Several months later, on 24 May 1940, Le Besnerais sent a letter to all Regional Directors and District Chiefs, giving them orders on how to denounce and deal with anti-national activities.[25] So although there are no recorded incidents of sabotage within the railway, milder forms of protest were common during this period of mobilisation.

The war took a sharp turn when Germany invaded the Low Countries on 10 May 1940. In six weeks, France, along with its railway system, was brought to its knees. It was not only the military invasion and the aerial bombings which caused problems: it was the wave of people fleeing the Germans, a wave which came crashing down onto the transport system. There are no exact statistics on how many people fled Belgium, the Netherlands, Luxemburg and North-east France in those six weeks.

---

[21] SNCF/303/LM/7: Note pour le Conseil de Discipline in Disciplinary Council 1940 (3 Apr. 1940).

[22] SNCF/505/LM/105: Comptes rendus hebdomadaires (1°) (20 Jun. 1939).

[23] SNCF/25/LM/256: Letter (30 Aug. 1939) from Le Besnerais to Directeur du Service Central du Personnel.

[24] Thomas, *Des trains contre les Panzers* (1999) 45.

[25] According to the laws of 24 Jun., 1 Sept., and 25 Sept. 1939, cheminots would be immediately fired if they were involved in 'the distribution and circulation of foreign tracts' or 'the publication of any information which might encourage the actions of a foreign power', or if they were involved in communist activities despite the dissolution of communist organisations. SNCF/25/LM/256: Letter (24 May 1940) from Le Besnerais to many.

The national statistics gathered in August 1940 are not wholly accurate, since by that point many refugees had already returned home, or had not bothered to register.[26] Ten million people is the most recent estimate. In any case, refugees were counted in millions, not thousands.

The mass exodus took the French by surprise. Although they had prepared themselves for evacuation, no one anticipated numbers on this scale.[27] The wave of refugees was triggered in large part by fear, as horrific memories of 1914–18 came rushing back.[28] This was especially true of those living in Northern France, where the Germans had made the strongest impact.[29] In April, the cheminot Cieran wrote an article in *Notre Métier* describing the Germans' arrival in Lille in March 1914: 'thousands of homes were set on fire, entire neighbourhoods. It was the beginning of a terrible ordeal which would last until 1918'.[30] Pierre Blairet's father, a cheminot himself, warned his wife and children that they would have to flee before the Germans put Verdun *à feu et à sang* – to blood and fire – like they had done twenty-five years ago.[31] Simone de Beauvoir encountered refugees 'who spoke of children with severed hands'.[32] Since then, academics have come to understand that this was probably an exagerration: 'Mothers experienced the exodus through the imagery of the previous invasion, especially rapes and mutilated children'.[33] As the refugees moved into Central and Southern France, their fear spread like wildfire. Adding to this chaos was relentless German bombing: the shrill noise, the smell of smoke and fire, the sight of wounded or dead bodies was the materialisation of imaginary fears.[34]

---

[26] Statistics suggest there were about 2.5 million refugees in Aug.1940, see Jean Vidalenc, *L'Exode de Mai–Juin 1940* (Paris: Presses Universitaires de France, 1957) 425–6. Today, most historians refer to 10 million refugees throughout the entire exodus.

[27] The lack of preparation in 1870–1871 and 1914–1918 had created chaos in certain areas. In order to prevent this, prefects began to design basic evacuation plans after the signing of the Munich agreement. A first wave of preventative evacuation from Alsace-Moselle in September 1939 went relatively smoothly, and new plans were made in February 1940 although no one wanted to alarm the population or appear defeatist. See Marchand, *Les chemins de fer* (1924) 55–6; Valérie Laisney-Launay, *L'Exode des populations Bas-Normandes au cours de l'été 1944* (Caen: Centre de Recherche d'Histoire Quantitative, 2005) 27. Vidalenc, *L'Exode* (1957) 29, 262–4.

[28] See John Horne and Alan Kramer, *German Atrocities, 1914, A History of Denial* (London: Yale University Press, 2001).

[29] For more on the memories of the Great War under Vichy, see Richard Cobb, *French and Germans, Germans and French: A Personal Interpretation of France Under Two Occupations 1914–1918/1940–1944* (Hanover, NH: University Press of New England, 1983) 3–32.

[30] M. Cieran, 'Souvenirs de l'arrivée des Allemands à Lille au début d'Octobre 1914', *Notre Métier* (15 Apr. 1940).

[31] Pierre Blairet, *Cheminot* (Paris: Editions du Rocher, 1998) 46.

[32] Cited in Horne and Kramer, *German Atrocities* (2001) 403.   [33] *Ibid.*

[34] Henri Amouroux, *La Grande Histoire des Français sous l'occupation, vol. 1, Le Peuple du désastre, 1939–1940* (Paris: Laffont, 1976) 378.

Myths about fifth columnists and 'ferocious German parachutists' only fuelled these fears, and 'it did not matter that there was no harm done. From now on, fear dictated the terms'.[35]

Once people had decided to flee, they headed straight for the trains, and the situation soon grew chaotic. A British war correspondent described the situation in a Belgian station: 'trainload after trainload leaving the station; a lot of red blankets about, giving it a hospital note; children – white, tired, and dirty. Some of the trains have been bombed and machine-gunned – one or two hit. The Belgium Red Cross are giving free meals'.[36] Similar scenes spread to France, especially in Paris where all trains were centralised. Consequently, Parisian stations soon became sites of confusion and chaos. At best, people trying to make connections in Paris were exhausted and confused. There was an attempt to organise the transfers by designating meeting points and centres, but by June, scenes in train stations had gone from difficult to tragic.[37] The main doors of central Parisian stations such as the *Gare Montparnasse* occasionally had to be closed so that those already on the platforms were not pushed onto the tracks by incoming masses.[38] On 10 June, one traveller wrote:

The train [to Bordeaux] leaves in 4 hours time. About 20,000 people have gathered outside the station, most of them are sitting on their belongings. It is impossible to move, the heat is unbearable. (...) Crying children are all round, and the many babies in arms look like they are being crushed to death. The Police Officer in charge of the entrance gates orders all babies to be handed over to the Police inside. This human baggage is gradually passed over the heads of the crowd by outstretched arms, and the babies are assembled within the station gates, until the mothers can get through to collect them.[39]

Stations suddenly emptied when the German troops arrived on the outskirts of Paris, and statesmen and railway personnel were evacuated from Paris. The masses deserted the Parisian stations as quickly as they had come. The Director of Personnel, Jean Barth, was the only SNCF director to remain in Paris. In his journal, he described the scenes in the *Gares du Nord, de la Villette, de Rambouillet*: 'the empty buildings, pillaged and ransacked, remained as testaments of a deeply painful exodus'.[40]

[35] *Ibid.*
[36] James Lansdale Hodson, *Through the Dark Night, Being Some Account of a War Correspondent's Journeys, Meetings and What Was Said to Him, in France, Britain and Flanders during 1939–1940* (London: Victor Gollancz Ltd., 1941) 177.
[37] Pierre Miquel, *L'exode: 10 mai–20 juin 1940* (Paris: Plon, 2003) 155; Hanna Diamond, *Fleeing Hitler: France 1940* (Oxford: Oxford University Press, 2007) 35–8.
[38] Bruno Carrière, 'Les rails de l'Exode' in *La Vie du Rail* (7 Jun. 1990) 46.
[39] Cited in Diamond, *Fleeing Hitler* (2007) 58.
[40] AN/72/AJ/473: Journal de Barth, Director of Personnel (12–27 Jun. 1940).

Outside Paris, train stations became sites of death and destruction. On 10 May alone, the stations in Boulogne, Lille, Valenciennes, Dunkerque, Charleville, Calais, Hazebrouck, Saint-Amand, Orchies, Laon, Hirson, Lens, Liévin, Avion, Hénin-Liétard, Douai, Givet, Compiègne, Pontoise, Conflans and Villerupt were all hit by German bombs. A week later, the station in Tergnier was completely destroyed and dozens of civilians were killed. One ex-cheminot recalled the scene at Montereau on 15–16 June: 'There was no one left in this dead station, apart from a few bodies sprawled along a platform'.[41] Railway lines were also targeted, and when tracks were severed this meant huge delays. Trains became so unreliable that people did not think twice about fleeing by car, by bicycle, or for so many, on foot. The photographs of women and children fleeing on foot are amongst the most famous images of the exodus.

Despite this chaos, Crémieux-Brilhac described railway workers as 'level-headed and dedicated'. Henri Amouroux congratulated the SNCF for its ability to manage both the military transports and the evacuation of a panic-stricken population. Vidalenc and Diamond, whose works focus specifically on the exodus, underlined the almighty efforts of the cheminots and the French railways despite the terrible circumstances.[42] Whilst these claims are rooted in truth, they conceal the shadier side of their experiences. Gabriel Bonnin, an apprentice railway worker at the time, was working in the Noisy-le-Sec depot when cheminots were ordered to evacuate in June 1940.[43] With three of his friends from the SNCF, he took the last train from Noisy and went off to 'raise hell'. They stole bottles of liquor from an unsupervised shop, drank so much that they soon reeked of Ricard, and flirted with a group of girls for most of the journey. They eventually reached Brive-la-Gaillarde, where they were expected to work in the stations and depots in the area. But instead, Bonnin and his friends worked as little as possible. 'It was the Tower of Babel,' he declared, 'there were whore houses, we got a priest completely drunk...'.

This piece of oral history adds a new dimension to the traditional discourse of cheminots in the war. So far, stories of the exodus have come from written sources signed by travellers and engineers, press articles or historical works. This interview thus fills an interesting gap in the historical sources.[44] Of course, by boasting about the amounts of

[41] Carrière, 'Le Rail de l'Exode' (1990) 47.
[42] Amouroux, *La Grande Histoire des Français*, 1 (1976) 379. See also Diamond, *Fleeing Hitler* (2007) 33–37; Vidalenc, *L'Exode* (1957) 262.
[43] Interview Bonnin (2008).
[44] For more on oral history, see Alessandro Portelli, 'What Makes Oral History Different' in Robert Perks and Alistair Thomson, eds., *The Oral History Reader* (London: Routledge, 1998) 63–74.

alcohol he drank or the girls that he met, Bonnin may have been trying to
show off rather than to give an accurate record of the events. Still, his
testimony helps to develop a new narrative of freedom and frivolity,
rather than work and patriotism. These themes are present in broader
studies of individual experiences, notably in the works of Diamond and
Vidalenc, but they were never mentioned in conjunction with cheminot
history.

Marc Bloch was the first to dare criticise the cheminots in the 'strange
defeat':

> Could anything have been more *kleinbürgerlich*, more *petit bourgeois*, than the
> attitude adopted in the last few years, and even during the war, by most of the
> big unions, and especially by those which included civil servants in their ranks?
> (...) I saw something of the way in which the Post Office workers and the
> railwaymen behaved both during and after the war, and the spectacle was not a
> very edifying one. (...) In most of the cities of western France during the month of
> June I saw hordes of wretched men wandering the streets in an effort to get back
> to their homes. All of them were carrying loads far heavier than they could cope
> with, and why? Simply because the railway stations had seen fit to close their left-
> luggage offices for fear of imposing on their staffs a few hours of overtime, or of
> rather heavier work than usual.[45]

Although Bloch was here ignoring the workers' increased work hours, his
remarks remain observant and insightful as they complement other archival documents describing the disciplinary problems at the time. Gustave
Roux, working for the South-West network, was given three years in
prison for defeatist attitudes and physical violence. Adolphe Viel stole
funds from the SNCF. Germaine Bougot abandoned her post on 16 May
1940.[46] Every month, dozens of similar cases about insubordinate
workers were brought to the attention of regional networks. Indeed,
cheminots continued with their lives and personal concerns, whether or
not these were in line with the patriotic attitudes imposed from above.

2   Rebuilding the nation

On 22 June 1940, Pétain signed an armistice with the Germans. This was
a crushing military and moral defeat, but also a physical one. The
bombings in May–June 1940 had disfigured France, not least its railways.
Over 542 engineering structures were significantly affected, and key

[45] Marc Bloch, *Strange Defeat, a Statement of Evidence Written in 1940*, translated by Gerard
Hopkins (London: Oxford University Press, 1949, c1946) 138–9.
[46] SNCF/303/LM/7: Disciplinary Council 1940 (28 Aug. 1940).

railway lines were severed at twenty or thirty different points.[47] Most of
the damage was localised in the East, where 260 tunnels, bridges, via-
ducts and other structures were destroyed, and 129 SNCF buildings
completely demolished.[48] The collapse of the railway system in mid-
June had only worsened the situation. Traffic was paralysed in many
parts of the country, causing severe shortages in industrial materials and,
more worryingly, food supplies. French and German authorities were
aware that it was necessary to rebuild the French national economy, and
for this they were fully prepared to invest in the reconstruction of the
railway system. Their goals were two-fold: to repair the damage, and to
restore pre-war elasticity in railroad traffic.

Faced with the gargantuan task of rebuilding the railway, the SNCF
needed as much personnel as it could get. However, an acute crisis in
personnel shortage threatened to hinder these reconstruction plans. On
the eve of the war, the SNCF personnel amounted to approximately
500,000 workers; however, between May and June 1940, 1,370 cheminots died, and 35,000 were taken prisoners.[49] Not only that, but thousands had joined the exodus and were nowhere near their jobsite. And so
in June–July, the SNCF management was already asking the Germans to
return their workers who were being held as prisoners of war (POWs).

Returning POWs was not necessarily the government's first priority:
indeed, Georges Scapini (the French Ambassador in charge of negotiating the conditions for the POWs) had even admitted to Otto Abetz (the
German Ambassador in Paris) that releasing POWs was 'not desirable in
a period of unemployment'.[50] However, the German authorities were
desperate to get the SNCF back on its feet, and they knew that skilled
railway workers could not merely be replaced by unskilled men and
women. As such, they were willing to make certain concessions in order
to ease the personnel crisis – indeed, Germans wanted to control the
SNCF but only from afar, enough to ensure that they could make the
most of the French economy without wasting men and materials on
setting up an intense supervisory system. About half of the cheminot
POWs were thus returned almost immediately to France, a promising
negotiation which showed not only Germany's ability to cooperate, but
also its understanding of the French railway and economic crisis. Eventually these negotiations came to a standstill: between November

[47] AN/72/AJ/415: Procès verbal de la séance du (7 Oct. 1943) 6.
[48] AN/72/AJ/2296: *La Région de l'Est de la SNCF de 1939 à 1945* (Imprimerie des Dernières Nouvelles de Strasbourg, 1947) 58.
[49] According to Ribeill, 730 cheminots died in enemy hands, and 640 were killed by wartime circumstances. Ribeill, 'L'accommodation sociale de la SNCF' (2001).
[50] Paxton, *Vichy France* (1975) 77–8.

1940 and February 1941 the number of cheminots still held captive stabilised at 17,000, and by the end of the war, there were 14,313 cheminot prisoners.[51]

After securing the return of (some) POWs,[52] the SNCF implemented a series of new measures: work hours increased from 2,408 to 2,558 a year; women called up in 1939 due to wartime pressures were asked to remain, and 42,000 more were hired[53]; and workers nearing retirement were also advised to stay on. Jean Berthelot was careful to underline that this measure was not intended to abuse the workers, for he was only too aware that these new demands might fuel negative attitudes amongst the workers. The rights which workers had managed to secure in regards to retirement age and working hours were being suddenly challenged, and there was a risk of causing strikes and protests, a situation which the SNCF could not afford in this critical time of reconstruction. And so, as he explained that retirement age could not remain at 55 but had to be pushed back, he was careful to explain that 'at a time when all French people must work to rebuild the country' they needed these men to stay and work.[54]

The repatriation of the 10 million people on the run was another logistical issue to be reckoned with. The Germans had demanded the repatriation of the population in Article 16 of the Armistice Convention, but it was not so simple: first, there were several million refugees. Second, very few railway lines had been repaired, and most were in a dismal state. Third, the demarcation line was patrolled by German soldiers who made sure that Frenchmen did not cross it unless they had an official authorisation. The only way to prevent total chaos was therefore to organise an official and efficient repatriation system. Travellers were prioritised according to profession and location, but prioritisations changed depending on national needs. Workers necessary for national reconstruction were generally at the top of the list: 'on 18 July, trains of 1,700 cheminots, 728 Peugeot workers, 450 employees from air force factories, 264 from *Air Liquide* and 106 from *Electro-Mécanique* all

---

[51] Jean Berthelot, *Sur les rails du pouvoir. De Munich à Vichy* (Paris: Robert Laffont, 1967) 150–1; See also report on the 1945 exercise cited in Bachelier Report, 1.2. Libération des cheminots prisonniers de guerre.

[52] AN/72/AJ/415: Mémento de la conférence tenue à la WVD (5 Jul. 1940).

[53] Cited in Ribeill, 'L'accommodation sociale de la SNCF' (2001). There is little specific information on what role(s) these women tended to undertake, although they would have been less labour-intensive. In disciplinary files pre-dating 1939, women are almost always cited as *gardes-barrières*.

[54] AN/72/AJ/414: Note (5 Jan. 1941) from Berthelot to Claudon, General Director of Transports.

left Bordeaux for Paris.'[55] Parisians were also prioritised, and between 26 July and 15 August millions of them returned home.[56]

Once again, stations became the centre of peoples' lives. Refugees sat in nearby cafés for hours on end, waiting seemingly forever, a glass of water in their hands and an eye on their luggage.[57] When refugees finally boarded the trains, the situation could turn sour:

> To prevent people storming the train, the Germans only let a few refugees on to the platform at a time. In the next moment it is our turn to climb into the cattle wagons in which several families are already installed more or less comfortably. Then another storm of cries breaks out. There are vehement protests. The people who have already comfortably settled themselves in a nice seat are not pleased to see more people come aboard and are not keen to squeeze together to make room for them. 'There is no room', they cry. 'Oh come on, of course there is', the others say; 'just push over a bit, you are taking the space of four people!'[58]

Sometimes they were supplied with only a single bucket in the rail cars to relieve themselves. The physical discomforts of repatriation were matched by the emotional tragedies of those who, after such extensive travelling, had lost either some*thing* or some*one*. Louis Le François began almost every entry of his diary by copying the personal advertisements he found in the daily papers. 'E. Aerts, ex-champion, refugee Rieux-Minervois (Aude), is looking for his son Jean,' 'Lieutenant Decourrière and his cyclists are looking for Adjudant Griffon and soldier Boulanger and their truck,' 'Blue coat, double lining, thrown into a military car in Gien. Return to ...'.[59] The SNCF was caught in the middle of this lost-and-found process, and in March 1941 it drew up a list of 13,000 people who still had not collected their bags and packages.[60]

There is no doubt that cheminots worked hard during this period. Immediately after Pétain's appeal of 17 June, they had started heading back to work. They were starting to return to Paris on 18 June, and management arrived soon after.[61] By 15 August 1940, 77 construction sites had been erected. Two weeks later, there were 108 sites. By mid-December, traffic

[55] Henri Amouroux, *La Grande Histoire des Français sous l'occupation, vol. 2, Quarante millions de pétainistes* (Paris: Laffont, 1977) 161.
[56] Diamond, *Fleeing Hitler* (2007) 153.   [57] Vidalenc, *L'Exode* (1957) 248–9.
[58] G. Adrey, journal entry cited in Diamond, *Fleeing Hitler* (2007) 154.
[59] Louis Le François, *J'ai Faim ... ! Journal d'un Français en France depuis l'Armistice* (Brentano's: New York, 1942) 21–6.
[60] Amouroux, *La Grande Histoire des Français*, 2 (1977) 161; Carrière, 'Le Rail de l'Exode' (1990) 48.
[61] Paul Durand, *La SNCF pendant la guerre: Sa résistance à l'occupant* (Paris: Presses universitaires de France, 1968) 112.

was back to normal.[62] In all, the SNCF spent 1,400 million francs in repairs. Robert Le Besnerais was extremely grateful to the cheminots for their unfailing efforts: 'I would like to give hommage to the devotion, the courage and the patriotism of our personnel who ensured a successful reconstruction', he stated in 1943.[63] Within this effort of reconstruction, the resistance to the occupier is not necessarily so obvious.

3   Values under Vichy

If cheminots seemed to embrace their role in the national reconstruction, what did they make of Pétain and the new Vichy government? It is well known that many French people accepted and even welcomed the new regime. This is in large part explained by the cult of Marshal Pétain, which was so central to the popularity of the Vichy regime in 1940. Pétain had successfully put an end to a war that most French people had never wanted in the first place. When Germans swept through Northern France, many officials had called for peace 'in order to prevent even more misery and ruin'.[64] Moreover, by offering himself to France on 17 June 1940, Marshal Pétain had made the ultimate gesture toward a disorientated people in need of a leader. 'With just a few messages expressed in a firm and familiar tone, he gave the French people much more than the status, the charter and the convention that they so wished. He gave them a reason to live.'[65] Finally, Pétain put an end to the Third Republic. The events of May and June had, for some onlookers, revealed the inability of the Republic to protect its population: many government officials had supplied the population with little information, no organisation and ultimately abandoned their posts.[66] Likewise, they had failed to re-arm and defend the country's borders: '... the myth of the German stroll through non-existent French defences became established. And with it, a repudiation of the Third Republic and a thirst of something different'.[67] Even Henri Frenay, the founder of the Resistance movement *Combat*, could justify Pétain's acceptance of an Armistice: 'Marshal Pétain was hindered by the Armistice convention. He could not act

---

[62] Bernard de Fontgalland, *Cheminot sans frontières: 50 ans de carnets de voyages à travers le monder* (I.A. Diffusion, 1988) 33.

[63] AN/72/AJ/415: Procès verbal de la séance du (7 Oct. 1943) 7.

[64] Cited in Crémieux-Brilhac, *Les Français*, 1 (Paris: Gallimard, 1990) 600.

[65] Paul Lombard, 'Le Maréchal et l'Armistice', *France* (Octobre 1943) 3.

[66] H. R. Kedward, 'Patriots and Patriotism in Vichy France', *Transactions of the Royal Historical Society*, vol. 32 (1982) 181.

[67] Paxton, *Vichy France* (1975) 21.

openly against Germany, but his intentions were clear. That which he could not do, *we* would do'.[68]

Pétain's legacy won over the hearts and minds of people all over the political spectrum, not least amongst the 'apolitical' technocrats who ran the SNCF. Jean Berthelot was the SNCF's Assisting Managing Director when Pétain asked him to replace Anatole de Monzie as Minister of Communication and Transports in September 1940. Berthelot, who considered himself an engineer and not a politician, was initially reluctant to accept the offer. However, Berthelot also greatly admired Pétain. After an inspirational conversation with the Marshal, he accepted the new position. 'When I told the Marshal that I regretted being taken away from my current post, he responded with paternal serenity: 'do you think that I, myself, would not have preferred to relax? I have certainly deserved to, but instead I have offered myself to France. (...)' Then the Marshal spoke very kindly of the cheminots. He knows them well; he observed them closely during the previous war. (...) By the end of the session, I decided that it was not time to back out, and that I had to look forward.'[69] In May 1941, Berthelot gave a speech expressing his admiration for the Marshal, who had managed to restore the principles of authority and hierarchy within the transport industry.[70]

The National Revolution – a programme dedicated to the moral, social and cultural reconstruction of France – promised a new future for France.[71] In August, Berthelot issued a radio message to every cheminot in France, asking them to support the National Revolution, and in particular his fight against communism.[72] Berthelot's support of the National Revolution was part of a broader current of thought. Vichy was constituted of specialists and technocrats, members of the intellectual elite who had dreamed of a government led by experts since the 1930s. They had all excelled at the *École Polytechnique* and other top schools, and were the brightest engineering minds of their times.[73] This handful of men included Jean Berthelot, Jean Bichelonne and Robert Gibrat, all of whom were involved with the SNCF during this period, either by working in the SNCF management, or in the Ministry of Communications and Transports. They wanted a revolution from above,

[68] Henri Frenay, *The Night Will End* (Sevenoaks: Coronet, 1976) 25–7.
[69] Berthelot, *Sur les rails du pouvoir* (1967) 95.
[70] AN/72/AJ/415: Séance plénière du Conseil Général des Ponts et Chaussées (14 May 1941).
[71] For more on the National Revolution see Paxton, *Vichy France* (1975) 136–233.
[72] AN/72/AJ/477: Appel radiodiffusé de Berthelot aux cheminots français (21 Aug. 1941).
[73] Limore Yagil, *L'Homme Nouveau et la Révolution Nationales de Vichy (1940–1944)* (Villeneuve d'Ascq: Presses Universitaires du Septentrion, 1997) 211–13.

one which would reconcile the worker and the employer, signalling the start of a new age of industrial production. Pétain's National Revolution provided them the opportunity to implement their ideals.

To be more precise, these men embraced corporatism, a philosophy which rejects individualism and liberal democracy and which became a key of the National Revolution. Of course, corporatism was one of the pillars of the *Charte du Travail*, Vichy's new labour charter. In fact, since the Paris Commune and especially after 1934, the ideas around social Catholicism, solidarity and corporatism developed throughout a small group of the French intellectual elite in which we could easily include Lyautey and Dautry.[74] The National Revolution, and the way it viewed, work, family and nation, also had serious paternalistic undertones. As Vigna says, 'paternalistic domination aims to celebrate natural communities such as family, business and the nation'.[75] And actually, Vigna points to the emphasis on sports, something particularly popular in big companies, not least automobile companies where they encouraged both the practice of sport and the spectacle of sport. As Dautry's personal archives show the *cités cheminotes* were largely designed on this model.

It is not so surprising that the SNCF – with its strict hierarchy – were receptive to the concepts of authority, discipline and hierarchy which are inherent to corporatist attitudes – but what about the cheminots? The new moral values issued by Pétain's National Revolution were integrated amongst the lower echelons of the SNCF. Indeed, distinctive features of the cheminot culture meant that, no matter their original political affiliations, railway workers were especially predisposed to accept the new regime's legitimacy, even when they did not fervently support it. It is impossible to measure the degree of support that each individual cheminot had for the regime, yet new research suggests that there was a cultural continuity between the pre-1940 railway milieu and Vichy's new moral order. Georges Ribeill's close study of the *Renseignements Hebdomadaires*, which replaced the company's official paper *Notre Métier* on 1 August 1940, shows that it made constant references to Pétain's speeches and radio messages. Ribeill was surprised by this, since the SNCF was, by nature, an apolitical company. However, the political values upheld by the National Revolution were also part of a familiar professional discourse. As Ribeill pointed out, 'the appearance of the slogan *Travail, Famille, Patrie* – Work, Family, Nation – on the five franc coin reminds us that the new motto was in complete accordance with the railway corporative ideal'.[76]

---

[74] Le Crom, *Syndicats, nous voilà!* (1995) 60–2.
[75] Vigna, *Histoire des ouvriers* (2012) 116.
[76] Ribeill, 'L'accommodation sociale de la SNCF' (2001).

Further parallels existed between cheminot traditions and Vichy's new moral order. Pétain's plan for a 'return to the land' reminds us of Raoul Dautry in the 1920s and 1930s, when he created the railway garden-cities. Of course these projects were very different in that one called for a full-on return to agriculture; still, the idea that a relationship with the land, the earth, the soil was important for individual but also collective well-being is important to underline. Vichy's doctrine on women as good wives and mothers also fell perfectly in step with the ideals the French railways had always promoted about women.[77] In the *Chantiers de la Jeunesse* (Youth Work Camps), these obligatory rural camps sponsored by Vichy to reform the French youth, Pétain imposed the 'Hébert method', an outdoor exercise routine being practiced in many railway centres since the 1920s.[78] And whereas Vichy's limitation of alcohol may have been a shock to many French people, railway managers had regularly enforced measures to curb cheminots' drinking habits since the nineteenth century.[79]

If there was a certain familiarity between the values of the cheminot milieu and those of the new government, it is difficult to say with any real certainty whether cheminots were actually swept up in the fervour of the National Revolution. A study of *Renseignements Hebdomadaires* suggests that cheminots regularly contributed photographs of their ideal homes and families, of their meetings with Pétain, or of their sports excursions and cultural activities; however, we do not know how voluntary this process was (see Figures 2.1 and 2.2). Perhaps the collection of photographs was orchestrated from the upper echelons of the SNCF. That being said, these photographs were regularly published in the *Renseignements Hebdomadaires*, reminding us of the professional values which overlapped with the goals of the National Revolution, and which cheminots appear to have continued to uphold under Occupation.[80] The fact that Pétain was an esteemed military figure, and that cheminots were particularly proud of their paramilitary status, might finally suggest that they would have welcomed his ascension to power.

---

[77] On women in the National Revolution, see Hanna Diamond, *Women and the Second World War in France, 1939–1948: Choices and Constraints* (Harlow: Longman, 1999).
[78] Interview André Brussière (26 Feb. 2008).   [79] Le François, *J'ai Faim* (1942) 35.
[80] In our beautiful cheminot families, we recently learned with great pleasure that M. Cailleux, replacement guard at Dampierre-Saint-Nicolas (Seine-Inférieure), had had a thirteenth child. *Renseignements Hebdomadaires* (22 May 1942); The beautiful family of Henri Charles, from the Verdun depot, after the birth of his fifth child. *Renseignements Hebdomadaires* (29 Jan. 1943); The beautiful family of M. Deletez, handler in Douai. *Renseignements Hebdomadaires* (19 Jun. 1943); M. Beauchet, roadmender at Hénin-Liétard, and his wife, level-crossing keeper at Courrières, surrounded by their 11 children. *Renseignements Hebdomadaires* (23 Jul. 1943).

Figure 2.1 In our beautiful cheminot families, we recently learned with great pleasure that M. Cailleux, replacement guard at Dampierre-Saint-Nicolas (Seine-Inférieure), had had a thirteenth child. *Renseignements Hebdomadaires*, 39 (22 May 1942). SNCF – Centre National des Archives Historiques.

However, the cheminot-led paper *Le Rail* reveals a pro-Vichy cheminot community. *Le Rail* was the bi-monthly paper of the *Corporation des Transports*, a trade union set up in 1923 to represent the interests of a group of conservative anti-CGT cheminots. The director, Rémi Wasier, had been a supporter of *Action française*. Already in 1934, they attacked Camille Chautemps and Léon Blum,[81] and were deeply critical of the left-wing 'cartel' which was in power. They supported the far-right street riots which took place on 6 February 1934, and subsequently wrote that the 'honest people' (the right-wing activists) had been thrown into jail whilst the real 'crooks' were still running free.[82] *Le Rail* then took a strong anti-Popular Front stand, and it was deadly against the nationalisation of the SNCF. Each copy made scathing criticisms of the new national railway company: 'It is said that the English parliament can do everything except for one thing: it cannot make a woman into a man (hum! hum! although nowadays we can see this happen...) And the SNCF, she can do everything but she cannot find a way to make trains

<hr>

[81] *Le Rail* (21 Jan. 1934).
[82] Rémi Wasier, 'La France contre les voleurs et les assasins', *Le Rail* (11 Feb. 1934).

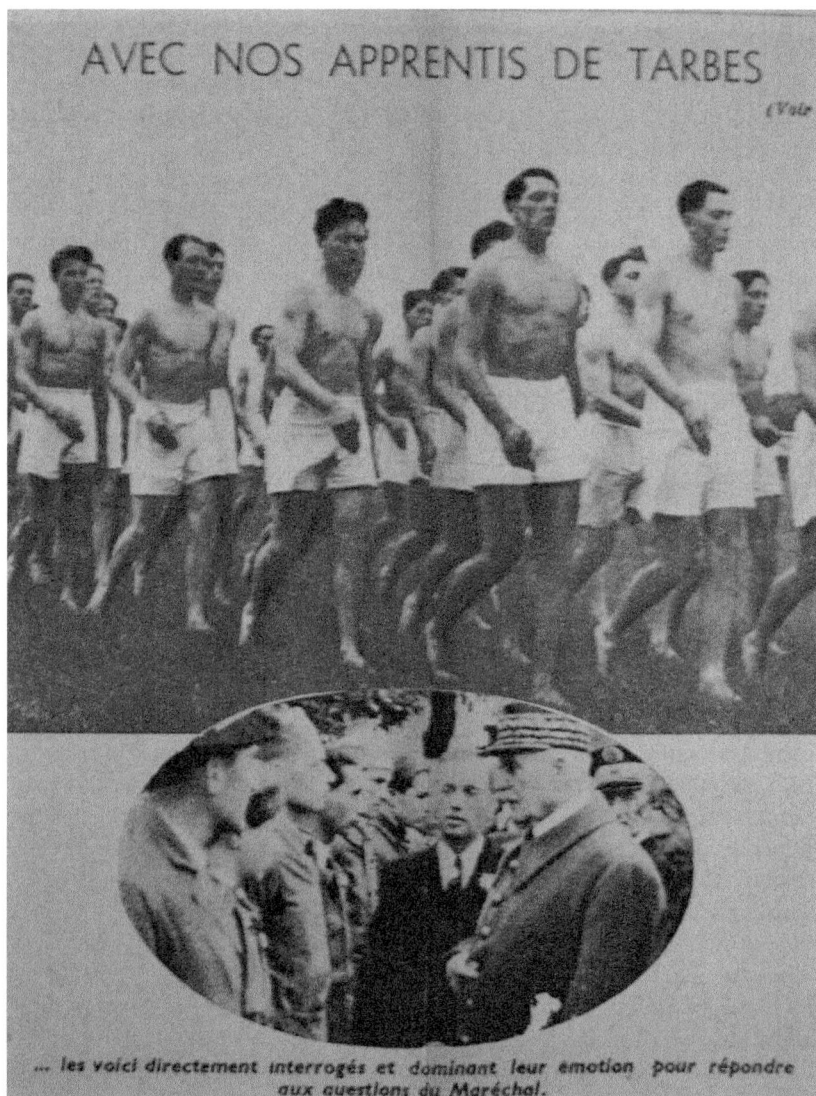

Figure 2.2 Our apprentices in Tarbes: Cheminot apprentices meet
Marshal Pétain, *Renseignements Hebdomadaires*, 9 (10 Oct. 1941).
SNCF – Centre National des Archives Historiques.

arrive on time in the North Region'.[83] It even criticised the SNCF's family policies, claiming, for instance, that the SNCF was 'not preoccupied by family conditions' when it came to deciding pay ranks and rises, and did not organise the holiday rota for its workers accordingly, or did not distribute travel passes to agents' parents.[84]

Wasier, his assistant André Gadin and the handful (a few thousand) of followers had found a government it wanted to work with. They regularly published suggestions for the *Charte des Cheminots*, keen to rid the trade union world of the 'false principles' it had abided by for so long.[85] On 1 February 1942, a giant portrait of the Marshal was printed on the front page, and below was a summary of the thirty-minute meeting between Pétain and the representatives of the *Fédération des syndicats du Rail* on 17 January 1942. Family values also made their way into the paper, in a rather humorous way. The edition on 15 March 1942 had two cartoons encouraging big families. The first showed a father asking his daughter whether she wanted a little brother or a little sister – 'Both!' she answered enthusiastically. In the other one, a group of big kids were telling a smaller boy that it must be so boring at home since he was an only child.[86] The overlapping concerns between *Le Rail* and Vichy's National Revolution cannot be ignored, and they confirm the cultural and even political conservatism of a small but non-negligible part of the cheminot community.

Finally, if some cheminots were able to cope with Vichy's new regime, it was also in part because of its anti-communist stanza. After the Nazi-Soviet Pact was signed on 23 August 1939, anti-communist sentiments erupted, as communists were denounced by the state for being anti-war and anti-national. The SNCF wholly abided by these measures. In a letter to the Director of Personnel (Barth), the Managing Director (Le Besnerais) quoted Monzie saying that 'we must make sure that our entire personnel, without a single exception, is able to carry out its patriotic duty, and that there is no indulgence towards our future enemies or their accomplices'.[87] Those who acted suspiciously were immediately suspended.

When Germany began its occupation of France, the wave of anti-communist repression lost some of its intensity precisely because of the Nazi-Soviet Pact. Upon their arrival in Paris, the Germans liberated several communists imprisoned during the Phoney War. It is even claimed that Otto Abetz, the German ambassador in Paris, personally received 'some very well-known leaders of the Communist Party' in his

---

[83] 'A la SNCF. Bruits et Potins', *Le Rail*, (15 Jan. 1938).
[84] 'Nos familles sacrifiées', *Le Rail* (1 Jul. 1939).
[85] 'La Charte cheminote', *Le Rail* (1 Dec. 1941).   [86] *Le Rail* (15 Mar. 1942).
[87] SNCF/25/LM/256: Letter (30 Aug. 1939) from Le Besnerais to Barth.

offices.[88] Moreover, 'in Wiesbaden, during the Armistice commission, the German and French delegations only mentioned the communists *once* in six months . . .'[89] This honeymoon period did not last. The Vichy government disbanded the French Communist Party (PCF) on 26 September 1940. Then, in November, *L'Humanité* mentioned the arrests of communists by Nazis.[90] By 1941, Special Sections were erected in the Free Zone's departmental courts-martial to act 'with exceptional rigour against "Communists and anarchists"'.[91]

The communist witch-hunt led by the Vichy ministers intensified after the summer of 1941, when Hitler breached the Nazi-Soviet Pact by invading Russia. Men and women suspected of belonging to the Communist Party were now being quietly arrested and interned into detention centres.[92] The Germans were also arresting an increasingly large number of communist suspects, and after 1942 they started putting more and more pressure on the SNCF to enforce harsher anti-communist surveillance.[93] A process of supervision and denunciation was also put into place in the SNCF, and Berthelot and Le Besnerais regularly voiced their anti-communist views.[94] It was well known that Berthelot had blamed the left-wing Popular Front for France's defeat, and he believed communists to be 'natural enemies of the public order, whose goal is to create a revolutionary chaos.'[95] In July 1941 he wrote a letter to the Chairman of the SNCF, Pierre-Eugène Fournier, stating that 'it is vital, in our current situation, to destroy communism in France'.[96]

Despite his fierce anti-communism, Le Besnerais knew that imposing excessive anti-communist measures within the SNCF put the efficiency of the railway at risk. Indeed, if cheminots were ordered to search for communists amongst their colleagues, or if anti-communist repression affected

[88] See Roland Gaucher, *Histoire secrète du Parti communiste français, 1920–1974* (Paris: Albin-Michel, 1974) 310–1.
[89] Amouroux, *La Grande Histoire des Français*, 2 (1977) 419–20. Emphasis in the original.
[90] Amouroux, *La Grande Histoire des Français*, 2 (1977) 431.
[91] Paxton, *Vichy France* (1975) 224.
[92] Jean-Pierre Azéma, *1940 l'année terrible* (Paris: Seuil, 1990) 313.
[93] SNCF/25/LM/1934: Letter (23 Sept. 1942) from HVD to Direction Générale; Statement (22 Oct. 1942) released to all Directeurs d'Exploitation des Régions.
[94] *Ibid.*, Letter (8 Mar. 1942) from Lepage, Chef de dépôt, to Richard, Chef d'Arrondissement de Paris (Traction). Depot, workshop and station chiefs were given different instructions from, on one hand, the SNCF management, and on the other, the local German authorities. As a result, they often got confused as to the exact procedure they were required to follow when denouncing communist activities. The Directors were aware of such problems and were adamant that their company orders trumped those of the Gestapo.
[95] Cited in Bachelier Report, 3.7.2.
[96] SNCF/25/LM/1934, Letter (3 Jul. 1941) from Berthelot to Fournier.

them in large numbers, there was a real risk that the entire community would rise in protest, causing real havoc on the railways. Already in October 1941, Le Besnerais had nuanced his position, insisting in his report that the spread of communist propaganda in the SNCF 'amounted to just a few isolated cases'. He even suggested that lifting morale amongst cheminots would be more effective than using repressive measures.[97] By awarding several hundred cheminots with military honours and citations, Le Besnerais hoped to prevent them from being roped into communist activities.[98]

Indeed, not all cheminots embraced communism and/or the CGT. The trade union *La Corporation des Transports* had been anti-CGT since the interwar years, and under Vichy the newspaper would go on to slander communists who they associated with Gaullists, anti-militarist and anti-clerical groups.[99] In the Ariège, there were fewer than 300 cheminots in this department, due not least to the fact that there were fewer railway lines in this mountainous region bordering the Pyrenees.[100] As such, calls for strikes never reached this area, and the personnel seemed overall to be very contained. In fact, at Pierre Semard's commemoration ceremony on 11 March 1945, only forty people attended : 'M. Maury, who managed the *Patriote de l'Ariège*, deplored the absence of so many trade union members when he opened the ceremony.'[101]

The archives of the purges within the SNCF further reveal the plurality of political views and inclinations within the SNCF, not least towards the right. There were cheminots within the ranks of the *Parti franciste*, the *Parti Populaire Français*, or Marcel Déat's *Rassemblement National Populaire* (RNP). Others spread German propaganda, belonged to the *Milice*, held *Légion des volontaires français contre le Bolchévisme* (LVF) meetings in their homes, or supplied the Germans with arms and weapons.[102] After the Liberation, they would all have to take responsibility for these 'crimes'. Jean Agret, a skilled labourer in Toulouse, was arrested on 19 January 1945 for having belonged to Vichy's Milice and later condemned to 20 years forced labour.[103] Edmond Barthes was accused of

---

[97] *Ibid.*, Rapport du Directeur Général de la SNCF concernant l'activité communiste et les mesures prises contre elle au cours de la 2ème quinzaine de sep. 1941.

[98] Bruno Bachelot, 'La mise en place de la législation anti-communiste à la SNCF, Sept. 39–Nov. 42', masters thesis at the University of Maine (2002) 176.

[99] 'Les communistes à la SNCF', *Le Rail*, 12 (15 Sept. 1941).

[100] ADA/25/W/13: Letter (18 Oct. 1941) from Tuizat, Inspecteur Principal, to Commissaire Principal; Note of Intervention (24 Mar. 1953).

[101] *Ibid.*, Letter (12 Mar. 1945) from Inspecteur de Police to Commissaire de Police.

[102] ANMT/2004/040/009: Epurations (Cas individuels) Agents arrêtés depuis la libération et actuellement incarcérés.

[103] SNCF/303/LM/15: Jean Agret, Note (26 Mar. 1945) from Chef de la Division du Service Général to Chef des Services Administratifs.

belonging to the Milice. He was condemned to fifteen years forced labour, a fine of 502 Francs, was stripped of his citizenship rights for twenty years and ultimately ejected from the SNCF.[104] Jean Verneuil was condemned to death for having taken up arms against the French.[105]

4   Workers, unions and the *Charte du Travail*

Some cheminots also truly believed that they could work with Vichy to protect and even improve their interests. Indeed, ex-trade union leaders joined Vichy's efforts to create a new trade union system, also known as the *Charte du Travail*. Traditional historiographies of cheminots in wartime France examine resistance, communism, clandestine activities, but Vichy's single, legal trade union system remains 'virgin territory'.[106] This is largely because the *Charte* was never that popular at the time – neither the French or even the Germans ever really bought into it.[107] Moreover, the archives are scarce. To write an article on the topic, Georges Ribeill used documents personally given to him by the *Fédération CFDT des cheminots* in 1987.[108] Ultimately, the trade union leaders who supported Pétain's *Charte* are ignored in both history and memory. As Paxton wrote, most people still believe that trade unionism was completely dissolved in 1940 – the period thus remains stuck between two important moments in labour history, the Popular Front and the Liberation. The *Charte* is strikingly absent from historiography.[109] But a history of the *Charte* and those who supported it is essential. It shows above all 'that Vichy was not a block; that Vichy evolved; that Vichy was not a mere parenthesis; that the National Revolution cannot be reduced to Nazi institutions forcefully imposing themselves onto Vichy'. Most importantly, 'the Vichy regime was accepted as the effective government of the nation, even by those who hated it'.[110] Jean-Pierre Le Crom's book and the special volume in *Le Mouvement Social* (1992) are rare works on this topic.[111]

But what was this *Charte* ? The *Charte du Travail* was a social agreement embodied in a single unique trade union. French union

---

[104] SNCF/274/LM/002: Letter (30 May 1946) from Directeur Région du Sud-Ouest to Directeur du Service Central du Personnel.
[105] *Ibid.*, the sentence was never carried out.   [106] Ribeill, 'Les chantiers' (1992) 88
[107] Paxton's preface to Le Crom, *Syndicats, nous voilà!* (1995) 15.
[108] See footnote 9 in Ribeill, 'Les chantiers' (1992) 88.
[109] Paxton in Le Crom, *Syndicats, nous voilà!* (1995) 17.
[110] *Ibid.*, 8. In his book, Le Crom enters a line of historians who argue that Vichy was not a cohesive block, from Stanley Hoffmann to Daniel Lee: Hoffmann, *Decline or Renewal? France since the 1930s* (New York: Viking Press, 1974); Lee, *Pétain's Jewish Children* (2014).
[111] See Le Crom, *Syndicats, nous voilà!* (1995); Jean-Louis Robert, 'Le Syndicalisme sous Vichy', *Le Mouvement Social*, 158 (1992).

representatives would be organised in groups, or 'families', according to their corporate profession. The Professional Family of Transports was then further divided into seven different Organising Committees which represented smaller interest groups of local or internal transports by water, road and rail.[112] In these groups, employers, technicians and workers would work together to solve problems. However, unlike the quarrels of the 1930s, there could be no politics, no conflicts and strikes were strictly banned.[113] Of course, this was a deeply idealised vision which overlooked completely the existing tensions within professional 'families'. As mentioned in Chapter 1, the homogenisation of a group like the cheminots was impossible: there were too many hierarchies, too many different types of work, too many different interests. So was it possible at national level?

A widespread publicity campaign was set in motion in order to galvanise support for the *Charte*. Pamphlets, journalists and newspapers explained its structure, goals and outcomes. One recurring theme was that the *Charte* would bring an end to class struggle, considered one of the main causes of the defeat: '[C]lass struggle will disappear,' claimed Paul Rives in *Le Midi*.[114] Georges Servoingt, editor of the right-wing paper *L'Espoir Français*, explained that under the Third Republic, employers and employees had been at complete odds, each vying for his own personal interests, rather than thinking of the general good. The *Charte* was an attempt to bring together the employers and workers. There were also propaganda meetings, like those organised in Toulouse in early 1942[115], and speeches by some of the country's highest authorities. Pétain spoke twice to the working classes in March and May 1941, whilst Monseigneur Maurice Feltin addressed the public in 1942 reminding them that they needed to engage with the *Charte* and the new trade union system in order to restore the nation and carry out their Christian duty.[116] Linked to this social solidarity was the idea of national prosperity: 'The *Charte du Travail* guarantees the rights of everyone. In every company, managers, employees, workers

---

[112] ANMT/2002/026/023: *Les Familles Professionnelles: Transports (I)* (Paris: Bulletin de la Charte du Travail, Ministère du Travail, 194?) 12–4.

[113] *Ibid.*, Georges Servoingt, 'L'Aube de la Collaboration Sociale', *La Charte du Travail* (Lyon: Imprimerie du Salut Public, 194?) 1.

[114] ADHG/2060/W/82: Paul Rives, 'La charte du travail: conditions materielles de la paix sociale', *Le Midi* (8 Nov. 1941).

[115] *Ibid.*, 'Réunion d'étude et de propagande sur la Charte du Travail', *La Garonne* (29 Jan. 1942); 'Une réunion d'information sur la Charte du Travail', *Le Midi* (2 Feb. 1942); 'Ce soir aux Variétés ...', *La Garonne* (11 Mar. 1942).

[116] ANMT/2002/026/023: *Les Syndicats et la Charte du travail*, Lettre Pastorale de Monseigneur Maurice Feltin, Archevèque de Bordeaux Evèque de Bazas (Paris, Vichy: Editions du bur eau de la propagande ouvrière, 1942).

belong to the same 'Team' united by the same interests, run by the same disciplinary values, working towards the same goal: the property of the nation'.[117] On 1 May 1941, Pétain declared that the 'stability and harmony' encouraged by the *Charte* would 'bring about the hour of [France's] recovery'.[118]

The Propaganda bureau tried to recycle old terms and apply them to the *Charte*, thereby implying a continuation of old policies rather than a restructuring imposed by Germans and/or Vichy. 'The spirit of the charter is essentially revolutionary', it stated.[119] 'Thanks to the *Charte*', the workers would be able to fight against the 'injustice of the proletarian condition'.[120] At the meeting of the cheminot trade union on 1 March 1942, Pasquier, one of the main leaders, made a claim that the spirit of collaboration between ministers, workers, trade union members and managers had actually been in effect since 1920. The only thing that had really changed was that the Marshal was now the one they had to report to.[121]

Trade unionism did not disappear under Vichy, it got re-shaped – but why buy into it? There were the traditional reasons linked to anti-communism, pacifism and/or anti-parliamentarism which would explain why socialists would want to be involved in Vichy's new social project. However, Le Crom underlines two other major factors. First, because trade union leaders were looking to protect the rights workers had already managed to obtain. This was the case of Mentor Pasquier, a major militant within the *Fédération des Cheminots* who was nominated to the *Conseil National*, a Vichy-ist institution aimed at helping create a link between the government and the people.[122] In the first meeting he attended, Pasquier fought against the proposition to push retirement age back to 65 years old. In the second meeting, he successfully challenged the proposition to reduce transport allowances of railway workers.[123] The idea was making sure that rights which had been so

---

[117] ANMT/2002/026/058: Propaganda images for the Charte du Travail.

[118] ANMT/2002/026/023: *La Charte du Travail*, 2.

[119] *Ibid., Pourquoi la Charte du travail?* (Paris, Vichy: Editions du bureau de la propagande ouvrière, 194?) 2.

[120] *Ibid.*, 4.

[121] ADHG /2042/W/10: Letter (23 Mar. 1942) from Commissaire Divisionnaire, Chef du Service Régional des Renseignements Généraux to Préfet Régional.

[122] Phillippe Fabre has a good paragraph explaining the Conseil National. See Phillippe Fabre, *Le Conseil d'Etat et Vichy: le contentieux de l'antisémitisme* (Paris: Publications de la Sorbonne, 2001) 183.

[123] Le Crom, *Syndicats, nous voilà!* (1995) 221; see also Chevandier, *Cheminots en Grève* (2002) 172. Pasquier was dismissed from the SNCF after the war as a result of his actions under Vichy ; this decision was over-turned a few years later.

recently acquired were not thrown out during regime change, rather than full adhesion to Vichy.

The second main reason one might support the *Charte* resonates with earlier points: with the collapse of the Popular Front, the betrayal of the Hitler-Stalin pact, and then the military defeat, many felt that a new 'third way' needed to be found.[124] As Paxton wrote it is impossible to understand the receptivity of Vichy in left-wing circles without taking into consideration the political turmoil since 1936. Taking part in Vichy was more about 'the decline of the Popular Front, the struggles between communists and non-communists within the united trade unions, the failure of the 30 November 1938 strike, the war which no one wanted, the rejection of tried and tested formulas and the thirst for a new beginning'.[125]

So who were these men who supported the *Charte*? There was Marcel Roy in the metal industry, Parsal in agriculture, Liaud in the railways and many more. All of these men would be sanctioned at the Liberation for their involvement in the *Charte*, but was their enthusiasm for this project actually sincere ?[126] Some could be said to be active partisans of the regime, others were socialists who wanted a leading role in managing the trade unions and others still were just trying to protect the interests of a group of workers.[127] Indeed, the decision to back Vichy's *Charte* had not been straightforward, not least in the case of the cheminots.[128] In August 1940, the *Fédération* was already wondering whether it should abstain from being present in the regime's institutions, or whether it should take an active role in their construction and expansion. As we know, they opted for the latter.

Ultimately, entire sectors of French economy, society and industry remained largely untouched by the *Charte*, and the SNCF was one of them.[129] Because the railways were no ordinary company and/or industry, their workers came under slightly different rules which were yet to be devised. An official *Charte des cheminots* would eventually come into being after a tedious process of negotiation.[130] But even then, 'its link to the Transport Family was more theoretical than practical, and mostly consisted of certain liaisons'.[131] Meetings were organised to try and engage cheminots in the Charte, like the one organised by the *Syndicat des Cheminots* on Saturday 21 March 1942 in Toulouse. Mr Servière

[124] Le Crom, *Syndicats, nous voilà!* (1995) 220.   [125] *Ibid.*, 7–8.   [126] *Ibid.*, 227.
[127] Chevandier, *Cheminots en Grève* (2002) 173.
[128] Le Crom, *Syndicats, nous voilà!* (1995) 229.   [129] *Ibid.*, 388.
[130] See Ribeill, 'Les chantiers' (1992).
[131] ANMT/2002/026/023: *Les Familles Professionnelles: Transports (I)* 14.

presided the event, which opened at 21h15 with a minute of silence in honour/memory of the cheminots who were killed in the war and the POWs. Servière subsequently mentioned his disappointment that, as times had gotten tough, fewer and fewer people attended these meetings: only about one hundred attendees had showed up that day to hear about this Charte 'on which their trade union future is based'.[132] In his speech Pasquier acknowledged the difficulties in writing up the Charte, but argued how important it was to support it nonetheless: '... hasn't collaboration existed amongst the cheminots since 1920?', he pointed out. 'Haven't they always presented their grievances to the various governments via the Ministers of the PTT? Why would it be any different today. The government of the Marshal is the one which currently represents all of France.'[133] Ultimately, he deployed the propaganda tactics used by Vichy and emphasised the continuity between the interwar period and the Charte. The Charte, he claimed, only served 'to confirm a situation which has existed for twenty years already'.

Liaud and Pasquier were initially very involved in drawing up the Charte, but as the project developed, enthusiasm began to waver.[134] Numerous drafts were drawn up, but the large majority were deeply unsatisfactory. When one of the versions was submitted to Pétain on July 1942, the latter confided to Gibrat that he was annoyed that it engaged more with current structures of the SNCF rather than with the ideals they (Vichy) were promoting. Indeed, the Union Organising Committee was not buying into the National Revolution jargon. The February 1943 version of a Charte des Cheminots was eventually adopted, but it just as soon created opposition and growing resistance among the workers.[135] By winter 1943–44, the ex-trade union leaders wanted to lay the idea of a Charte des cheminots to rest completely.[136] At this stage, four new federal secretaries had in fact been elected , including Jean Descombes and Gérard Ouradou who were both socialists and secretly part of the Resistance group Libération Nord.[137]

There are others reasons why cheminots would never really become enthused by the Charte. Strikes and 'lock-outs' were banned, a government decision which hindered those who were so inclined, but also which threatened the theoretical freedom and masculinity of the workers.[138]

---

[132] ADHG /2042/W/10: Letter (23 Mar. 1942) from Commissaire Divisionnaire, Chef du Service Régional des Renseignements Généraux to Préfet Régional.
[133] Ibid.   [134] Le Crom, Syndicats, nous voilà! (1995) 229.
[135] Chevandier, Cheminots en Grève (2002) 171.
[136] Le Crom, Syndicats, nous voilà! (1995) 230.
[137] Chevandier, Cheminots en Grève (2002) 173; see also Ribeill, 'Les chantiers' (1992) 108–11.
[138] ADHG /2060/W/82: 'La Charte du Travail', Paris-Soir (3 Nov. 1941).

Moreover, Vichy's trade union system did not understand the deep-rooted pluralistic nature of the French workers. Supporters of the *Charte* claimed that internal divisions within trade unions had led to the fall of France[139], but to deny the distinctive and specific nature of the men working within and across professions was to underestimate individual agency. One could never force harmony on a community with uneven needs, interests and concerns.

If feelings towards the *Charte* varied, what is clear is that a portion of the cheminots – perhaps not most representative, definitely not the pro-soviet communists – nonetheless aligned their politics to Vichy trade union system. They saw it as a possible tool for negotiating better working conditions. On 31 January 1943, 71 trade unions were represented by 116 delegates in Toulouse. There, Liaud started the session by describing the *Fédération* as a modern and renovated trade union made up of a total of 480 unions in full boom.[140] It is not possible to assess if the local trade unions were, in fact, 'booming' at the time; nor is it possible to measure the degree of enthusiasm which these trade unions had for the *Charte*. It is, however, important to discuss how cheminots did, in fact, imagine a relationship with Vichy, although a real vision never materialised in itself.

Conclusion

In many ways, it appears that the cheminots responded positively to the call for war in 1939, more so in fact than other workers. The nation was once again calling upon them for its military success, and they were keen to defend France. The subsequent defeat, however, would prove to be deeply traumatic. Indeed, the combined trauma of previous political problems in 1938–9 and the current military defeat of 1939–40 set a particularly desperate tone throughout French society. In this atmosphere of exhaustion, humiliation and confusion, many began to consider that following the guidance of Marshal Pétain was, indeed, the best thing to revive the French nation. The cheminots were no different. They, too, were part of this society which ushered in Pétain and Vichy, and which even believed that they could bring about a new future for France.

---

[139] *Ibid.*; Jean Laborde, 'Echos du Monde: La Charte du Travail', *La Petite Gironde* (Monday 5 Nov. 1941).

[140] ADHG/2042/W/10: See article attached to letter (1 Feb. 1943) from Commissaire Principal, Chef du Service Départemental des Renseignements Généraux to Préfet Délégué.

This should not be understood to mean that Vichy had widespread, unwavering support. Yet the consensus was that the large majority of French men and women wanted to move forward, and they could only do this by working together. Indeed, if the French became more inward-looking during the Occupation, they also accommodated to the new regime out of basic principles of solidarity and survival.[141] We can see an upsurge of organised solidarity, not least in the working class. POWs associations, for instance, sprung up everywhere, and the French were encouraged to think of their fellow men in a foreign land, captive but alive. They sent them books, foods, letters, and most of all, hope. In fact, Vichy and Marshal Pétain derived much of their legitimacy from the idea that it had sacrificed itself for the good of the nation. For if France was militarily defeated, at least the horrors of war had been avoided. And now, the government told them, they could rise again by joining their strengths.

Far from confirming the popular image of the communist cheminot, a study of the Vichy period highlights the multiplicity of political and ideological leanings throughout the railway milieu. Equally, it challenges the idea that cheminots were resisters of the first hour, and shows on the contrary that solidarity was key in this period: solidarity with family, of course, but also with colleagues, workers and the nation. As has been seen, it was a running theme in the state and company propaganda, whether Berthelot wanted the cheminots to work harder than ever before, or Pétain wanted the workers to join the *Charte*. Behind these moralistic speeches about solidarity lay a strong corporatist, paternalistic undertone which probably annoyed some workers, but the fact that the railways were re-built in record time suggests a real level of cooperation. As it will be shown, not all cheminots agreed with Berthelot or Pétain. But much like in the First World War, the Second World War and the German Occupation initially pulled the nation together in a unifying moment. It was only later that cracks would start to appear.

---

[141] Philippe Burrin, *Living with Defeat: France under the German Occupation* (London: Arnolf, 1996, c1995).

3   Bahnofs[1]

Jean Barth, the Director of Personnel, was one of the only directors still in Paris after 13 June.[2] He kept a diary where he recorded his first interactions with the Germans: 'Friday 14 June – At 14h, two German Officers were escorted to my office by the concierge of *Gare St Lazare*: very polite, almost pleasant'. The officers declared that they wanted to get the trains running again in order to supply the civilian population, to which Barth answered that unfortunately all the men and material have been dispatched during the exodus. This response disappointed the Germans, but they openly agreed with Barth that, had the situation been reversed, they would have done the same.[3] Already, a courteous relationship was being established. A few days later, Barth met some more officers: 'At 10h30 I get a phone call that five German Officers are waiting for me in my office; I go back; one of them speaks remarkable French', he wrote. Apparently, this same officer 'knew all the senior civil servants of the SNCF'.[4] This specialist knowledge was sure to impress Barth.

Indeed, the first encounter with the Occupier was not necessarily a bad one. On 21 June 1940, Jean Guéhenno described scenes of civilians welcoming the Germans into Clermont: 'These poor people who had done six hundred kilometres not to see [the Germans] now ran to greet them'. 'Oh foolishness', he despaired.[5] Within a matter of hours, the rumours of barbarism and horror had evaporated into thin air, leaving room for curiosity and even contact. Léon Werth noticed that the pejorative term '*boches*' was suddenly replaced by soldiers, whilst Simone de Beauvoir recalled the friendly interactions with generous and flirty Germans as she walked back towards Paris.[6] These stories contrast

[1] In German, the word *bahnof* means train station. However, under Vichy, the term was reappropriated by the cheminots to designate the German railway workers who came to work in France.

[2] There is very little information on Jean Barth aside from his role as Director of Personnel.

[3] AN/72/AJ/473: Journal de Barth, Friday 14 June 1940.   [4] *Ibid.*

[5] Jean Guéhenno, *Journal des années noires 1940–1944* (Paris: Gallimard, 2002, c1947) 16.

[6] Burrin, *Living with Defeat* (1996) 23.

sharply with the myth of Franco-German animosity, so often displayed in films such as *La Grande Vadrouille* (1966), *Papy fait de la Résistance* (1983) and *Effroyables Jardins* (2002). Likewise, in *La Bataille du Rail* (1945), the relations between Germans and French cheminots were reduced to oppression, resistance and violence. This remained the official version of events for many years. In 1968, Paul Durand briefly mentioned that relations between cheminots and Germans occasionally benefited from a shared technical knowledge, but he still struggled to embrace the complexity of their relations. In the thirty-five-page section on Franco-German encounters, Durand primarily intended to prove the 'bitterness of the(ir) relations': 'Everywhere, cheminots look unfavourably on this enemy invasion', he wrote.[7] Maurice Choury's study similarly reduced Franco-German relations to cheminots' resistance to the *boches*.[8]

More recently, historians have emphasised the civil relations between the French and the Germans, not least amongst those working for the railways. Alfred Gottwaldt and Alfred Mierzejewski have argued that rapports between the French and German railway workers were generally civil on both sides, with the Germans acting as supervisors rather than as oppressors.[9] There was an *entente cordiale*, a cordial relationship, between these groups of workers whose profession bridged a historical gap of animosity. Such studies fall in line with broader works which explore behaviour under Vichy. In particular, Philippe Burrin drew attention to the idea of a 'correct attitude to adopt'[10] towards the Germans which '...boiled down to erecting a wall between the French and the Germans',[11] but he showed that the 'silent treatment' epitomised in Vercors' *Silence of the Sea* (1942) was not much more than an idealised interpretation of what was in fact a more ambiguous relationship between occupier and occupied.[12] The French built a number of different kinds

---

[7] Durand, *La SNCF* (1968) 159; 165.

[8] Maurice Choury, *Les cheminots dans la bataille du rail* (Paris: Librairie académique Perrin, 1970).

[9] Mierzejeski, *The Most Valuable Asset* (2000) 83–4. See also Alfred Gottwaldt, 'Les cheminots allemands pendant l'Occupation en France de 1940 à 1944' in Marie-Noëlle Polino, ed., *Une entreprise pendant la guerre: la SNCF 1939–1945* (Paris: Presses Universitaires Françaises, 2001).

[10] Burrin *Living with Defeat* (1996) 192.   [11] *Ibid.*, 192–3.

[12] Gildea, *Marianne in Chains* (2003); Sandra Ott, 'Duplicity, Indulgence and Ambiguity in Franco-German Relations, 1940–1946', *History and Anthropology*, 20.1 (2009) 57–77. To see the relationships between French women and German men, see Sandra Ott, 'The informer, the lover and the gift giver: Female collaborators in Pau 1940–1946', *French History*, 22.1 (2008) 94–114; Fabrice Virgili, *Shorn Women: gender and punishment in liberation France* (Oxford: Berg, 2002, c2000); Fabrice Virgili, *Naître ennemi: les enfants de couples franco-allemands nés pendant la Seconde Guerre mondiale* (Paris: Payot, 2009).

of relations with the Germans: commercial, artistic, strategic, amicable and, as we will see, professional.

Focussing on Franco-German relations within the railway can further nuance current understandings of French behaviour under Occupation. In the early days of the Occupation, white-collar but also blue-collar workers adapted to Franco-German cohabitation and professional collaboration. These rapports changed after the labour laws of 1942 and 1943, not least when French railway directors became more and more resistant to negotiation and compromise as they saw Germans encroach on their material, their personnel and their freedom. In contrast, a study of the experiences of French cheminots working in Germany nuances the 'dark' history of the STO.

1   A promising armistice and on-going negotiations

One of the great myths of the Franco-German Armistice was that it put the French – and the SNCF – under the German jackboot. Article 13 is often cited as the most severe clause in regards to the railways, yet a close reading shows that the SNCF was not just handed over for the Germans to control. The article stated that all military installations and stocks be handed over to the Germans; that the railways should remain in their current state and that it was forbidden to sabotage or destroy them further; and that the French had to gather enough personnel and material in the Occupied Zone to reconstruct the damaged system of communications, whether it be roads or railways. According to Jean-Pierre Masseret and Christian Bachelier, the German interpretation of this article implied that all railway organisations would be *at the disposal* of the German Chief of Transports, Werner Goeritz.[13] Two further articles referred to the railways: Article 15 stated that the French had to convey all German transports which passed through the Free Zone between the Reich and Italy, and Article 16 ordered the French state to organise the return of all the refugees via the railways.[14]

These clauses did not sound the death sentence of the French railway system. As Michel Margairaz recently wrote, 'when the Armistice Convention was signed on 22 June 1940, it did not provide enough information to specify the exact rapports between defeater and defeated

---

[13] Jean-Pierre Masseret, 'Ouverture du colloque' in Marie-Noëlle Polino, ed., *Une entreprise pendant la guerre: la SNCF 1939–1945* (Paris: Presses Universitaires Françaises, 2001); Bachelier Report, 1.1. Premier contacts avec l'occupant, juin–septembre 1940.

[14] The Franco-German Armistice of 1940 can be viewed at the Avalon Project, Yale University, available at http://avalon.law.yale.edu/ wwii/frgearm.asp.

within the railway milieu'. In fact, the Armistice was generally never quite as crippling or rigid as it has sometimes been described. The French Navy, for instance, was untouched by the Germans, and as Robert Paxton and Henry Rousso have pointed out, Vichy was convinced that negotiations would loosen the terms of collaboration.[15]

So if Germans had ravaged Poland and its railways in the September 1939 invasion, their agenda for France was very different: they mainly wanted to use French railway materials to restore the efficiency of their own deteriorating railways.[16] Indeed, despite overall economic growth since 1933, by 1937 the German national railways, the *Deutsche Reichsbahn* (RB), had started to see cracks in its own system. In late 1938 Julius Dorpmüller, the Managing Director of the Reichsbahn, had even taken 'the risky step of informing Hitler in writing that the Reichsbahn had reached the limit of its potential'.[17] Their railway crisis was caused by a number of factors. During the Nazi rearmament programme, the Reichsbahn had been side-lined from all official discussions mapping out future economic and military goals. As a result, the Reichsbahn was left to adapt to increasingly disproportionate demands. Combined with the fact that the Reichsbahn was being mismanaged, this meant that by 1939–40 the Reichsbahn was unable to keep up with military expansion in the East. The situation only worsened after the difficult winter of 1939.[18] Therefore when Germany invaded the Low Countries in 1940, it was only interested in using the French and the Belgian railways 'as reservoirs of rolling stock for the Reichsbahn'.[19] As Ulrich Herbert pointed out, this would ideally be achieved 'with minimal input from the part of the German military, financial and administrative services'.[20]

And so the doors were left open for discussion. Almost immediately after the Armistice was signed, a Commission was born to interpret its various articles and supervise its implementation. The Commission was placed in Wiesbaden in Germany, and a French delegation was sent there to represent France's interests, with Jean Berthelot representing

---

[15] '... multiple evolutions after June 1940 gave the Pétain government both the incentive and the opportunity to try to buy its way out of the harsh armistice into some less restrictive, more normal arrangement'. Paxton, *Vichy France* (1975) 59; '... the various protagonists, and in particular the French, believed in a space of negotiation, despite or because of the armistice'. Henry Rousso, 'Bilans et Perspectives' in Polino, ed.,*Une entreprise pendant la guerre* (2001).
[16] 'Dorpmüller attempted to absorb [the Ostbahn] completely within the RB'. Mierzejeski, *The Most Valuable Asset* (2000) 79.
[17] *Ibid.*, 55.   [18] *Ibid.*, 87.   [19] *Ibid.*, 84.
[20] Cited in Gottwaldt, 'Les cheminots allemands' (2001).

the railway transports.[21] Fears that the Germans intended to further augment their control over the railways were soon dissipated. The Bachelier Report clearly explains Berthelot's encounter with Lieutenant-Colonel Theilacker in Wiesbaden, where the latter assured him that the Germans had no intentions to take over the French railways. Whilst military transports would be directed by the German authorities alone, the French would be the only ones to actually carry out these transports. The bottom line was: German control, French execution. And this, he highlighted to Berthelot, was obviously only for military transports: 'it is evident that once this [military] priority is satisfied, materials can be used for public transports'.[22]

To supervise the French transport and communications system, the Germans set up a centralised body in Paris which did not infringe too aggressively on the SNCF. The *Wehrmacht Verkehrsdirektion* (WVD) was run by Colonel Werner Goeritz, a decorated senior Nazi military official who died in 1958.[23] This institution supervised all transport systems, and Hans Münzer, who had been part of the RB since 1906, oversaw the railway system from within a specialised service. The WVD was then subdivided at the regional level into the *Transportkommandanturen* (TK). Each TK in Nantes, Bordeaux and Rennes also contained a specialised service to supervise the regional railway activities, known as the *Eisenbahnbetriebsdirektionen* (EBD).[24] An initial contingent of 28,500 railway workers from the RB was sent to Belgium and France in 1940. This, however, was only a temporary measure, and by spring 1941 only 4,000 RB workers supervised a workforce of about 400,000 people.[25] The Germans had put in place a national as well as a regional supervision system of the French railway, but had refrained from the total occupation of railway services that they had undertaken in Poland.

Fruitful discussions were also taking place outside of Wiesbaden. On 5 July 1940, Berthelot, Colonel Paquin, and Colonel Goeritz's representative, General Gerke, met in Paris to iron out some questions about the interpretation of the Armistice. The minutes of this crucial meeting show

---

[21] For a bigger view of the overarching developments of Franco-German exchanges in 1940 over the Armistice, not least in Wiesbaden and Montoire, see Paxton *Vichy France* (1975) 51–91.

[22] Cited in Bachelier Report, 1.1.

[23] Not much else is known about Goeritz, although it is important to note that the WVD would eventually become the HVD when Nazi police forces took control over the military services.

[24] AN/72/AJ/477: Letter (5 Jul. 1940) from Harrand, French Delegate of Transports, to Directeur du Service Central du Mouvement. See also AN/72/AJ/415: Mémento of WVD Conference (5 Jul. 1940).

[25] Mierzejeski, *The Most Valuable Asset* (2000) 147.

that most of the French desires were confirmed. The SNCF was assured that its personnel would be able to travel easily, and the Germans even acknowledged that this would lead to better running of the service. The Germans also re-confirmed that, once military transports were carried out, material and personnel could then be used to transport goods and people for French purposes. Above all, the Germans assured the French that they would not requisition material if it was too detrimental to French interests. When the French mentioned the administrative and logistical problems they foresaw regarding the small area in Northern France which had been placed under the transport authorities in Brussels, the Germans insisted that the matter was being 'looked into'.[26] A few days later, Berthelot hinted that even more agreements had been confirmed in person: 'some assurances', he said, 'can only be given orally'.[27]

Of course the situation was not always smooth sailing. On 30 June 1940 there were already complaints that the Germans prevented agents from returning to their posts in certain Parisian stations. They had furthermore ordered lights to be shut off completely between 22h and 6h, thus banning all transport movement during that time.[28] By 10 July, Le Besnerais was writing to the Minister of Public Works, Ludovic-Oscar Frossard (an ex-PCF member succeeded by Jean Prouvost the following day), to highlight the problem: whilst there was a general consensus to get the trains running normally, German instructions limited what they could do, especially in the Occupied Zone.[29] Some of the requests which came from the WVD indeed appeared slightly unrealistic and very time consuming, not least when they asked Le Besnerais to have every daily report translated into German. Le Besnerais was not afraid to reject this demand and to instead offer to make a single tableau with the key railway terms translated into German; it was then up to them to piece together the reports.[30]

But still, the Germans seemed co-operative on the big issues, not least the return of POWs. In 1940 there were approximately one and a half million French POWs, and although the Armistice stated that none would return before the end of the war, the French would relentlessly try to negotiate their return.[31] Of course releasing POWs was not ideal in

[26] AN/72/AJ/415: Memento (5 Jul. 1940).

[27] *Ibid.*, Letter (8 Jul. 1940) from Berthelot to Ministre des Travaux Publics.

[28] SNCF/26/LM/0020: Difficultés Rencontrées par la SNCF pour la reprise de l'Exploitation (30 Jun. 1940).

[29] *Ibid.*, Letter (10 Jul. 1940) from Le Besnerais to *Ministre des Travaux Publics*.

[30] *Ibid.*, Correspondence (7 and 23 Jul. 1940) between WVD and Le Besnerais.

[31] Although the Armistice initially stipulated that POWs would remain in captivity until the end of the war, the French government managed to obtain some concessions over time. These were not deemed sufficient, and the French would continue to demand the release of more POWs. See Jackson, *The Dark Years* (2002) 127, 174, 179.

a period of such high unemployment, but their return remained a very big bargaining chip. As Scapini underlined at the time, 'some results from Montoire' in favour of releasing POWs were 'essential for the stability of France'.[32] On 16 November it was agreed that POWs with more than four children could return, and in May 1941 negotiations on more releases were started.

Whereas the Scapini mission struggled to get POWs returned to France, a third of the 35,000 cheminot POWs were back within a few weeks of the Armistice. This exceptionally high level of return is largely down to the strategic importance of the railways themselves. As specialist workers, they could not be spared if France was to ensure rebuild its communications system. The German understood this condition perfectly: 'we plan on releasing railway employees currently being held prisoner, who worked in the SNCF before the war, in occupied territory, so that they can return to their post,' they promised.[33] '[It was] even better than I had dared hope for' said Berthelot, delighted by the negotiation.[34]

Yet cracks soon began to appear in this POW scheme. By August 1940 only a portion of cheminots had returned, some of whom even continued to have POW status.[35] This meant that, despite being home, they had to report to the local *Kommandantur* once or twice a week. Another situation arose in December whereby POWs residing in the Forbidden Zone had been freed but were unable to get access to their homes.[36] By February 1941, the privileges cheminot POWs had originally received – asking for leave, for example – were being dismissed.[37] Moreover, discussions about the possibility of returning all cheminots had come to a complete standstill. In July, Le Besnerais sent the WVD a list specifying the workers who needed to be returned to the SNCF most urgently to ensure the good running of the service, and he even went to discuss this in person with Colonel Von Tippelskirsch. By the autumn, his requests had still not been granted, and Le Besnerais was warning that 'the good running of the public service and especially of the military

[32] Paxton, *Vichy France* (1975) 78.
[33] Berthelot, *Sur les rails du pouvoir* (1967) 78. See also AN/72/AJ/415: Mémento (5 Jul. 1940).
[34] Berthelot, *Sur les rails du pouvoir* (1967) 78.
[35] SNCF/206/LM/1: Letter (1 Aug. 1940) from Barth to Directeur d'Exploitation des Régions.
[36] *Ibid.*, Letter (5 Dec. 1940) from L'Huillier, Chef du Service de liaison, to Lamiral, Chef d'Arrondissement de Traction à Vesoul.
[37] *Ibid.*, Letter (19 Feb. 1941) from Kessler to L'Huillier (Ingénieur Principal, Représentant de la SNCF-EBD à Nancy).

transports depends, in large part, on the outcome of our request [for the return of POWs]'.[38]

In August 1941, the question of POWs remained absolutely central to SNCF managers.[39] Reading through the issues of the SNCF newspaper *Renseignements Hebdomadaires* between 1940 and 1944 shows the quasi-sacred place cheminot POWs held within the company: the SNCF did everything to maintain links with those still captive in Germany, and in fact stealing from a POW parcel was one of the most serious crimes on the railway.[40] And so Le Besnerais continued to press the Germans on the subject of the liberation of all cheminot POWs. In March 1942 the Germans seemed to entertain this idea; however it is more likely that they were using it as leverage to get more benefits from the SNCF. Indeed, Paquin complained that whilst Germans claimed to be looking into the liberation of the POWs, they were simultaneously requesting 9,500 more workers for Germany.[41]

So although the SNCF initially held a privileged position in regards to the return of the POWs, it was soon reduced to the same kind of pressures and bargaining as the Vichy government; likewise, whilst it may have had some benefits in regards to the demarcation line, these should not be overstated. Indeed, cheminots and the running of the railways in general continued to suffer from the severance of France into separate territories. Initially, cheminots were granted easy access to the *Ausweis* (identity card) necessary to cross these virtual frontiers which separated France; but this relative mobility had strict limitations. The regulations around the *Ausweis* were especially tight to prevent any abuses. Cheminots could not, for instance, make use of their *Ausweis* when they were on leave unless it was to reach their permanent home address.[42] Moreover, they had many different types of passes, and only approximately 23,000 cheminots had permanent ones which allowed them free passage at any time.[43] Generally, their *Ausweis* allowed them mobility within a certain time limit. There was also the frequent administrative blip which might make it impossible for

---

[38] SNCF/26/LM/0036: Letter (18 Nov. 1941) from Le Besnerais to Scapini.

[39] *Ibid.*, Letter (7 Feb. 1942) from Berthelot to Fournier.

[40] 'Lets continue to watch over the POW parcels', *Renseignements Hebdomadaire* (1 May 1942). For more information on contacts between POWs, their families and the SNCF, see *Renseignements Hebdomadaire* (28 Nov. 1941); (13 Feb. 1942). SNCF/206/LM/1: Avis de Service (12 Jul. 1943), Liaison avec les agents prisonniers de guerre ou détachés en Allemagne et avec leurs familles.

[41] SNCF/26/LM/0036: Letter (3 Mar. 1942) from Paquin to Secrétaire d'Etat aux Communications.

[42] ANMT/202/AQ/236: Letter (11 Oct. 1942) from Chef de la Division Centrale du Mouvement-Voyageurs to Chef du Service de l'Exploitation de la Région du Nord.

[43] *Ibid.*, Letter (5 Nov. 1941) from Barth to many.

workers living in one zone and working in another to move freely. These blips generally got taken care of, but they could take some time. Still, the cheminots' *Ausweis* was a precious commodity, and it is no wonder that one agent 'forgot' to hand his back after he was fired from the SNCF.[44]

But the Germans were not always to blame for the difficult conditions of the Occupation, and Franco-French rapports could be equally tense. On 24 June 1940, Jean Jardin and his son were trying to track down railway materials so that they would not be seized by the Germans. However, when they arrived in Trouville, it was not the Germans who posed problems but the hostile hoteliers, who refused to return the material until they received full payment.[45] A few months later, the SNCF only received part of the coal it had requested from the Direction of the Mines. When he found out about this, Berthelot wrote a stern letter to René Belin in the Ministry of Production demanding that the SNCF receive the totality of the requested amount. He then stormed off to Vichy to voice his outrage and ensure that this would never happen again.[46] And whilst the Ministry of *Ravitaillement*, or Supplies, wanted to ban family parcels in order to prevent the spread of the black market, Berthelot thought that this was a terrible idea which would 'unnecessarily attract widespread unpopularity against the government'.[47] Indeed, the interests of the French clashed frequently.

Ultimately, a civilised Franco-German cohabitation seemed plausible in those early days of 1940. Despite apprehensions and annoyances, the path towards cohabitation was paved with negotiation and even cooperation. On Christmas Eve of 1940, the SNCF headquarters received a very cordial letter from the WVD informing them that they would need a station to be closed for military purposes. And, already a step ahead, the Germans specified some nearby routes which could be used instead to prevent a traffic jam.[48]

2   Bahnofs

Examining Franco-German rapports in the lower echelons further proves that a spirit of cohabitation existed throughout the French railway

---

[44] *Ibid.*, Letter (19 Jun. 1941) from Cambournac, to Chef du Service de l'Exploitation.
[45] The exact circumstances of this incident are, unfortunately, unknown, since Jardin does not detail them in his book. However, it appears that hoteliers would somehow have been in a position to 'hold hostage' these machines. Pascal Jardin's memoirs are cited in Bachelier Report, 1.1.
[46] AN/72/AJ/414: Note (23 Sep. 1940) from Berthelot to Claudon, Directeur Général des Transports.
[47] *Ibid.*, Note (5 Apr. 1941) from Berthelot to Jusseau.
[48] SNCF/26/LM/0020: Letters (24 and 28 Dec. 1940) between WVD and Direction de la SNCF.

services. In many ways, this is not surprising: as mentioned earlier, there were in fact few Reichsbahn workers in France. Even at their peak (in the first and last months of occupation) they did not make up one tenth of the total of cheminots. In fact, most railwaymen had no direct contact with the RB workers. The ex-cheminot Marcel Redempt explained that 'We did not see the German presence amongst us, there was generally a German cheminot in an office, often the office of the depot chief, but the rest, we didn't see them'.[49] Jean-Claude Huckendubler, who worked for six months in the station at Fontainebleau in 1943 where 'we could not feel the war', never saw a single German railway worker.[50] Indeed, since Germans were only there to ensure that raw goods and railway materials requested by the Reich were being effectively dispatched, they were concentrated in railway centres dedicated to the transportation of goods. A station like Fontainebleau, which primarily took care of passenger trains, was of little interest to them.

Even when they worked together, cheminots did not feel threatened by their German counterparts. Whereas the soldiers who had marched into the French villages were typically strong and young, German railwaymen were by and large older men nearing retirement age. Many had been wounded during the previous war and even spoke a bit of French, which was especially good for making polite conversation with the cheminots.[51] Some were not railway professionals, but had worked in a related industry. This did not matter since their duties were limited to supervision and required no technical skills.[52] Mr Brussière described the German who worked in his workshop as a *gros pépère*, or fat boy, who, in the mornings, would do his surveillance round and then settle down for a little drink. This was hardly the symbol of Germanic efficiency and brutality.[53]

It is thus no coincidence that, while cheminots pejoratively referred to the German occupiers as *les boches*, they called the German railway workers *les bahnofs*, which means railway station. Testimonies and interviews consistently reflect the spirit of camaraderie which existed amongst French and German railway workers. 'They were *ch'minots*, just like us', said Robert Lebrun. 'They were *ch'minots* themselves!' echoed Brosset. Creusot considered them 'sort of like colleagues', while Bonnin stated that 'a *ch'minot* is a *ch'minot*, whether he's French or German!'[54]

[49] AHICF: Interview transcript, Marcel Redempt (19 Oct. 1999) 12.
[50] AHICF: Huckendubler (1999) 4–5.
[51] Interview Roger Charbonnier (24 Apr. 2008).   [52] AHICF: Huckendubler (1999).
[53] Interview Brussière (2008).
[54] Interviews Robert Lebrun (7 Feb. 2008), André Brosset (23 Feb. 2008), M. Creusot (4 Mar. 2008), Bonnin (2008).

The ties sometimes exceeded professional cordiality. Towards the end of the Occupation, a small group of French cheminots tried to recruit the *bahnofs* to join the resistance by spreading some propaganda tracts in German.[55] In another case, a German chief intervened on behalf of a French cheminot who was being threatened by a Gestapo agent.[56] But there were limits, too, to the cordial relationships. 'Relations between French and German cheminots were cordial,' said Lebrun, 'up until the moment that they spotted something wrong'.[57] Brussière remembered one particular incident when a *bahnof* had had his revolver stolen. 'Now it was serious. There was no joking about'. The Gestapo came to investigate the situation, and for forty-eight hours cheminots feared a potential hostage situation. It turned out that another *bahnof* had stolen his colleague's revolver – rumours were that he was sent to the Eastern front.[58] These admissions reflect the complexity of the situation, and it is very true that certain individuals within the German supervision system terrorised the French cheminots. Dr Lagerhausen had been assigned to a post at the EBD in Lille from the start of the Occupation until late 1941, after which he was sent to WVD Brussels. Violently anti-French, he was considered the *Nazi de service*, the local Nazi. 'The French cheminots who came into direct contact with Lagerhausen describe him as the perfect example of the detestable occupier'.[59]

Towards the end of the Occupation, criticisms began to appear on both sides. When speaking about the railways in late 1943, one war correspondent wrote in *Die Reichsbahn*: 'In Germany, there already exists a sound and reliable system [...]. It is not the case in France. Notions of punctuality and reliability are not as deeply rooted into the culture of French civil servants as they are in ours, and as a result we never have any guarantees'.[60] Likewise, cheminots from the depot in Cherbourg lodged complaints against the *bahnofs* in 1944. 'The German teams refuse to prepare their machines. When they come back into the depot they do not empty the ashtray (...) [a cheminot] complained that the Germans ate, drank and talked loudly in his office'.[61] These negative reports were a direct consequence of the huge influx of Reichsbahn personnel from 1943 onwards. The number of *bahnofs* on French soil, which was still stable at 6,500 in late 1942, had rocketed to 34,000 by the end of the

---

[55] SNCF/25/LM/1934: Correspondance relative aux menées antinationales.
[56] AN/72/AJ/497: Pierre Watelet.   [57] Interview Lebrun (2008).
[58] Interview Brussière (2008).
[59] AN/F/14/16943: Report (28 Jan. 1946) from Ministre des Travaux Publics et des Transports to Ministre des Armées.
[60] Cited in Gottwaldt, 'Les cheminots allemands' (2001).
[61] AN/72/AJ/474: Report (31 Jan. 1944) Visite du Dépôt de Cherbourg le 19 Jan. 1944.

Occupation.[62] Large contingents arrived in January 1944: 1,000 arrived in Marseille, 1,500 in Dijon and 2,000 in Avignon. Afterwards they were dispatched into small groups on specific depots, workshops and stations in the nearby towns.

Still, these tensions were limited, and the influx of Reichsbahn workers towards the end of the Occupation posed no real threat. In fact, morale was so low amongst these new workers that they put very little pressure on French cheminots. A contingent of Reichsbahn workers had arrived in Dijon in miserable conditions: none of them had any idea as to their whereabouts, and kept asking where this town called 'Dijon' was located. They were relieved to find out that they were nowhere near the coast. They had travelled four long days with almost nothing to eat, and only wanted an end to this disastrous war.[63] Despite their new railway uniforms, some of them were not specialist railway workers.[64] In fact, some were not even German. The Reichsbahn had occasionally brought foreign railway workers to France before 1944, but this became quite frequent during those last few months of the Occupation. There were 450 Polish and Russian workers in the Haguenau depot, 400 Ukrainians in the Montigny workshops and 300 Russians in Bischheim.[65] When one chief engineer in Béziers was asked how he felt the Reichsbahn presence impacted him in 1944, he simply answered that 'nothing has changed for the SNCF traffic'. In fact, the arrival of 150 German cheminots in February 1944 in Béziers was 'nothing serious': they were all old men, and only there to supervise the French.[66]

3   The Impact of 1942

1941 marked a global turning point in the war. The German army invaded the Soviet Union in June, and although it never managed to go beyond Moscow, the war suddenly escalated in both space and nature. This move Eastwards also triggered a radical new phase in Nazi racial policies. In December 1941, the Japanese attack on Pearl Harbour further re-mapped the war as America became fully involved in the conflict. As the war turned into a truly global affair, the fissures in Hitler's imperial fantasies and logistical plans began to emerge.[67]

---

[62] These numbers are cited in Gottwaldt, 'Les cheminots allemands' (2001).

[63] AN/F/14/13698: Report Côte d'Or, Dijon (31 Jan. 1944).

[64] *Ibid.*, Report Vesoul (22 Apr. 1944).

[65] AN/72/AJ/2296: *La Région de l'Est de la SNCF de 1939 à 1945* (1947) 101. It must be noted, however, that Haguenau and Bischheim were in the annexed part of Alsace, so the situation was different in these Nazified areas no longer considered to be French.

[66] AN/F/14/13698: Report Béziers (7 Feb. 1944).

[67] This becomes particularly evident when reading chapters 6, 7 and 8 in Mark Mazower, *Hitler's Empire : How the Nazis Ruled Europe* (London: Allen Lane, 2008).

But it was in 1942 that these fissures began to develop into dangerous cracks. Indeed, by late 1942, the Allies had landed in North Africa, and the German army was suffering heavily on the Eastern Front. France was far from unaffected by these global shifts; yet within the nation itself, the emergence of labour laws was cataclysmic. The labour laws implemented in France in 1942–3 had serious consequences which affected not only the working classes but the entire population in France. It is crucial to understand how they escalated and intensified over a period of twelve months, for these laws were possibly the most influential factor on popular opinion at the time.

It all started with Pierre Laval's return to power on 18 April 1942. Laval had been involved in high politics since the 1930s: initially a supporter of the left, his allegiance gradually turned towards the right until, following the 1940 defeat, he became the one of the most important men in the Vichy regime. In those first few months of Occupation, Laval was in fact too German-friendly, and his negotiation tactics, amongst other things, risked alienating French popular opinion. In December 1940, Pétain ejected him from the government and replaced him with François Darlan, thereby disappointing the Germans who loved having Laval fight their corner in the negotiations. Eventually, Pétain would feel pressured to dismiss Darlan and re-integrate Laval into the government, and so, on 18 April 1942, Laval became Prime Minister of France.

One of the first things Laval did when he returned to government was to create the *Relève* programme. In May 1942, the German Minister of Labour, Fritz Sauckel, requested 350,000 French workers to work in Reich territory. Laval agreed to send 250,000 volunteer workers, but for every three workers sent to Germany, one French prisoner would be returned to France. In hope of rallying public support for this *Relève* programme – which in French means changeover – Laval organised a welcome ceremony in the *Gare de l'Est* for the first train of returning prisoners on 11 August where he was present himself; still, he was unable to mask the dark reality of this labour scheme.[68] Prefect reports showed growing popular discontent at the time: 'it was departure, conscription, and deportation which became the keywords in the last few months of 1942, not return, relief, or compensation'.[69]

The unpopularity of the *Relève* meant that few men volunteered to work for Germany. In the eyes of the public, Laval's bargain with Sauckel had only confirmed Vichy's declining power and Germany's domination, and as a result quotas for volunteer workers were never reached. Something

[68] Jackson, *The Dark Years* (2002) 220.   [69] Kedward, *In Search of the Maquis* (2003) 4.

needed to be done: on 4 September 1942 a new law declared that men aged between 18 and 50, as well as single French women between 21 and 35, could be subject to compulsory labour in the service of the nation. As Patrice Arnaud points out, this law did not explicitly mention the transfer to Germany. Indeed, men and women could be employed in the *Organisation Todt*, which meant that workers stayed in France but worked on projects dedicated to German interests.[70] Still, the growing demands of the German military needed to be met, and the pressure to recruit foreign workers in Germany was constantly increasing. Following intense negotiations with the Germans, Laval eventually enforced the STO in February 1943: now, all men aged 20 to 22 were sent to work in Germany.

The *Relève* was not, however, the first instance of French workers leaving for Germany.[71] As early as 1941, the Reichsbahn were asking for volunteer French cheminots; that September the SNCF abided and sent over a few hundred volunteers to Germany.[72] The request kept increasing, however, and this irritated the French railway directors. Robert Le Besnerais, who strongly disapproved of any measure which disrupted his workforce, tried to deter cheminots from leaving. He did not threaten to sack anyone who voluntarily left for Germany, but he made it clear that they would be seriously jeopardising their pension rights and other professional privileges. Berthelot also sent the German authorities a list of 4,648 cheminots, all POWs still in Germany who could work for the Reichsbahn if they were immediately released.[73] Moreover, rather than send out its permanent agents, Le Besnerais proposed that the SNCF begin a fast-track training programme which would prepare workers for work in Germany. He predicted that the cheminots in the workshops and depots could train up to 1,000 train drivers a month – the rest of the quota would then be filled by sending a few hundred volunteers. On the eve of the *Relève*, in February 1942, the Germans asked for more train drivers and workers, but Le Besnerais pointed out that they already had 18,000 cheminot POWs which they could use, and 4,840 were precisely the type of skilled workers the Germans were asking for.[74] The *Relève* put added pressure on these

[70] Arnaud, *Les STO* (2010) 9.
[71] A lot of data has been published in Durand's book, see Durand, *SNCF* (1968) 290–308.
[72] It is important to note that the exact numbers of volunteers are unknown. However, according to Arnaud, of the approximately 24,400 railway workers who went to Germany to work, 94% were 'requisitioned', or *'requis'*, whilst the remaining 6% would have been volunteers. See Arnaud, *Les STO* (2010) 48.
[73] SNCF/505/LM/185: Letter (30 Apr. 1941) from Le Besnerais to WVD; Note (6 Feb. 1942) written by Berthelot.
[74] SNCF/26/LM/0036: Note sur l'envoi de cheminots français en allemagne (6 Feb. 1942) from Berthelot.

negotiations for railway personnel, but in the Autumn of 1942 Berthe-lot's replacement, Robert Gibrat, managed to obtain the status of 'irreplaceable workers' for some skilled cheminots. This status, however, did not concern all railwaymen.

The law of 4 September 1942 would be the next brutal step in Vichy's labour service campaign, except this time it would draft list of specific workers who were obliged to depart for Germany. As it might be expected, these conscription lists caused outrage, and Vichy's credibility and legitimacy was beginning to dissolve. As recruitment problems con-tinued and Germans added pressure for more workers, the government decided to enforce widespread compulsory labour service, and the Forced Labour Service (STO) was inaugurated in February 1943. By the spring, Germans had requested 60,000 more workers to be sent to Germany, including 10,000 cheminots. While the SNCF management objected, the Minister of Industrial Production, Jean Bichelonne, sug-gested taking more cheminots out of certain services, and replacing them with women.[75] Bichelonne was a rising star from the *École Polytechnique*, where he had graduated from twenty years earlier. He was considered to be one of the up and coming French technocrats, obsessed with the modernisation of France, and he played central roles in the nation's economic collaboration.[76] In 1942, he held several ministerial posts one of which involved replacing Robert Gibrat, and the suggestion to replace cheminots with women was part of his tactic to please both the SNCF and the Germans. In December 1943, for example, Bichelonne had agreed with Le Besnerais that it was absurd to have to hire German mechanics to work in France when hundreds of French mechanics were being sent to Germany.[77] And yet, the outcome of his negotiations with the Germans show that he would continue to send workers.

It is commonly believed that the cheminots were exempt from the STO, but it is only in late February 1944 that the SNCF became a *Sperr-Betrieb (S)* industry, a 'protected plant' was considered vital to German interests.[78] As such, its workers were spared from deportation to Germany.[79] Until then, the SNCF had been affected by all labour laws which emanated from German and French authorities. It was only in

[75] AN/72/AJ/1927: Minutes of Ministerial meeting (18 Aug. 1943) 2.

[76] For more information on Bichelonne, there is Guy Sabin's subjective account, *Jean Bichelonne 1904–1944* (Paris: France-Empire, 1991). Baruch offers a particularly more piercing insight into this persona, Baruch, *Servir l'Etat français* (1997) 370–1.

[77] AN/72/AJ/1927: Minutes of Ministerial meeting (7 Dec. 1943) 2.

[78] *Ibid.*, Minutes (15 Feb. 1944) 5; (28 Feb. 1944) 6.

[79] Ulrich Herbert, *Hitler's Foreign Workers: Enforced Foreign Labor in Germany Under the Third Reich* (Cambridge: Cambridge University Press, 1997) xvii.

June 1943 that the HVD Paris (*Haupt Verkehrsdirektion*) had asked that the SNCF be able to protect some of its workers in particular departments from being affected by the STO laws.[80] Indeed, the SNCF's national but also international strategic significance meant it could not spare its skilled workers so easily. By February 1944, the company was finally granted this status.

After 1942, relations between the Germans and the SNCF management soured considerably. This was not only due to the intensification of labour laws as described above, but also to other pressures which Germans were exerting on personnel and material. Already in August 1942, Robert Gibrat saw his role as a careful balancing act between pleasing the Germans and understanding the SNCF's limitations.[81] When the HVD tried to impose work on Sundays in October 1943, their request was met with outrage amongst the SNCF. First, the Germans had no right to make last minute requests. Second, the increase of work hours seemed counter-productive. Of his own initiative, the Chairman of the SNCF Pierre-Eugène Fournier – who had been the head of the *Service du contrôle des administrations provisoires* (SCAP) in 1940–41, which was notably in charge or the aryanisation of French businesses[82] – explicitly wrote in a letter that it was his 'duty to point out that increasing working hours in the workshops would be inopportune from all points of view' at this point in time.[83] The affair eventually had to go up to the highest French authorities since neither the HVD nor the SNCF had the right to decide over the matter.

After 1942, as tensions were mounting to reflect the growing difficulties of wartime conditions, Franco-German mistrust amongst the transport services became more and more visible. Sometimes the altercations were relatively polite. In October 1942, Poncet asked the Germans to stop sending their locomotives to be cleaned in France – at least for some time. 'We are going to go through an extremely difficult period', he wrote, and the Reichsbahn should expect a reduction in the repairs of material from France.[84] However, the SNCF was particularly sensitive

---

[80] Cited in Bachelier Report, 5.2.3. Le classement de la SNCF comme S-Betrieb.

[81] SNCF/26/LM/0036: Letter (29 Aug. 1942) from Robert Gibrat to Munzer.

[82] To find out more about the SCAP, see Antoine Prost, Rémi Skoutelsky, and Sonia Etienne, eds., *Aryanisation économique et restitutions* (Paris: Documentation française, 2000) 16–21; Jean-Marc Dreyfus, *Pillages sur ordonnances: aryanisation et restitution des banques en France, 1940–1953* (Paris: Fayard, 2003); Laurent Joly, *Vichy dans la 'Solution Finale': histoire du commissariat général aux questions juives* (Paris: Grasset, 2006) 104–7.

[83] SNCF/26/LM/0036: Letter (14 Oct. 1943) from Fournier to Ministre, Secrétaire d'Etat à la Production Industrielle et aux Communications.

[84] Cleaning the machines was crucial for upkeep and safety, and the Germans were, according to this document, sending their locomotives to be cleaned – not merely repaired – to France. SNCF/303/LM/22: Letter (15 Oct. 1942) from Poncet to HVD.

on matters of personnel, and it would not hesitate to bluntly discourage the HVD's requests. On 22 December the HVD Paris asked that the SNCF only fire its personnel once the decision was approved by the German Chief of District and Traction; Le Besnerais refused. Such an act would not only breach important personnel laws established by the Inspector of Labour and Transports, but it would also be irrelevant: already the SNCF was firing people only under unique circumstances since it could not, in wartime conditions, dispose of its personnel which was a precious commodity, so what was the problem?[85] Allowing this request to go through would only undermine the authority of the railway chiefs and directors.

By early 1943, the negotiation process was time-consuming and tense. It is not that Franco-German rapports had been exclusively cordial beforehand, but up until that point, the language of negotiation was far less aggressive. The sometimes heated correspondence suggests that as the Germans were intervening on matters of personnel more and more frequently, the SNCF became determined to defend its interests. The Germans, for instance, were putting pressure on the SNCF to have its cheminots carry out surveillance duties alongside the Germans (in view of preventing sabotages): Le Besnerais repeatedly insisted that this was not possible: 'I have already had to underline many times that (...) [the SNCF] cannot ask its personnel to carry out what is in fact police surveillance in order to prevent attacks which relate to public order'.[86] At times the Germans would try and circumvent the agreements and impose some surveillance rules at a local level, even in the Free Zone, but these could be spotted and halted.[87]

One of the major arguments used by the SNCF throughout the negotiations was that the Germans' requests would disrupt the lower ranks of the SNCF, and that this disruption posed a great threat which should not be underestimated. This was certainly the case during the talks of mixing driving teams, when the Germans wanted to maximise efficiency by augmenting German presence on rolling transports. But when they suggested to team up French and German locomotive engineers and drivers, the SNCF directors erupted in anger. In a furious letter to Bichelonne, Fournier wrote that 'assigning French train drivers to team up with German locomotive engineers would raise big problems, and cause great agitation. French agents would be particularly shocked by the

[85] SNCF/26/LM/0036: Letter (23 Dec. 1943) from Le Besnerais to HVD.
[86] SNCF/26/LM/0020: Letter (5 Aug. 1943) from Le Besnerais to Minister.
[87] *Ibid.*, Letter (31 Dec. 1943) from Fournier to Ministre, Secrétaire d'État à la Production Industrielle et aux Communications.

fact that German mechanics are being used to conduct French trains while French cheminots have been forcefully sent off for forced labour to Germany'.[88] This does not mean that there was no collaboration, however. In 1941, the SNCF personnel assisted German military authorities in controlling the travellers getting off the trains at certain stations.[89] Likewise, the Germans too could be wary of Franco-German collaboration: in August 1943, they discouraged the collaboration of German and French surveillance teams for the preparation of railway convoys.[90] So although Fournier's letter to Bichelonne suggests that the SNCF wanted to protect its workforce, it is perhaps more likely that mixing teams to drive locomotives was the real issue here. Indeed, it was the idea of maintaining an illusion of control over the exploitation of the railways. If locomotives, the symbol of railway power, were driven by Germans, then this illusion was burst.

4   Working in Germany

The daily lives of the 24,400 cheminots who worked for the Reichsbahn open yet another door of investigation into Franco-German relations.[91] Now the history of foreign workers in Germany is a very sensitive one. For a long time Edward Homze's study was the only one which existed on Western workers in Germany.[92] Indeed, the subject of foreign workers and even of POWs had been ignored because German historians were interested in far greater crimes in the camps.[93] Likewise, the broader history of French workers in Germany has taken a long time to free itself of post-war myths. Immediately after the war, the STO were a 'taboo' subject: since they had worked *for* Germany, their stories paled in comparison to the far more heroic tales of resisters, and were thus sidelined from the grand narrative of the war. One ex-STO recalled his arrival in *Gare de l'Est* when he returned from Germany: 'a cheminot came towards us and he rested his hand on my shoulder. Prisoner or worker? he asked. Worker, I answered. He suddenly pulled back his friendly hand and distanced himself. Like a bond had just been

[88] AN/72/AJ/474: Letter (7 Dec. 1943) from Fournier to Bichelonne. Same letter also held in SNCF/26/LM/0036.
[89] SNCF/303/LM/22: Application du couvre-feu; Report (19 Sep. 1941) from Service Central du Mouvement to Mouvement Sud-Ouest.
[90] This was in order to prevent sabotages and such incidents. SNCF/26/LM/0020: Letter (18 Aug. 1943) from Keyner to Direction Générale de la SNCF.
[91] This number comes from Arnaud's study, *Les STO* (2010), 48.
[92] Herbert, *Hitler's Foreign Workers* (1997) 5–6.   [93] *Ibid.*, 3.

broken'.[94] In 1971 Jean-Marie d'Hoop tried to break the taboo in an insightful article intended to show that ex-STO were also victims of Nazism.[95] However, the picture he painted was too dark. Perhaps it was the need to counterbalance the clear hostility towards the history of the STO, or perhaps it was the lack of sources, but the myth of industrial collaboration was largely dismissed only to let room for the myth of victimisation.

After a boom in Franco-German economic histories of the Second World War in the 1980s and 1990s, historians began to question the lives of the 'forced' workers themselves.[96] A conference held in Caen in 2003 confirmed that the 750,000 forced labourers had not been the only ones to work for the Germans: what about the civilian and POW volunteers? What of those who worked for the *Organisation Todt*? What about those who worked in S-plants? Working for Hitler was not an anomaly, and hundreds of thousands of men in fact 'volunteered' in one way or another to carry out this work.

The question of voluntary work in Germany is especially interesting in the case of the cheminots. The *Relève*'s immediate lack of success showed the shifting moods amongst the French population, and after the 4 September 1942 many young Frenchmen began to evade conscription[97]; still, it would be wrong to assume that everyone rejected the conscription to Germany. A Department Head, or *Chef de Service*, wrote to Le Besnerais asking him what to do when agents requested to leave the SNCF to go work on the Reichsbahn without having been conscripted.[98] Such was the case of Paul Chausson who, despite being in the Free Zone, requested to be transferred to Germany in August 1942, possibly because his current job at the SNCF was under threat. The Director of Personnel Barth personally responded to Chausson's request saying that the conscription only concerned the Occupied Zone,

[94] Jean-Pierre Vittori, *Eux, Les STO* (Paris: Messidor/Temps Actuels, 1982) 14–5.
[95] Jean-Marie d'Hoop, 'La main d'oeuvre française au service de l'allemagne' *Revue d'histoire de la deuxième guerre mondiale*, 81 (Jan. 1971) 83–4.
[96] Vittori, *Les STO* (1982); Ulrich Herbert, 'Good Times, Bad Times' in Richard Bessel, ed., *Life in the Third Reich* (Oxford: Oxford University Press, 1987); Rémy Desquesnes, 'L'organisation todt en France 1940–1944', *Histoire, Economie et Société*, 11.3 (1992) 535–50; Ulrich Herbert, 'Labour and Extermination: Economic Interest and the Primacy of Weltanschauung in National Socialism', *Past and Present*, 138.1 (1993) 144–95; Richard Overy, *War and Economy in the Third Reich* (Oxford: Clarendon Press, 1994); Herbert, *Hitler's Foreign Workers* (1997).
[97] SNCF/206/LM/4: Report n°50 (17 Nov. 1942) from Belfort Depot; SNCF/206/LM/2: Letter (22 Oct. 1942) from Inspecteur de la main d'oeuvre des Transports to Chef de Dépôt Belfort.
[98] SNCF/303/LM/1: Départs d'Agents en Allemagne (15 Jul. 1942).

and so he would have to wait until the search for volunteers (possibly) extended to the Free Zone.[99]

In July 1943, 100 cheminots were invited to Germany as a thank you for the courage they had shown in the past few months despite the worsening wartime conditions. The trip was expected to last eight to ten days in September. It was a group visit 'on a strictly professional level', where cheminots were able to enjoy 'some of Germany's natural beauties, big provincial towns and some of the biggest industrial and railway centres'.[100] The SNCF's Central Services drew up a list of potential names and then distributed them to the regional directors who contacted the men directly.[101] It was expected that some would refuse, so the list was slightly longer than the number of places actually allocated. Some responses were positive: in Tours, three cheminots accepted.[102] In the South West region, however, none of the eight invitees went: indeed, whereas one had initially accepted the offer, he later retracted his acceptance claiming that he could not go because his daughter was ill. It is very possible that his sudden retraction had little to do with his daughter's health, and was in fact a consequence of peer pressure.[103] Ultimately, the invitation was not as successful as anticipated, so it was extended to cheminots who had been wounded (either as a result of the war, or in a professional accident).[104]

More recently, scholars have also challenged the quality of life for those who went to work in Germany. Patrice Arnaud (2010) and Helga Elisabeth Bories-Sawala (2010) have nuanced the lives of French workers in Germany and clearly shown that the lives of those working in Germany were not always doom and gloom.[105] Picaper also told the stories of those Frenchmen who had had liaisons with German women during their stay

---

[99] *Ibid.*, Letter (13 Aug. 1942) from Barth to Directeur de l'Exploitation de la Région Ouest.

[100] SNCF/303/LM/22: Note attached to letter (28 Aug. 1943) from Chef de la division du service général to Arrondissement Matériel et Traction Montluçon et Bordeaux.

[101] *Ibid.*, Letter (23 Aug. 1943) from Barth to many.

[102] *Ibid.*, Charles Dubarry and Emile Pommier, Letter (30 Aug. 1943) from Ingénieur chargé du Dépôt to Ingénieur C.A.M.T., Tours; Jean Blanchis, List (undated) Liste d'Agents invités à prendre part à un voyage en Allemagne.

[103] *Ibid.*, Handwritten note (4 Sept. 1943).

[104] *Ibid.*, Letter (28 Aug. 1943) from Chef de la division du service général to Arrondissement Matériel et Traction Montluçon et Bordeaux; See also Bachelier Report, 5.5.2. Le discret voyage d'Allemagne des cheminots français.

[105] Patrice Arnaud, *Les STO: Histoire des Français requis en Allemagne nazie, 1942–1945* (Paris: CNRS Editions, 2010); Helga Elisabeth and Bories-Sawala, *Dans la gueule du loup: les Français requis du travail en Allemagne* (Villeneuve d'Ascq: Presses universitaires du Septentrion, 2010).

in Germany.[106] The love stories, which often ended in marriage and children, remind us of the new possibilities which awaited French workers in Germany – possibilities which many seized. Still, it is difficult for some to tear themselves away from former myths. Jean-Pierre Harbulot, for example, focuses almost exclusively on the difficulties and struggles of life in the Third Reich. Whilst his work is enlightening due to some good sources, it is a bit too one-sided and reveals nothing of the nuances underlined by Arnaud and Bories-Sawala.[107] Moreover, whereas Harbulot mentioned friendships amongst Frenchmen from different backgrounds, he largely overlooked interactions with German workers.[108]

Following in the footsteps of this recent scholarship, we must equally revisit the myths of the cheminots who worked for German railways. Durand initially described their departure as a quasi-death sentence: 'over the course of the Occupation, approximately 12,000 agents who were invited to go work in Germany would leave the SNCF often to never return'.[109] But new sources suggest that cheminots' lives in Germany were not so tragic. Indeed, conditions were tough, but interactions with Germans were not necessarily unwelcome.[110] Arnaud cited several examples of alliances made between nationalities, especially when they worked side by side. The Frenchman Henri Court was working alongside Paul, a German, in the Reichsbahn drawing workshop at Zweibrücken. They discovered their mutual passion for poetry and bonded over this significant cultural tie.[111] The cheminot Marcel Blanchard created quasi-filial bonds with his supervisor.[112] 'Relations between German and French workers were not so bad', echoed Henri Perrin. 'I saw many teams work very well through real camaraderie. One German brought his French co-worker white bread and cake each week'.[113]

The basic descriptions of life in Germany are as varied as the men who went there. Izard and Rey worked in smaller stations or depots of

[106] Jean-Paul Picaper, Le crime d'aimer, les enfants du STO (Paris: Syrtes, 2005).
[107] See Jean-Pierre Harbulot, Le Service du Travail Obligatoire: La région de Nancy face aux exigences allemandes (Nancy: Presses Universitaires de Nancy, 2003). Harbulot's work is enlightening and he gathers some good sources; however, it continues to embrace some of the older myths of STO victimization and reveals nothing of the nuances which Arnaud and Bories-Sawala underline in their work.
[108] See Harbulot, Le Service du Travail Obligatoire (2003) 463–78.
[109] Durand, SNCF (1968) 287.
[110] Cold and isolation were difficult to endure, whilst fines handed to workers could sometimes cost them their whole weekly salary. Arnaud, Les STO (2010) 49, 137.
[111] Arnaud, Les STO (2010) 115.
[112] Marcel Blanchard, memoirs in Les cheminots dans la guerre et l'Occupation, témoignages et récits, Revue d'Histoire des Chemins de Fer, Hors Série, 7 (Mar. 2004).
[113] Arnaud, Les STO (2010) 121.

approximately 3–600 people, Séiké and Tencé worked in large railway junctions amidst thousands of workers.[114] And whilst Van Cleef worked mostly with Germans in the locomotive depot in Engelsdorf, Person assessed that the personnel in Karlsruhe was extremely mixed: '20% German, Alsatians and Lorrains, 20% French, 20% Belgian and Dutch, 20% Italians, and 20% Russian, Spanish, Czech, Slavs'.[115] Even for these three cheminots who worked in the same Reichsbahn depot in Korn-westheim in 1942, timetables varied significantly depending on where you were allocated: Brun worked eight hours a day with one rest day every eight days; Weingand was working sixty-hour weeks with one rest day every thirteen days, a much harsher regime than had been initially advertised; and Rich was on fifty-five-hour weeks with one rest day every nine days.[116]

Some had it harder than others. Many foreign labourers complained about the bunk beds in wooden barracks,[117] and aside from the cramped surroundings there was the lack of heating and hygiene.[118] The parasites were so bad in Rich's barracks that they could only manage a few hours of sleep every night.[119] It would appear that conditions degraded over time, especially after the bombings. Violette, who had initially been happy with his heated barracks, his hot water and his indoor toilet, saw the conditions deteriorate drastically after his living space was bombed.[120] Food was the other constant complaint. They rarely got enough to eat through their employers alone, and had to rely on ration tickets, packages from home, and even the black market to make up for this.[121] According to Weingand, whereas the food was good in restaurants, what they received in the workplace was unhealthy.[122] For Ferrand, if the SNCF could help with one thing, it was to improve the food supplies: he was fed up with potatoes and boiled cabbage.[123] Problems then varied from place to place, from person to person. Van Cleef found the winters especially hard, whilst Besson was frustrated by the language barrier. For Rich, distance was difficult to overcome: with his brother being a POW, Rich needed to return home and take his place as the head of the family.[124]

The news from Germany was not all bad, however. If the food was not always sufficient it was at least decent, and some considered their living

[114] SNCF/26/LM/018: Jean Izard (Nov. 1944); Georges Rey (undated); François Séiké (undated); Georges Tencé (Nov. 1944).
[115] *Ibid.*, Marcel Person (undated); Roger Van Cleef (1944).
[116] SNCF/206/LM/3: Edmund Brun (1943); Georges Weingand (1943); Jean Rich (1943).
[117] *Ibid.*, Arsène Ferrand (1942).   [118] *Ibid.*, Brun; SNCF/26/LM/018: Person.
[119] SNCF/206/LM/3: Rich.   [120] SNCF/26/LM/018: Jean Violette (undated).
[121] SNCF/206/LM/3: Ernest Grab (1942); Brun; Rich.   [122] *Ibid.*, Weingand.
[123] *Ibid.*, Ferrand.
[124] SNCF/26/LM/018: Van Cleef; Raymond Besson (1942) SNCF/206/LM/3: Rich.

conditions satisfying.[125] Furthermore, unlike forced workers, volunteers could be trusted to go into private housing where conditions were surely better.[126] Some French workers, such as Weingand and Laude, benefitted from this, and it is perhaps no coincidence that their reports on the conditions are slightly more positive than the rest: Laude found that supplies such as clothes and shoes were satisfying, and that he had enough food from his employer.[127] Weingand, who was not yet in private housing but was about to go, felt he did not suffer from an absence of rest days. In fact, his general impression was that there was a 'good camaraderie with the German chiefs and workers and other foreigners'.[128]

One important aspect of their period in Germany was that the large majority of cheminots worked on the Reichsbahn, with only one in twenty workers stationed in other industries. Continuity in professional skill was extremely important for the morale. Coquelard, who described himself as a 'modest cheminot', felt relatively isolated 'in this unknown land', but 'the railway was the only thing which was not an enigma to me'.[129] Indeed, living in bad conditions did not mean that the workers could not somehow appreciate their professional experience; far from it. Ferrand's complaints did not stop him from being in awe of the modern German work posts which had such luxuries as central heating and *vestiaires lavabos*. Not only that, but he found a certain camaraderie amongst his fellow German workers: 'not encountering any difficulties with the Germans, his colleagues are very helpful'.[130] Lipp, who spent nine months working on the Reichsbahn in 1942–43 and who joined the resistance on his return, asked to be sent out to Germany after the war when the French occupied a chunk of West Germany: 'I would like to volunteer to go to Germany; my knowledge of German language and work customs could be useful to my corporation who I am sure needs more workers'.[131] Furthermore, whilst some cheminots claimed that there was a general animosity towards Germans, especially amongst the non-volunteers, others suggest that this was directed more towards supervisors and figures of authority.[132] Indeed, the Germans identified as being problematic were the head of the Camp, or his ex-Waffen-SS subordinate, or the SS in charge of their work station.[133] The average German railway worker does not seem to have been a threat.

[125] SNCF/206/LM/3: Léon Cousy (1942); Paul Guéritot (1942); Ferrand; Besson.
[126] SNCF/26/LM/018: Tencé; Izard.   [127] *Ibid.*, Laude.
[128] SNCF/206/LM/3: Weingand.   [129] SNCF/26/LM/018: Georges Coquelard (1946).
[130] SNCF/206/LM/3: Ferrand.
[131] SNCF/25/LM/1933: Letter (25 Jun. 1945) from Bernard Lipp to Chef du Personnel Exploitation.
[132] SNCF/26/LM/018: Izard; Violette.   [133] *Ibid.*, Person, Van Cleef.

And whilst the French may have been more reluctant to volunteer in 1940–41 than other nationalities, they were amongst the most appreciated workers in Germany itself. Homze pointed to a political scientist in the US Army who stated that the French were amongst certain 'favoured nationalities', and as such were relatively well treated.[134] In fact, 'a pilot study of French workers by the United States Strategic Bombing Survey (USSBS) indicated that the French, as might be expected, showed considerable understanding of the German population and especially the working class of the Reich'.[135] According to Homze, the comments of one Frenchman best summarized the conditions for French foreign workers: 'we worked hard, too. The German workers liked us, and we got along with most of them. But we had so little to eat'.[136] In contrast, it was well-known that Eastern workers were treated more harshly than anyone else. Even amongst Western workers there was a hierarchy to be followed: initially, the Danes and the Belgians worked just as hard as Germans, whilst the French worked less hard and propagated Marxist propaganda. However, the Dutch were the most troublesome workers. After Autumn 1941, German labour reports showed shifts in attitudes: the French and Belgian workers were described as 'industrious' and 'willing', and the attitudes of the Danes and the Dutch were improving. If there was any problem it was amongst the French and Belgian women: one officer in Stuttgart wrote 'it is not an exaggeration when it's said that you rather rarely find a decent French woman'.[137]

Homze relied heavily on the USSBS records which, as Overy warns us, should be handled with care; still, many reputable scholars have since confirmed these impressions.[138] Milward thus wrote that if no foreign worker worked as hard as a German worker, the French were actually considered more efficient than others. In fact, Speer wrote down in one of his reports that French workers were 'the best of all foreign labour', and that they were 'rivalled only by Russian woman workers'.[139] And if there seems to be an evolution of working conditions between 1940 and 1944, it is not as obvious as expected. Ulrich Herbert's research of the Autumn 1941 period indicated that 'the majority of civilian workers from the West, in particular the Belgians and French, were performing to the general satisfaction of their employers and the authorities. They were receiving relatively high wages and, as far as can be gathered from the

---

[134] Edward Homze, *Foreign Labour in Nazi Germany* (Princeton: Princeton University Press, 1967) 293.
[135] *Ibid.*   [136] *Ibid.*   [137] *Ibid.*, 55–6.
[138] Overy, *War and Economy* (1994) 26, 30–1, 261.
[139] Alan Milward, *The New Order and the French Economy* (Oxford: Clarendon Press, 1970) 274.

documentary evidence, lived under conditions that were little different from those of a German worker, at least in between the campaign in France and the end of 1941'.[140] And according to Richard Overy, the high levels of productivity were sustained through 1944 despite a more reactionary, less disciplined, and less productive foreign workforce.[141] As such, rumours of 'sabotage' should not be overestimated.

But how did the French get along amongst themselves? Some testimonies embrace a slight romanticisation of French – and cheminot – solidarity and resistance. Person's report, for example, portrays the French as anti-fascists who did not get on with Central Europeans or Italians. They all committed various acts of resistance, he wrote, whether it was simply by not obeying orders or carrying out small acts of sabotage.[142] This is confirmed in other testimonies. Big acts of sabotage and escape attempts were, if not completely unheard of, at least far more rare.[143] Small acts of passive resistance are, however, frequently referred to. Tencé, for example, underlined that the French, Belgians and Dutch never actually refused to work, but they would do 'slow work', or would frequently go to the doctor's office.[144]

However, rapports amongst Frenchmen were not completely straightforward. Van Cleef recalled that the French ex-POWs who were supposed to make requests on behalf of the workers for more food and materials, never did: their position was an advantageous one, he stated, why compromise it?[145] In contrast, Rey remembered about thirty French volunteers of 'questionable morals' who used to go to the doctor's office a lot.[146] Even Person wrote that some Frenchmen – not cheminots, he specified – abandoned their work because they were so tired, but they were soon made to go back to work. Indeed, the cheminots in particular, he stated, were more hardworking than others: they did not need to so many rests, for instance.[147] So although it is especially worth noting that Person was trying to project an image of passive resistance, he was equally concerned with upholding the image of cheminots as excellent workers with incorruptible ethics.

Conclusion

The Occupation was obviously not a period of peaceful cohabitation, far from it. However, the post-war depictions of Germans as 'savages' are

---

[140] Herbert, *Hitler's Foreign Workers* (1997) 105.
[141] Overy, *War and Economy* (1994) 366.   [142] SNCF/26/LM/018: Person.
[143] *Ibid.*, Izard; Violette; Van Cleef.   [144] *Ibid.*, Tencé.   [145] *Ibid.*, Van Cleef.
[146] *Ibid.*, Rey.   [147] *Ibid.*, Person.

not always an accurate reflection of Franco-German relations. This is not to downplay the hardships of deportees, prisoners of war and forced labour workers; but it is key to see how life went on, in both Germany and France. The links that cheminot POWs maintained with the SNCF during their internment were, for instance, key (See Figure 3.1). Likewise, it is important to underline the cordial relationship between the French and German cheminots in France. Their professional collaboration was not always seen as a crutch. Historically, the railway milieu had strong international ties, not least amongst the upper echelons. Raoul Dautry made frequent trips to Great Britain to examine their railways; railway magazines were frequently publishing news and photographs of the latest advances in railway technology around the world (not least America); international railway timetable meetings were held annually, where leading engineers and directors would meet from all European countries; the SNCF paper was inspired by a German Reichsbahn poster when designing its own campaign aimed at cheminot wives (See Figure 3.2). Although the upper echelons seemed to fit into an international network of railway specialists, the amount of international exposure and interaction is less clear at the lower echelons. Still, one can imagine that a shared professional knowledge would have helped

Figure 3.1 A cheminot POW in Stalag I-A sent two photos of an exhibition which he and his fellow cheminots built in the camp. *Renseignements Hebdomadaires*, 62 (27 Nov. 1942). SNCF – Centre National des Archives Historiques.

Figure 3.2 'Women, do your duty'. Drawings inspired by a Deutsche Reichsbahn Poster. *Notre Métier*, 1 (15 May 1938). SNCF – Centre National des Archives Historiques.

establish communication and even bonds. This is precisely what one witnesses during the Occupation.

The professional bonds shared by French and German cheminots were key during the Occupation, but they need to be understood within their full complexity. Indeed, Franco-German rapports changed over time according to the different circumstances. Despite a general air of negotiation and cohabitation, tensions in the upper echelons escalated as the war went on. This phenomenon was not mirrored so perfectly amongst the lower personnel, however. French and German agents had a shared experience of being blue-collar workers with similar hardships and shortages; this was very different to the conditions of high-ranking agents. More so then Reichsbahn agents, it was the abusive power of high-ranking men which cheminots detested most, whether French directors, railway chiefs or German officers. As the following chapters will argue, their professional frustration would remain a central feature throughout the Occupation.

But if the study of the relationship between French and German railway workers sheds considerable light on the complicated relations with the occupier, it is also a strong reminder of France's role in the overarching story of Nazi-Occupied Europe. Indeed, two of the main topics of friction between, on the one hand, the SNCF managers and workers, and on the other, the SNCF managers and the Germans, were the German seizure of both railway material and railway men. Indeed, the seizure of the SNCF's personnel and material is a major part of the story of the French railways during the Second World War, but also of France itself. Whilst the history of Eastern Europe during the Nazi Occupation was shaped by unprecedented mass murder, violence and terror, the history of Western Europe was shaped largely by the total draining of economic and industrial abilities. In the New Order, France was to be drained of its economic resources in order to provide the Reich territory with all of its needs. The SNCF case shows how the pilfering of France affected bureaucrats and workers alike, but it also serves as a stark reminder that if the daily conditions of the occupation were never as brutal or harsh as those in Eastern Europe, France was in many ways being sentenced to death through economic draining.

4   Theft

Cheminots seemed to adapt swiftly to Vichy, maintaining a real professional consciousness despite the circumstances. In November 1940, the French Police Commissar in Lyon believed there was nothing to fear from them: 'The communist elements, and especially the railway workers, do not overtly express their opinions and they avoid commenting on governmental decisions; in some private conversations you can even hear that "a drastic change has occurred within the regime, but as long as the interests of the workers are being considered, then it is all for the best"'.[1] But even in this early period of relative passivity, a handful of cheminot acts of dissidence were being reported. In late June 1940, some cheminots in Poitiers redistributed goods originally destined for British soldiers to the local hospitals, and sent more such material to the Free Zone, instead of handing them over to the German authorities. Two cheminots were arrested as a result, one of whom was deported to Buchenwald.[2] In August 1940, one cheminot mislabelled a German freight car so that it ended up in the wrong location: he was the first cheminot sentenced to death.[3]

Indeed, a brief overview of upper-management announcements in 1940–41 indicates a growing concern over cheminot dissidence. On 25 June 1940, Le Besnerais reminded the cheminots not to disrespect the Germans: 'there is no need for me to remind SNCF cheminots (...) [that they] must maintain decency and dignity when, whether in correspondence or conversation, they come into contact with the occupier: [these values] have always been traditional amongst us'.[4] The following month, he published a more explicit statement by the *Wehrmacht*

---

[1] ADR/45/W/35: Report (Nov. 1940) from Police Commissar in Lyon. Special thanks to Daniel Lee for this reference.
[2] Durand, *La SNCF* (1968) 365.
[3] AN/72/AJ/2296: Préface: Discours prononcé par Mr André Auroussseau, Président-Général de Résistance-Fer (25 Jan. 1984) in Jacqueline Thirion, 'Le Printemps Fleurira'.
[4] SNCF/25/LM/240: Ordre du Jour n°34 (25 Jun. 1940).

Verkehrsdirektion (WVD) Commander, Goeritz, reminding cheminots that they had to 'strictly abide to these principles so that the German Military Authorities never have to envisage applying the sanctions outlined by [Goeritz]'.[5] Yet by mid-August, reminders became orders: 'it is formally forbidden to make, or witness, injurious inscriptions attacking Germany or its leaders, whether it is on material or buildings; if inscriptions of this type appear despite this, they must be immediately removed'.[6] And on 4 December 1940, Le Besnerais actually threatened to revoke any cheminot caught smuggling people (especially POWs) or letters across the demarcation line.[7]

The intensification of these threats made against 'disobedient' cheminots suggests that their own misconduct was slowly swelling. Yet amidst a variety of acts of dissidence – mislabelling trains, mocking the Occupiers, tagging anti-national or offensive inscriptions on railway sites – one particular form stood out: employee theft. Already in October 1940, Cambournac, the Director of the North Region, was commenting that 'Thefts are being frequently carried out to the detriment of the clients or the SNCF, and it is with great sadness that I notice that cheminots can be counted amongst the thieves'.[8] Indeed, between 1939 and 1942, the number of cheminots brought to the South-West Region's Disciplinary Council (SWDC) for stealing doubled. And by early 1942, employee theft had become a 'leprosy' within the railways.[9] Directors were even receiving letters from the public claiming that they could no longer count on the railways. Terrified that this epidemic of theft could seriously threaten the reputation of the railways, the leadership's response could not have been more clear: 'it is in our best interest to immediately remove the thieves from our service', wrote Barth.[10] Whilst not all thefts resulted in immediate dismissal, the large majority were.[11] As will be seen, repression of cheminot theft became central to SNCF concerns and policies.

But why did employee theft within the SNCF rise to such a great extent under Vichy? As has been shown so far, the cheminots tend to be a uniform body of workers with implacable professional values and a unique loyalty to their machines, their colleagues and the railway milieu.

---

[5] *Ibid.*, Ordre du Jour n°35 (24 Jul. 1940).
[6] SNCF/25/LM/240: Ordre du Jour n°36 (18 Aug. 1940).
[7] *Ibid.*, Ordre du Jour n°38 (4 Dec. 1940).
[8] *Ibid.*, Ordre Régional n°37 (31 Oct. 1940).
[9] *Ibid.*, Ordre Régional n°105 (23 Feb. 1942).
[10] SNCF/303/LM/2: Letter (21 Oct. 1941) from Barth to many.
[11] SNCF/25/LM/240: Etat numérique menseul des agents mis en cause pour vols le 1ᵉʳ janvier 1941 (situation au 15 Nov. 1941). The table shows that although dismissals were not the *only* punishment for theft, they were the most common form of punishment.

The cheminots were bound together by a professional code of conduct which prioritised obedience, security and hard work. Their lives were run with punctual precision dictated by their watches; their pristine uniforms were worn with great pride – it thus seems very out of character for cheminots to begin stealing the goods which they had been entrusted to transport. This long history of professional discipline does not, of course, exclude instances of defiance. Strikes had taken place, and daily acts of insubordination were denounced. Some cheminots were punished for being absent from their posts, others for being drunk on the job or for having falsely claimed to be too ill to work and then later found walking around in town at a leisurely pace.[12] In peacetime, these consisted of the majority of insubordinate acts. In 1920, acts of theft represented fewer than 1% of punishments.[13] In wartime, however, it was slightly different: during the First World War, general acts of dissidence continued but theft became more and more prominent in 1916 and 1917, the most difficult years of the war.[14] Although a comparative study of theft in the two world wars would deepen our understanding, cheminot theft statistics in 1914–18 seem incomparable with those of 1939–45. The link between war and theft is undoubtedly true, but there seems to be something slightly more complicated going on during the 1940s.

1   Approaches and methods

What do they do, those who have no space to organise themselves, to voice their concerns, to exert their power? Those who are constantly 'in the enemy's field of vision'?[15] These people, according to Michel de Certeau, cannot use strategies of overt resistance and defiance. First, because they are far too visible. Second, because they require a level of power and organisation which some workers do not have. As such, they resort to everyday, hidden, subaltern tactics of defiance. 'Power is bound by its visibility', but 'ruse is possible for the weak' precisely because of its invisibility.[16] Those in spaces of power could utilise 'strategies', but 'tactics, in contrast', could only be deployed by those whose power and visibility has been removed: 'Strategies gamble on the resistance which the establishment of a place or locus offers to the wear and tear of time; tactics on the contrary put their faith in a skilful utilization of time, and of

---

[12] SNCF/243/LM/10: Registre des Punitions et Gratifications (1914–1918).
[13] *Ibid.*, Registre des Punitions et Gratifications (1920).
[14] *Ibid.*, Registre (1914–1918).
[15] Michel de Certeau, Frederic Jameson and Carl Lovitt, 'On The Oppositional Practices of Everyday Life', *Social Text* n°3 (Autumn 1980) 6.
[16] *Ibid.*, 6.

the opportunities it offers as well as the place it can introduce into the very foundations of power'.[17]

Yet how does one measure these hidden tactics of ordinary men and women? Are tactics such as theft clearly identifiable in history? Scholars interested in theft throughout history consistently refer to the inherent difficulties of such a study. For one, data is extremely hard to obtain. Herrick Chapman described the difficulty in obtaining records of invisible misconduct: 'it is impossible to say how many workers, technicians, engineers, or even employers took part in sabotage or in schemes to slow down production'.[18] He is not alone in raising this problem. For Robin Kelley, theft is an 'elusive' form of resistance particularly hard to trace.[19] Hollinger and Clark acknowledged 'the difficulties in determining the amount of employee theft'.[20] In the case of the railway workers, how many times did a cheminot slow down his work intentionally to disrupt traffic? How many times did he drink on the job without getting caught? How many pieces of coal did he smuggle home?

Not only that, but the conclusions we can draw are tentative at best. Historians who look at hidden forms of working-class deviance in the workplace offer a range of different reasons for their actions: the re-appropriation of time and labour, of leisure and goods, for instance. Selina Todd has warned against overstating working-class resistance to employers, arguing instead that 'distracting themselves from the monotony of the labour process was the aim of many young workers. Their talking, singing and joking, disliked and often forbidden by employers, provided distraction from tedious work, was a means of re-appropriating work time, and undermined supervisors' authorities'.[21] It might seem easier to conclude that stealing occurred out of economic necessity, but as it will be shown there are still too many nuances to reduce it to monetary and material compensation alone. Of course, to know which specific reason most impacted individual workers at individual moments is impossible. The lack of data, but also the multiplicity of individual behaviours and independent circumstances makes it very hard to trace precise patterns of behaviour.

---

[17] *Ibid.*, 7.
[18] Herrick Chapman, *State Capitalism and Working-Class Radicalism in the French Aircraft Industry* (Oxford: University of California Press, 1991) 253.
[19] Robin D.G. Kelley, '"We are not what we seem": rethinking black working-class opposition in the Jim Crow South', *The Journal of American History*, 80.1 (Jun. 1993) 91.
[20] Richard C. Hollinger and John P. Clark, *Theft by Employees* (Lexington, Mass.: Lexington Books, 1983) 4.
[21] Selina Todd, *Young Women, Work and Family in England, 1918–1950* (Oxford: Oxford University Press, 2005) 160.

So why study theft at all? In the 1980s, scholars of social science, anthropology and philosophy were pointing to the importance of studying alternative, invisible, unorganised forms of resistance, which are the only forms of protest possible in atmospheres of intense supervision. According to Robin Cohen, these included an array of actions from sabotage to psychological responses, stopping through drug use and feigning sickness.[22] For James C. Scott, workers devised 'hidden transcript(s)' to challenge authority, and in doing so created 'a dissident political culture that manifests itself in daily conversations, folklore, jokes, songs, and other cultural practices'.[23] Subaltern activities thus lie at the heart of the history of everyday life.

Moreover, working-class history cannot be reduced to trade unions, their leaders and their members. As Michael Seidman pointed out, working-class parties, structures and representatives do not necessarily embody the many facets of working-class frustrations and concerns.[24] So if one wants to understand the story of workers from a bottom-up perspective, looking only at political structures can be seriously misleading. Furthermore, not all workers can benefit from structured representation. The history of domestic workers is one without unions or representatives, a similar situation to the history of working-class women who often (but not always) appeared disengaged from politics and labour relations because of low trade union membership. As such, scholars must turn to subaltern activities in order to better understand the stories of these unrepresented workers.[25]

Turning away from the study of trade unions is particularly relevant in regards to the cheminots in the Second World War. First, not all cheminots were members of trade unions, and even those who were did not necessarily pay their dues, suggesting a certain disengagement. Second, if

---

[22] Robin Cohen, 'Resistance and Hidden Forms of Consciousness Amongst African Workers', *Review of African Political Economy*, 19 (Winter 1980) 8–22.

[23] Scott is cited in Kelley 'We are not what we seem' (1993) 77. See also James C. Scott, *Weapons of the Weak: Everyday Forms of Peasant Resistance* (New Haven, London: Yale University Press, 1985).

[24] According to Seidman, certain studies have shown 'that working-class organisations such as the PCF were *partis passoires* [or sieves]; through them workers and others passed with little active involvement, as they did in major political parties and unions during the Popular Front. Historians began to question the closeness of the relation between workers and their organisations or between workers and their ideologies...'. Seidman, *Workers Against Work* (1991) 9.

[25] The relationship between women, their work and the unions is explored by Todd in chapters 5 and 6, whilst Kelley describes how black domestic workers faced 'considerable barriers to traditional trade union organization', and had to devise new 'hidden transcripts'. See Kelley 'We are not what we seem' (1993) 89; Todd, *Young Women* (2005) 145; 166–7.

trade unions were not completely dissolved under Vichy as was discussed in Chapter 2, they were seriously disrupted nonetheless. Having lost the traditional structures and institutions through which they could express their grievances, what did the cheminots do? It is thus crucial that we look elsewhere for expressions of cheminot frustration.

At times, it may seem like the lack of concrete evidence around employee theft can leave the historian to only make a series of educated guesses, rather than to draw scientific conclusions. Yet this chapter is rooted in a thorough study of disciplinary reports from the SWDC between 5 January 1939 and 8 December 1941.[26] It is rare to find such a regular and detailed record of employee misconduct, and examining them very closely gives us a far more specific idea of what was happening. The files contain basic data on all the cases which went before the SWDC during this period: name of cheminot, rank, residence, and type of 'misconduct'. Out of 480 different cases in this period, 303 involved incidents of theft.[27] A series of questions then need to be asked: why were cheminots brought to the SWDC? How significant was the phenomenon of theft amidst other forms of misconduct ? Who (in terms of their hierarchical role and rank) was stealing ? When were they stealing ? What were they stealing ? This gives a much clearer idea of acts misconducts, and especially theft, during this crucial period from Phoney War to Occupation.

The statistics drawn from these records were then cross-referenced with other sources, including statistical reports, the SNCF newspaper *Renseignements Hebdomadaires*, public announcements and posters, and when possible, cheminot testimonies. This range of sources allows us to test theories more accurately. At times, the sources confirm the effect of wartime shortages on attitudes and behaviour; at other times, they remind us of the significance of working-class struggles and identities which, in a time of occupation, were heightened rather than dispelled. As Barry Godfrey has remarked in his own work, one cannot get exact answers to questions of employee theft due to the limitation of sources; yet one can see a pattern in psychological resistance and opposition to work, to the employer and the supervisory system.[28]

---

[26] SNCF/303/LM/7: Disciplinary Council reports from 1939, 1940 and 1941 of the South-West Region.

[27] These numbers on based on the author's own calculations, who tried to be as diligent as possible in this analysis. Any mistakes are my own.

[28] Barry Godfrey, 'Law, factory discipline and 'theft': the impact of the factory on workplace appropriation in mid to late nineteenth-century Yorkshire', *British Journal of Criminology*, 39.1 (1999) 61.

2   Theft in wartime – or tactics of the ordinary worker

In times of war and occupation, luxuries almost disappear and basic commodities are rationed. Consequently stealing, like the black market, becomes a part of everyday life.[29] This is not so surprising since traditional codes of conduct – of what is acceptable, and what is not – change in during conflicts. Expectations and tolerance levels shift to accommodate to the difficult conditions which characterise war and occupation. In the 1940s, France was no different.

The rise of employee theft in the SNCF mirrors the changing norms in wartime. Indeed, the SWDC records show not only an increase in disciplinary cases between 1940 and 1942 (See Figure 4.1), but within those, the cases regarding theft almost doubled in number (See Figure 4.2). Further statistics from 1941 show a similar phenomenon in other regions. That year, the number of dismissals in the East Region for theft alone climbed from 32 cheminots in January–March to 193 in October–December.[30] In the West Region, 200 cheminots were dismissed within the first eight months of Occupation.[31] In the South-East Region there were 932 cases of cheminots caught stealing between January and November that year, and over 80% of these thefts took place within the railways themselves.[32] Whilst stealing was considered illegal in peacetime, in wartime it became a quasi-necessary supplement to daily rations and shortages.

These statistics beg an important question: were cheminots actually stealing more, or was theft more criminalised under Vichy? In other words, does the rise in disciplinary cases brought before the SWDC reflect a real increase in general cheminot misconduct, or is it just the case that the SNCF leadership was buckling down on misconduct during this period? These are important questions which, unfortunately, cannot be answered with absolute certainty. However, if one considers the historic disciplinarian nature of the SNCF leadership, then it is unlikely that they would ever have been lenient to any kind of theft going on in the railways. Indeed, the safe transportation of both travellers and goods was central to the reputation of the railways. If the railways were unable to ensure safe and secure transport, then their reputation was tarnished. The dangers of railway travel already terrified

---

[29] For more information on the link between war and theft, see Lowell S. Selling, 'Specific War Crimes', *The Journal of Criminal Law and Criminology*, 34.5 (1944).

[30] SNCF/25/LM/240: Ordre Régional n°102 (5 Jan. 1942).

[31] *Ibid.*, Affichage de tracts pour prévenir des punitions affligées en cas de vol (Mar. 1941).

[32] *Ibid.*, Etat Numérique Mensuel des Agents mis en cause pour vol du 1 Jan. au 31 Oct. 1941.

Total

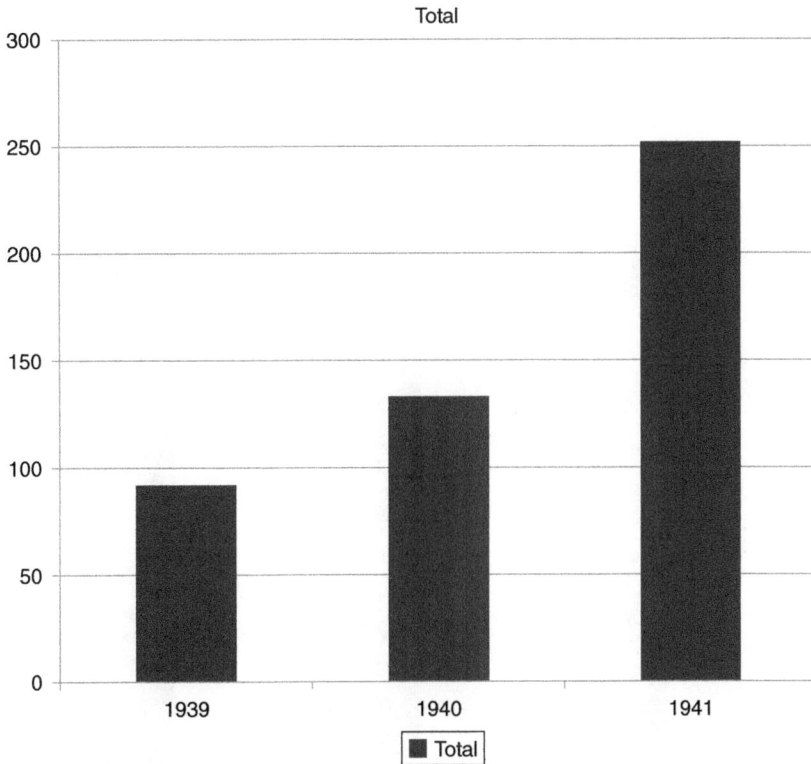

Figure 4.1 Total number of cases brought to the SWDC, 1939–41.

many people in the nineteenth century – the unreliability of the transport of their goods and luggage would only further dampen their
enthusiasm for railway transport. It is for these reasons that the railways
were such a highly disciplinarian milieu, and as a result I would be
confident to suggest that the steep rise in disciplinary cases in the
Second World War was not as much a change in attitude on the part
of the leadership, but rather on the frequency of acts of misconduct
being committed.

Some evidence helps back claims of an actual rise in cheminot theft.
Indeed, by identifying what cheminots stole between 1939 and 1941 it is
possible to see a shift in the type of things which they stole – a shift which
reflects the growing shortages of the Occupation, and the growing need
for basic (and luxury) products. Overall, the tableau of thefts under
Occupation is very coloured. There was the useful coal to keep you
warm, clean and civilised which, in large quantities, you could sell on:

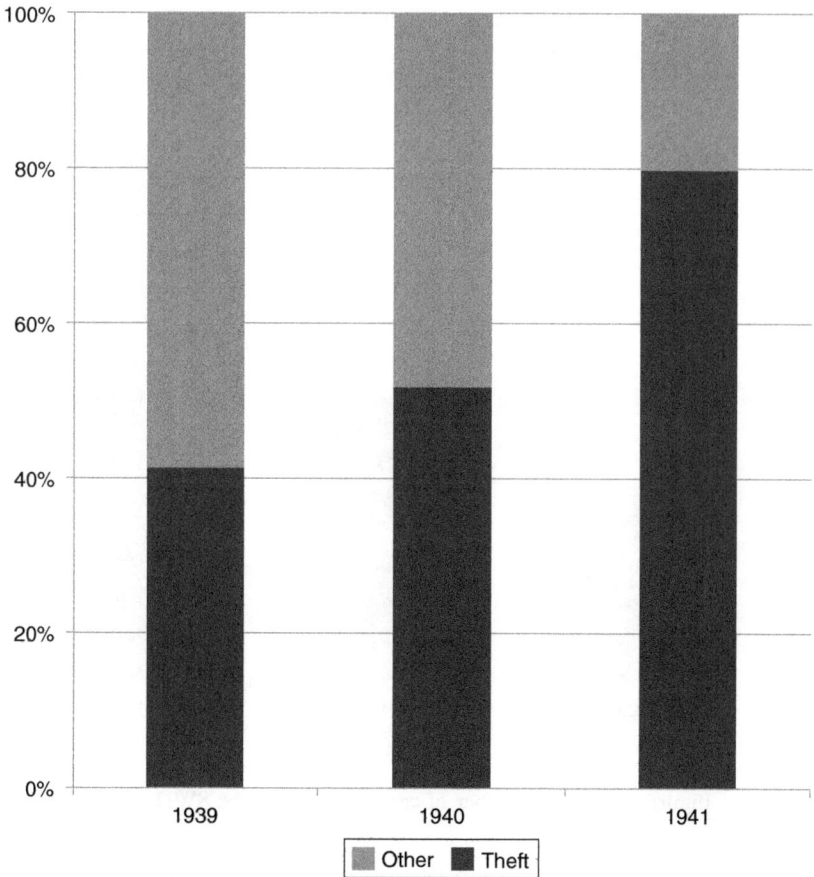

Figure 4.2 Cases regarding theft brought to the SWDC, 1939–41.

one cheminot stole 50kgs of coal,[33] and another stole 350kgs.[34] There was the enjoyable champagne, sugar, jam, whiskey, cheese, soap, curacao liquor, shoes, and salad bowls.[35] And there was the less expected: two

[33] Charles Aubert Huot from the Belfort depot was given 15 days of imprisonment and 600 francs fine for stealing those 50 kilos of coal. SNCF/206/LM/6: Mesures Disciplinaires dossiers d'agents (Vols), Vol des années 1940; Fiche de Renseignements Concernant un agent passible d'une sanction disciplinaire soumise à la décision de M. le Directeur Général.

[34] This large quantity of coal was stolen by an unskilled worker in Bethune. SNCF/25/LM/ 240: Poster, 68 agents dismissed for theft in May 1943.

[35] Details of what was stolen were often included in the posters denouncing cheminots recently dismissed for theft. Ibid., Poster, 68 agents dismissed for theft in May 1943.

horses and a horse-drawn carriage.[36] And yet, patterns can be detected. In 1939 and 1940, over 50% of the theft cases involved money, materials and clothing and shoes, whereas thefts of bikes, wood and coal increased significantly in 1941. Moreover, in 1941 items which had been previously absent from the SWDC files suddenly appeared with considerable frequency: animals, petrol, tobacco and even private parcels were now being stolen by cheminots. Of course, discerning what people steal is a complicated enterprise; despite the regular, detailed and systematic records at our disposal, these only tell us about *known* cases, leaving a vast space for unknown, un-archived crime. And even when the records are relatively complete, there remain many cases where the information is too vague to categorise. Indeed, general inscriptions in the SWDC files sometimes only mentioned 'theft to the prejudice of the SNCF', 'merchandise' or 'materials', giving no clear indication of what cheminots were actually stealing. That being said, the findings we do have show a strong link between theft and wartime. Indeed, what was being stolen in 1941 was exactly the basic commodities which were becoming increasingly rare during the Occupation: meat, petrol, tobacco.

This may come as a surprise since cheminots were often considered more advantaged than other workers. Cheminots were not plagued by unemployment; as skilled workers they received slightly higher wages than many other workers; as manual workers they got more rations; their free transport costs also meant they could go to the countryside to obtain the goods which they needed. But as Herrick Chapman commented in his study of the aviation industry, 'even relatively good wages for long term employees in aviation did not insulate people from the hunger, cold and sense of insecurity that plagued working-class France during the Occupation'.[37] The same can be said for the cheminots.

By stealing basic goods such as meat, wine and coal, cheminots were not just alleviating shortages – they were also reaffirming masculine identities of the provider. In a time of shortages and hardships, and following a humiliating defeat, the sense of emasculation was extremely strong in France.[38] The presence of the hyper-masculine German Nazi was threatening to many Frenchmen; Vichy's own National Revolution

---

[36] The *cantonnier* stole these from a private owner, rather than the SNCF. He was not fired, but given 4 months imprisonment. *Ibid.*, Poster, Révocations pour Vol au cours des mois de juillet et août 1941.

[37] Chapman, *State Capitalism* (1991) 247.

[38] For more information on masculinity under Vichy, see Luc Capdevila, 'The Quest for Masculinity in a Defeated France, 1940–1945', *Contemporary European History*, 10.3 (Nov. 2001) 423–45; Joan Tumblety, *Remaking the Male Body: Masculinity and the Uses of Physical Culture in Interwar and Vichy France* (Oxford: Oxford University Press, 2012).

which emphasised physical sport culture and a return to nature was an effort to revive this masculinity. The cheminots, who were an almost all-male community of over 400,000 manual workers between 1940–44, were already participating in this renewal of physical education; but by stealing, they were redefining their masculine 'roughness', which was unlike the moral bourgeois notions of masculinity (strength, self-control and self-discipline). And by providing for their families in times of shortages, workers were in many ways re-appropriating the domestic sphere which had, by this stage, come under the shadow of German Occupation.[39]

Historians have given other explanations for theft in wartime, not least profit. Fabrice Grenard and Jacques Delarue have shown how the black market thrived throughout France during the Occupation. Far more than a peripheral market, it was central to the daily life of almost all people, and even the government.[40] Indeed, the failure of the rationing system meant that the population felt justified to recur to alternative methods to obtain what they needed. A shift in moral codes – what was acceptable, and what was not – was taking place all over France due to the pressures of war and occupation. Clandestine networks were thus erected, not least to cross the demarcation line. People with easy access to goods were involved in these networks: as Lynne Taylor has shown, farmers, whole-salers, merchants and retailers found themselves in very good places to carry out some black marketing. Taylor's study also emphasizes the centrality of SNCF employees to black market organisations and net-works: indeed, their ability to cross borders and access raw materials was extremely attractive. Barriers were set up at train stations so that surveil-lance and police authorities could better access these smuggling hot-spots. In January 1942, a black market cell was uncovered amongst the cheminots for smuggling coal. Apparently, five cheminots from Jeumont

---

[39] A good discussion of masculinity in the railway milieu is Paul Michel Taillon, '"What We Want is Good, Sober Men:" Masculinity, Respectability and Temperance in the Railroad Brotherhoods, c.1870–1910', *Journal of Social History*, 36.2 (2002) 331. For more on masculinity and working-class culture, see Martin Francis, 'The Domestication of the Male? Recent Research on Nineteenth- and Twentieth-century British Masculinity', *The Historical Journal* 45.3 (2002) 637–52; Martin Johnes, 'Pigeon Racing and Working-class Culture in Britain, c. 1870–1950', *Cultural and Social History*, 4.3 (2007) 361–83; David L. Collinson, "Engineering Humour': Masculinity, Joking and Conflict in Shop-floor Relations', *Organization Studies*, 9.2 (1988) 181–99; Lois A. West, 'Negotiating Masculinities in American Drinking Subcultures', *The Journal of Men's Studies*, 9.3 (2001) 371–92.

[40] Fabrice Grenard, 'Les implications politiques du ravitaillement en France sous l'Ocupation', *Vingtième Siècle. Revue d'histoire*, 94 (2007) 199–215; Jacques Delarue, *Trafics et Crimes sous l'Occupation* (Paris: Fayard, 1968).

would clandestinely order coal from Belgium and then redistribute the coal in packs of 500–1,000 kgs amongst 137 cheminots.[41]

Theft also carried a heavy paramilitary significance. As John Sweets pointed out, theft in the *maquis* was widespread: 'From an early date, Vichy authorities, aware of the frequent disappearance of substantial quantities of explosives, gasoline, ration coupons, and other materials useful to the *maquis*, have tried to limit those losses by various means'.[42] In order to prevent these thefts, extra security was organised during the transport of these goods from one place to another. Still, many operations were successful. Cheminots may not be the main instigators in such incidents, but they facilitated *maquisard* theft operations. In a post-war ceremony, the cheminot Georges Buttard boasted about one such incident. He had learnt that a train expected to arrive in Ambrieu contained an entire freight car overflowing with cigarette cartons: 'We stopped the train [before it reached the station] and just started unloading. Everyone on the train was helping [us]: the handler, the conductor, the driver, and even the track layers, standing nearby'. To make their colleagues appear innocent, they 'got some rope to tie up their hands, and they marched towards the town pretending that the train had been hijacked'. The result? '5,000 *maquisards* were more than happy to smoke to the health of the *boches*'.[43]

If cheminots stole, it was also because of their close proximity to large quantities of goods across France.[44] Already in the nineteenth century, the birth of the railway had seen a shift in existing criminal trends: with goods and people moving all across the nation, the opportunities for theft significantly increased. Railways in particular 'offered employees the opportunity to take goods as well as money, and goods in transit were vulnerable to theft. Drink, of any variety, seems to have been a favourite target'.[45] In a time of shortages, the massive movement of goods and materials was all the more vulnerable. The ex-railway workers Jean-Claude Huckendubler and Bernard Le Chatelier described how easy it was for cheminots to get hold of, and potentially re-distribute, goods and materials. Cheminots working in the depots had the best access to large quantities of goods and materials, and in the big transfer stations and depots they would see kilos of Roquefort, beetroot and potatoes pass

[41] Lynne Taylor, 'The Black Market in Occupied Northern France, 1949–1954', *Journal of Contemporary history* (1997) 163, 159–60.
[42] Sweets, *Choices in Vichy France* (1986) 216.   [43] AN/72/AJ/495: Georges Buttard.
[44] The theme of proximity re-emerges in cheminot resistance activities.
[45] R. W. Ireland, '"An increasing mass of heathens in the bosom of a Christian land": the railway and crime in the nineteenth century', *Continuity and Change*, 12.1 (May 1997) 62.

under their noses. For those working on locomotives, such as Mr Charbonnier, it was easiest to steal coal. 'Getting supplies wasn't always easy', said Le Chatelier, 'but I have to say that the personnel in the depot helped us a lot'. And when there were a few generations of railway workers in a single family, they could combine forces and significantly increase their booty.[46]

The importance of location comes into full light when analysing which cheminots were most involved in theft. According to the SWDC records, handlers were involved in a third of employee thefts. As it so happens, handlers held one of the lowest ranks on the railroad, and they needed no qualifications to enter the SNCF. Their strong prominence amongst thieves suggests two things: that they were younger and had less to lose from stealing, and that their sense of allegiance was less strong than that of other cheminots.[47] But locomotive engineers were second in line, with *cantonniers* (roadmenders) close behind them. The most common thieves amongst the cheminots were thus a combination of low-ranking, young men, with little loyalty to the SNCF, and more established and respected cheminots. This point about loyalty is further confirmed by other statistics in December 1941: out of 390 cases, only a third were committed by non-permanent staff.[48] Moreover, if one considers the theft statistics across the SNCF in 1942–44, the permanent staff was more active in theft than auxiliaries or those working in collaborating companies (Figure 4.3).

What is interesting to note is that the majority of cheminots involved in employee theft physically worked alongside the railway tracks, whether in stations, or on the roads. According to the archives, it was these workers who were brought to the Disciplinary Council, rather than the workers who were subject to the constant supervision in the workshops or the depots. The explanations for who stole cannot, therefore, be reduced to age, inexperience and disloyalty alone; they also had to with location. This could explain why workers in highly-supervised, fixed workshops feature low amongst the culprits.

As previously mentioned, these statistics raise all sorts of problems. The disciplinary records can only tell us about known crimes, and even then, some of the data is too vague to allow us to draw definite conclusions. Furthermore, to truly understand the phenomenon of theft, a systematic study of the disciplinary records in other regions is wanting,

---

[46] Interview Robert Charbonnier; AHICF: Interview transcript, Bernard Le Chatelier (19 Nov. 1999) 14; Huckendubler (1999) 4.

[47] Youth and a lack of loyalty are two defining characteristics amongst employee thieves. See Hollinger and Clark, *Theft* (1983) 6–9.

[48] SNCF/25/LM/240: Nombre d'arrestations pour vol en décembre 1941: 390. Répartition, par Région des sanctions à la suite de ces arrestations.

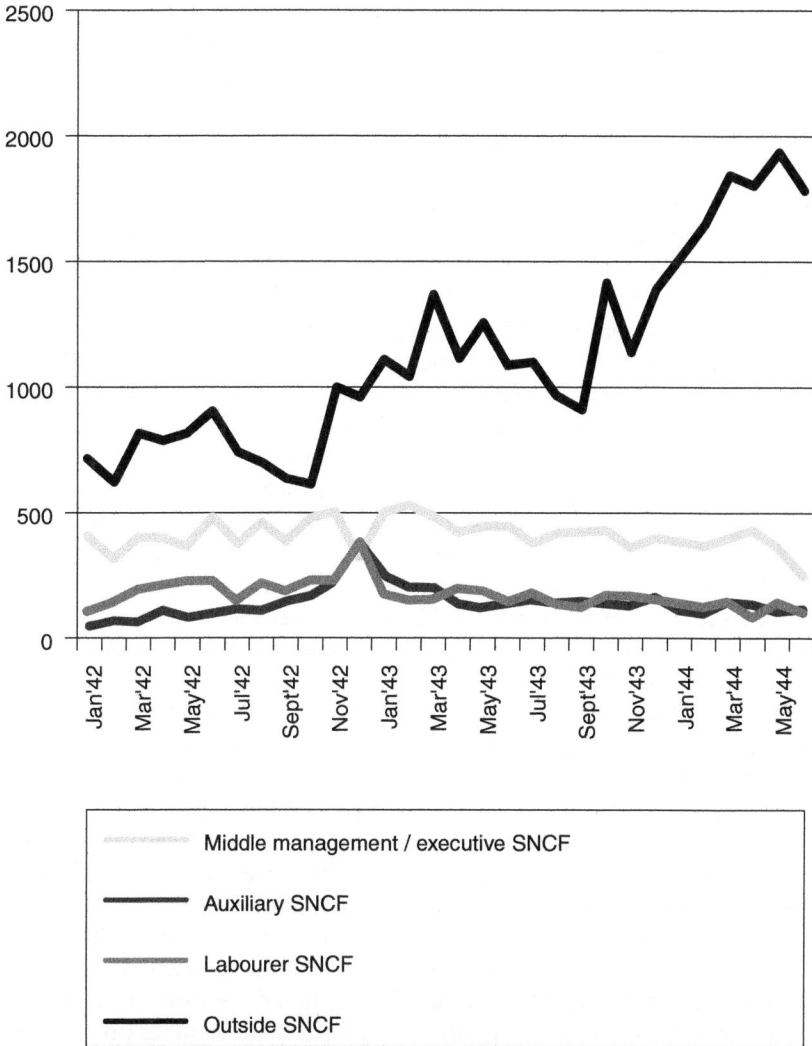

Figure 4.3 Those caught for stealing from the SNCF, January 1942–
May 1944.[49]

as is one of the pre-1939 and post-1942 period. But even if one were able
to obtain all of this 'missing' information, it would still be impossible
to make definitive assumptions on the motivations behind theft.

[49] SNCF/25/LM/240: Statistique des vols, Révocations d'agents, Personnes Appréhendées
1942, 1943, 1944.

The societal conditions which push historical actors to act (or not) in certain ways are always up against the power of individual agency, and this is an unknown factor.

In the case of cheminot theft during the Occupation, there is an additional problem with statistics. When examining the archives on theft in the railways, I came across charts tracing theft in the 1942–44 period – right when the SWDC records ended. These statistics are particularly fascinating: first, because they cover the whole territory; second, because they include data on thefts from the SNCF committed by cheminots and non-cheminots and finally, because they show very different patterns of theft between the two groups. Whereas non-cheminot theft regularly increased after November 1942, cheminot theft fell slightly (Figure 4.3). In 1943, Le Besnerais' announcement reflected this phenomenon: 'As we know, many thefts are committed by those outside of the railways, and if, unfortunately, some cheminots gone astray end up following bad examples (...) there is no doubt that the personnel overall condemns such going-ons'.[50] His usual disciplinarian tone from earlier announcements had been washed down.

In many ways, the rise of non-cheminot theft from 1942 onwards reinforces previous claims about links between theft and economic hardship. Indeed, everything from 1942 onwards became more complicated, such that by 1943 the relatively stable situation of 1940–41 was a distant memory. But if the increasing hardship enabled a significant rise in theft, why was this only affecting the non-cheminots? After all cheminots' lives, too, got a lot harder after 1942. Firstly, cheminot repression intensified, with the large majority of arrests, deportations and killings of cheminot taking place in 1943 and 1944. Secondly, cheminots were still front row witnesses to the German seizures of French industrial and agricultural goods. By 1944, almost half of the SNCF's material was in German hands,[51] although the exact numbers of materials destined for Germany is difficult to assess.[52] From their work stations, cheminots saw hundreds of thousands of tonnes of wheat, iron, cattle, rabbit skins, wood, wine, and even bicycles being sent to Germany.[53] Thirdly, if the Relève in 1942 and then the STO in 1943 did not hit cheminots as hard as other professions, the idea that cheminots were *exempt* from these hardships is largely false. As previously stated, it was only in early 1944 – a year after the STO was introduced – that SNCF became an 'S' industry and its workers were not

[50] *Renseignement Hebdomadaire* (29 Oct.1943).
[51] Lartilleux, *Le Réseau National* (1948) 23.
[52] See Ribeill, 'Trafic sous contraintes' (2007) 170–4.
[53] Long lists of goods being transported reveal the diversity of the railway transports. See AN/72/AJ/2296: Transports de produits et matières premières pour l'Allemagne (Oct. 1943–May 1944).

forced to leave for Germany. Finally, the aerial Allied bombings which targeted railway infrastructure to hinder German military movements in 1943–44 caused considerable destruction to cheminot homes and workplaces, putting their lives in danger on a daily basis. If anything, the situation in 1942–44 was dire for the railway community.

Another plausible explanation might be that, after 1942, the SNCF leadership was less inclined to discipline their workforce. As such, it was not that cheminot theft stabilized, but rather that they were being less criminalized for it. Indeed, the railways were coming under more and more strain due to lack of material and pressures from the Germans. In fact, as it will be further discussed in Chapter 6, the SNCF leadership took a more explicitly protective attitude in regards to their personnel after 1942. The particular strains which cheminots were facing in this period risked breaking their morale, but the SNCF needed them now more than ever. As such, high-ranking but also mid-ranking cheminots may have been less inclined to discipline workers in these dark times, using a carrot rather than a stick approach. Still, the disciplinarian tone against theft was very present. After all, a company-wide anti-theft prevention campaign was launched in 1943. Moreover, as previously stated, the history of discipline and punishment within the SNCF would suggest that it is unlikely that a radically *laissez-faire* attitude would emerge during the war.

There is one final crucial point to make: the stabilisation of theft coincided with the re-emergence of clandestine trade union movements and underground resistance networks. As the next chapter will show, activism became more directed, more focussed, more organised after 1942 and especially 1943. As such, cheminots were more empowered after 1942, able to develop strategies of resistance and opposition rather than relying on tactics of everyday life. This does not mean that they would do away with subaltern behaviours completely; however, the re-emergence of underground trade unions and resistance groups may have helped channel their frustration into more active protest.

Ultimately, explaining employee theft in the railway milieu under the Occupation also requires us to consider the long-term ideological causes. Amongst the working classes, theft was a reflection of the complicated relationships between employee and employer, between worker and occupation, between individual men and collective unions. Their interests did not always coincide, and theft was a manifestation of workers' frustration. According to Lawrence and Robinson, 'workplace deviance as a form of frustration against organizational power'.[54] Through quantitative data,

---

[54] See Lawrence and Robinson, 'Ain't Misbehavin'' (2007) 378–94.

Lawrence and Robinson prove something which other scholars have already picked up on. But their choice of language is less focussed on terms such as 'resistance' and 'opposition' to management, and they really develop the notion of 'frustration'. Defining theft as an act of frustration better portrays cheminots' subaltern activities. The term resistance is too problematic to be appropriate because it is too closely linked to the idea of the French Resistance and does not accurately reflect the phenomenon itself.

3   Cheminot theft: a question of morality

It was one thing to steal coal, wood, wine or soap from the railways; it was quite another stealing from the parcels destined for French POWs. These did not constitute the majority of thefts, but their growing frequency was deeply problematic for moral reasons. Indeed, by stealing from POW parcels, cheminots were committing a deeply anti-patriotic gesture. 'There is nothing more precious than what we are entrusted to give prisoners of war and not a single [parcel] should ever go missing'.[55] And yet, POW parcels were tampered with. Le Besnerais could not hide his horror: 'I have witnessed that despite the heinous nature of these acts, and despite the numerous warnings that their chiefs gave them, some railway workers continue to steal from the packages destined for prisoners of war'.[56]

The status of POW parcels is largely explained by the status of POWs themselves. Prisoners of war were central to Vichy's diplomatic negotiation strategies. They were also national heroes and martyrs, and stealing products destined for them was considered a very serious crime. In the posters listing cheminots convicted for theft, those who had stolen from POW parcels were highlighted in bold and underlined. They were identified, isolated and fired immediately. In the second trimester of 1943, 103 cheminots were disciplined for theft in the South-West Region, yet three of them – two low-ranking employees and one train engineer – were caught stealing POW parcels. Their punishments were by far the most brutal: on top of being fired, two were sent to 15–20 years of forced labour, and one spent five years in solitary confinement.[57]

The theft of POW parcels reminds us that stealing had deep moral implications which went beyond the strict legal code: this was not just about breaking the law, but about breaking basic moral principles. Of

[55] 'Continuons à veiller aux colis de prisonniers', *Renseignements Hebdomadaire* (1 May 1942).
[56] SNCF/25/LM/240: Ordre du Jour n°43 (12 Mar. 1942).
[57] *Ibid.*, Poster 'Révocations pour Vols pendant le Deuxième trimestre 1943'.

course, in wartime, one must expect for a shift in norms of acceptability. Yet morality did not disappear completely – it remained deeply entwined with cheminot theft. The SNCF's anti-theft campaign was a strong reminder of the SNCF's desire to 'keep the cheminots' moral sense awake'.[58] Entitled the Prevention Service, it was launched in October 1943 and was rooted in the idea that repression was not enough to curb employee theft: the only way to truly prevent crimes was to change mentalities.[59] The Prevention Service had two aims: first, a material aim, which required a more intense system of supervision as well as self-supervision. Increasing surveillance was an obvious solution in particularly vulnerable sites. Extra men were sent to certain main train stations where thefts had repeatedly occurred, such as Lille.[60] Certain goods were more protected than others, too: goods cars were particularly vulnerable, and parcels were put under tight surveillance.[61] Surveillance issues also intersected with German interests and demands: the WVD fully supported these methods, even at times calling out for a tightening of security themselves.[62]

The second aim of the Prevention Service was a moral one, which consisted of psychological and educational activities.[63] Of course, this was a long-standing technique of working-class disciplinary strategies which showed the leadership's ability to exploit the fears and concerns of the cheminots to their own advantage. Moral pressure had frequently been applied to the cheminots. For example, posters listing the cheminots caught for stealing and subsequently dismissed were regularly pasted on SNCF walls in full view of employees.[64] The content of the posters varied from region to region, with some debate about whether or not cheminots should be named as well as shamed. Le Besnerais believed that posters should occasionally indicate the rank and residence of the guilty cheminots.[65] Similar problems were occurring in the postal services, and certain ministers wanted to divulge individual names so that

---

[58] *Renseignement Hebdomadaire* (29 Oct. 1943).

[59] 'L'Angoissante question des vols (suite)', *Renseignement Hebdomadaire* (5 Nov. 1943) 1.

[60] ANMT/202/AQ/201: Letter (approx. 6 Nov. 1941) from Chevrier to Latouche.

[61] *Ibid.*, Letter (approx. 3 Nov. 1943) from Chef de Service de l'Exploitation to Chef de Service VB.

[62] *Ibid.*, Letter (undated) from Directeur de Service Central du Mouvement to Directeur de l'Exploitation de la Région Nord.

[63] 'L'Angoissante question des vols', *Renseignement Hebdomadaire* (12 Nov. 1943) 1.

[64] SNCF/25/LM/240: The poster listing '68 agents dismissed for theft in May 1943' has, in the top right corner, a typed indication of where the poster should be pasted: 'Place on sites non-accessible to the public'.

[65] *Ibid.*, Letter (14 Mar. 1941) from the Directeur du Service Central du Mouvement to many.

other workers could fully understand the consequences they would face if ever involved in theft.[66] Although it is not known if this was implemented uniformly throughout the PTT, names were shown when the theft involved POW parcels.[67]

If psychological intimidation was everywhere, it was also imbued with manipulation and paternalism. By tugging at the strings of their professional ethos, the leadership was hoping to educate, enlighten and improve cheminot mentalities of the time. Accusations against their general misconduct were veiled in compliments about their professionalism, their integrity and their patriotism:

> I have had many opportunities to express my satisfaction with the way the cheminots carried out their duties during the war and the reconstruction. (...) But at the moment I can see certain signs of carelessness: appearances are not always what they should be, thefts are far too frequent, incidents in the exploitation as well, negative propaganda against discipline has been noticed in several establishments. (...) and yet, our profession is our life and that of our children. The honour and future of our corporation are at stake (...) one must side-line the culprits and punish them without hesitation or indulgence, but it is especially important to warn and counsel [the cheminots] in order to avoid errors.[68]

Not only that, but management played on the nationalism of the times, reminding cheminots that theft was not just a crime, but a national offence: 'every single thief prejudices the French and them alone'.[69]

The core values of cheminot integrity and honesty were brought to the forefront of the SNCF's campaign to fight theft, and the SNCF newspaper was full of references to cheminot professionalism and nationalism. Theft 'dishonoured' he who committed it, and these hard times were no excuse for such behaviour.[70] The first page of the 14 January 1942 *Renseignements Hebdomadaires* issue was heavy with rhetoric on honesty and integrity, a desperate attempt to gain access into the cheminots consciousness and bring them back from the 'dark side':

> It would seem that a wind of madness is blowing through certain places, troubling and disorienting spirits which had until now been considered honest, even annihilating amongst certain cheminots, close to retirement and with an irreproachable past, the sacred honesty which they had developed throughout their long careers. And there are some who just let go and let themselves fall... they pinch something once, twice... "just a few trifles (with

---

[66] *Ibid.*, Letter (11 Dec. 1942) from V. Di Pace, Secrétaire Général des Postes, télégraphe et téléphone (PTT) to the Secrétaire d'Etat à la Justice.
[67] *Ibid.*, Letter (Apr. 1943) from Inspecteur Général des transports to Le Besnerais.
[68] *Ibid.*, Letter (19 Aug. 1941) from Le Besnerais, probably to many.
[69] *Ibid.*, Ordre Régional [de l'Est] n°102 (5 Jan. 1942).
[70] 'A Propos ... Des Vols', *Renseignement Hebdomadaire* (19 Dec. 1941).

this war, these shortages, are we not ... excusable?)" And then one gets bolder. Suddenly, one takes "something which is worth it", and then it's done: one has become a thief.[71]

This slippage into dishonesty threatened to contaminate not only the corporation, but also the home: 'Before thinking of himself, every cheminot must think of his children and of the moral code he must impose without fault in his own home'.[72] Long diatribes on cheminot integrity were complimented by short rhymes, easy to remember, intended to act as mottos by which one should live their lives: 'Opportunity makes the thief, No unsupervised parcels', 'Scattered parcels.... Stolen parcels!'[73] Some were even accompanied by small cartoon images, further infantilising the cheminots[74]

After the war, when theft was still a problem, similar strategies continued to be used. Through humour, cheminots were infantilised and coaxed into creating their own surveillance system. The Bogy and Tampon comic strip still played on this theme in the post-war period. When Bogy and Tampon stop to read an SNCF poster – 'Cheminots, participate in the surveillance of transports carrying wine' – Bogy suddenly gets an idea. He convinces Tampon to climb into an empty wine barrel. 'Don't be scared', he says, 'I'll be with the police nearby'. Tampon, who has crawled into the barrel, eventually falls asleep. When two thieves begin to drill a hole into the barrel, the drill pokes Tampon's bottom, and he wakes up jumping out of the barrel, yelling 'Ow!! Thieves!!!' The last scene is a comical reunion of Bogy and Tampon, the latter telling his friend that he will have to help apply some bandages as he strokes his sore bottom. In the background, the two thieves are chained together, being taken away by the police[75] (See Figure 4.4).

The SNCF encouraged cheminots to play a part in the theft prevention campaign itself, a pre-existing method deployed by the Prevention Service. In December 1943, cheminots were invited to design and submit posters which would be useful for a nation-wide theft prevention campaign. The drawings were to be divided into two sections: one examining 'moral' prevention, the other 'material' prevention. The awards were enticing: first place won 5,000 francs, second place 2000, third place 1500, all the way to place 25, which won 100 francs. Was it this promise

---

[71] 'A certains Cheminots avant qu'il soit trop tard!', *Renseignement Hebdomadaire* (16 Jan. 1942).
[72] 'A certains Cheminots avant qu'il soit trop tard!', *Renseignement Hebdomadaire* (16 Jan. 1942).
[73] *Renseignement Hebdomadaire* (26 Nov. 1943).
[74] *Renseignement Hebdomadaire* (10 Dec. 1943).   [75] *Notre Métier*, (29 Mar. 1946).

Figure 4.4 Bogy and Tampon catch thieves on the spot: 'Poster: Cheminots, take part in the campaign to supervise wine transports; Bogy: 'I have an idea !'; 'Bogy: 'Don't worry, I'm not far, and with the police'.; Nightime, two shadowy figures . . .; Tampon: 'Ow !! Thieves !!'; Tampon: 'You'll have to put some ice packs !' *Notre Métier*, 52 (29 Mar. 1946). SNCF – Centre National des Archives Historiques.

of awards which encouraged cheminots to send in their proposals? Or were they, too, as horrified by theft as the leadership were?

Whether spontaneously or coercively, poster designs were submitted. The jury met on 15 February 1944, and ten days later the three winners had their posters printed in centre page of the *Renseignements Hebdomadaires*.[76] The poster (see Figure 4.5) which won second place is especially interesting for its *tutoiement* – the use of the informal '*tu*' rather than the more formal '*vous*'. This is a further reminder of the forced familiarity towards, or even infantilisation of, railways workers. A few weeks, from 6 to 22 March, all submitted posters were on display at the *Gare de Lyon*. Le Besnerais, along with other Directors including Barth and Tuja, went to see the exhibition, and applauded the efforts and creativity of the cheminots.[77]

The SNCF's continued insistence on moralising cheminot theft undoubtedly shows their paternalistic traditions. And yet, it also suggests that they believed this kind of moralising would work. If the cheminots' moral compass had shifted during the war and Occupation, it had not been completely broken, and the directors were determined to use this to their advantage.

Conclusion

One should be careful not to romanticise cheminot theft, and especially to associate it with active resistance to the occupier. A story involving the ex-cheminot Georges Perruche, highlights the fine line between theft and

---

[76] *Renseignement Hebdomadaire* (25 Feb. 1944).
[77] *Renseignement Hebdomadaire* (3 Mar. 1944).

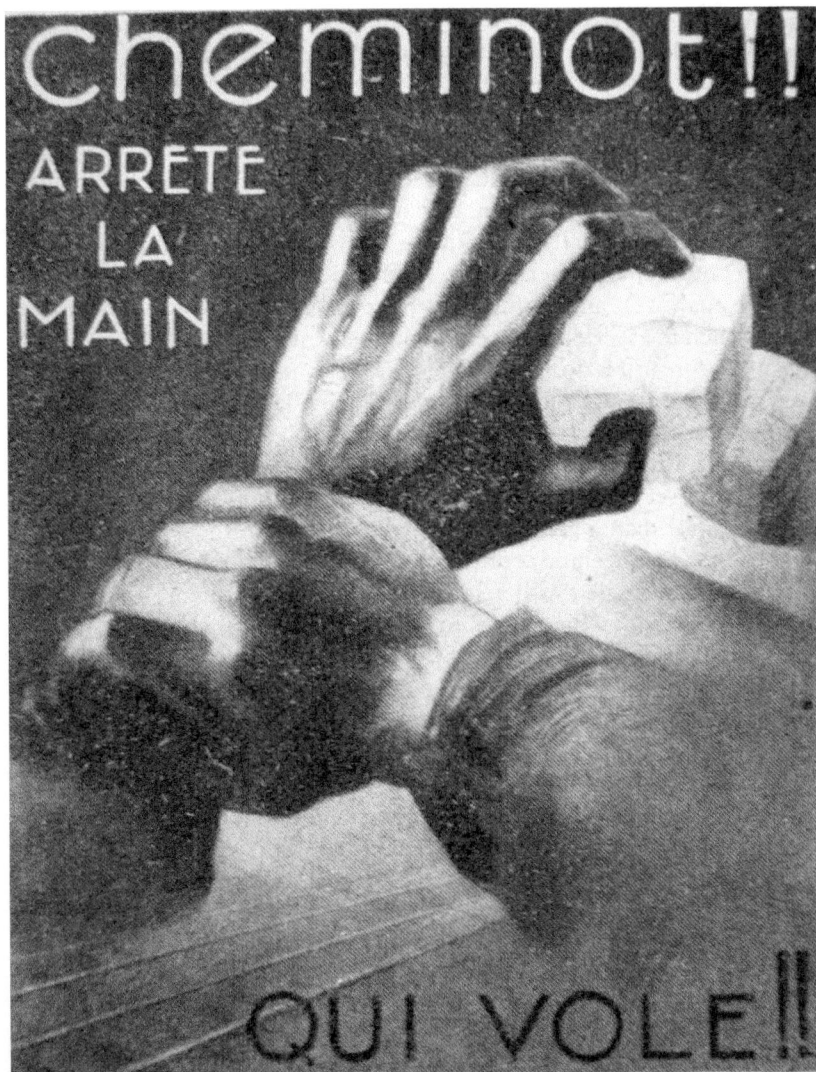

Figure 4.5 'Cheminot!! Stop the hand which steals!!' Runner up poster for the Prevention Service Poster Competition, 1944. *Renseignements Hebdomadaires*, 25 Feb. 1944. SNCF – Centre National des Archives Historiques.

trickery.[78] Perruche was the station master at Pont Tarbier. Early one morning in June 1944, he was approached by a German who asked him in a very thick accent if he could leave his luggage in the main office. He assured Perruche that he would pick up the bags that very night. The cheminot accepted, but was immediately struck by how heavy they were. Once he and his colleagues had hauled the bags upstairs to his office, curiosity got the better of them: they opened the luggage to find countless bottles of good French wine. Within a few minutes they had devised a plan to pour out a quarter of each bottle (they kept what they poured out for personal use), and to fill them back up with water and push in the cork. When the German officer served the wine on the following day at a big luncheon of Nazi officials, the pale and tasteless liquid enraged his superiors. He had to return to the wine merchant, a local collaborator, who was forced to replace all the bottles at his own expense. 'Shortly after the Liberation', wrote Perruche, 'this little anecdote appeared in the press, and everyone was laughing!' Perruche's story is closer to a great practical joke than a great robbery, but it speaks to the varied nature of (and motivations behind) subaltern activities of the time. And although this story is entangled with acts of anti-German resistance – not least in his own re-telling of the story – employee theft was much more complex.

Still, the study of subaltern activities, and of employee theft in particular, gives a fresh understanding of the cheminot community. It shows that so many cheminots – not just the young or the unskilled – were frustrated with their work, their bosses, the railways. They were angry at the Germans, yes, and at Laval and his Vichy cronies, too – but the drastic rise in employee theft visibly shows the tensions within the very community which was supposed to be the symbol of family, unity and patriotism. And this is a very different perspective from that of obedient, hard-working, resisting cheminots. For employee theft tells us a slightly different story to theft alone. As Godfrey has underlined, employee theft suggests that workers are defying the supervisory system, their bosses and their work itself. So if wartime necessity drove them to steal from their employer, then this also says a lot about their changing relationship between the cheminots and their workplace.

This changing relationship between cheminots and the workplace will become more and more evident in the following chapters, especially as cheminots engage in sabotage. However, at this stage, does employee theft suggest a total break in tradition? It is important to understand that, despite its radical nature, employee theft was not a total breakdown of the

[78] AN/72/AJ/497: Georges Perruche.

esprit cheminot. If one looks closely enough, the *esprit cheminot* was present in these repeated acts of insubordination. The interviews I ran allowed me to see how cheminots working in different sites often shared their booty in this classic spirit of professional solidarity. This was not only in the interviews, but in many of the anecdotes cited in this chapter. The very fact that the SNCF directors prosecuted those cheminots who simply *used* stolen goods shows that a network of exchange and distribution was rife amongst the cheminots. The *esprit cheminot* is thus a much more fluid concept which got moulded to different occasions and circumstances. As the following chapters will show, it remained intertwined with further acts of defiance and even of resistance.

5   Protest

Subaltern acts of protest were bubbling below the surface from 1940 onwards, and theft was only one amongst other manifestations: humour, pranks, slow work, bad work, all were tactics which became increasingly widespread throughout France. The proliferation of these small, hidden, individual acts of everyday resistance is particularly obvious in cheminot history.[1] Aside from mentioning the big strikes, Durand and Choury enumerated the myriad individual acts of cheminot resisters. Louis Armand – a well-educated chief engineer at the SNCF who fought in the resistance before becoming the SNCF's Managing Director in 1949 – praised Durand's ability to emphasise the 'essentially clandestine activities, the typical aspects and principal objectives of cheminots' individual resistance'.[2] More recent studies by Georges Ribeill, Christian Chevandier, Serge Wolikow and Laurent Douzou have also underlined the significance of cheminots' everyday resistance, their methods of protest and disobedience.[3] Indeed, the clandestine and individualistic nature of cheminot resistance has never been denied.

However, Armand also believed that the sum of these individual acts showed 'a quasi unanimous consensus of the entire corporation of about 400,000 agents, a consensus where active participants found, at many dramatic moments, the same protection they would have had under cover of the maquis'.[4] This fit into his broader effort to portray cheminots as a uniform body of resisters under the banner of *Résistance-fer*, an (alleged) network of cheminot resisters during the Occupation. *Résistance-Fer*, or Res-Fer, has often been considered as *the* active cheminot

---

[1] Chevandier provides a good overview of cheminot resistance studies in *Cheminots en Grève* (2002) 174–80.

[2] Preface by Louis Armand in Durand, *La SNCF* (1968) viii.

[3] Chevandier, 'La résistance des cheminots' (1997); Ribeill, 'Les Cheminots face à la lutte armée' (1996); Wolikow, 'Syndicalistes cheminots' (2001); Douzou, 'La résistance des cheminots' (2001).

[4] Durand, *La SNCF* (1968) viii.

resistance group during the Occupation, not least by eminent historians.[5] However, the nature of Res-Fer is much more ambiguous. Even ex-cheminots and ex-resisters are unsure about its origin: 'Apparently it existed before [the end of the occupation]', said Lebrun, 'but I didn't know anything about it. After the war, it had an important social role'.[6] 'Ah, listen, I think it was created after the war (...) I think that those who were part of the Resistance unified to form the movement *Résistance-Fer*, I think that's how it went', commented Le Chatelier.[7] Jean-Yves Boursier recorded unique testimonies from the Migennes train depot, which declared that 'there had been no such thing as a 'cheminot resistance' or *Résistance-Fer*, no collective action against the occupier'.[8]

In fact, there was no such thing as a nation-wide, company-wide, organised cheminot resistance network. Res-Fer was an association created after the liberation, on 27 December 1944, to unite railway workers who had resisted the German occupier.[9] It not only maintained links between ex-resisters, but it also gave financial and moral support to the families of those cheminots who had been deported or killed by the Nazis.[10] That being said, there was an attempt to unify the cheminots into a single resistance network – but it was not very successful. Until the spring of 1943, the network *Ceux de la Libération* (CDLL) was the only resistance network to include a formal 'Rail' – or *Fer* – division led by Lucien Bourgeois. That spring, Roger Coquoin, the head of the CDLL, put Bourgeois in charge of detaching cheminots from all resistance networks and to unite them into a separate railway network. Liaisons were made with other resistance groups, notably *Combat* and the *Noyautage des Administrations Publiques* (NAP).[11] Indeed, the NAP, was one of the only other networks to have a special railway section known as NAP-Fer led by René Hardy.[12] But this attempt to unite all these cheminots into one coherent, separate network failed. First, because cheminot resistance and protest activities were far too fragmented and disparate.

---

[5] One example is Kedward, whose major contribution to resistance studies and French history is indisputable, and who equates *Résistance-Fer* to cheminot resistance. See '*Résistance-Fer*' in the index in Kedward, *In Search of the Maquis* (2003) 338. He is far from being the only one, and many other leading historians of Vichy France have also been unaware of the much more complicated nature of Res-Fer.

[6] Interview Lebrun.   [7] Interview Le Chatelier.

[8] Boursier, *La Résistance* (1993) 11.   [9] AN/72/AJ/2280: *Journal Officiel* (7 Jan. 1945).

[10] *Ibid.*, Résistance Fer, Union des Cheminots Résistants, Statuts: Buts de l'Association.

[11] The NAP's controversial role in the resistance – simultaneously working with Vichy and supplying information to the Free French and Allies – is mentioned in Matthew Cobb, *The Resistance: The French Fight against the Nazis* (London: Simon & Schuster, 2009) 129–30.

[12] Chevandier, *Cheminots en Grève* (2002) 180–1. Chevandier also acknowledges the complicated origins of Res-Fer.

Second, because loyal ties between the cheminots and the resistance groups they belonged to could not easily be severed.[13]

To what extent does the absence of a uniform resistance in the SNCF challenge the idea of cheminot resistance? After all, if only 1% of cheminots were part of *Résistance-Fer* after the war, does this mean that the myth of cheminot resistance is completely hollow?[14] Explaining individual and collective acts of protest and resistance is a strong reminder that there is more than a kernel of truth behind the myth of cheminot resistance. Moreover, by tracing the motivations which lay behind these protests, is it possible to gain a slightly different understanding of cheminot resistance?

1   Subaltern activities and individual protest

Before discussing structure and ideology, it is crucial to understand the subaltern activities which the cheminot are so well-known for. Under Vichy, the French national press was heavily censored, and anti-German and anti-Vichy jokes were forced to remain in the private sphere. The only jokes permissible in the press were satiric allusions to the trials of daily life, such as rationings and curfew. Historians therefore have to rely on testimonies which are full of such anecdotes:

One winter evening in 1940–41, I was walking down the canal in my home town Charenton, (. . .) when I was suddenly accosted by two Wehrmacht soldiers. In very bad French, they asked me if I knew a café where they could have some fun with the local girls (. . .) I nodded at them enthusiastically 'Ja! Ja! There is a house with a big red lantern outside, and inside are lovely young ladies in red hoods!' 'Gut! Gut!' they cried excitedly. I took them down a little street and then pointed them in the direction of Rue des Quatre Vents saying 'House on the left!' And my two idiots scrambled up the hill [towards what was actually the Police Station] instead of young ladies, they came face to face with sneering policemen![15]

Such pranks, if they happened at all, are probably exaggerated with hindsight. However, the fact that they are being *told* in the first place reveals a deep-seated desire to show off Gallic cleverness. There was an underlying pleasure having tricked, deceived or outwitted the Germans, and the re-telling of such stories alone provided a euphoric rush of superiority.

Humour allowed for a re-appropriation of dignity, but there were other ways to show one's power. As previously mentioned, *ralentissage*, or 'slow

---

[13] AN/72/AJ/2280: Note succinte sur les origines de Résistance-Fer (24 Mar. 1950).
[14] Figure extracted from Georges Ribeill '*Résistance-Fer*, du "réseau" à l'association: une dynamique corporative intéressée?', *Revue d'histoire des chemins de fer*, 34 (2006).
[15] AN/72/AJ/495: Darphin.

work', had been a traditional tactic of protest for centuries, and the method successfully re-emerged during the Occupation. According to Mlle Josse who worked as a liaison officer in the war, 'never before did parts take so long to be assembled – never before did so many tools vanish into thin air'.[16] Even coded BBC broadcasts encouraged cheminots to engage in slow work.[17] Other methods of resistance required a similar break from the railway tradition of obedience and discipline, such as mislabelling cars. Freight cars transporting goods always had a destination label stuck on the side, which indicated the station it was supposed to be sent to. By altering these labels, or taking them off completely, freight cars ended up in wrong cities, or else they were considered empty and were sent back to the depots. The labels which had been peeled off were also forwarded to London, to the Allied Headquarters, so the Allies could keep track of transport movements. It was the start of a 'label war' within the railways.[18]

I was carrying out my little individual acts of resistance, hijacking freight cars full of ammunition which were destined for the German aviation camp in Samoussy. It was not a dangerous affair, since I would simply remove the destination labels. As a result the freight cars were considered empty and were sent to the triage station. Of course once it arrived there, people noticed that it was full, but since there was no indication of the destination long exchanges ensued between the RB services and the Wehrmacht about where it should be sent. The freight cars would eventually end up at the correct destination, but at least the transport would have been seriously delayed.[19]

Mislabelling required so little preparation that it could almost be accidental. Julien Berçaïts, a sixteen-year-old apprentice working in Bordeaux, was strolling alongside a parked train during his night shift when a man jumped out from under the rail cars and gestured to the terrified boy: 'listen mate, take these labels and stick them on the train cars, like me!' Too frightened to object, Julien mechanically began sticking the labels on the train – it was so dark he could not even read what was written on them. It was only a few days later that he found out that the train cars he had labelled had ended up in the wrong destination. To his surprise, he had participated in the resistance.[20] Yet mislabelling freight cars was not so easy, and careless mistakes meant that goods destined for French use were lost or sent to the wrong location. Cars full

---

[16] AN/72/AJ/496: Mlle. Josse.
[17] Cécile Hochard and Bruno Leroux, *La Lettre de la Fondation de la Résistance: Les cheminots dans la Résistance* (Fondation de la Résistance, 2005) 8.
[18] Durand, *La SNCF* (1968) 354–5.   [19] AN/72/AJ/495: François Depoorter.
[20] AHICF: Interview with Julien Berçaits; *L'inacceptable* (2000) dir. Claude Binsse.

of animals – destined for the general food supply of the French population or for the Wehrmacht – were found stranded in remote locations as a
result of careless mislabelling.[21] In April 1944, for example, two freight
cars with 20,000 kgs of bread destined for French civilians went to
waste.[22]

Other illegal gestures included the clandestine transportation of goods
and people. In 1940, prisoners of war who escaped from the makeshift
camps often relied on the good will of cheminots to hide them on trains
and get them across the demarcation line. And during those first weeks of
the Occupation, when only 300 letters were allowed across the demarcation line per day, cheminots smuggled letters by hiding them in their
breast pockets.[23] When the packages got bigger, they hid them inside
their locomotives.

One could go on enumerating these acts to ask the same questions:
why did cheminots commit individual acts of resistance? Was it within
their nature? Not quite. One of the main reasons to explain this cheminot
involvement in resistance activities, whether subaltern or organised, is
location. According to Ribeill, cheminots could be involved in resistance
activities because they had the technical knowledge, the institutional
significance and the strategic positioning. Indeed, the cheminots' strategic position was crucial: Christian Bachelier and François Marcot both
argue that if cheminots were involved in the organised resistance, it was
largely because the Resistance needed their knowledge and resources.
They therefore sought out the cheminots themselves.[24] Indeed, cheminots were working on one of the most valuable instruments for German
economic and military survival. As such, they could hinder it on a daily
basis and annoy the Germans. Sometimes they did it for the organised
resistance, at other times, by themselves.

Another burning question is how to interpret these gestures? To what
extent do they form 'resistance' to the occupier? Jacques Sémelin differ-
entiated civilian resistance – non-violent and non-military forms of resistance – from military resistance – more organised and thereby more easily
identifiable.[25] Civilian resistance can take on multiple forms, which vary

[21] Durand, *La SNCF* (1968) 355.   [22] AN/72/AJ/495: Lucien Barbier.

[23] Paxton, *Vichy France* (1975) 53.

[24] Bachelier Report, 6. *Le développement de la résistance des cheminots, 1943–1944*; François
Marcot 'Pour une sociologie de la Résistance: intentionnalité et fonctionnalité' in
Antoine Prost, ed., *La Résistance, une histoire sociale* (Paris: les Editions de l'Atelier-
Edition ouvrières, 1997).

[25] Jacques Sémelin, 'Résistance civile' in François Marcot, Bruno Leroux, Christine
Levisse-Touzé, eds., *Dictionnaire Historique de la Résistance* (Paris: Robert Laffont,
2006) 691–3; See also Jacques Sémelin, *Unarmed Against Hitler, Civilian Resistance in
Europe, 1939–1943,* (Westport, CT: Praeger Publisher, 1993, c1989).

greatly in risk, efficiency and even motivation. According to Sémelin, civilian resistance 'was rarely directed against the occupation forces openly', instead, it aimed to 'preserve the collective identity of the attacked societies (...) [It] offered a privileged means to dig a trench between military domination, which was the actual state of affairs, and political submission, which was a state of mind'.[26] The anthropologist James C. Scott further argues that, under a repressive regime, these daily acts of defiance and disobedience – what he calls 'everyday resistance' – are at the heart of popular resistance.[27] They are generally used by peasants or the working class, who have no other means of protesting. Unfortunately, such unorganised, individual, opportunistic acts of resistance are often overshadowed by 'real' resistance, which is organised, collective and selfless.[28]

Considering the dangers and tensions of the time, and the censorship that limited the freedom of expression, tricks and practical jokes can certainly be seen as acts of everyday resistance to the Germans. One did not need to be part of an organized resistance group in order to participate in popular resistance against the Occupier. Indeed, in 1997, François Marcot declared that 'the multiplicity of actions carried outside of official organisations (...) prohibits us from reducing the Resistance to the organisations which existed'. However, Marcot also saw the need to limit the definition of 'resistance': 'one does not resist "in one's head," resistance is an action'.[29] Pierre Laborie also saw the importance of this link between action and idea. The idea of resistance needed to precede the action of resistance. Indeed, 'an act of compassion can save the life of a clandestine individual or a Jew: yet if it is carried out with no intention to harm the occupier or his accomplices, then it remains first and foremost an act of compassion'.[30] It is impossible to say whether these everyday tactics of opposition combined both idea and action, but they still fit a broader picture of dissidence, defiance and risk.

The proliferation of acts of misconduct, disobedience, trickery and even individual resistance under Vichy can thus largely be explained by the frustrations of the Occupation and the strategic positioning of the cheminots; we also need to consider that, for most of 1940–42, there was an absence of official structures through which cheminots could express their grievances, whether the trade union movements or organised resistance.

---

[26] Sémelin, *Unarmed Against Hitler* (1993) 3.
[27] Scott, *Weapons of the Weak* (1985) 28–37.   [28] *Ibid.*, 292.
[29] François Marcot, 'Pour une sociologie' (1997) 22, 21.
[30] Pierre Laborie, 'Qu'est-ce que le Résistance?' in Marcot et al., ed., *Dictionnaire* (2006) 35.

Understanding this absence is crucial in explaining the rise of employee theft in 1940–42, but also the proliferation of subaltern activities described above. The word 'absence', however, should be explained. First, there was no actual 'absence' of trade union structures. Vichy did not destroy the unions it sought to change them. Second, this 'absence' was as much about a change in structure as it was about a growing disinterest from the grass-roots. In May 1940, the cheminots themselves were less concerned with their trade union rights than with other more pressing matters, not least the exodus, the defeat and the reconstruction of the nation as well as their own lives. Indeed, as Chevandier stated, the widespread disinterest in trade union activity was 'largely due to the fact that cheminots had other preoccupations'.[31] This disinterest would change over time, however, and with it we can see a visible step from subaltern activities of everyday resistance to active protest.

2   Politics, patriotism and professional frustration

The transformation of cheminot protest from subaltern, individual activities to active, organised protest is not clearly linear. There was no definite moment when everything changed; in fact, the two co-existed throughout the Occupation – involvement in organised resistance happened, albeit at a minority level, from 1940, whilst theft, practical jokes and *ralentissage* would continue until the Liberation. As it has already been underlined, *Ceux de la Libération* had a 'Rail' division from the onset led by Bourgeois.

However, there was a perceptible shift into more active resistance in 1942–43. Chevandier points to certain phenomena which were more important in the early years of the Occupation than others: absenteeism was higher in 1940–41, whilst the number of small sabotages (sending a package to another destination) was higher in 1942, 1943 and 1944. Equally, if some claim that the first cheminot strikes took place on 11 November 1940 at the Ivry workshops, this stoppage may merely be confused with other 11 November manifestations.[32] According to Chevandier, one of the first visible strikes was in Oullins in October 1942, a response to Laval's 4 September 1942 labour law. Although it did not last for more than a day, the October 1942 strike marks the beginning of a period of increasing localised strike action amongst the cheminots: 14 July 1943 (Tergnier and Villeneuve Saint Georges), 20 September 1943 (Sotteville-les-Rouen), 26 May 1944 (Marseille) and 7 March 1944

---

[31] Chevandier, *Cheminots en Grève* (2002) 160.   [32] *Ibid.*, 185.

(Vitry workshops).[33] There was a similar increase in railway sabotage during this 1943–44 period, although this will be discussed at a later point.

These studies point towards an intensification of methods: but why, exactly, does this intensification occur in the cheminot milieu? A close and careful reading of clandestine publications found on railway sites illuminates the reasons behind the intensification of cheminot protest activity.[34] The body of archives under investigation consists of underground tracts, newspapers, pamphlets and leaflets found on railway sites and handed over to the SNCF Central Services in Paris, between March 1942 and December 1943. Most were in depots, others found along tracks, others pasted on walls of common areas like the locker rooms.[35] Others still were found inside, or thrown from, trains. Some were hidden in bathrooms, in offices, and occasionally they were posted directly to the home of middle-management cheminots. The thick, colour-printed pamphlet *Le Maréchal* – which was made to look like it celebrated Pétain, but in fact included many subversive quotes and drawings in the central pages – was sent by post and under SNCF envelope to the station master in Veynes and the head of the information services in Gap.[36] One cannot know who planted such material: was it local resistance groups? cheminots themselves? other workers living and/or working in the vicinity? Outsiders obviously had ways of bringing this material to the railway sites, since one could easily access a train station; not everyone, however, could paste a tract in a workshop bathroom. We can thus assume a degree of complicity and/or initiative from within the railway milieu.

This body of archives shows a regular flow of left-wing underground press. Copies of *La Vie Ouvrière* – the biggest CGT paper originally launched in 1909, banned in 1939, back up and running illegally in February 1940, was producing over 250 illegal issues by 1944 – and *L'Humanité* – another underground revue born from the PCF in 1904 but banned in 1939 following the Nazi-Soviet pact – regularly appeared in railway sites. Cheminot underground press, like *Le Cheminot Syndicale,* also became more frequent after 1942, with its third issue appearing in February 1943.[37] Many were aimed at cheminots, whether they were published by cheminots themselves – *Le Travailleur du Rail, La Tribune des Cheminots, Le Cheminot Syndicale* – or by left-winged groups – especially *La Vie Ouvrière*

---

[33] For more examples see Chevandier, *Cheminots en Grève* (2002) 190–6.
[34] SNCF/25/LM/258: Tracts anti-nationaux 1942–1943. In this chapter, all subsequent tracts, newspapers and letters were found in 25/LM/258, unless stated otherwise.
[35] Letter (10 May 1943) from Lourdin accompanying the 'Cheminots de Perrigny' tract.
[36] *Le Maréchal.* [37] *Le Cheminot Syndicale,* n°3 (Feb. 1943).

and *L'Humanité*. And yet, the cheminots were not the only ones targeted in these tracts. Many were aimed at workers and French people in general, and some at women.[38] Seeing as there were almost no women in the SNCF, this is a strong reminder that the railway was being used as a method to spread propaganda, not just to recruit potential resisters, strikers or union members.

Cheminots were ordered to collect and record any such anti-government, anti-German or anti-national tracts found on railway sites, and then to inform the railway managers as well as the local authorities. This meant that middle management was involved in the wider process of the oppression and surveillance of cheminots, a position which compromised their reputation on a number of levels: they were working against the cheminots, siding with upper management, collaborating with French and even German authorities. Some worked diligently: on the morning of 16 September 1942, the Department Head of Gargan station found a number of tracts lying along the tracks.[39] He added these to the ones he had found the night before, and made careful note of them in a letter which he sent to upper management and local authorities (These included Renard, an SNCF regional director, the Police Commissar of Noisy-le-Sec, the Police Commissar of Livry and the German Surveillance Services of Noisy-le-Sec.) But others took a different approach to this call for surveillance of 'anti-national' activities. In a letter to the Police Commissar in Marseille on 6 November 1942, one chief wrote 'According to the SNCF instructions, I am handing over 5 tracts herewith which were discovered in the buildings of my district'. However, the 'anti-French' tracts he attached were not what the government had in mind: 'Frenchmen! Avoid the Jews, ...'; 'England betrayed Europe' ; '25 years of Bolshevism Plague of the World'.[40] Hopefully, those who read this letter had a good sense of humour.

If the context of these tracts is difficult to determine with exact precision, a careful study of their content shows clear patterns in the kinds of tactics cheminots and workers were encouraged to adopt. Firstly, there was a call to refuse departure for Germany. Given the time frame of the tracts under investigation – from Summer 1942 to December 1943 – it is

---

[38] A tract dedicated to metalworkers was found in October 1942 in the ateliers of La Folie; the tract *Femmes de France* was found stuck on a wall of the refectory in Nice-St-Roche in November 1942; *Femmes que deviendrez-vous?* was found in a depot in Nantes on 30 April 1943; *Le Cri des Femmes* was found in the Lyon-Mouches depot in October 1943.

[39] Letter (Sept. 1942) from Renard, Directeur de la Région Est, to Renz, EBD Paris-Est.

[40] Letter (6 Nov. 1942), from Chef du 3è arrondissement du Matériel to Commissaire de Police in Marseille. This letter was transferred all the way up to Central Services.

not surprising that a lot of the space was devoted to the *Relève* in Spring
1942, the law of 4 September 1942 and of course the STO law in
February 1943. 'You will not go to Germany. Your work will not contribute to worsen and prolong vile hitlerian enslavement (. . .) there are
enough French prisoners of war and there is no need to increase those
numbers. (. . .) You will stay in France', wrote *Combat* in July 1942.[41]
Following the September law, one tract called for civil servants to inter-
fere with the lists announcing the designated workers.[42] Messages were
also directed specifically at the cheminots: 'Not one cheminot for
Hitler !'[43] ; 'Resist by all means possible !'[44] And in May 1943, *Combat*
published a letter from one cheminot exposing Vichy's lies about good
salaries, food and housing in Germany: 'For food it's juice at 8 in the
morning, for lunch a plate of potatoes and red cabbage and a piece of
bread of 300 grams which is supposed to last until the following day. So
you understand what I'm saying ... I sleep in a wooden barrack. They
have given us two covers, some straw and that's it, so I sleep without any
sheets ...'.[45]

This call to refuse departure for Germany was accompanied by a
language of death and slavery. The *Vie Ouvrière* described German
factories as 'factory-graves'[46], and those in Vichy, not least Laval, were
repeatedly denounced as slave traders: 'The slave traders in Vichy'[47]; 'the
slave trader Laval wants the deportation of the cheminots!'[48] This language of the death and exploitation of French workers by both the Nazis
and the French was powerful, but the discourse of patriotism was equally
prominent. Indeed, by evading conscription, young French men were
not only avoiding death and slavery, but they were also acting as honourable Frenchmen and good patriots. Those who rejected the deportations
were real Frenchmen living according to republican values: 'Do not
forget that you are French, and thereby inheritors of our most noble
traditions of freedom and heroism'.[49] In contrast, those who left were
cowards: 'Protest against the ignoble deportations (. . .) which bring

---

[41] 'Travailleurs!', *Combat*.   [42] 'Fonctionnaires Français', *Combat*.
[43] 'Pas un cheminot pour Hitler' was the headline in *La Tribune des Cheminots*, Seine-
Inférieure (Oct. 1942); The Comité Populaire des cheminots signed a small tract under
the same title.
[44] 'Cheminots!', the Front National de Lutte pour l'Indépendence de la France.
[45] 'Lettre d'un cheminot de Valence', *Combat* (Mar. 1943). Of course, whether this letter is
authentic is a different matter; what is important here is its presence alone.
[46] *La Vie Ouvrière*, n°88 (May 1942).
[47] 'Cheminots!', Comité Populaire des cheminots Batterois.
[48] 'Le Négrier Laval veut la déportation des cheminots! A l'action!', Comité populaire des
cheminots de la région Picarde.
[49] 'Cheminots', Région Communiste du Vaucluse.

shame on all those who accept them'.[50] Interestingly, leaving for Germany was also betraying the class struggle: 'Laval wants to "designate" cheminots to go work in Germany ... But cheminots will not betray France and the working class'.[51]

Aside from refusal to leave, the tracts also called out for actual physical violence. A discourse of bloodshed was embedded in a deep and explicit hatred of the Germans, who were systematically referred to in pejorative tones, such as 'the accursed *boche*'[52] or the 'hitlerian barbarians'.[53] But if calls for violence were there, but they remained vague. When the *Tribune des Cheminots* called for revenge against their murdered colleagues, they did not explicitly order cheminots to kill the Germans – in this particular instance, they threatened those chiefs who might be '*boche* enough' or 'cowardly enough' to designate men to go work in Germany with a 'punishment to reflect their treachery', but no explicit call for blood.[54] Likewise, the *Comité du Front National* shouted 'Death to the slave traders. Death to Traitors. Death to the *boches* ...'[55] In fact, it could be argued that the memories of French martyrs were used to stir up violent protest, rather than murder. But if the *Comités Populaires des Cheminots* did not talk about murder as such, the call for a violent destruction of material and infrastructure was powerful: 'let us follow the path shown to us by our dear departed [Pierre Semard]: let us do nothing which can serve the enemy, lets sabotage transport, blow up bridges and tunnels, destroy locomotives, refuse to drive trains transporting materials destined for Germans'.[56]

One of the most recurring themes in this body of literature is the call for strikes. In a time of oppression – when challenging the authorities so visibly was to risk one's job, one's liberty, if not one's life – going on strike was an extremely dangerous act, only adding to the historical fear of redundancy. Tracts thus spent a long time justifying them. Strikes were portrayed at many things: an act of protest against the conscription to Germany, for instance. 'Protest in depots, workshops, on the tracks, everywhere against the departures for *Bochie*', wrote the *Tribune des Cheminots*.[57] Strikes were also a protest against the arrest of fellow colleagues arrested by 'Vichy's Gestapo', like the call for strike on

[50] *Ibid.*   [51] *La Tribune des Cheminots*, Seine Inférieure (Oct. 1942).
[52] *Le Cheminot Syndicale*, n°3 (Feb. 1943).
[53] 'Les barbares hitlériens obligent les juifs à porter un signe distinctif', undated, PCF.
[54] *La Tribune des Cheminots*, Seine Inférieure (Oct. 1942).
[55] Small colourful tracts (blue and red writing) in support of the Comité du Front National.
[56] Three small, typed tracts, all from Comité Populaire des cheminots and urging to commemorate Semard's death on 7 March.
[57] *La Tribune des Cheminots*, Seine Inférieure (Oct. 1942).

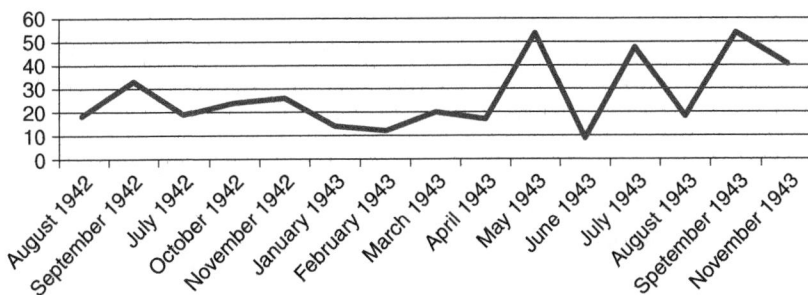

Figure 5.1 Monthly estimate of tracts forwarded to the SNCF Central Services between July 1942 and November 1943 (Missing: Dec. 1942 and Oct. 1943).[58]

28 December.[59] These calls for strike also had a strong republican undertone. Chevandier is right to emphasize this link between patriotism and strikes, and the statistics extracted from the archives clearly indicate that the amount of reported tracts peaked in those months where national, republican holidays coincided with calls for strikes: July (14 July, Bastille day), September (20 September, Valmy) and November (11 November, Armistice).

In anticipation of 14 July 1943, the communist tracts were especially eloquent about the link between strikes and patriotism: 'Our forefathers fought with courage during the great Revolution and all throughout the history of our people. Like them, you will ensure that the 14 July 1943 will be a grandiose day which marks our advancement towards liberation'.[60] This republican anniversary was followed by other commemorations which not only honoured the memory of past French victories, but specific victories against the Prussians in 1792, and the Germans in 1918. In anticipation of the commemoration of Valmy in September 1943, the illegal CGT and the *Mouvements Unis de la Résistance* decided to call a general strike on 20 September. The *Syndicat des Cheminots de la Corrèze* explained why: 'Comrades, 20 September 1792 is one of the great dates of history: It is the first victory of armies of the French Revolution against the foreign coalition. Our collective action on 20 September 1943 must signal the first collapse of Nazism and our first step towards national liberation. Comrades, onwards on 20 September! Four

[58] Results based on the statistics from all the tracts sent to the Central Services between June 1942 and December 1943.
[59] 'Cheminots ... Alerte', typed tract.
[60] 'Cheminots', Région Communiste du Vaucluse.

our right to life; For a better life, a more humane life'.[61] These were big claims, but big claims which others believed in too. The strike was backed by many other trade unions, not least the *Organe régional du Comité Limousin du Front National*,[62] and the *Fédération des Cheminots*.[63] The CGT *Syndicat des Cheminots de St-Etienne* called for a general strike on 11 November 1943 using equally nationalistic and historic overtones: 'Cheminots ! Go on strike on 11 November, so that 1943 can be a new 1918 for the despised *boches*'.[64]

Left-wing landmarks such as 1 May coincided with strikes.[65] A general strike was called in May 1943 'to sabotage production destined for the enemy'.[66] And on 28 May 1942 *L'Humanité* published a call to commemorate the 71st anniversary of the Commune de Paris on 31 May.[67] Even the victories of 1936 were used to generate enthusiasm: 'only organised action can put us on the path to victory like in 1936'.[68] Considering the absence of cheminots in 1936, it is somewhat ironic that a tract found in December 1943 shouted to all 'French Cheminots" to 'act, united like in 1936 hand in hand'.[69] Cheminot and communist martyrs, most frequently embodied in Pierre Semard, were often used as rallying cries for strikes. On 11 November 1942 the PCF in the Gard published a tract telling cheminot to 'arm yourselves for the supreme effort ... Pierre Semard, you will be avenged ...'.[70] Pierre Semard was both a symbol of the communist *unitaires* and the cheminot community. To stir up strikes in May 1943, the *Bureau illégal de l'Union des syndicats de la Région Sud-Est* wrote: 'Cheminots from the PLM remember the words of our great Pierre Semard before he was shot: "I know the cheminots well, I am sure they will do nothing which could be useful to the enemy. (...) not one deportation train must go (...) Prepare yourselves for the insurrectional strike for the liberation of the French soil'.[71] The *Organe de Défense des Cheminots Lyonnais* talked about how the 1st of

[61] 'Appel aux cheminots corréziens', Syndicat des Cheminots de la Corrèze.
[62] *Valmy*, n°1, Organe régional du comité limousin du Front National (Sept. 1943).
[63] 'Camarades Cheminots', Union des syndicats de la région parisienne (Fédération des Cheminots/CGT).
[64] 'Cheminots! Dans l'action fêtons le 11 Novembre !', Syndicat des Cheminots de St-Etienne, CGT.
[65] *La Vie Ouvrière*, n°88 (May 1942); *La Tribune des cheminots*; Three small tracts all signed un groupe de syndiqués, Le Front National and PCF.
[66] Small tract, unsigned.   [67] *L'Humanité*, n°164 (28 May 1942).
[68] 'Camarades, le bureau illégal de l'union nord vous parle', Union des Syndicats de la R.P., Fédération des Cheminots, CGT.
[69] 'Cheminots Français', Fédération Nationale des Cheminots, signed Crapier and Dupuy.
[70] 'Cheminots!', PCF, Région du Gard.
[71] '... A tous les cheminots', Bureau illégal de l'Union des syndicats de la Région Sud-Est.

May could not be day of 'festivity', but rather a day where they remembered Pierre Semard, as well as other victims, who the common enemy had deported or killed.[72]

But ultimately, the call for strikes on national commemoration days was regularly accompanied by a far more specific professional agenda in listing professional grievances and claiming grievances. This is not unusual: in the First World War, strikes were also organised to improve working conditions. As mentioned in Chapter 1, the cheminot strikes in Marseille in 1917 revolved around salaries, working hours and the integration of female personnel. In fact, 1917 saw the broader cheminot community unify and unionise.

It is thus less surprising that calls for strike were also made during the Second World War were also motivated by working-class concerns: 'Against the 24 hour weeks !'; 'protest against extra working hours by going on strike, and occupy workshops, depots and train stations'; 'Demand that your grievances be met ! Demand a pay rise'.[73] There were many tracts claiming better working conditions, like the one launched by the *Union des Syndicats de la R.P. – Fédération des Cheminots*/CGT in late 1943. It started off by outlining the deplorable conditions of the cheminots – their low salaries, the growing hardships, a decreasing buying power – explaining that this was caused by Vichy and the Railway Board.[74] Going on strike was the only way that cheminots could claim their rights. On 1 December 1943, at 13h45, the cheminots in the La Villette depot ('100%' of them, apparently) stopped working to claim better working conditions.[75]

The call for Corsican cheminots to strike on 20 September 1943 thus included a detailed list of seven claims which included the return of deported colleagues, the liberation of the territory and the fall of the pro-German clique in Vichy; its two leading claims, however, were the abolishment of the sixty-hour week, and the return to a forty-hour week.[76] A couple of months later, when the *Syndicat des Cheminots de St-Etienne* called for a strike on 11 November, they also included the demands for 'increase in our salaries and pensions, 500 grams of bread per day for everyone'.[77] In fact, during the strikes of

[72] *Le Travailleur du Rail*, Organe de Défense des Cheminots Lyonnais.
[73] 'Comité populaire des cheminots de la région parisienne', typed tract.
[74] 'Camarades, le bureau illégal de l'union nord vous parle', Union des Syndicats de la région parisienne (Fédération des cheminots, CGT).
[75] 'Appel aux cheminots' by the CGT.
[76] 'Appel aux cheminots corréziens', Syndicat des cheminots de la corrèze.
[77] 'Cheminots! Dans l'action fêtons le 11 Novembre!', Syndicat des Cheminots de St-Etienne, CGT.

11 November 1942, the cheminots in Grenoble put forward their *cahiers de revendications*, or list of demands, at the same time as they went on strike. Again on 20 September 1943, the *Fédération des Cheminots* encouraged cheminots to submit their list of demands at the same time as their strike.[78] The calls to strike on the working-class holiday of 1 May also included similar professional claims. The *Travailleur du Rail* printed the need to claim a 50% salary increase,[79] whilst small slips of paper passed around that same month made specific claims about salaries and soap: 'Cheminots, metalworkers, workers from all corporations, draw up your list of demands. Salary increase of 50%. Supplies of work clothes. Extra rations of soap. For all of these demands general strike on 1 May'.[80]

3   Trade unions and class struggle

These calls for strike are strong reminders that strike actions are rooted in working class traditions, a remark made by the *Comité Limousin du Front National* in its first underground publication: 'traditional weapon of the working class, the strike has become the necessary instrument for national liberation'.[81] In fact, references to class struggle are sewn into much of this underground cheminot press. In December 1942, the *Tribune des Cheminots* wrote that 'the Liberation of the proletariat will be the work of the proletariat itself'.[82] The *Travailleur du Rail* urged cheminots to stand up – '*Debout*' – 'to win the battle for freedom and social progress'.[83] References were also made to the broader fight against fascism, and the need to ally with those fighting the class struggle in Italy and Portugal.[84]

Not only that, but SNCF management, and the bourgeois industrialist elite in general, were often targeted in the press. The tract aimed at the *Cheminots Champenois* cried out 'It is up to you to thwart enslavement plans of the SNCF Trustees and the *boches*'.[85] The amalgamation of Laval and Vichy 'thugs' with the Germans is quite common in the

---

[78] 'Camarades Cheminots', Union des Syndicats de la région parisienne (Fédération des cheminots, CGT).

[79] *Le Travailleur du Rail*, Organe de Défense des Cheminots Lyonnais.

[80] 'Cheminots, metallos, ouvriers de toutes corporations' signed un groupe de syndiqués.

[81] *Valmy*, n°1, Organe régional du comité limousin du Front National (Sept. 1943).

[82] *La Tribune des cheminots*, Organe du Comité Populaire Central des Cheminots (Oct. 1942).

[83] *Le Travailleur du Rail* (Sept. 1942).

[84] 'Camarades, le bureau illégal de l'union nord vous parle' Union des Syndicats de la région parisienne (Fédération des cheminots, CGT).

[85] 'Cheminots Champenois …'.

underground press, but this specific reference to SNCF management less so. And it is in fact hugely revealing. Many criticisms were laid at the feet of their Ministers: 'If *Monsieur* the Minister of Transports believes that a 1310Fr supplement is necessary to help the grade 10 agent compensate inflation, then in our eyes, the same increase is even more necessary for the agent at Grade 1'.[86] And scathing remarks about the SNCF were not far behind : 'Whilst the SNCF sacrifices our health and even our lives to save a few tons of coal, the *boches* fuel up and daily trains [of coal] head out to fascist Italy', wrote the *Tribune des Cheminots* in November 1942.[87] Later that year, the *Syndiqués du Dépôt de La Chapelle* criticised the SNCF management for wanting to 'raise productivity whilst [its cheminots] were suffering more and more from restrictions'.[88] The SNCF managers were blamed for low salaries, growing hardships and decreasing buying power.[89] Their meagre attempts to distribute supplemental wages were considered laughable: 'the SNCF and Vichy is mocking the cheminots', they wrote.[90] In Grenoble, a harrowing caricature of an 'anonymous' middle-manager was circulated: 'he is small, greyish, and wears gold trousers. Few brains, just enough to understand that he must obey the orders of the Depot Chief (. . .) He admires the Belins, the Liauds and other hitlerian agents like them, gets his mandate not from the workers but from their enemies, Bosses, Vichy and Co'.[91]

Repeated calls for unionisation in cheminot tracts further underline the socio-professional nature of strikes and organised protest. Few liked the *Charte du Travail*, dubbed the '*Charte* of Enslavement'[92], and preferred joining the clandestine unions sprouting all across the nation. Those cheminots involved in the *Charte* themselves – Liaud, Pasquier, and others – were described as 'a bunch of renegades [who] have common cause with Pétain, Laval, Hitler and Mussolini'.[93] They were described as 'fascists', 'collaborators', 'valets of hitlerism' and

[86] *Le Travailleur du Rail* (Sept. 1942).
[87] *La Tribune des cheminots*, Organde des Comités Populaires de défense des Cheminots du Nord (Nov. 1942).
[88] 'Camarades', Syndiqués du Dépôt de La Chapelle.
[89] 'Camarades, le bureau illégal de l'union nord vous parle', Union des Syndicats de la région parisienne (Fédération des cheminots, CGT).
[90] *La Tribune des cheminots*, Organe illégale de la Fédération des Travailleurs du Chemin de Fer, CGT (Oct. 1943).
[91] 'Cheminots, pour vos revendications faites grève et manifestez la 11 novembre'.
[92] 'Cheminots de Perrigny'.
[93] *La Tribune des cheminots*, Organde des Comités Populaires de défense des Cheminots du Nord, dated Nov. 1942.

'anti-French'.[94] And so the underground press was rife with calls to create local trade unions, and to join the old national trade unions which was regrouping underground. Initially there were different regional *Comités Populaires des Cheminots* (Havre, Seine-Inférieure, Picarde, Région Parisienne).[95] 'Unionise en masse', wrote *Le Travailleur du Rail* in September 1942, urging them to create grass-roots groups and present their collective grievances to their Department Heads.[96] 'Lets all unify', wrote *La Tribune des Cheminots*, encouraging cheminots to join local (illegal) trade unions.[97] 'Cheminots', the PCF cried, 'Unify in your large *Comités Populaires*, form your *Comités d'Unités'.*[98] No one was to be excluded from these committees: 'Socialists, communists or Christians, Unify (...) Establish your list of demands and have your elected representatives present it to your Department Head'.[99] 'Do you think you can improve your living conditions by yourself? Do you think you can resist the slave traders Laval and Pétain alone?' asked the *Comité Populaire des Cheminots*. 'Our unions and our action can change your living conditions', they promised.[100] It was like the spirit of the Popular Front was there again – except this time, the cheminots would take part in this national unifying moment.

What really started the mass unionisation was when the *Fédération des Cheminots*, a branch of the CGT, re-surfaced in 1943. From then on, there was a real effort to get more cheminots to join the unions. 'French Cheminots!', they cried, 'You hold an honourable post, be on the edge of the fight, unify in your unions, your technical sections, your *Comités d'Unités*. (...) 'Onwards, for your grievances! Onwards, to chase out the invader and punish the traitors! Long live the *Fédération Nationale des Cheminots!* LONG LIVE FRANCE!'[101]

The *Fédération* was led by communist militants who had been key characters in cheminot trade unions before the war.[102] First, there was

[94] 'Camarades Cheminots', Région Sud du PCF; 'Cheminots Français', from the Fédération Nationale des Cheminots, signed Crapier and Dupuy; *Syndiqués, anciens syndiqués, écoutez la voix de votre fédération*, by the Fédération Nationale des Travailleurs des Chemins de Fer.
[95] 'Appel aux cheminots havrais', *Comité Populaire des Cheminots du Havre*.
[96] *Le Travailleur du Rail* (Sept. 1942).
[97] *La Tribune des Cheminots*, Seine-Inférieure (Oct. 1942).
[98] 'Cheminots', Région Sud du PCF.
[99] *La Tribune des cheminots*, Organde des Comités Populaires de défense des Cheminots du Nord (Nov. 1942).
[100] 'Unissons-nous dans le syndicat!', Comité Populaire des Cheminots.
[101] 'Cheminots Français', from the Fédération Nationale des Cheminots, signed Crapier and Dupuy.
[102] 'Ecoutez la voix de votre Fédération!', from the Fédération Nationale des Cheminots, signed Crapier and Dupuy.

Lucien Midol and Jules Crapier. Midol had been imprisoned since the start of the war since he did not reject the Nazi-Soviet pact, and after being transferred to a prison in Algeria was freed in February 1943 by the Allies. This is when he began to get involved in the rebirth of the trade unions. Crapier, however, stayed in France. After the defeat he was arrested for trying to organise local trade union committees, and was transferred from prison to prison for years. In June 1942 he escaped and picked up his activities where he left them off. In July 1943, he was named as the head of the national direction of *Comités Populaires Cheminots* and later was put in charge of trans-regional connections within the PCF. Raymond Tournemaine (North) and Georges Wodli (Alsace-Lorraine) were also involved, as was Marc Dupuy (South-West). Together with Wodli, Dupuy was responsible for launching the *Tribune des cheminots* in December 1940, and was later given major responsibilities in reforming the trade unions in the Free Zone.[103]

There is no doubt that the Occupation unified workers, not least the cheminots, around a common anti-German battle cry. But unions also spoke to the very specific, material concerns of ordinary workers. The main concern was salary. Indeed, cheminots' salaries were capped due to shortages and wartime conditions, meaning that they could not adapt to inflation, and more importantly could not buy goods on the black market to supplement daily needs. Cheminots demanded a fixed rate per hour – 'lets demand a 5fr increase per hour'[104] – but also more substantial sums – 50% increase of salary.[105] Employers were not oblivious to this, but the small increases they allowed were ridiculed. In *La Vie Ouvrière* in 1942, they described the 13–15% as 'an embarrassment, a provocation'.[106] In October 1943, the *Tribune des Cheminots* mocked the 'laughable increase applied to the cheminots'.[107] But there were other issues besides salaries: cheminots were tired of having no new clothes, no soap. 'During 60 hours of the week we are forced to work in oil, dust (...) we've had enough of having an empty stomach and being covered in rags'.[108] The cheminots in the Perrigny depot make a very specific list to meet their needs, demanding extra clothes, new shoes, soap, thread, cotton, tobacco, pasta, fat, meat and potatoes, '500 grams of bread per

[103] See Midol, Crapier and Dupuy in Goergen, *Cheminots et Militants* (2003).
[104] Series of small, square-shaped tracts.
[105] *La Vie Ouvrière*, n°88 (May 1942); *Le Travailleur du Rail*, Organe de Défense des Cheminots Lyonnais.
[106] *La Vie Ouvrière*, n°88 (May 1942).
[107] *La Tribune des cheminots*, Organe illégale de la Fédération des Travailleurs du Chemin de Fer, CGT, (Oct. 1943).
[108] 'Cheminots du dépôt de Perrigny'.

day as well as one litre of wine'. They wanted to live off the produce of their own country, and not to be 'at the mercy of accidents and illnesses brought on by weakness' and fatigue.[109] Aside from bread, wine was a central issue, not just for cheminots, but for all workers: 'What worker can buy 1 litre of Wine *appellation contrôlée* at 32 francs ? In France, 1st producing nation, the *boches* steal 13 million hectolitres'. Workers were re-appropriating not only a produce of leisure and pleasure, but also one which embodied national identity: '1 litre per day for workers. 8 litres per month for the entire population. Prepare 1 May, Day of struggle and Action. Lets get the invader who steals our wine !'[110]

It is fascinating to see how the three major trade union papers – the *Cheminot Syndicaliste, Le Travailleur du Rail* and *Le Tribune des Cheminots* – combined these professional concerns and demands with an overarching patriotic discourse, so dominant in the *culture de l'occupé*, the culture of the occupier. The *Cheminot Syndicaliste* simultaneously denounced the sixty-hour week and the forced labour service : 'Down with the 60h and the Deportations'.[111] Alongside denunciation of deportations and killings, there were complaints about 'extra working hours' and requests for '500 grams of daily bread'.[112] The third publication of the *Cheminot Syndicale* tied the ideas of syndicalism and liberation together : 'Long live the union, long live the liberating struggle for the independence of France'.[113] In February 1943, *La Voix du peuple* described the cheminot struggle as both 'for their demands and 'for the liberation of France'.[114]

So although there is no doubt that ideas of patriotism, liberation and politics were important in the active protest of the cheminots, their professional demands played an equally central role. They were always present within the background of the cry for protest and revolt, for violent action and for strike. After all, the cry to constitute the cheminots' *Comités d'Unités* – which served as underground local trade unions – was embedded in this cry for demands: 'The *Comité du Syndicalisme Indépendant* is being constituted. A manifest of the working class will soon be published. We must join the unions en masse. We must draw up our demands. We must engage in the struggle to see them met'.[115]

It is finally key to point out how cheminot trade unions mobilised the memory of communist martyrs to ignite adherence to and involvement in

---

[109] *Ibid.*   [110] 'Nous voulons du vin', small tract by Comité Patriotique.

[111] *Le Cheminot Syndicaliste,* Comité Populaire des Cheminots du Sud-Est (Jun. 1943).

[112] *La Tribune des cheminots,* Organe du Comité Populaire Central des Cheminots (Oct. 1942).

[113] *Le Cheminot Syndicale,* n°3 (Feb. 1943).

[114] *La Voix du Peuple,* Organe des Comités Populaires de la Région Parisienne.

[115] *Le Cheminot Syndicale,* n°3 (Feb. 1943).

resistance, not least Pierre Semard. The death of the ex-cheminot and communist leader, Pierre Semard, in March 1942, caused uproar throughout the entire railway community.[116] Pierre Semard had been excluded from the *Fédération* in September 1939 because of his anti-war sentiments.[117] The following month, he was accused of embezzling the trade union's funds by a fellow cheminot, Jarrigion. Although evidence against him was weak, Semard was found guilty and was sentenced to three years in prison. However, instead of releasing him once he had finished his sentence, the Germans transferred Semard to an internment camp in Gaillon. Soon after, he was taken as a hostage, and shot by the Germans on 7 March 1942. Before his execution, Semard wrote a letter to all communists, and his fellow cheminots.[118]

Dear Friends,
    I have the opportunity to tell you my last words, since in a few moments I will be shot. I await death calmly. I will show my executioners that communists die as patriots and revolutionaries. My last thoughts go with you, comrades in the struggle, with all the members of our Great Nation, with all French patriots, with the heroic fighters of the Red Army and their chief, the great Stalin. I die with the certitude that France will be liberated. Tell my friends, the cheminots, that they should do nothing to help the Nazis [and their allies]. The cheminots will understand me; they will hear me; they will act; I am certain of this. Farewell dear friends, the time has come to die. But I know that the Nazis [and their allies], who will shoot me, are already defeated, and that France will continue its great battle. *Long live the Soviet Union! Long Live France!* Pierre Semard.

Although the letter did not encourage active resistance, it did tell the cheminots to refrain from assisting the Nazis. Also, it assured readers the France would be liberated, and Nazis defeated.

Despite Semard's complicated history with the railway trade union, news of this poignant letter soon spread, as did news of his death. He became the greatest cheminot martyr. As has been mentioned, numerous tracts used his name as a rallying cry for protest and resistance. Suddenly, it did not matter that Semard had been shunned by the railway union before the war. He now incarnated all those who had been sentenced to death, as well as future innocent victims.

But Semard was not alone: 'sabotage machines, switches, cut the transmission cables. Remember Pierre Semard and Jean Catelas'.[119]

---

[116] Xavier Vigna, 'La mémoire de Pierre Semard chez les cheminots CGT' in Wolikow, *Pierre Semard* (2007) 261–84.
[117] Wolikow, *Pierre Semard* (2007) 37–8.
[118] Letter translated from website, http://lacausedupeuple.chez-alice.fr/pcf/pcf1.html, retrieved on 20 Sep. 2010.
[119] 'Camarades Cheminots ...', PCF Région Ouest.

'On this day [20 Sept. 1942]', wrote the *Travailleur du Rail*, 'cheminots must show themselves to be at the forefront of the liberation battle. They will avenge Pierre Semard and Jean Catelas and other patriots who have fallen under the *boche* fire or under the blade of the Guillotine'.[120] Jean Catelas, Raymond Tournemaine and Georges Wodli would also be mobilised to ignite passions. Tournemaine's trajectory within the resistance was not obvious, much like Semard. A communist militant who did not refuse to acknowledge the Nazi-Soviet Pact, he was imprisoned in April 1940 and transferred to various camps and prisons throughout the Occupation. He finally escaped in May 1944, and was immediately reinserted at the head of the *Fédération*. But Catelas and Wodli were seen not only as communist martyrs but also as heroic resisters. Catelas, a militant communist and active syndicalist, was involved in the first flurries of resistance activities after the defeat. He was involved in the clandestine publication of *L'Humanité*, and wrote an open letter to the cheminots in Amiens in 1940 asking them to continue the struggle amidst clandestine trade union groups. Arrested in May 1941, he was guillotined on 24 September of that year. Wodli was an active member of the PCF and in 1941 became involved in reconstituting the underground party. He led the Mario group in Eastern France where he organised railway sabotages, clandestine passages and other activities. After escaping arrest a first time, he was arrested by the Gestapo in October 1942 and later transferred to the Schirmeck camp in Alsace. He died at the hands of the Gestapo in Strasbourg.[121]

It is important to outline the lives of these men whose ties with the communist party and railway trade unions are sometimes stronger than with those of the resistance – nonetheless, their story was deeply entwined with the fight against Nazism and the Occupation. In their tract of July 1943, the *Comité Populaire des Cheminots de la Côte d'Or* honoured the memory of Pierre Semard, Jean Catelas and Tournemaine before crying out 'Death to the fascist bandits ! Long live France!'[122] *La Vie Ouvrière* listed the names of Semard, Catelas and Timbaud to project their call for violence: 'honouring these heroes is good ; avenging them is better'.[123] Local heroes were also added to the lists of martyrs regularly drawn up in the press, and their names were also rallying cries for active protest such as strikes. To stir the cheminots they described specific attacks, such as the death of a cheminot death in Besançon who was shot

[120] *Le Travailleur du Rail* (Sept. 1942).
[121] See Tournemaine, Cateslas and Wodli in Goergen, *Cheminots et Militants* (2003).
[122] 'Cheminots Dijonnais', Comité Populaires des Cheminots de la Côte d'Or.
[123] *La Vie Ouvrière*, n°88 (May 1942).

by Nazis on 15–16 September 1943: 'the cheminots from Besançon were shocked by this new Nazi crime, and they reacted vigorously, stopping work for twenty minutes to attend his funeral as a sign of protest'.[124]

Conclusion

A study of the archives confirms the significance of cheminots' everyday resistance to the Occupier. It was not only an individual, passive resistance: many cheminots were tied to existing resistance networks beyond the SNCF, such as *Combat* or *Ceux de la Libération*. Not only that, but the rise of trade unions allowed for organised pockets of resistance to spread throughout the railways. Indeed, the re-emergence of trade unions gave cheminots an underground structure through which they could voice their patriotic, political and professional outrage.

So even if the network *Résistance-Fer* never fully materialised during the occupation itself, this does not mean that cheminot resistance activities lacked structure. Indeed, the absence of a single coherent cheminot resistance organisation does not mean that all cheminot activities can be reduced to spontaneous, individual acts. The problem with an over-reliance on the individualistic nature of cheminot resistance is that it embraces the impact of individual agency but overlooks the broader connections with ideology, politics and actual resistance networks. Understanding cheminot resistance is thus about navigating between these two tensions – agency and structure, the individual and the collective – and understanding how they interacted continuously throughout the occupation. More than anything else, a certain coherence can be detected in the motivations for the emergence of organised cheminot networks of resistance – whether they were individual, collective or tied to bigger resistance movement – especially after 1943, following the re-emergence of trade unions. And here again, we can detect the importance of anti-work, anti-employer attitudes amongst the cheminots.

More interestingly, the step into active resistance – and especially strikes and professional grievances – shows that, after several decades of absence from the scene of active working-class protest, the 1943–44 period was a moment of renewal for the cheminot community. They cried out in opposition to Vichy's labour service, to the Nazis' crimes against the French population, but also to the SNCF's mismanagement of resources. Indeed, professional interests were at the core of protest methods and motivations, and they helped to cement the patriotic and

[124] *La Tribune des cheminots* (Oct. 1943).

political enthusiasm which brought people together against a common
enemy: the German invader, the men in Vichy, and the 'unpatriotic',
'treacherous' management/trade union leaders, who for decades had
oppressed the workers, and who now appeared to enable the pillaging
of France.

Of course, if these archives tell us about the enthusiasm of some
cheminots for active protest and strikes, they do not tell us about actual
cheminot involvement. And involvement, in fact, was far from straightforward. Chevandier wrote that in October 1942, when the first traceable
strike broke out in Oullins, there was in fact a lot of division over whether
or not they should go on strike. Indeed, Oullins housed a wide range of
cheminots who wanted to go on strike – communists, Christians, socialists – but others were more cautious. Such divisions had always been
visible in the 1910 and 1920 strikes, and they would continue to be there
in 1947. This is of course a phenomenon which reaches far beyond the
cheminots: Hobsbawm commented on this division between strikers and
'blackleggers' (those who refused to strike) amongst the nineteenth-
century working classes: even where 'the habit of solidarity, which is
the foundation of effective trade unionism', was strong, like in the coal
mines, 'the danger of blacklegging is always acute' amongst men and
women who could not do without their salary, and thereby refused to
strike.[125] In Vichy France, the dangers involved in strikes were very much
present. That being said, the Occupation managed to change fears, to
shift the moral dilemmas around active and violent protest was especially
true in regards to active resistance methods such as industrial sabotage.

[125] Hobsbawm, *Labouring Men* (1986) 9.

6   Sabotage

If the cheminots were involved in passive and active protest, in individual and collective resistance, to what extent did they take part in railway sabotage? As discussed in the first chapter, cheminots were uncomfortable with violent resistance and industrial sabotage since the late-nineteenth century. Instinctively, a cheminot was reluctant to destroy his professional tool – when Robert Lebrun chuckled in his interview and declared that 'the guys who drove the steam locomotives loved their machines even more than their wives!' he was only half joking.[1] And yet, towards the end of the Occupation, the railway system became crippled by explosions, derailments and bombings. Sabotage – the industrial, violent, machine-breaking kind – was threatening not only to hinder the German military effort – which was the desired effect – but was also making it more and more difficult for the French economy and society to survive.

The myth of *Résistance-Fer* and the film *La Bataille du Rail* may aggrandize and heroise cheminot resistance, and the traditions of the nineteenth century may have been deeply engrained within the mindset of this professional corps, but this does not mean that cheminots did not get involved in active and even violent resistance. Indeed, the increasingly difficult conditions of the occupation put the railways and its workers under considerable strain. As frustrations were mounting, so too were networks of resistance and information services. The cheminots became involved in a variety of different networks which all participated in the gradual paralysation of the railways, not least in 1943–44. At other times, they took matters into their own hands and sabotaged tracks and materials. Their resistance may not have been uniform, but it was often embedded in a variety of local, professional, political and patriotic structures all across France.

In order to understand cheminot sabotage in Vichy France, it is not enough to look at the enumeration of sabotages across the territory, or to examine the different operations organised by the Allies of the French

---

[1] Interview Lebrun.

143

Resistance in the run up to the D-Day landings. One must also understand the contexts of the time which allowed for a change in mentality amongst the railway milieu. Indeed, the shift from an aversion to industrial sabotage to a participation – at all levels – in sabotage operations reveals the changing moral codes of the time. As such, railway sabotage was deeply linked to questions of morality, professionalism and protectionism – not only in the lower echelons of the SNCF, but also at the top ranks.

1   The Deterioration of the railways

When thinking about the rising number of cheminot saboteurs towards the end of the Occupation, the first thing to consider is the deterioration of living conditions in general. After 1942, the political and economic circumstances of the Occupation became far more strained. The *Relève*, the round-ups of Jews, the intensification of the communist witch-hunt, the increasing number of arrests and deportations, the food shortages and the entrance of German troops into the Free Zone in November 1942 made people question whether or not Vichy had their best interests at heart. Moreover, cheminots faced a number of professional drawbacks after 1942, with a growing crisis in railway material and personnel. This deterioration of living standards revealed the realities and limitations of Franco-German collaboration: as the frustration of the French mounted, and as resistance networks became more organised, widespread and inter-connected, the urge to combat the conditions of the Occupation grew throughout French society.

Aside from these general conditions, the deterioration of the railways in particular goes a long way in explaining the escalation of violence within cheminot resistance. By 1942, important changes had occurred within the SNCF, reminding the cheminots of the restrictions of occupation. In June 1942, the *Wehrmacht Verkehrsdirektion* (WVD) – which had supervised the railways until that point – was replaced by the *Haupt Verkehrsdirektion* (HVD). The main difference was that the railways were no longer under the command of the military, but of the *Reichs Verkehrsministers* (RVM), the Reich's Ministry of Transport.[2] This had been a largely logistical decision in order to maximise efficiency across the Eastern and Western territories, and reflected the growing importance of the Third Reich ministries in running the occupied territory. Despite this change in name, the structure remained intact. Still, the SNCF felt threatened that the Reichsbahn might further infiltrate the French railways. This breached the terms reached by the Armistice commission in

---

[2] Bachelier Report, 4.1.4. Haupt Verkhersdirektion, Paris.

Wiesbaden, yet there was no coordinated effort to protest against it. Secondly, on 11 November 1942, immediately following the Allied invasion of North Africa, German officers crossed the demarcation line in an armoured train. They were initially stopped by the French authorities, but eventually Vichy agreed to let the Germans cross the line. In order to protect the SNCF's sovereignty, French cheminots took over all German transports in the Free Zone.

By late 1943, the SNCF faced innumerable problems. In a speech given in October, the general manager Robert Le Besnerais painted a dark picture of the current state of French railways:

In the Department of Material [and Traction], everyone made gargantuan efforts to keep up with the repairs. Until the end of 1942, it just about handled the situation. However, in the past few months, the situation has become critical. The war is causing more and more destruction, buildings are being destroyed, there is less personnel because workers are being sent to Germany, and there are not enough supplies.[3]

The increase in German seizures meant that, by 1944, almost half of the SNCF's material was in German hands,[4] and 40% of rail traffic in France was destined for German goods.[5] In addition, workshops announced that the repairs on locomotives and freight cars would be delayed by a year. A mountain of repair work had piled up after Albert Speer had insisted that the railway material returned to the SNCF (often in a terrible state) must be repaired in France.[6] Furthermore, bombings and sabotages caused immense destruction, such that repair shops were submerged with work.[7] Even by working round the clock, French cheminots were unable to keep up with the rate of repairs.

The acute shortage of material meant that the SNCF was unable to sustain national transports. During the autumn and winter of 1943, there were not enough locomotives and freight cars to collect and distribute coal. Supplies became dangerously low, and workers worked bank holidays to prevent a national catastrophe.[8] There was such a great need for the transportation of goods and supplies that the SNCF reduced the number of passenger trains around the Christmas holidays.[9]

---

[3] AN/72/AJ/415: Procès verbal de la séance du 7 Oct. 1943, 11.
[4] Lartilleux, *Le Réseau National* (1948) 23.
[5] Cited in Ribeill, 'Trafic sous contraintes' (2007).
[6] AN/72/AJ/1927: Minutes of Ministerial meeting (20 Dec. 1943) 4. In this chapter, all subsequent references to the Minutes of Ministerial meetings will be referred to as 'Minutes'.
[7] *Ibid.*, (6 Mar. 1944).
[8] *Ibid.*, (20 Dec. 1943, 4. See also 6 Sep. 1943; 13 Oct. 1943; 2 Nov. 1943).
[9] AN/72/AJ/415: Procès verbal (7 Oct. 1943).

At the same time, the SNCF was facing a grave financial crisis. The Germans' massive material demands caused the most serious financial problems, a situation exacerbated by the 2,500 million francs they still owed the SNCF in 1943.[10] By the summer of 1944, the railway had a deficit of six billion francs. The problem was twofold: first, German payments were always late, and they often did not cover the entire bill. Second, the German transport rates in the Northern zone were considerably lower than in the Free Zone. When prices had been negotiated in 1940, they had been downsized in the name of collaboration. But a few years later, the so-called collaboration had turned into exploitation. Moreover, with inflation and the deterioration of the railway system, the company raised prices for the German seizures of material, a strategy that made no difference, since payments were constantly pushed back.[11]

The situation was made even more difficult because of cheminots' low morale as a result of the forced labour service. While a number of irreplaceable workers were exempt from it, basic employees still followed an intense training period for several months, and were then shipped off to work for the RB in Germany. The SNCF even hired new workers in order to train them to work in Germany. The SNCF management described the prescription of its labour force as a 'bloodletting', whereby the Germans were slowly draining the life out of the French railway.[12]

One cannot underestimate the effect of the pillaging of the French railways. In fact, the German seizure of men and material from within the SNCF reflects the centrality of France within the Nazis' New European Order. The reliance of French manpower to support the German economy was already discussed in Chapter 3, and here again we can see how French goods were necessary not only for the German economy but also for the German military. As Mazower has explained, Hitler's imperial vision did not overlook France. Whilst entire populations were destroyed in Eastern Europe, in the West the brutality of the occupation took on a more economic, rather than human, form.[13]

Finally, the increasing number of arrests and killings also put added pressure on the community. Indeed, the persecution of cheminots – whether they were deported, shot, killed in bombings, imprisoned, held

[10] AN/72/AJ/1927: Minutes (23 Mar. 1943).
[11] SNCF/505/LM/257: Letter (28 Apr. 1944) from Fournier to Bichelonne, 3.
[12] AN/72/AJ/1927: Minutes (31 Mar. 1943). See AN/72/AJ/1927 and 1929 for more information.
[13] See chapter 9 in Mazower, *Hitler's Empire* (2008).

hostage or injured during the war – materialises in the archives. In regards to numbers, Thomas Fontaine is currently working with the SNCF and the AHICF to trace all deported cheminots between 1940 and 1944.[14] In terms of cheminots who were persecuted and died under the Occupation, there is already a thick file in the SNCF archives. Six nominative lists indicate that 1636 cheminots were killed as a result of German persecution.[15] Of these, 743 agents were arrested by Germans and died in deportation; 489 agents were arrested and shot by Germans; 326 agents were arrested by Germans and were still missing; 39 agents were arrested by Germans and were presumed to have died in deportation; 34 agents were arrested by Germans and died in France ; 5 agents were arrested and killed in bombings. These nominative lists included names of the individual cheminots, the towns where they worked, which region they were affiliated to, what position they held within the SNCF, their date of arrest, their date of death and sometimes the reason for their arrest.

Examining these lists more closely shows the intensification of cheminot arrest, shootings and deportation over time. Of the 489 railway workers shot during the Occupation, there were only 12 victims in 1941 compared to 77 in 1942. The method of shootings also changed by 1942, and collective violence became much more frequent: 5 cheminots were shot on 1 October; 3 on 28 October; 5 on 21 November; 9 on 30 December. Moreover, if cheminots were mostly targeted for communist/political activities in 1941 and 1942, by 1944 mass arrests and deportations were becoming more and more widespread. Entire towns were besieged in 1944, such as Maillé (Indre-et-Loire), Ascq (Nord), Tulle (Corrèze) or Robert-Espagne (Meuse), and cheminots were frequently amongst the victims of these massacres. Hostages were also taken after sabotage or resistance activities. On 14 July 1944, when the railway workers rallied in Vitry, a Parisian suburb, to celebrate Bastille day, French and German police forces swooped into the town, rounded up nine workers and deported them East. Three of these were cheminots, and they died in deportation. If these collective reprisals spread fear and panic across the cheminot community, they also spread anger.

---

[14] Thomas Fontaine's previous work on the deportations is highly recommended to understand the politics of deportations: Thomas Fontaine, 'Déporter. Politiques de déportation et répression en France occupée, 1940–1944', doctoral thesis at Paris 1 (Paris 1, 2013).

[15] These statistics were established from a file in the SNCF. SNCF/25/LM/1940: Nominative list of agents who died (or no news) under the Occupation. This table only reflects certain reasons in order to show the evolution of political arrests and then arrests as part of reprisals on the population. All data analysed by author.

Table 6.1 *Total of cheminots arrested/died by year.*[16]

Year of arrest	Number of arrests	Number of deaths/no return
1939	1	
1940	31	0
1941	159	12
1942	219	118
1943	353	96
1944	755	593
1945	5	434
Unknown	113	384

2   Recruiting cheminots for sabotage

As the war wore on, the pretence of a so-called collaboration was no longer working: the French were truly living under an enemy occupation who did not have their best interests at heart. But it would take more than pure frustration to turn cheminots into industrial saboteurs. First, cheminots were recruited by networks of resistance which generally originated from outside of the SNCF. From the beginning of the Occupation, they were targeted by the military intelligence services in London who considered them as key informants. Indeed, obtaining information on the railway networks was always a priority because, as Mierzejewski wrote, 'the German economy simply could not function without extensive and efficient rail transportation'.[17] The Allies were thus fully aware that if they managed to knock down this major pillar, the Third Reich would collapse. The *Bureau Central de Renseignements Alliés* (BCRA), or Central Bureau of Intelligence and Operations, was established within De Gaulle's Headquarters on 1 July 1940, and it liaised with the Intelligence Services (linked to the Foreign Office) and the Special Operations Executive (SOE, linked to the War Office).[18]

Cheminots could easily gather the necessary military information from their work posts. Whether it was a station or a triage centre, they wrote down their observations on all transport-related issues. They indicated

---

[16] It is important to underline that the arrest of one cheminot in October 1939 in Loches could not have been carried out by the Germans. As such, the claim that these statistics are based on arrests by *Germans* should be considered with caution.

[17] Mierzejewski, *The Most Valuable Asset* (2000) 163.

[18] Sébastien Albertelli and Guillaume Piketty, 'Bureau central des renseignements et d'action' in Marcot et al., eds., *Dictionnaire* (2006) 94–6. The Special Operations Executive organised popular uprisings and sabotages throughout Reich territory. See also Michael R. D. Foot, 'Special Operations Executive' in Marcot et al., eds., *Dictionnaire* (2006) 111–3; Foot, *SOE in France* (2004).

German military movement by writing down the schedules of German current transport flow, *Transports en cours d'opérations*,[19] or gave updates on the construction of temporary railway lines in northern France which were being built between 1943 and 1944 for German use.[20] Many entries offered basic descriptive information about warehouses and machinery, information with which the Intelligence Services could draw up large regional and national maps and familiarise themselves with the territory. Information gathered by cheminots was passed on through a chain of resisters until it finally reached the BCRA offices. The delivery process could take up to several months, but a continuous relay of information formed an impressive amount of data which was then analysed by military strategists looking to drop bombs on railway infrastructure.

When specific plans to destroy the transportation and electrical facilities in France were drawn up by BCRA in March 1942, the Allies needed cheminot informants more than ever. Cheminots were generally recruited through personal networks both within and outside the SNCF. The cheminot Meuniez, for example, would have had strong suspicions that his friend and colleague Lucien Barbier was engaging in civilian resistance. After a meeting of SNCF regional inspectors which they both attended in August 1942, he approached Barbier and some others, telling them he needed trustworthy people to pass information to the Allies, and Barbier readily accepted.[21] French resistance networks also wanted to create ties with the cheminots, and Kleiber Deleghier was approached by a member of the resistance group *Organisation Civile et Militaire* (OCM).[22] Others integrated resistance networks through more spontaneous and personal channels. Bachelier listed a few of the cheminots identified by Paul Durand – Mourgue was in Vény, Monnier and Hemes were in Vengeance, Casez was in the MUR, *Voix du Nord* and OCM, and Chaudot and Guyader were in the *Francs-tireurs Partisans* (FTP)[23] – and shows the importance of these networks within the overarching history of railway sabotage in this period.

Cheminots had many different roles within sabotage operations, all of which were tied to their functions. Some sent in sketches and drawings of specific parts of the railway lines which should be targeted, such as tight bends and wooded areas. Since it was more difficult for breakdown cranes to gain access to these spots, damages would inevitably take longer to repair. Others explained how to best sabotage a train. On 1 June 1943, René Hardy from the MUR wrote a memo on railway sabotage.

---

[19] AN/72/AJ/2297: Report on Railway Resistance, (Jun. 1940–1944).
[20] AN/3/AG/2/236: Results of bombings (Mar.–Jun. 1944).
[21] AN/72/AJ/495: Lucien Barbier.   [22] *Ibid.*, Deleghier.
[23] See Bachelier Report, 6.1.6. La Résistance Organisée.

'Sabotages must only be carried out with extreme caution so as to not endanger the lives of our cheminot comrades, but also cause maximum destruction'. Hardy's tone was very directive, and there was no room for spontaneity. Indeed, the plans to sabotage the railways were, within the networks, of military precision. They had to be conducted in 'perfect order' according to a specific plan whereby 'A team of *Groupes-Francs* liaised directly and at all times with the SNCF employee who could supply information about timings' and other technicalities. Above all, these sabotage – and those involved – were not to be confused with the efforts being made towards D-Day.[24]

The plans to sabotage the railways en masse were already being openly discussed within the ranks of *Combat* in late 1942.[25] René Hardy, René Lacombe and Henri Garnier Ledoux were in charge of forming sabotage teams, not least through the NAP. After Hardy's suspected involvement in Jean Moulin's arrest, however, he was replaced by a leading member of *Combat*, Jean-Guy Bernard. Bernard and Louis Armand liaised together to create special information networks all across France. As previously mentioned, this was part of an attempt to unite all the cheminots into one separate 'Rail' network which was considered fundamental for the development of massive sabotage plans on the eve of the Allied landings: the *Plan Vert*, or Green Plan.

If the Allied and Resistance networks needed the cheminots for their sabotage plans, the cheminots also began to realise for themselves that sabotage may be the best strategy not only to save the war, but also to protect the railways. To fully understand this phenomenon, however, it is necessary to go back and briefly consider the threat of bombs in this period. France was bombed throughout the war, but bombing intensified more seriously in 1942, when the Allies began to bomb industries which were benefitting the Third Reich. So although aerial bombings were initially well-received – French people understood that the Allied victory was in their interest – things deteriorated over time. As Simon Kitson pointed out, by the summer of 1943 'a greater hostility towards air attacks was evident'.[26]

Workers were particularly vulnerable to aerial bombing, and certain professions were more exposed than others: factory workers, miners and cheminots. According to Vigna, the effect of these bombings was often that the bonds between workers and their companies were reinforced, a

---

[24] *Ibid.*   [25] *Ibid.*

[26] Simon Kitson, 'Criminals or Liberators? French Public Opinion and the Allied Bombing of France, 1940–1945' in Claudia Baldoli, Andrew Knapp and Richard Overy, eds., *Bombing, States and Peoples in Western Europe 1940–1945* (London: Continuum, 2011) 285; See also Lindsey Dodd's chapter in the same book, '"Relieving Sorrow and Misfortune"? State Charity, Ideology and Aid in Bombed-out France, 1940–1944', 75–97.

bond which was encouraged by the *Charte du Travail*.[27] One incident in Marseille showed how the fear of bombings even managed to suppress local workers' protest. According to the Prefect of the Bouches-du-Rhône, the Marseille bombing in late May 1944 had interrupted the on-going local strikes and scared the workers back to work. In a letter to Laval, he wrote that 'the psychological shock of the bombing on the Marseille area did – it must be said – play a part in the complete return to work'.[28]

According to Richard Overy, even bomb commanders were uneasy with the devastation they were causing.[29] Indeed, by 1943 the Allies were deeply concerned by the limited success of their aerial attacks which often missed the railway infrastructure they were targeting and would destroy nearby civilian infrastructure.[30] On Sunday 18 December 1942, a bomb on St Quentin's railway station caused nine deaths, five of which were cheminots, yet the SNCF buildings were almost intact.[31] On 8 March 1943, 10% of the actual railway target was hit in Rennes, while 300 civilians and cheminots were killed.[32] On 15 March 1944, the bombing of the Laon-Soissons railway line killed fifteen civilians.[33] Similar tragedies were repeated all over French territory, counting many cheminots and their families amongst the victims. A map of Tergnier would show that the cheminots' homes were always very close to the railway junctions so that, if a bomb missed its target by a few meters, they were the most likely victims. The Allied Headquarters in London wrote: 'we must try to spare the French network in itself because SNCF workers have already suffered a great deal under American bombs. Although the morale is good for the moment, it would undoubtedly fall if cheminot families keep on being affected'.[34]

Aerial bombings were not only dangerous, they were also considered ineffective. Since bombers often missed their targets, they only caused minor damages which took a few hours to repair, or at best several days. In those cases the German trains were given complete priority, while the

---

[27] See Vigna, *Histoire des ouvriers* (2012) 149–50.
[28] ADBR/76/W/218: Letter (1 Jun. 1944) from Prefect to Chef du Gouvernment, in file on various strikes in May 1944.
[29] Richard Overy, *The Bombing War: Europe, 1939–1945* (Allen Lane, 2013) 556–82, 582.
[30] Yves Machefert-Tassin, 'Le bilan des bombardements aériens des installations ferroviaires en France, leurs conséquences stratégiques et humaines: tactiques incohérentes, résultats discutables, victimes civiles exorbitantes et destructions à long terme inutiles?' in Polino, ed., *Une entreprise pendant la guerre* (2001).
[31] AN/3/AG2/236: Résultats de bombardements, Note n°5, Saint Quentin (17 Dec. 1942).
[32] Machefert-Tassin, 'Le bilan' (2000).
[33] AN/3/AG/2/236: Résultats de bombardements, Hirson Station (15 Mar. 1944).
[34] AN/3/AG/2/234: Report (6 Jun. 1943) France-Air, Objectifs pour Bombardements.

Figure 6.1 Consequences of aerial bombing on railway materials: Délivrance (near Lille) Bombing on 4 September 1943. SNCF/PNV/ 103919. SNCF – Centre National des Archives Historiques.

French transports were brought to a standstill. Armed with their professional knowledge, cheminots could indicate which tactics could result in the long-term damage necessary to hinder German transports.

3   Sabotage

In this atmosphere of fear and frustration, and with the growing plans of the Allies and the French Resistance to paralyse the railways, sabotage seemed the best way to simultaneously target the German transports and prevent pointless damage on the rail network. Indeed, the trick about sabotage was doing it responsibly: material should be damaged enough to cripple German transports, but not so much that it harmed civilians or that it completely destroyed the material which France needed to rebuild itself after the Liberation. Cheminots were equipped with the professional expertise to accomplish this. Leaflets were even drawn up to spread their techniques throughout the French population, with detailed images accompanied by simple instructions. There were a number of methods to choose from: shifting a track, blocking a switch, cutting out a section of a track by using explosives, damaging the breaks by cutting off

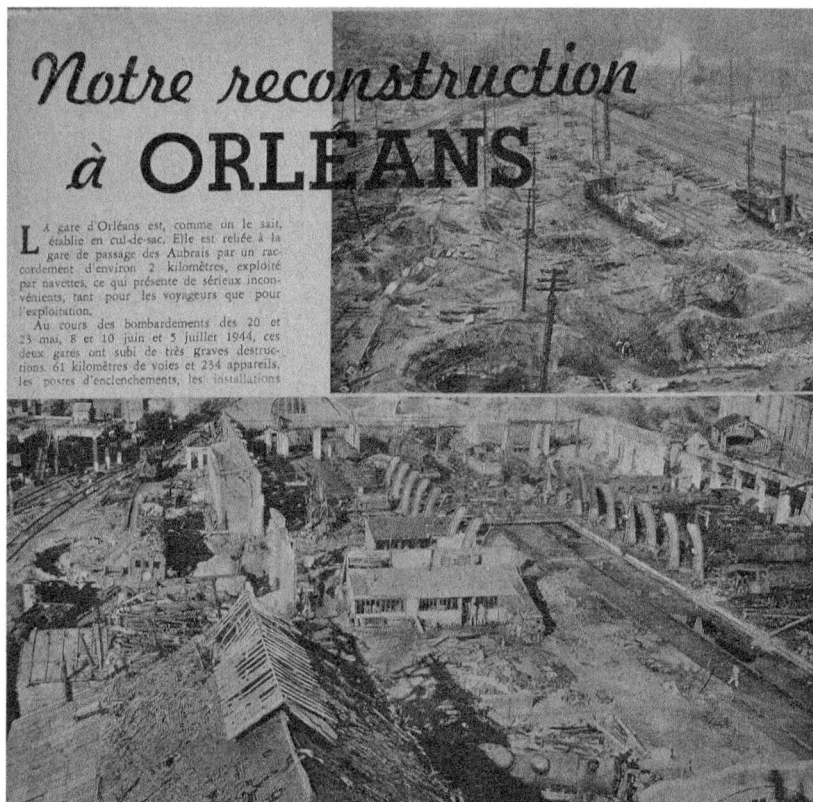

Notre reconstruction
à ORLÉANS

L A gare d'Orléans est, comme on le sait, établie en cul-de-sac. Elle est reliée à la gare de passage des Aubrais par un raccordement d'environ 2 kilomètres, exploité par navettes, ce qui présente de sérieux inconvénients, tant pour les voyageurs que pour l'exploitation.
  Au cours des bombardements des 20 et 23 mai, 8 et 10 juin et 5 juillet 1944, ces deux gares ont subi de très graves destructions. 61 kilomètres de voies et 234 appareils, les postes d'enclenchements, les installations

Figure 6.2 Consequences of aerial bombing on Orléans depot and station. *Notre Métier*, 49 (1 Mar. 1946). SNCF – Centre National des Archives Historiques.

air supplies to the pump. And tips were given on which types of sabotages gave which results: 'to cause delays, you must derail the train in a tunnel or in a long bend. To destroy a train, choose an embankment so that the machine will drag the other cars down'.[35]

Of course not all sabotages were so effective. This is especially true of the non-cheminots who planned the railway sabotages, which included resistance groups and *maquisards*.[36] A police report dated February 1943 even recorded a sabotage in the Northern town of Lievin carried

[35] AN/3/AG/2/234: Leaflet on sabotage (6 pages).
[36] Kedward, *In Search of the Maquis* (2003) 63–4.

out by children, who had 'loosened the brakes on a rake of carriages with twenty cars lined up (. . .). These cars came crashing down everywhere and have caused serious damages'.[37] The damage caused by these children was considerable, and one can doubt its usefulness for the overarching effort to fight the Germans. Even cheminot sabotages – although allegedly more carefully planned – could have terrible consequences: the railway sabotage in Ascq on 1 April 1944 had been planted by a small group of local cheminots, and it triggered a collective reprisal where over eighty men from Ascq were massacred by the SS that very night.[38]

But to what extent did cheminots overcome their initial resistance to sabotage? When a reporter remarked to Louis Armand in 1984 that 'cheminots had some big psychological barriers to overcome [because] destroying [their] professional tool must have been excruciating', Armand responded that the protection of railways from bombing was greater than anything. 'I agree [with your statement], but destroying it ourselves was better than seeing it destroyed by aerial bombings' he declared.[39] Armand downplayed cheminots' psychological barriers to sabotage, and many were still reluctant to engage. This is not least because sabotage risked the lives of colleagues and innocent civilians. Locomotive drivers were the first victims of derailments: when a train was sabotaged on the night of 5–6 October 1943, dozens of Italian prisoners of war were burnt alive in the terrible explosions and the three cheminots driving the train were crushed to death.[40] After having sabotaged a railroad track, François Depoorter realized that the train about to be derailed was driven by a friend: 'Seeing him, I regretted having decided to derail the train, because I knew full well that the train driver was the first victim of derailing. However my patriotic spirit took over, and I did not tell him anything, but shook his hand, for longer than usual, and let him go to his destiny'.[41] In the end Depoorter intervened to try and prevent the derailing, and no one was hurt. The risk of collective reprisals was also palpable. In late December 1942, ten hostages ('communists') were taken in Avion (Pas-de-Calais) following a railroad sabotage and an attack on a German soldier.[42] By 1944, the collective

---

[37] AN/F/7/14881: Police Information, February 1943 Report (Dec. 1942–1943).
[38] See Ludivine Broch, 'Martyred Towns at the Liberation: The Case of the Massacre d'Ascq' in Broch and Carrol, eds., *France in the Era Global Wars* (2014) 50–72.
[39] 'Un Entretien avec Louis Armand, Président d'Honneur de '"Résistance-Fer"', *La Vie du Rail* (1984) 7.
[40] AN/3/AG/2/235: Informations Diverses (Sabotage) 1943, 2–3; AN/72/AJ/495, Debachy.
[41] AN/72/AJ/495: François Depoorter.
[42] AN/F/7/14881: Informations de la Police Nationale (Jan. 1943).

reprisals that swept over the country counted amongst the greatest civilian tragedies of the Occupation. Railway sabotage caused the death of 86 men in Ascq on 1 April 1944, and the death or deportation of 231 civilians in Tulle on 9 June that year. Faced with such violence, many cheminots made a conscious decision not to engage in sabotage. Chanteloup, who worked near St Brieuc in the Department of Exploitation, began his resistance activities in 1941 and eventually became an informant for the Allies. However, he never engaged in sabotage activities because he knew that they were often followed by brutal reprisals against the civilian population.[43]

Still, some cheminots were determined to sabotage the railways, not least in preparation for Allied landings. In October 1943 Roger Charbonnier and two other cheminots, Robert Lebrun and Roger Chouin, decided to sabotage the rail tracks in Tergnier. Not one was over twenty years old. They gathered a large number of explosives and, one night, set them off in the park area, destroying machinery and infrastructure. The Germans were completely enraged, and the following morning summoned all of the cheminots in Tergnier. An SS Officer asked that the culprits step forward, but Charbonnier, Lebrun and Chouin remained quiet. Thirty fellow railway men were taken hostage and imprisoned for several weeks, until they were eventually released. The exploits of these three cheminots are proudly displayed in the local museum, along with a black and white photo taken fifty years later of the three of them, arm in arm (See Figure 6.3). During their interviews Charbonnier and Lebrun were questioned about how they had felt knowing that men were being held hostage for a crime they had committed – what about solidarity? Lebrun admitted that had any of the hostages been executed, he would have felt very uneasy.[44] On the other hand Charbonnier bluntly declared: 'You can't get sentimental in those situations – it's the laws of war'.[45] One cannot help but wonder: if the hostages had been deported or killed, would their responses have been different?

The dismemberment of the railway network truly began between December and February: hundreds of locomotives were sabotaged, 491 successful derailments were organised, 265 freight cars were completely destroyed, over 100 pieces of heavy equipment (such as breakdown cranes and water towers) were damaged and 11 turntables were impaired. By early 1944 military intelligence services were preparing for the Allied landings by designing different action plans which would paralyse all forms of communication and transport after the landings.

[43] AN/72/AJ/495: Chanteloup.   [44] Interview Lebrun.   [45] Interview Charbonnier.

Figure 6.3 Three ex-cheminots and saboteurs: Roger Charbonnier, Robert Lebrun and Roger Chouin, Tergnier, 1998. With special thanks to the *Musée de la Résistance et de la Déportation en Picardie*, Tergnier.

They were coded as follows: the *Plan Violet* would paralyse the telephone lines, the *Plan Bleu* the electrical system, the *Plan Tortue* (which became *Plan Bibendum*) the roads, and finally the *Plan Vert* the railway network.[46] These plans were supposed to be launched the minute Allied soldiers stepped foot on the Normandy beaches, but even before that date there was a steady increase in bombardments and sabotage to prepare the field. After having been reduced between December 1943 and February 1944, bombings picked up again in the spring of 1944 with 48,400 tons of bombs falling on France between March and July.[47] According to Yves Machefert-Tassin, only 8% of those bombs hit railway infrastructure. The intelligence services had obviously registered the cheminots' dislike of bombings: 'it is absolutely necessary to understand the scorn felt by the cheminots [with regards to disasters of aerial bombing], which, if it

---

[46] Bruno Leroux, 'Plans d'action en France (déclenchement et exécution)' in Marcot, et al., eds., *Dictionnaire* (2006) 744–6.
[47] AN/3/AG/2/236: Réclamations contre les bombardements.

develops, could cause us to lose our closest collaborators'.[48] However, they had also been impressed by the efficiency of sabotage. An official SNCF report stated that between January and August 1944, more than 3,000 machines were damaged or destroyed. In fact in the spring of 1944, sabotages became so typical after the Allied landings that minor sabotages were no longer being registered.[49]

But it was the Allied landings in June 1944 which unleashed a wave of resistance and protest activity which had been brewing for several months. On 5 June 1944, and hundreds of coded messages on the BBC sparked the start of the action plans, and notably of the *Plan Vert*. For weeks Louis Armand, Jacques Chaban-Delmas – who worked in the Ministry of Industrial Production under Bichelonne but was deeply involved in supplying information to the Free French during the Occupation[50] – and British officials had been preparing for the moment when the simultaneous destruction of the French railway would completely cripple the Germans in their retreat.[51] However after the landings, unexpected difficulties arose. These were briefly mentioned in an interview with Louis Armand: '[The plan was not fully put into place.] We organised the *Plan Vert* at a time when we thought we could distribute a number of explosives and weapons across France. But when the time came, there were very few parachute drops'.[52]

It was then that the spontaneous and fragmented nature of cheminot resistance came into full swing. For weeks the familiar phrases over the radio – 'He is strict but fair' or 'The first snag costs two hundred francs' – had indicated the events to come.[53] But when no parachute drops came, the local resisters were still determined to paralyse the railway network. The only difference was that, now, they had to rely more heavily on the cheminots, whose methods of sabotage did not require weapons and explosives. This slightly chaotic improvisation of sabotage meant that the specific directives from above were rarely met; however, as Chevandier wrote, 'the failure of the *Plan Vert* ironically revealed its true success'.[54]

What was irresponsible in 1940 was patriotic in July–August 1944. Since last minute resisters had never had any links to organised groups

[48] See table 1 in Machefert-Tassin, 'Le bilan' (2001).
[49] AN/72/AJ/485: sabotages et avariés au matériel moteur (Jan.–Aug. 1944). Kedward underlines that regional summaries of 'incidents' (theft, arrests, sabotage, etc.) were often incomplete. Numbers were lowered to give 'an overall reassuring tone'. See Kedward, *In Search of the Maquis* (2003) 78.
[50] Chaban-Delmas would become a leading Gaullist political figure in post-war France.
[51] Chevandier, 'La résistance des cheminots' (1997) 157.
[52] 'Un Entretien avec Louis Armand', *La Vie du Rail* (1984) 7.
[53] 'Un Entretien avec le Général Koenig Ancien Commandant en Chef des Forces Françaises de l'Intérieur', in *La Vie du Rail* (1984) 4.
[54] Chevandier, 'La résistance des cheminots' (1997) 157.

they relied on opportunities. Barthe, a train driver in South-West France, was driving a train full of German soldiers and Russian prisoners on 1 August 1944. Throughout the entire Occupation, Barthe had not considered undertaking any resistance activity. But on that summer day, when the station master at Naucelles warned him that *maquisards* had placed explosives on the tracks several hundred feet away, Barthe decided to contribute to resistance activities and drove straight into the trap. Luckily, he survived to tell the tale of how he had participated in the explosion of four passenger cars full of enemy soldiers.[55]

4   Protecting saboteurs

Since it risked endangering the local population, sabotage, like aerial bombings, had a negative effect on public opinion. In October 1943 the BCRA received an alarming report: 'The recent derailing on the passenger train Paris-Marseille has caused several civilian deaths, creating considerable distress amongst the population. We must take immediate measures before the population turns against the *réfractaires* and the *groupes francs*'.[56] The derailing in question had occurred on 7 October 1943 and dozens of passengers were killed. Vichyist press used this incident to spread its anti-resistance propaganda, distributing an official explanation of the tragedy which was printed in the evening papers:

A train heading towards Dijon with medical supplies for French prisoners in Germany was derailed because of sabotage on the railways lines. (...) Just a few moments later, the Paris-Marseille-Monaco coming from the opposite direction hit it at full speed, colliding with the freight cars lying across the tracks. The locomotive and five carriages were derailed, and a tank car went up in flames. So far there are 31 dead, including the train driver (...) and twenty critically injured. Once again, French lives have been taken as a result of terrorist activities. Innocent victims, peaceful travellers are added to the 'tableau de chasse' of these criminals.[57]

The facts in this press release were somewhat manipulated, since it failed to mention that the train to Dijon was carrying Italian STO workers forcibly sent to Germany, and that the German guards on the train had prevented cheminots from intervening to help them after the first derailing.

---

[55] AN/72/AJ/495: Elie Barthe.

[56] *Groupes francs* were mobile squads who specialised in armed attacks and sabotage, whilst *réfractaires* were men who actively refused to comply with the forced labour laws. AN/3/AG/2/235: Note (16 Oct. 1943) concernant le moral de la population en France à la suite des sabotages et attentats contre les transports ferroviaires.

[57] AN/3/AG/2/235: Report WEZ 16/35603, France Politique, La catastrophe ferroviaire de Sennecey-le-Grand (Ce qu'en ont dit la radio et la presse Vichyssoise et la réalité.)

Still, it is important to underline that the reports in the BCRA files confirm that anti-resistance sentiments were real – and anti-sabotage sentiments were undoubtedly present within the cheminot community. In the winter of 1943–44, one report commented on cheminots' uneasiness with railway sabotage: as resisters attached to official networks increased the amount of railway sabotage to try and disrupt German traffic, France's general economy was suffering the consequences. As such, these acts were disturbing the cheminots: 'The majority of the SNCF's low- and mid-level personnel, agents between levels 1 and 15, are entirely convinced by our ideas and goals, and like us they have a deeply engrained hatred against the 'boche'. Yet because they love and know their profession well, they cannot understand why there is no halt to these sabotages. The cheminot knows better than any Frenchman that these acts with limited objectives cannot really disturb the enemies transports that much, since these always have absolute priority over all other transports in France'.[58]

But how did SNCF directors react to railway sabotage, and to the growing dissidence amongst cheminots? Initially it was quite a shock: Le Besnerais, like Jean Berthelot, refused to believe that cheminots were actually the ones involved in railway sabotage. 'A cheminot never sabotages his professional tool', declared Berthelot in 1941, and there was a need to distinguish between 'cheminots engaged in propaganda' and the 'active saboteurs who came from outside the railway milieu'.[59] But aside from this incredulity, and beyond its obviously devastating effects on railway, workers and passengers, sabotage was a very costly phenomenon. According to official reports, a big sabotage cost the SNCF between 10 and 20 million francs. The incident in Varennes, for instance, had cost 18 million. Not only were there material repairs which could cost a small fortune, but in addition, a dead traveller cost about 300,000 francs, while a severely wounded traveller cost 200,000 francs.[60] Such a phenomenal financial burden could be softened not only by increasing ticket prices, but also by adding an additional tax on ticket sales to cover insurance costs in the event of sabotage.[61]

The first natural instinct to dealing with saboteurs was repression, with French and German authorities undertaking mass arrests. Thirteen cheminots were arrested by the Germans after a sabotage as early as July

---

[58] AN/3/AG/2/235: Report WEZ/16/35.600, France Politique, Deux rapports sur l'effet produit par les actes de sabotage.

[59] Bachelier Report, 3.7.6. L'engrenage ds sabotages et des otages, septembre-décembre 1941.

[60] This is probably in terms of life insurance.

[61] AN/72/AJ/1927: Minutes (17 Nov. 1943, p. 3; 26 Nov. 1943, p. 5).

1941.[62] But sabotage carried on nonetheless, and the next obvious solution was to add more guardsmen along railway lines and in certain 'sensitive' areas. Initially, prefects played a large role in assigning the guardsmen, but the steady increase of sabotage called for more forces.[63] As a result, in the winter of 1943, 12,000 guards were hired as well as 3,500 young men from the *Chantiers de la Jeunesse*.[64] Then, in January 1944, Germans brought in thousands of their own workers to guard the railway lines in highly sensitive areas such as the Alps.[65]

However, when the HVD suggested transferring railway personnel to guard the tracks, the SNCF management categorically refused because of its personnel shortage. They knew that asking cheminots to denounce their colleagues would create deep internal divisions which would only further weaken the professional corps. Directors did not threaten cheminots either. Instead, they tried to dissuade railway workers from sabotage by putting up posters of monthly sabotage victims, thereby tugging at their humanitarianism and empathy.[66]

The way that the upper management dealt with railway sabotage reflects a broader change in their attitude towards the Germans. Indeed, as Germans began to encroach on the liberties of the SNCF, the protection of the national railway – and its workers – became the priority. While the WVD had initially limited itself to supervising the activities of the SNCF, the HVD wanted more control. In July 1943 the German authorities requested technical information on the layout and distribution of French railway in the Southern Zone, information which, according to the Kohl Agreement, it was not entitled to.[67] Likewise, when the Germans tried to change the Priority Transports list, Bichelonne declared that he was uninterested, 'because it would mean opening the door for German civil servants to come in and take over, at every level of the company'.[68] Moreover, every opportunity was good to request the return of the railway men still held prisoners in Germany, as well as the return of French railway material.[69] In February 1944, Bichelonne lost his temper, and declared that the number of workers that Münzer from the HVD was requesting to transfer to

---

[62] Bachelier Report, 3.7.5. Cheminots! J'ai dû me résoudre à frapper certains d'entre vous.
[63] AN/72/AJ/1927: Minutes (13 Oct. 1943). For more about *gardes des communications*, see AN/F/7/14913: Corps de Gardes de Communications, SNCF (1941–1944); AN/F/7/14919: Groupe de Dijon.
[64] AN/72/AJ/1927: Minutes (13 Oct. 1943; 7 Dec. 1943).
[65] AN/F/14/16943: German cheminots in France.
[66] AN/72/AJ/1927: Minutes (24 Jan. 1944).   [67] *Ibid.*, (26 Jul. 1943).
[68] *Ibid.*, (7 Dec. 1943).
[69] *Ibid.*, (30 Aug. 1943; 7 Oct. 1943; 26 Nov. 1943; 7 Feb. 1944).

another service was 'completely delusional', and that no such agreement had ever been made.[70]

The greatest fear of the SNCF management was that cheminots' morale would drop, and that the collapse of the railway community would bring on the collapse of the entire transport system. They therefore took many steps to preserve the railway community and uphold general morale. When Laval mentioned to the SNCF that they were considering reducing the holiday allowance of its employees, management declared this completely unjustifiable.[71] Work hours had already been largely exceeded, and certain depots and stations were kept open on Sundays and bank holidays in an attempt to catch up on the already frightening delays in the transport system. Therefore when Germans asked the SNCF to impose 60 hour weeks on even *more* stations and workshops, Le Besnerais said that this was out of the question. But the Managing Director was all too aware that the transport crisis was worsening, and that the only way to improve the situation was not to hire more unskilled workers, but rather to exploit better experienced cheminots. Le Besnerais therefore said that increasing the number of work hours to 60 was a possibility, only if cheminots' rations were increased accordingly.[72] According to Jean Bichelonne, ensuring better food rations 'was the best way to show solidarity in these difficult times'.[73] During the winter of 1943, Le Besnerais made almost weekly requests to increase meat, tobacco and wine rations, as well as additional shoes and uniforms. Therefore when the HVD requested a reduction in the length of snack breaks, SNCF management categorically refused.[74]

SNCF management was especially aware of the disastrous psychological effects of arrests and hostage-taking, which were so often a consequence of railway sabotage. Although in spring 1943 Le Besnerais had been looking to arrest certain communists, by Spring 1944 discussions on the negative effects of brutal German reprisals had taken central place in the weekly meetings held at the Ministry of Communications.[75] Interventions were made in specific cases, for example when chief engineers

---

[70] *Ibid.*, (28 Feb. 1944).   [71] *Ibid.*, (13 Aug. 1943).

[72] *Ibid.*, (31 Mar. 1943; 10 May 1943).

[73] *Ibid.*, (13 Sept. 1943). Bichelonne also believed that better food rations would prevent the spread of communism.

[74] *Ibid.*, (17 Nov. 1943).

[75] *Ibid.*, (25 May 1943; 12 Jul. 1943); (17 Apr. 1944): 'Le Besnerais has signalled an incident in Moulin-Neuf. Work was stopped after the French police came to arrest two foreign workers. One of them was killed when he tried to escape. Six delegates from Personnel came on site to try and intervene, but they were arrested by German police, which has created a lot of havoc'.

were threatened with arrest and imprisonment, or when cheminots considered to be innocent were arrested.[76] When seven cheminots were condemned to death for resistance activities in 1943, the directors stepped in and asked that they be released. Their relentless efforts were successful since the cheminots in question were ultimately pardoned; however they were deported to Germany, and, unbeknownst to anyone in France, were shot in Buchenwald.[77]

The Massacre of Ascq – mentioned only briefly so far – is a fascinating example of how upper management did not treat railway sabotage as a straightforward crime which needed to be repressed and punished. A minor railway sabotage against a train carrying men form the 12th SS Panzer Division had triggered the massacre of 86 men on 1–2 April 1944 in the town of Ascq. The affair caused outrage across the region and France: the murder of 86 innocent men dragged out of their homes in the middle of the night had clearly been a disproportionate response to a sabotage which had not even injured anyone. And amongst these victims, there were 21 cheminots. The grass-roots railway community seized the incident to mobilize popular resistance against the Germans, but the SNCF management was also outraged. Indeed the crime in Ascq breached official agreements regarding the repression of French cheminots. In November 1943, the German authorities had assured the Ministry of Communications and the SNCF Management that cheminots would no longer be victims of German reprisals. Too often, railwaymen had paid the price for resistance activities, as they were on site when sabotage occurred, and would be taken hostage or brutalised in myriad ways. Thus following the incident in Ascq, Bichelonne wrote to the German Chief of Transports to underline how the SS had violated the 1943 agreement. The Chief of Transports denied any violation, but presented his personal regrets for the incident in Ascq. He then assured Bichelonne that no other similar incidents would occur.[78] It is unlikely that Bichelonne was convinced by this.

When the Germans sentenced the original Ascq 'saboteurs' to death in June 1944, the SNCF sent over top managers to attend the funeral – indeed, seven out of the eight saboteurs had been cheminots. Fewer than forty people in total attended the funeral of the saboteurs in June 1944, probably because many Ascquois blamed the saboteurs as well as the Germans for the massacre. But amongst those were the Director of the

---

[76] *Ibid.*, (30 Aug. 1943). On this particular occasion they also mentioned Lang. See Chapter 7.

[77] *Ibid.*, (29 Nov. 1943). These men were most likely condemned to death by a German tribunal, since Bichelonne asked Munzer to pardon them.

[78] AN/3/AG/2/342: Letter (4 Apr. 1944) from Bichelonne to Fournier.

North Region, Mr Lemaire, a top railway engineer from the *Ponts et Chaussés*, Mr Etienne, and an SNCF inspector, Mr Latouche. Their presence goes a long way in showing the seriousness of the matter: even saboteurs were being honoured as martyrs by the SNCF leadership.[79]

Conclusion

The phenomenon of railway sabotage is a cornerstone of Vichy memory, but following on from discussions of nineteenth-century working-class protest we are familiar with cheminots' anti-sabotage, anti-violent rhetoric. The cheminots are far more known for their striking action, and the moral dilemmas they face when sabotaging are familiar to specialist historians. '... even in 1944 the clandestine press of the *Fédération des Cheminots* alluded to the heartbreak which a cheminot had to overcome when driving his locomotive towards derailing or destruction', wrote Bachelier.[80] For by sabotage we do not mean 'disruption' here – ultimately, thefts, strikes, mislabelling cars, *ralentissage*, all of these forms of protest 'sabotaged' the German war effort; rather, we are talking about industrial sabotage, machine-breaking. Breaking machines was a tradition amongst working-class employees to get messages across to their employers, notably that they were dissatisfied with the machines themselves.[81] This, of course, explains why cheminots – whose work originated in machines themselves – had not initially adopted this method of protest. For them, machines were one of the most-loved parts of their job.

However during the Occupation cheminots could take part in industrial sabotage, thereby redefining their relationship to protest, their machines and the railways altogether. But if the increasing number of railway sabotages in 1943–44 shows a shift in cheminots' behaviour, they were still professionally responsible in their sabotages, being careful not to pointlessly destroy their equipment or to risk the lives of innocent civilians. As such, did cheminots really break with tradition? It is more likely that the Occupation broadened the limits of their professionalism, shifted their mentalities and re-defined their collective values.

Of course, the history of cheminot sabotage begs the question: why did cheminots engage in sabotage activity, but never sabotage the Jewish convoys? In many ways this question has already been partially answered here: cheminots did not instigate as much as they facilitated sabotage. As

---

[79] Locals, however, saw them as traitors for having endangered the town. See Broch, 'Martyred Towns' (2014).
[80] Bachelier Report, 6.1.1. De 1941 à 1943, la montée des résistances.
[81] Hobsbawm, *Labouring Men* (1986) 7. See Chapter 2 on machine breakers.

such, if the Allies or resistance networks did not instigate sabotage of the Jewish convoys, then there is little chance that cheminots would have instigated it themselves. Moreover, this chapter has underlined cheminots' on-going concern with protecting travellers and colleagues: it was one thing to sabotage a goods trains, but transports carrying hundreds of people, no matter who they were, were far more problematic. Yet in order to fully grasp the complicated history of Jewish convoys and railway sabotage, it is key to further investigate the relationship between the cheminots and the Jewish question, the SNCF and the Final Solution.

7   Shoah

Sabotage was an important moral issue at the time of the occupation; today, however, the Jewish deportations are the obvious moral problem. There is no doubt that the SNCF took part in the deportations: between March 1942 and August 1944, the SNCF deported 76,000 Jews from France in 79 convoys.[1] Studies have explained this participation in very different ways over the years. Kurt Werner Schaechter was the first to publicly denounce the company's implication in the Holocaust. More measured studies by Christian Bachelier and Georges Ribeill have nuanced the SNCF's role in the decision-making process of the Jewish deportations form France. These largely confirm the findings of Raul Hilberg, Serge Klarsfeld and Alfred Mierzejewski who portray the SNCF more as a cog in the wheel of the Final Solution rather than as an active participant – a facilitator, not an instigator.

Determining the precise role of the SNCF in the Final Solution has important historical consequences; and yet, this only tells part of the story. Two major issues frame discussion of the SNCF and the Holocaust. The first concerns the issue of the SNCF and the deportations, and more specifically its disputed role within the Final Solution. The logistics of organising the Jewish deportations lie at the heart of contemporary preoccupations about SNCF history. There is a need, therefore, to understand the organisational process that led to the deportation of France's Jews. The limitation of sources, however, makes this a difficult task. Few documents in the SNCF archives directly relate to the Jewish deportations. This is largely due to the fact that the Holocaust transports were never central to the SNCF's operations – as it will be explained, the percentage of trains used to deport Jews was minimal in comparison to the total traffic flow. Accordingly, the Final Solution did not affect the

---

[1] According to *Mémorial de la déportation des Juifs de France* (Paris: Serge et Béate Klarsfeld, 1978). The Mémorial de la Shoah website explains the variations in number: www.memorialdelashoah.org/index.php/en/archives-and-documentation/encyclopedia-of-the-shoah/frequently-asked-questions.

SNCF greatly in terms of material or manpower. Administrative and corporate archives are thus not the place to find emotional or moral discussions of what was happening to the Jews. This does not mean, however, that we cannot piece together the story of the deportations from the SNCF's perspective relying on other sources.

The second main issue is that of the Jewish personnel within the SNCF. Very little is known about Jews in the SNCF, not least because there were so few of them.[2] According to Georges Ribeill, there were approximately 141 Jewish personnel, a small number which is not fully verifiable but which is probably not far from reality.[3] I was able to determine the names of twenty-eight Jewish cheminots, and was fortunate to locate additional details about the lives, families and work of twenty five of these workers. This involved cross-referencing numerous lists, records and dossiers in hope of finding a single name, a single reference. The quantity and quality of the information varies for each cheminot, but creating individual files is of vital importance in understanding how the persecution of Jews was carried out within the SNCF.

What, exactly, do the stories of these twenty-five Jewish cheminots tell us about cheminots, the SNCF and the Jewish question? To what extent can their stories help us to clarify issues surrounding the SNCF and the deportations? How can they help explain the absence of sabotage of Jewish convoys? The Jewish question in the railways is not limited to the deportations themselves, and the lives of the Jews working for the SNCF during this period allow us to get a new and a much closer insight into the mentality of the SNCF directors and cheminots vis-à-vis the Final Solution. First, one must explore the impact of the Holocaust on the SNCF personnel at all hierarchical levels, from the antisemitic laws in 1940–41 to the intensification of persecution in 1943–44. By tracing the administrative bureaucracy, we get a better sense of how the lives of these Jews was affected, but also about how non-Jews in the SNCF reacted to the persecution of their Jewish colleagues. It is then possible to discuss the highly sensitive issue of the deportations, underlining past historiographical work but also emphasising new material which captures the realities of the time.

---

[2] The low number of Jews within the SNCF reflect the overall rates of Jews in national ministries. Marc Olivier Baruch used a primary source listing the amount of Jews in all ministries affected by the 1940 and 1941 antisemitic laws, and the Ministry of Transport and Public Works ranked 8th according to how many Jews were affected by these laws (see 'Bilan d'Application des Statuts des Juifs (Avril 1942)' in Baruch, ed., *Servir l'Etat Français* [1997] 655). It could also reflect the fact that foreign workers were not really visible within the ranks of the SNCF, and as such foreign Jewish working class men and women would not have been involved in the railways.
[3] Ribeill, 'L'accommodation sociale de la SNCF' (2001).

1   Antisemitic laws 1940–41

The stirrings of legislative antisemitism began in the summer of 1940, with French – not German – legislation. At the time, the Germans were busy outlining the details of their economic and political collaboration with Vichy, and it was only on 27 September 1940, more than three months after the Fall of France, that their first antisemitic law was implemented in the Occupied Zone. The law defined Jews according to German standards, forbade them to return to the Occupied Zone and required them to register with their local sub-prefecture.[4] In the meantime, the French were already spinning a web of exclusionary legislature aimed at foreigners, communists, free masons and Jews.[5] The law of 22 July 1940 reviewed and/or repealed all naturalizations since 1927; the law of 27 August which annulled the Marchandeau law; the laws of 17 July, 16 August and 10 September which stated that one could only work in the public service, medical profession and the bar respectively if one had a French father.[6] These laws were founded on the idea that France needed to be built by Frenchmen and Frenchmen alone. By implementing them, Marc Olivier Baruch argues, civil servants 'became antisemites', 'not in the racist and agitated way of militant Nazism, but like the well-educated people that they were, and at varying degrees'.[7]

Vichy implemented its first antisemitic statute on 3 October 1940, just days after the new German law of 27 September. But if it was possibly responding to this first German law to simultaneously show independence and willingness to collaborate, Vichy was also just building on its xenophobic programme of the summer of 1940. The statute symbolised a significant turn in French policy towards Jews, and it is famously regarded as the first brick laid by the French government on the road to complicity in genocide. As Tal Bruttmann neatly summarised, the statute had three major functions: it defined Jews; it excluded them from the public sector; it side-lined them from the private sector.[8] However, the implementation of this statute was uneven. First, who was Jewish? According to the statute, one had to have either three Jewish

[4] Marrus and Paxton, *Vichy France and the Jews* (1995) 7.
[5] There is a debate about how far the laws of summer 1940 were aimed at Jews. For Renée Poznanski, they were, but others are less sure.
[6] Marrus and Paxton, *Vichy France and the Jews* (1995) 3–5. These laws were published in Claire Andrieu, ed., *La perséceution des Juifs de France, 1940–1944, et le rétablissement de la légalité republicaine: Recueil des textes officiels, 1940–1999* (Paris: La Documentation Française, 2000).
[7] Baruch, *Servir l'Etat français* (1997) 150.
[8] Tal Bruttmann, 'La Mise en œuvre du statut des Juifs du 3 octobre 1940', *Archives Juives*, 41.1 (2008) 11–24.

grandparents, or two Jewish grandparents and a Jewish spouse. But the statute said nothing about how to identify Jews; it was up to the administrations themselves to identify the Jews working in their services. The absence of a centralised bureau to overlook the implementation of this statute would lead to further disorganisation and confusion. Second, the public and private sectors were affected very differently. In regards to the former, one was not necessarily dismissed: only certain roles were completely forbidden to Jews, whilst others were only partially affected, or even not at all. As for the latter, the private sector began to be affected in 1940 but this law was expanded in June 1941.[9]

The SNCF was naturally affected by the statute. Six men in particular were subject to the new regulation: Jacques Eisenmann (*Ponts et Chaussées* engineer detached to the SNCF), Henri Lang (Assisting Director in Tracts and Buildings Department of the South-West Region and engineer at the *corps des Ponts et Chaussées*), Jean Lévy (Director of Central Department of Material and Traction), Pierre Lévy (Engineer *Ponts et Chaussées*), Robert Lévi (Director of Fixed Installations) and Stein (Track Engineer in Rouen). A seventh man, Paul Ehrmann, received a letter on 16 December 1940 barring him from the *corps des Ponts et Chaussées* in accordance to the October statute. Le Besnerais immediately objected: Ehrmann could not possibly be barred, he was not Jewish, nor were his wife and parents. 'I am much obliged to ask you to fix the error made in regards to this civil servant as quickly as possible', wrote Le Besnerais.[10] In the end, Ehrmann was confirmed a 'non-Jew', and he was reinstated in his ranks of the *Ponts et Chaussées* in January 1942. Ehrmann is a rare case.

The men affected by the first statute were not brutally excluded from the SNCF, although this is not so uncommon.[11] One of the most well-known cases within the SNCF was the gradual expulsion of Henri Lang, whose family was originally from Alsace-Lorraine, and had been in France for many generations. Born in 1895 in Rambervilliers, he was a studious young man who entered *Polytechnique* before the outbreak of the war in 1914, at which point he joined the French army. During the Great War, Lang distinguished himself from his peers in numerous battles, not least Verdun and the Somme, and his exploits led him to receive some of the highest decorations in France including the *Légion d'Honneur*. His life

---

[9] Daniel Lee explores the complicated nature of Jewish 'identity'. See Lee, *Pétain's Jewish Children* (2014) 14–6.

[10] APSNCF: Paul Ehrmann, Letter (11 Jan. 1941) from Le Besnerais to Berthelot.

[11] Likewise, the expulsion of the *Banque de France*'s Jewish personnel 'was not carried out in a brutal fashion'. Dreyfus, *Pillages sur ordonnances* (2003) 181.

after the war was paved with professional success: Lang finished his studies and became an engineer with a seat at the *Ponts et Chaussées* before becoming exclusively involved in the railways. By the 1930s, Lang was one of the most esteemed directors in the SNCF. His personal life, too, was a rich one, although fraught with hardships: Henri married Jacqueline Hirsch after the war, and two of their four children would die in childhood. But his family life was nonetheless a pleasant one, in which education and music were key, while religion was largely ignored in the home and their children were never raised in the Judaic faith.

The 3 October statute saw Lang lose his seat as professor at the *corps des Ponts et Chaussées*, and he was demoted within the SNCF. Yet Lang was part of a network of influential individuals who were ready to help him ride out these laws. By December 1940 his activities at the SNCF were reduced to the study of the electrification of the railways, but requests for a special exemption were being brought forward. Other Jews also benefitted in similar ways. Pierre Lévy, who had devoted his life to the railways, was put into early retirement but maintained his personal as well as professional ties with the railway elite.[12] Robert Lévi's story runs parallel to Lang's own life much more clearly: also a French Jew firmly implanted in the country's technocratic elite, Lévi was as devoted to France as he was to his job.[13] The two men shared the same circle of highly placed friends, and Lévi also received some support during this early period. In regards to Jean Lévy and Stein there is very little information. If the former was probably able to go to in the Free Zone and North Africa, the latter was arrested the same day as Lang, but there is no traceable information about their families.[14]

So if the lives of the SNCF's Jewish personnel undoubtedly changed after 3 October 1940, they were still well-respected and even supported by their peers. Their lives were tied on personal levels to those of Raoul Dautry, the great technocrat and ex-railway director who would take a prominent role in French politics both before and after the occupation; Frédéric Surleau, who after a long career in the railways became Assisting Managing Director of the SNCF from 1937 to 1939 and would reappear in political circles after the war; Maurice Lemaire, a railway engineer who became the Managing Director of the SNCF after the war; Jean Tuja, Regional Director of the South-East; and Jean Berthelot, the Minister of Transport and Communications from 1940 to 1942. In fact,

[12] Nathalie Bibas, *Henri Lang, 1895–1942* (Paris: Editions LBM, 2012) 145.
[13] See 'Robert Lévi (1895–1981), Souvenirs' in *Mémoires d'ingénieurs, destins ferroviaires* (2007) 213–346; Interview transcript, Bernard Lévi (2000).
[14] Interview transcript, Eisenmann (2000) 13.

Lang's daughter, Catherine de Béchillon, remembered how Robert Le Besnerais had also been a close family friend: 'I have memories of him coming to the house for dinner, on a number of occasions, just like that. He was a bit gruff, and he was also diabetic I think, he had some health problems, so every time he came around there was always talk about some special diet'.[15] Catherine later became close friends with his nephew, Daniel Le Besnerais, when they met at an SNCF summer camp in 1944.[16]

In June 1941 a second statute defined who was Jewish or not and further distanced Jews from public service and French national life. One of the main problems was that these antisemitic laws threatened to disqualify highly trained and gifted professionals. Berthelot was only too aware of this, and he sent a letter in support of Henri Lang. Indeed, according to article 8 of the June 1941 statute, certain Jews could be acquitted from this law if they had rendered exceptional services to the state or their family had been in France for at least five generations: 'M. Lang [has] distinguished himself as a man with remarkable efficiency, initiative, and judgement. (...) As a technician of superior professional worth and morals, M. Lang has always carried out his numerous projects with great success (...) projects which, in addition to their technical value, contain an important architectural value'.[17] Berthelot also wrote highly of Robert Lévi's professionalism in support of his exemption: 'Mr Robert Lévi is an undisputable authority in questions of construction and all technical matters related to the railways (...) [He] is one of the most knowledgeable people in matters of triage, and he has made the most significant contributions to the modernisation of French train stations'.[18] Just like those targeted by the statutes themselves, French technocrats were confident that the state would ultimately protect its most loyal subjects. The best solution was thus to rely on the administrative protocol which could reverse the legislation affecting friends and colleagues.

Of course, these interventions which played by the rules of the law guaranteed nothing. As Poznanski has underlined, the application process for exemptions was a terrible ordeal which often took months, and was rarely successful.[19] It was not Jewish employees but their superiors, who had to hand in the application dossiers to their relevant ministry. The Minister would give his opinion on the matter, and then transfer the

---

[15] Interview transcript, de Béchillon (1997) 9.   [16] *Ibid.*
[17] APSNCF: Henri Lang, Letter (16 Aug. 1941) from Berthelot to the CGQJ, séction des dérogations.
[18] APSNCF: Robert Lévi, Letter (7 Aug. 1941) from Berthelot to CGQJ.
[19] Poznanski, *Les Juifs* (1997) 141–2.

dossier to the *Commissariat Général aux Questions Juives* (CGQJ), an institute created in March 1941 to deal specifically with the Jewish question. There, the documents proving length of service or exceptional services were verified before the Minister would write an official report. The dossier was then forwarded to the *Conseil d'État*, which would determine the ultimate course of action. If accepted, the dossier was sent back to the relevant Minister who presented it to the Marshal. Ultimately, Pétain had the final say. The procedures were long, and rarely successful. By mid-August 1941, eighty-two Jews working in the SNCF were to be fired; thirty maintained in their positions for a while (including Robert Lévi and Henri Lang); twelve cases were still being investigated; thirteen were not unaffected by the laws for the time being.[20]

The arrest of Henri Lang in December 1941 brought home the real dangers Jews faced in Vichy France. In May, August and December 1941, 8,700 Jews were arrested in Paris, a fifth of whom were French Jews.[21] These operations were, as Klarsfeld clearly explains, launched by the German authorities with the assistance of the French police, and they were a direct response to a series of anti-German attacks. The December arrests targeted the French in particular, those Jews who held positions of power and authority. On the morning of 12 December 1941, German soldiers came to arrest Lang at his home, a scene witnessed by his wife and two daughters. Without any indication of why they were taking him, where he was going and when he would return, Lang was given a few moments to pack a suitcase and to say a brief goodbye to his family.[22] Lang soon found several family members – his brother-in-law Pierre Hirsch and a distant cousin Jean Léon – and colleagues – Pierre Lévy, a retired engineer from the North Company and Pierre Bloch, an old student from *Ponts et Chaussées*.[23] On the night of 12–13 December, along with 300 other Jews from the Drancy camp, this group of 743 men were transferred by train to the Compiègne camp.[24]

Following Lang's internment, Robert Lévi was advised by his colleagues to leave the Occupied Zone and hide in the Free Zone. And yet the Chairman, Fournier, refused to give him an official post in the Free Zone. He accepted Lévi's request to go on leave without pay, at which point Lévi crossed the demarcation line illegally with his wife and lived

[20] AN/72/AJ/477: Letter (9 Aug. 1941) from Fournier to Berthelot.
[21] Serge Klarsfeld, *Vichy-Auschwitz: La 'solution finale' de la question juive en France* (Paris: Fayard, 2001, c1993) 15.
[22] Bibas, *Henri Lang* (2012) 11–17. The arrest is very briefly (and broadly) referred to in an interview with Lang's daughter, see Interview transcript, de Béchillon, 2–3; To read about the operation itself, see Klarsfeld, *Vichy-Auschwitz* (2001) 36–8.
[23] Bibas, *Henri Lang* (2012) 14.   [24] Klarsfeld, *Vichy-Auschwitz* (2001) 36.

off of his retirement package from the *Ponts et Chaussées*.[25] Several years later, Lévi would comment on this period of his life : 'When leaving Paris for the Free Zone in 1942, I thought that maybe one day I could be on the side of the Allies, and that then I could work got the interests of the SNCF (I could not bear a grudge for the ignoble way the SNCF's Chairman behaved with me)'.[26] If the mixed support from the SNCF leadership comes to light here, it is Lévi's professional ethos, and his unwavering commitment to the railways, which truly shines through in this passage.

Throughout Lang's internment, first in the Royallieu-Compiègne camp, then later in Drancy, his wife as well as his colleagues at the SNCF continued to push for his exemption. He spoke of it a lot in his letters home during this period, mentioning also the visit he received from his friend Jean Tuja (Regional Director of the South-East). Lang was deeply concerned that this visit had somehow disappointed Tuja – that it had led him to believe that Lang could no longer be as professionally active as he had previously been. He specifically disclosed these feelings in a letter to his wife:

During my brief encounter with Jean T. I was so moved that I could barely get my thoughts straight. This made him doubt my alertness and my abilities. Would you and he both be reassured if I told you, once more, that I am perfectly able to work as hard as I used to? I would have liked to talk to him more about the railways, and he will have to come back and see me about this. I would like to know how the big Lyon-Marseille works are going, and those projects which we cared for like our children![27]

The emotion and devotion expressed in this letter are a strong example of the professionalism of this Jewish technocrat – a sentiment which also animated Robert Lévi, as mentioned earlier.

Lang was deported on the first convoy to Auschwitz on 27 March 1942 and died in the camp shortly after.[28] His family, however, would only come to know this after the war. In the meantime, they remained very much in touch with the SNCF. Lang's daughter, Catherine de Béchillon, described the support she and her family received. After having passed her philosophy exams at the secondary college Notre Dame de Sion, Catherine had the opportunity to go in the Free Zone. This was organised in collaboration with her school and the SNCF : 'the SNCF was in

[25] 'Robert Lévi' (2007) 340.   [26] *Ibid.*, 270–1.
[27] Letter (19 Mar. 1942) from Lang to his wife, cited in Bibas, *Henri Lang* (2012) 61.
[28] Lang was not gassed, since gassing immediately upon arrival was not yet implemented at Auschwitz. The exact date and circumstances of his death are uncertain, but according to his daughter he died soon after his arrival in Auschwitz.

charge of organising special trains so that children could go and spend their holidays with family members in the free zone'. The nuns at Notre Dame de Sion helped her obtain a false *Ausweis* using the identity of another student, and Catherine ended up in Lyon for 27 months. There, she was frequently in contact with Jean Tuja, who invited her every time he was down there: 'he always insisted that I go and see him, and since he was a very busy man with little time on his hands I joined him at big dinners, with all the SNCF managers, and non-SNCF managers, the swankiest people one could imagine, and me, at barely sixteen years old, I was participating in these dinners'.[29] Catherine's later enrolment to the *Baccalauréat* in Lyon was also the result of a direct intervention from Frédéric Surleau: 'so you see', she said, 'this is how I was 'entangled' with the SNCF'.[30] In the meantime, her mother and younger sister stayed in Paris, hiding in a small room with no electricity for two years, helped by the nuns from Notre Dame de Sion and other friends. Lévi's family had a similar trajectory, with his wife and son spending most of their time in the Free Zone, their contacts with the SNCF maintained.[31]

Jacques Eisenmann, Lévi's cousin, had quite a different experience. Eisenmann had been officially expelled from the SNCF following the law of 17 July 1940 which banned French people with foreign fathers from the civil service, although his own testimony ties his expulsion from the SNCF to his Jewish identity.[32] He believed that the SNCF sent him to the Free Zone after 1940 to get rid of him.[33] After a short stint in Moulins prison, however, his friend Dherse, the 'big boss' at Sollac, gave him a job and Eisenmann would stay in Lyon for the whole duration of the war.[34] In an interview in 2000 he gave vivid descriptions of Le Besnerais – 'I do not know [if he had any political affiliation]. I believe he would have agreed with any government' – and Berthelot – 'we made fun of him. The cheminots made fun of him. (...) he had beautiful handwriting and a sharp mind'.[35]

---

[29] Interview transcript, de Béchillon (1997) 4.   [30] *Ibid.*, 5.

[31] Bernard, his son, spent his time in Lyon where he finished his exams at *Polytechnique* and in 1943 joined the Resistance. In the meantime, his parents moved on to Marseille, and his father was left 'stranded' in North Africa when the Allies landed there. Unable to return to France, he stayed there for the rest of the Occupation working with the Free French. This was much to the dismay of his wife, who felt quite abandoned in Marseille, and would remind him of this after the war. Interview Lévi (2012); Interview transcript, Lévi (2000).

[32] Interview transcript, Eisenmann (2000) 4. It is unclear as to whether Eisenmann understands which law he was affected by. Another element to complicate his statement is that, when he joined the Armaments Ministry in 1939–1940 with Dautry, he was asked whether he wished to return to the SNCF, and he said he was never coming back. See Interview transcript, Eisenmann (2000) 8–9.

[33] *Ibid.*, 9.   [34] *Ibid.*, 10.   [35] *Ibid.*, 16, 23.

It would appear that most of the exemption requests were unfulfilled, with the exception of Henri Lang. In August 1943, the Minister Bichelonne was still making pleas for Lang's release. According to one report, Bichelonne was to 'intervene on behalf of Mr Lang, who Mr Morane has been mentioning, although he fears that it may be a hopeless case'.[36] In 1943, Marshal Pétain reinstated Lang in his seat at the *Ponts et Chaussées*.[37] At this point, he had been dead for months in Auschwitz.

2   **Radicalisation of persecution and the intensification of arrests**

The radicalisation of persecution began in the summer of 1942, with the infamous Vel d'Hiv roundup and the official launch of the Final Solution in France. But these decisions and actions were largely taken beyond the realm of the SNCF. Of course, the SNCF was tied to the deportation convoys which will be discussed at a later point. For now, we must continue to investigate how the intensification of persecution affected Jewish personnel within the railway company.

When Mussolini was overturned in September 1943 and the Germans penetrated the zone previously occupied by the Italians, a new phase of persecution began. Until then, the Italians had managed to protect Jews within their zone from German arrests; now, they no longer able to do so. The massive arrests in Nice in the autumn of 1943 signalled a change in command, and are a clear indication of the new antisemitic politics in France. But in fact we can witness an effervescence of arrests all over the French provinces: Bordeaux, Toulouse, Poitiers, Dijon, Reims, Troyes, Nancy, Moselle, Meurthe and Meurthe-et-Moselle.[38] Indeed, whilst Jews in the Paris area had been the most vulnerable in 1942, this was no longer the case in 1943–44. Now, it was in the provinces that mass and/or individual arrests were taking place.

It is important to underline that the radicalisation of Nazi persecution was not completely successful, in part because the Germans did not have the full support of the French. If Laval and Bousquet had assisted them in 1942, they now had more ambivalent attitudes.[39] And so whilst the fall of Mussolini could have signalled a new dawn for antisemitic persecution in France, the French government did not unanimously or whole-heartedly

---

[36] AN/72/AJ/1927: Minutes from Ministerial meeting (30 Aug. 1943).
[37] Interview Transcript, Catherine de Béchillon, (1997) 3.
[38] Klarsfeld, *Vichy-Auschwitz* (2001) 331–4.
[39] Bousquet and then Laval seem to show far more reluctance to compromise over the Jewish question; see Klarsfeld, *Vichy-Auschwitz* (2001) 319 (Bousquet), 331 (Laval).

support this persecution. This area of history is, with good reason, a slippery terrain: one must not be misled to think that the French government opposed the deportations of the Jews in 1943–44. Indeed, Klarsfeld has shown the involvement of individual French prefects and/ or policemen in the arrests and deportations in 1943–44, men who were driven either by personal advancement or the prospect of a financial reward. The involvement of the Milice is also noteworthy.[40] However, a shift in cooperation was notable. More importantly, it is absolutely key to understand that the numbers of Jews arrested in 1943–44 never reached the Nazis' desired quotas[41]. This had a lot to do with the fact that Jews were warned in advance of arrest, had time to go into hiding, relied on Jewish self-help networks or sometimes benefitted from the support of ordinary French men, women or resisters. All of these factors must be taken into account to understand this wave of arrest and persecution.

So how would the lives of the Jewish cheminots change under this new phase? How would the SNCF react to the radicalisation of Jewish persecution? At a time when Germany was occupying the whole territory, and when fewer deportation convoys Eastwards were being organised, how would the SNCF become affected by the escalation in antisemitic policy? The selection of Jewish men working amongst the lower ranks of the SNCF tells a very different story to that of Lang, Lévi and the others. Indeed, whilst the technocrats were heavily affected by Vichy's antisemitic statutes, as well as the 1941 reprisal arrests[42], most Jews working for the SNCF would fall victim to the radicalisation of persecution in 1943 and 1944. This does not mean that these men were not affected by the statutes: Salomon Chich, Sabétaï Toross and Robert Aron all lost their positions after the law of 2 June 1941.[43] However, their arrests in 1943 and 1944 reflect a very different aspect of Jewish persecution in France, and, ultimately, also a new and fatal stage of their lives.

Eighteen Jewish cheminots have been identified amongst the lower personnel, from blue-collar professions such as workers, labourers or clerks, to positions of greater responsibility, such as locomotive engineer or supervisor of rounds. Most of these men are French, although some

---

[40] Read chapter 9 in Klarsfeld, *Vichy-Auschwitz* (2001) 299–326.

[41] On 10–11 Jan. 1940, they arrested 228 Jews in Bordeaux, when the quotas had originally been for over 400. Klarsfeld, *Vichy-Auschwitz* (2001) 330.

[42] For more on reprisals and arrests in 1941, see André Kaspi, *Les Juifs pendant l'Occupation* (Paris: Seuil, 1997, c1991) 212–7; Poznanski, *Les Juifs* (1997) 257–60 ; Klarsfeld, *Vichy-Auschwitz* (2001) 15–42.

[43] APSNCF: Salomon Chich; Sabétaï Toross; Robert Aron.

come from North Africa (Salomon Chich, Sadia Lévy and Elie Molina), Germany (Jean-Louis Wolkowitsch) or Russia (Gabriel Touviès). They lived in different areas: four of them we do not know, but the others scattered in Epernay, Levallois, l'Aisne, Villeneuve, Houilles, and Lyon. Two came from Bordeaux, and four from Paris. Their differences in locality are further compounded by the diversity of age, which ranged from late twenties to early fifties at the outbreak of the war. And yet, despite these differences, and despite their French origins, their fate under Vichy was largely bound in tragedy, with the majority dying in deportation.

Of the eighteen, three cases are difficult to trace: we do not have any real information on Isaac Soudarski, André Lévy or Raymond Weil. Of the fifteen cases we do know about, six were arrested for being Jewish before September 1943. One was arrested on 30 August 1941 (Elie Molina), one during the Vel d'Hiv roundups (Salomon Chich), one for resistance activities in 1942 and shot at Mont Valérien (Jean-Louis Wolkowitsch). Three were arrested between March and 13 September 1943 (Gabriel Touviès, Alphone Asch and Daniel Kahn).[44] The arrests of the remaining eight Jewish cheminots all took place after September 1943 in various forms: some were arrested as a result of mass local arrests in early 1944 (Ferdinand Allant and Georges Boudin in Bordeaux, Aron in Lyon); some were arrested with their families (Sadia Lévy, Boudin); some were arrested from home (Allant) whilst others were arrested at their place of work (in the Epernay workshops).[45]

Following the arrests, a system of information, intervention and support was carried out across the SNCF through a combination of centralised and localised efforts of different divisions, management and personnel. Indeed, the arrest of any cheminot required their superior to fill in an official form entitled 'information to be given in the case that an SNCF agent is arrested by German authorities'.[46] In this form they gave the agent's basic details (name, rank, residence, date and place of birth) as well as some additional information such as familial status, professional qualities, military services and political affiliations. The details of

[44] APSNCF: Salomon Chich; André Lévy; Elie Molina; Gabriel Touviès; Raymond Weil; Jean-Louis Wolkowitsch. See also Maurice Wolkowitsch, 'J'avais un frère aîné ...' in *Les cheminots dans la guerre et l'Occupation, Témoignages et récits*, Revue d'Histoire des Chemins de Fer, Hors Série n°7 (2004), pp. 248–55; the CDJC has information on Alphone Asch and Isaac Soudarski.
[45] SNCF/303/LM/11: Ferdinand Allant (Agents arrested by the German authorities); Georges Boudin (Agents arrested by the German authorities). APSNCF: Robert Aron; Sadia Lévy.
[46] *Ibid.*, Allant; Boudin.

his arrest were also recorded: date, reason, sentence, trial date, reasons to ask for pardon, place of internment. This information was then sent up all the way to the Head of Central Services Division, allowing the leadership to keep a close eye on its personnel.

Once the middle management had alerted the Central Services, wheels could then be set in motion to help the internees. In the days that followed his arrest, Ferdinand Allant's superior wrote to the local prefecture asking them to release him on the basis that, first, he was an indispensable and reliable worker, and second, if his mother was indeed Jewish, his father was Catholic, as were his wife and children.[47] The Prefecture considered him Jewish, however, and Allant did not pursue the matter himself. He was deported to Drancy, from where he was liberated in late August 1944.[48] Allant's colleague Georges Boudin had also been arrested on 11 January 1944. Unlike Allant, Boudin's 'Jewish' status was unquestionable, and although the reasons for his arrest remained murky at first, they assumed it was because of his Jewish status. One letter from the CGQJ suggests that requests to free both Allant and Boudin were made by the Head of the Prisonner Department, but no intervention was possible.[49]

A big administrative problem arose when agents got arrested: who would their salary/pensions get paid to? What was their family status? Would the SNCF need to come to their assistance? Elie Molina, for instance, was single, and so there was no one (wife and/or children) that they could give the money to.[50] It was to be put on hold. However, further investigations revealed that Molina's father, a blind war veteran, had largely depended on his son. So in April 1942, the SNCF gave Mr Molina a lump sum of money to help cover his expenses. Allant's whole salary went to his wife, whereas Boudin's salary was put on hold since he had no children and was arrested with his wife.[51] For Gabriel Touviès, they ended up tracking down his daughter who was back in Paris after the war, the only one of her family to survive deportation. The process to retrieve her father's pension, however, would turn out to be a bureaucratic nightmare.[52]

---

[47] *Ibid.*, Allant, Letter (7 Jun. 1944) from Delbos to Ingénieur Chef des ateliers de Bordeaux.

[48] *Ibid.*, See the correspondence in Allant's file from Jun. to Sept. 1944.

[49] *Ibid.*, Boudin, Letter (14 Feb. 1944) from Commissaire Général aux Questions Juives to Head of Prisonner Department at the SNCF.

[50] APSNCF: Elie Molina, Letter (15 Apr. 1942) from Chef de la subdivision de la comptabilité to Directeur du Service Central du Personnel.

[51] SNCF/303/LM/11: Allant, Letter (Jan. 1944) from Pesez, Chef de la Division du Service Général, to Directeur des Ateliers de Bordeaux; Boudin, Letter (Feb. 1944) from Pesez to Chef des Services Administratifs.

[52] APSNCF: Gabriel Touviès, Note (Levallois, 2 Aug. 1944) Arrondissement Batignoles Matériel. See L. Broch 'Paperwork for Non-returning Deportees: Bureaucracy and

The various SNCF divisions and personnel who were tied to the targeted cheminots carried out official procedures of intervention by staying neatly within the limits of the administrative protocol: they declared the arrest, intervened on behalf of the agent or organised financial assistance for the families left behind. This is not so surprising: why would any emotions come across in the literature? Official SNCF correspondence was not the place to discuss the Jewish question, or even broader questions of morality (when these were not linked to professional conduct).

And yet, a close examination of the archives lets us peer into the tensions, fears and distress which the radicalisation of Jewish persecution triggered within the ranks of the SNCF. Indeed, just like the arrest of Henri Lang sparked a wave of anxiety in the ranks of the upper management, the arrest of Allant reveals real concern for the fate of this agent. At first glance, the official correspondence regarding his intervention reveals nothing more than mundane paper pushing : 'Following our transmission PB1 on 14 January 1944. I am honoured to attach herewith the copy of a letter from the head of the Subdivision of Supply in regards to the conditions in which the supervisor Allant Ferdinand (...) has been incarcerated by the Germans'. However, two separate messages are scribbled on one of the notes. The first: 'Take note, act quickly ...'; the second: 'When regarding the incarceration of an agent please intervene immediately (....) we must be diligent in order to save [him] a few days of detention, always very difficult to endure on a moral and physical level, if it is not in fact a matter of life or death'.[53] There is clearly, here, a level of understanding of the critical nature of the situation, as well as a real anxiety and fear about Allant's fate. Those pushing papers knew only too well that his arrest and internment were bad signs of things to come.

We find this concern elsewhere, especially in the documentation after the liberation when SNCF pension funds were being distributed to families of deceased agents. Since there were so many cases of no-returns, whereby death was in no way certified, a lot of post-war paperwork involved tracing agents' family members and identifying who to pay pensions to or, in case it was needed, who to support with benefits. As previously mentioned, Boudin was arrested at the same time as his wife, and both died in the camps. As such, the Chief Inspector of Material and

Tragedy After the Liberation' available at http://lfhm2014.com/2014/01/06/paperwork-for-non-returning-deportees-bureaucracy-and-tragedy-after-the-liberation-by-ludivine-broch/.
[53] SNCF/303/LM/11: Allant, Letter (May 1944) from Pesez to the Chef des Services Administratifs. The emphasis is in the original document.

179

Traction Workshops (South-West) wrote that 'Boudin's parents aged 90 and 86 are asking if they can receive the sum which is due to their son since his internment. I would be very much obliged if you could look into what can be done immediately to help sort this interesting matter'.[54] However, if the allocation of Boudin's salary could not be carried out at this stage (he was still noted as missing in Germany), they suggested giving 1,000 francs to help the elderly parents.[55] This sum is then disputed in a subsequent letter, when the Head of the Department of Material and Traction writes by hand agreeing to send them 1,000 francs, and on the bottom of the document, however, you see scribbled the words 'that's slim'; the original sum is then crossed out, and someone has written 2,000 instead.[56] The many messages in this letter suggest a level of understanding of the difficult situation of Boudin's parents, and a worry about their welfare. The humanism of the men working within the various divisions of the SNCF does, at times, come across, piercing through the administrative language which otherwise dominates the archives.

But were these concerns for Boudin, Allant and the others based on the fact that these men were Jewish? Or were they concerned because these were cheminots? I would argue that it was the latter. This of course is not because those working for the SNCF disliked the Jews; in fact, without wanting to draw any universal conclusions in regards to the SNCF or railwaymen, there are no more traces of virulent antisemitism in the SNCF than there are of philosemitism. What emerges from the archives is a concern for colleagues and their families, a concern which was linked not only to a real professionalism and a community spirit, but also to the radicalisation of the persecution of cheminots which coincided with that of Jews.

If cheminots became more concerned with the fate of their Jewish colleagues it is not so much because they realised the intensification of *Jewish* persecution per say, but rather that they saw the intensification of repression throughout French society, and not least amongst their own personnel. As previously mentioned, the SNCF management described the forced labour service as a 'bloodletting'.[57] They were seriously feeling the burden of German economic pressures. They tolerated less and less the relentless threats against their personnel. Indeed, SNCF directors

[54] *Ibid.*, Boudin, Letter (9 Apr. 1945) from Ingénieur to Chef du Bureau Principal Régional de la Solde. The emphasis is in the original document.
[55] *Ibid.*, Boudin, Letter (3 May 1945) to Monsieur Chef du Service MT.
[56] *Ibid.*, Boudin, Letter (May 1945) signed Barois.
[57] AN/72/AJ/1927: Minutes (31 Mar. 1943).

had rushed to help the seven cheminots condemned to death over the sabotage in Ascq in April 1944, showing a real shift in their attitude towards sabotage acts and the Germans themselves.[58]

This section will close with a letter which captures the tensions between knowledge and complicity, between racial and professional repression, between the leadership and the cheminots. In particular it reveals the entanglement between the persecution of cheminots on the one hand, and Jews on the other. In late March 1943, the Director of the North Region, Cambournac, wrote an urgent letter to Robert Le Besnerais:

I believe I must inform you about an incident which took place on 25 March at the Bourget station between a German officer and our personnel. On 25 March, the DA 901 train transporting Jews from Bourget-Drancy to Novéant was supposed to leave the Bourget station at 8h55. However, following a communication error, this train was ordered for Bourget for 26 March instead of 25. At around 6h30 on 25 March, the Bourget station was told by the local German surveillance team that the train was due for the 25th and not the 26th. Measures were immediately taken to organise this train as quickly as possible. After boarding, the train drove off at 10h45, thus with a delay of one hour and fifty minutes. It is during the formation of this train that Mr Benoit, Station Master at Bourget, was grossly insulted by an German officer in conditions which are described in the attached report.[59]

Although the letter opens with a reference to the Jewish convoy n°53 – which went to Sobibor, not Auschwitz, and contained over 100 children – it is principally focussed on the interaction between the German officer and the cheminot Benoit. Towards the end, Cambournac explodes in frustration: 'Such procedures cannot improve relations between the Occupation authorities and our agents who are already working under very difficult conditions. You will surely find it necessary to alert the HVD Paris of this affair or even to approach the German military authorities so that an enquiry on this officer's behaviour can be opened'. Cambournac wrote another letter reporting the incident directly to the Germans, the WVD, on 30 March 1943. He directly warned them that such 'incidents' must stop at once if they were to expect the trains to run on time.[60]

This correspondence is significant for two main reasons. First, it shows the raw emotions of the Director of the North Region. In this letter, Cambournac is reeling with anger over the mistreatment of one of his agents. Indeed, the incident between the cheminot and the German officer symbolised much more than a mere insult: it was about a general

---

[58] *Ibid.*, Minutes (29 Nov. 1943).
[59] ANMT/202/AQ/201: Letter (31 Mar. 1943) from Cambournac to Le Besnerais.
[60] *Ibid.*, Letter (30 Mar. 1943) from Cambournac to Wehrmacht-Verkehrs Direktion (WVD).

frustration over the miscommunication in Franco-German operations, the disrespect of French material and personnel and the growing threat on railway workers who were all too often the victims of German abuse. Second, the backdrop to this letter is the Holocaust. The mere mention of Jewish trains is a rarity in SNCF correspondence, let alone in either internal letters within the company, or letters directly to German officials. Is the mention of the convoy merely a logistical detail, or does Cambournac's fury also include a general disgust over the entire situation: the last minute scheduling of Jewish convoys, the deportations themselves and the unjustified pressures the cheminots were being put under?

Despite being both shocking and obscure, this letter should not be misunderstood for an explicit proof of indifference to the Jewish convoy. Rather, it reveals the frustrations of employers, frustrations which were rooted in professional concern but were no less emotional or intense. The fragility of the railways and its community in the Second World War was generating greater unity in professional interests and concerns, one which overlooked class as much as it did race. If anything the letter confirms earlier conclusions: that the protection of cheminot personnel – Jewish or not – was the most pressing concern.

3   Deportations of summer 1942

It is important to bear in mind the predominance of this bureaucratic, professional outlook when discussing the Jewish deportations. If the deportations from France are today a hallmark of national memory, at the time they were considered part of an on-going occupation, but had no real specificity to them. Between March 1942 and August 1944, 79 convoys left from France to Nazi concentration and extermination camps, and the SNCF's involvement – whether firing Jews or deporting them – would remain first and foremost administrative. Logistics and professionalism prevailed. Tracing the layers of the bureaucratic process reveals the extent of the SNCF's involvement that occurred separately from those of the Nazi officials in Berlin, the men in Vichy, the prefects and the local population.

The role of the Reichsbahn in this web of organisation merits to be briefly underlined before discussing the deportations from France. The persecution of Jews took a radical turn in 1941 as a specific plan for the Final Solution began to unfold.[61] Adolf Eichmann, head of Jewish

---

[61] The unfolding of the Final Solution falls beyond the realm of this book. For more information, see Christopher Browning, *The Origins of the Final Solution : The Evolution*

affairs, received orders in regards to the Final Solution which he then passed on to a complex web of individuals who worked under him. Raul Hilberg has traced – in considerable detail – the line of command to order these convoys: Eichmann's immediate subordinates were Rolf Günther, in charge of the general evacuation process across Europe, and Franz Novak, who linked the RSHA with the Reich Transportation Ministry and the RB to organise the details of railway transportation. The transports were then organised by the RB, whose central offices liaised with administrative bodies set up in occupied territories to supervise national railways. In France, for instance, the RB controlled the HVD in Paris.[62] Indeed, the RB were central in controlling the flow of convoys all across the Reich territory, and Hilberg's study underlines how the deportations played to the beat of the German railroads. Of course, one must be careful not to reduce the Holocaust to railway convoys: as recent scholarship shows, the map of the murdered Jews of Europe reaches far beyond the limits of the concentration camps: homes, streets, prisons, ghettos, mass graves scattered all over Europe became sites of genocide.[63] Likewise, Jews were also transported by truck, by boat and by foot, not only by train.

But if Hilberg's study showed that the RB was central to the Final Solution, Alfred Mierzejewski later demonstrated that the Final Solution was never central to the RB. The Jewish deportation transports were integrated into an already efficient system, fitting into a tight schedule which organised millions of convoys across Europe. Jewish convoys were a needle in a haystack: 'The Reichsbahn ran an average of 30,000 trains per day in 1941 and 1942, declining to about 23,000 trains per day in 1944. In contrast, the [Deutsche Reichsbahn] operated an average of just under two Jewish transports (...) per day'.[64] Far from having any kind of priority, Jewish convoys were considered 'special trains', which an official directive on 14 July 1941 defined as 'not absolutely essential to the war effort'.[65] Deportation trains did not have priority over railway

---

of *Nazi Jewish policy, Sept. 1939–Mar. 1942* (Lincoln: University of Nebraska Press; Jerusalem: Yad Vashem, 2004); Florent Brayard, *La 'solution finale de la question juive': la technique, le temps et les catéfories de la décision* (Paris: Fayard, 2004); Peter Longerich, *Holocaust : The Nazi Persecution and Murder of the Jews* (Oxford: Oxford University Press, 2010).

[62] Hilberg discusses the organisation and funding of the Jewish transports; see Hilberg, *The Destruction of the European Jews* (2003) 424–33.

[63] See, for example, Timothy Snyder, *Bloodlands: Europe between Hitler and Stalin* (London: Bodley Head, 2010).

[64] Alfred Mierzejeski, 'A Public Enterprise in the Service of Mass Murder: The Deutsche Reichsbahn and the Holocaust', *Holocaust Genocide Studies*, vol. 15, n°1 (2001) 36.

[65] Guckes, 'Le rôle des chemins de fer' (1999) 68.

equipment, either. Therefore, if no freight cars or locomotives could be allocated due to wartime pressures, the deportations were put on hold.

In order to implement the Final Solution in France, Eichmann relied on two components: the network of local SS organisations, and Vichy. Indeed, '[the RSHA's] central office was in Berlin, but it realized its full power and potential on a local level'.[66] Helmut Knochen had been sent to Paris soon after the Armistice was signed, where he became Head of the Gestapo. Within his services, Theodor Dannecker was appointed head of the Jewish Affairs Department. Knochen and Dannecker organized Jewish persecution in the Occupied Zone with mass round ups and internments in 1941.[67] To this end, they worked closely with Vichy police officials and minsters. At the same time, Vichy also initiated anti-Jewish legal policies. Moreover, in March 1941, it had created the CGQJ, placing the renowned antisemite Xavier Vallat at its head. Dannecker was therefore right to assume that Vichy would be willing to cooperate in the deportation of Jews from its territory.

On 11 June 1942, Eichmann invited the representatives of Jewish Affairs from France, Belgium and the Netherlands, to Berlin to discuss the deportations from Western Europe. For several months now, Germany had been deporting its own Jews. In the meeting, Eichmann explained that they were having problems requisitioning enough railway equipment to continue these deportations. It had therefore been decided to halt these deportations temporarily, and to focus on deporting Jews from Western occupied territories.[68] At the end of that meeting, Dannecker promised Eichmann 100,000 Jews, almost a third of the Jewish population in France.[69] When Dannecker returned to Paris on 15 June, he issued an important note outlining the guidelines for the upcoming deportations. The major terms of the deportations had already been decided at the meeting in Berlin: over a period of three months, 40,000 Jews would initially be deported. They would be allowed to take their own personal belongings on the journey, while the French would have to

---

[66] Michael Wildt, 'Generation of the Unbound: The Leadership Corps of the Reich Security Main Office', Paper presented at a lecture at the International Institute for Holocaust Research at Yad Vashem on 23 Jan. 2002 (Jerusalem, Yad Vashem, 2002) 20.

[67] On Dannecker, see Klarsfeld, *Vichy-Auschwitz* (2001) 38–42.

[68] Likewise, deportations from France were halted during the winter of 1942 for lack of railway equipment. In view of this lapse in the deportation programmes – which was due to the growing need for railway equipment on the eastern front, which was made more difficult by winter conditions – German officials tried to increase the rate of deportations from France in September 1942. This was unsuccessful. See Bachelier Report, 4.3.5. Les déportations de juifs de France en 1942.

[69] Klarsfeld, *Vichy-Auschwitz* (2001) 69–72.

provide (and pay for) food and water to last 15 days for each individual Jew. Each deportation convoy would consist of '1 locomotive, 3 passenger cars for the security guards, and 20 freight cars'.[70] Over the next ten days, Dannecker was involved in a series of other meetings where the projects and plans for the deportations were refined. Klarsfeld's detailed overview of these meetings underlines Dannecker's initial crucial role in the organisation of the deportations from France.[71] On 26 June, 1942, he had drawn up a 'set of rules (*Richtlinien*) for the deportation of the French Jews' whereby he not only determined who exactly would be deported (according to age limit and nationality), but also the exact list of things which Jews could bring with them : 'two pairs of socks, two shirts, two pairs of under drawers, a towel, a cup, a spoon, etc.'.[72]

Hilberg rightly stated that, by the end of June, 'the transport difficulty was partially overcome' – indeed, the doubts over whether or not there was enough railway material to deport Jews had been discarded, and everything was being put into place to start the deportations imminently. As Bachelier has shown, from mid- to late-June Dannecker was liaising with the HVD Paris to organise the first convoys. However, now that the trains were ready, they had to be filled. On 16 June, Bousquet confirmed that he would help German authorities gather the desired number of Jews. However, on 26 June 1942, in an unexpected twist, Laval retracted Bousquet's offer to assist the Germans in these operations in both the free and occupied zones.[73] Did the leaders in Vichy suddenly get a guilty conscience for handing over Jews to their worst enemies? In light of the Bousquet-Oberg accord which followed shortly after, and which permanently tied the French forces into the Nazis' system of repression and extermination, the possibility of an internal moral dilemma is unlikely. Rather, the population was uneasy in 1942, and support for Pétain and his regime was shifting. Vichy was concerned that an overt Franco-German collaboration would encourage more social upheavals.[74]

Dannecker was deeply preoccupied by the government's sudden retraction. He wrote to Karl Oberg, supreme head of the SS and the French police, and to Helmut Knochen, Secretary General of the Gestapo, sharing his concerns. Without the assistance of the French police, it would be extremely difficult to gather and deport 100,000 Jews. First, there was a human shortage of German police, since so many had

---

[70] Bachelier Report, 4.3.5.   [71] See Klarsfeld, *Vichy-Auschwitz* (2001) 72–84.

[72] Hilberg, *The Destruction of the European Jews* (2003) 406.

[73] Klarsfeld, *Vichy-Auschwitz* (2001) 86; 97.

[74] Another possible reason behind Laval's sudden hesitance was his personal vexation that Bousquet had not followed diplomatic decorum when failing to inform Laval of the offer he had made to Heydrich earlier in May. Klarsfeld, *Vichy-Auschwitz* (2001) 86.

been called to the Eastern front. Second, without the local geographical knowledge, or the mastery of the language, it was almost impossible to carry out searches.[75] Therefore, if the French were unwilling to hand over the Jews from the Free Zone, Dannecker would be unable to meet the quota he had promised Eichmann. However, on 3 July, Laval and Pétain both agreed to proceed with Bousquet's original offer.[76] The Bousquet-Oberg accord was confirmed, and the imminent deportation of 22,000 Jews from the Occupied Zone was announced.[77]

On 10 July, a meeting was held in Darquier de Pellepoix's office, who had replaced Xavier Vallat as the new Commissar of Jewish Affairs in May 1942. That day, the French and the Germans planned the round up of the Vel d'Hiv. It took place on 16–17 July 1942, and saw the immediate arrest of 13,000 Jews by 9,000 French police.[78] Ribeill notes that one SNCF representative was present at this meeting – 'probably a senior civil servant from the Central Services of Movement' – yet his actual role seems passive more than anything else – His presence was dictated by the need to regularly empty Drancy as indicated in the 8th instruction: 'The first transport must leave on 21 July, at latest on 22 July. (...) Other convoys will follow at 2-day intervals, which means a total of 3 convoys per week'.[79] A representative of the SNCF (name unknown) was present at a crucial meeting on 10 July 1942. Alongside Dannecker, his colleagues, representatives from the Prefecture of the Seine, the Police Prefecture, and the director of the Vel d'Hiv, the first Jewish convoy as part of the Final Solution was arranged to leave France.

Summarising the decision-making process of the deportations from France reveals how, within this web of organisation emanating from Berlin, Paris and Vichy, no decisions were actually made by the SNCF,

---

[75] On the importance of the French police, see Marrus and Paxton, *Vichy France and the Jews* (1981) 241–3. For more information about the police, see Simon Kitson, 'The police and the deportation of Jews from the Bouches-du-Rhône in August and September 1942', *Modern and Contemporary France*, vol. 5, n° 3, August 1997, 309–19.

[76] Klarsfeld, *Vichy-Auschwitz* (2001) 107–9. Aside from this intervention, Marrus and Paxton argue that Pétain was not as directly involved as Laval in the deportations, and he would occasionally intervene on behalf of some personal acquaintance or war veteran. On the other hand, Laval followed the affairs closely and generally supported the deportations of Jews (Laval did, however, make distinctions between French and foreign Jews) as long as it meant that he could maintain a certain bargaining power in the endless power struggles with the German authorities regarding an array of issues. Marrus and Paxton, *Vichy France and the Jews* (1981) 261–2.

[77] The exact number of Jews from the Free Zone was still unknown. CDJC/XXVb-52: Letter (7 Jul. 1942) from Dannecker to Knochen.

[78] Marrus and Paxton, *Vichy and the Jews* (1981) 250.

[79] Georges Ribeill, 'A propos du wagon couvert K, dit "wagon à bestiaux": de la réglementation militaires à ses détournements', *Historail*, 4 (2008) 70.

not even choosing cattle cars to deport the Jews. In fact, choosing cattle cars to transport people en masse was not as rare as one might think. Cattle cars were first used to transport men in wartime during the Franco-Prussian war in 1870–71: indeed, although built for transporting goods, these cars could efficiently transport people en masse. In article 48 of the General Rules of 1 July 1874, it was declared that Type 'K' cattle cars would be used to transport soldiers, prisoners or wounded men.[80] In fact, during the exodus of May–June 1940, the SNCF had had to use type 'K' cars to deal with the massive population movement. The historian Jean Vidalenc related the story of one woman who was in charge of escorting a hundred orphans from the *Gare d'Austerlitz*. She boarded a freight car along with the children, and was traumatised by 'the horrid race of refugee trains ... the sliding doors are closed and those inside cannot open them anymore'. In some rail cars, the refugees barely had a single sanitary bucket: '... one refugee wrote to the prefect of Aveyron demanding that each goods wagon being used for the purpose of repatriation include a bucket or some appropriate installation for hygiene purposes'.[81]

The Germans were initially undecided as to whether or not they should use cattle cars for the Jewish convoys – indeed, the demand for goods' transport throughout Europe was so high that material was not easily spared. So after cattle cars were used for the first time to transport Jews on 5 June 1942, the HVD Paris was instructed to go back to using passenger cars, like they had on 27 March. Heinz Röthke, who had recently been nominated to replace Dannecker as head of Jewish Affairs, underlined that this change called for an excessive amount of security. According to estimates, a convoy of freight cars required 16 guards (including one leader), whereas a convoy of cattle cars required 200 guards.[82] So if the HVD had been advised to use traveller cars in order to save freight cars for goods transports, Röthke argued that they could not expect to mobilise the large number of men to supervise such cars under short notice. This point would have been decisive, and cattle cars became the norm.

These sources are a strong reminder that Germans controlled the transports from Drancy to Auschwitz, and that the SNCF was nothing more than a cog in a wheel; however, the transfer of 13,000 Jews from

---

[80] Ribeill, 'A propos du wagon couvert K' (2008) 72.

[81] See A. Jacques, *Pitié pour les hommes*, cited in Vidalenc, *L'Exode* (1957) 262–4. Diamond, *Fleeing Hitler* (2007) 154.

[82] CDJC/XXVb-28: Telegram (16 May 1942) from Guenther to Knochen; CDJC/XXVb-86: Letter (20 Jul. 1942) from Röthke to Eichmann.

internment camps in the Free Zone to Drancy between August and October 1942 was carried out by the French. Did this mean that the SNCF have more space for manoeuvre? Not quite. As Bachelier has pointed out, the decision-making process was a well-oiled machine which had been set in place for earlier deportations and transfers. In 1940, the local Nazi Party leaders of recently annexed Baden and Saar-Palatinate, Gauleiters Wagner and Bürkel wanted to purge the area of non-Aryans. Heinrich Himmler, Chief of the SS, agreed to send thousands of Jews into the French non-Occupied Zone.[83] The subsequent deportation of almost 8,000 Jews from Bade-Palatinat in nine mass convoys on 22 October 1940 would be one of the SNCF's first involvements in deportations of Jews. In another example, the French railway company was involved in organising mass transports of North African workers in 1941.[84] The latter case set a precedent which would be repeated to a certain extent with the upcoming Jewish transfers: 'The procedure starts with a governmental decision which triggers the gathering of the administrations involved. Amongst them, there is a sponsor, the [Ministry of] Interior, and those who execute the orders. During the execution of the order itself, the Technical Delegation of the SNCF is linked to the Ministry of Interior via the general management of the Ministry in charge of transports. This intermediary eventually disappears'.[85]

The SNCF became directly involved in the Jewish transfers from the Free Zone on 15 July 1942, at a meeting organised by the Ministry of Interior in Vichy to plan the arrests of Jews in the Free Zone and their transfer to the Occupied Zone. Bachelier suspects that Dannecker attended the meeting since he was in the Free Zone at that time, but his presence is unverified. The SNCF's Head of the Technical Delegation was present, however.[86] He underlined the need for discretion, and suggested naming these special transports 'transports IATP (Israélites allemands, tchécoslovaques, polonaise)', after the Jewish, German, Czechoslovak and Polish deportees it contained. He also voiced his concern about the lack of rigid programming: contrary to their reputation of punctuality and rigidity, Germans tended to modify their plans at the

---

[83] According to Eichmann, this was an impulsive request on behalf of Himmler, and his own Bureau IV B 4 had to organize the transport with the RTM (Reich Transportation Ministry). Jochen von Lang, ed. *Eichmann Interrogated, Transcripts from the Archives of the Israeli Police* (London, The Botley Head Ltd, 1983) 72.
[84] Bachelier Report, 4.3.1. Les convois de juifs expulsés d'Allemagne vers la zone libre, octobre 1940 ; Bachelier Report 4.3.7.
[85] Bachelier Report, 4.3.7.
[86] *Ibid.*, Bachelier later refers to this man – the head of the Délégation Technique in Vichy, as a Mr 'Schultz' (or spelled 'Schutz').

last minute, and this seriously disrupted the general railway traffic.[87] So as long as they did not alter the established programme, there would be no problem.

Several decisions about the transfers were made at that meeting, for example, that the trains would cross the demarcation line at Chalon and Belfort, and that they would use third class carriages. It is unclear who exactly was making these precise suggestions, and soon after 'the Technical Delegation informed the SNCF Central Movement Services' with these plans. This service subsequently submitted a timetable on 24 July. But according to Bachelier, 'A second meeting was organised on the 27th. New principles were laid out for the transfer from the southern zone: Drancy was the destination; the line would be crossed at Chalon; convoys would consist of third class carriages (...); Marseille would be avoided; in Toulouse and Avignon, convoys would be sealed outside of the stations'.[88] Again, it is unclear exactly how these decisions were made, but we see a very real pattern. First, nothing was fixed from the start, and a number of changes were made along the line. For example, the first transports were originally organised for 8, 12, 14 and 20 August – from the camps in Gurs, Le Vernet, Noé, Le Récébédou, Rivesaltes, Les Milles, Nexon, Vénissieux, Nice, Saint Sulpice, Septfonds, Casseneuil and Montluçon to Drancy – but at the last minute, the dates were brought forward to 6, 8, 10 and 12 August.[89] Such last minute changes deeply irritated the SNCF, who was fastidious about punctuality. Indeed, when the timetables were disrupted, the SNCF did not fail to blame the shortcomings of the local authorities, or the indecisiveness of the Germans.

Second, a series of meetings initiated by the Ministry of Interior in the summer of 1942 were the starting point of this decision-making process. Thus, decisions were made in Vichy by the highest authorities, and the SNCF delegation present at these meetings then informed the Central Movement Services of the decisions and procedures to follow. The latter then accommodated the logistics accordingly. In fact, the Central Services of the SNCF were made aware of the details of the transfer transports at the same time as other local authorities. Indeed, '[o]n 1 August, the SNCF delegation in Vichy informed the Central Services of

---

[87] *Historique de la Délégation technique SNCF de Vichy 1940–1942*, 59. The document is reproduced in Bachelier Report, Annexe II: Des comptes rendus ferroviaires des déportations.

[88] Bachelier Report, 4.3.7.

[89] AN/F/7/15088: Handwritten Report, 'Réunion chez Mr Foucade – Mr Schutz'. See map of French internment camps for Jews in Anne Grynberg, *Les camps de la honte: les internés juifs des camps étrangers français 1939–1944* (Paris: Editions La Découverte, 1998) 9.

Movement and its delegations in Lyon and Limoges. That same day, Henry Cado, director of the National Police, wrote a series of telegrams to prefects and Police intendants in the Southern Zone detailing the preparation of transports'.[90]

Apart from the timetables, the SNCF's Central Movement Services did not decide very much. The planning of the convoys – number of cars, hay, pitchers, toilet buckets – all came from the Ministry of Interior.[91] Likewise, the allocation of food stuffs: Laval wrote directly to the Minister of Agriculture and Supplies on 29 July 1942 with orders to prepare provisions for the Jewish transfer convoys. In the interest of maintaining public order, '. . . it is absolutely essential that each individual concerned must be supplied, before departure, with enough vital goods to last the entire journey. Therefore, I ask that, two days before the planned departure, you distribute extra rations to the camps of Gurs, Le Vernet, Les Milles, Rivesaltes and Récébédou, in order that those concerned will have enough to last them 48 hours. I must insist on giving the lodgers an appropriate food supply, which will last them their entire transport, as this will prevent any kind of incident'.[92] Once these transports reached the demarcation line – usually at Chalon-sur-Saône[93] – the supplies they had been given (covers, pitchers, toilet buckets) were returned to the French authorities, who then sent them back to the camps.[94]

Prefects often criticised the SNCF for their conduct of the Jewish transports from the Free Zone to Drancy. The Prefecture of the Basse-Pyrénées complained about the SNCF's inadequate performance in these transports: 'The SNCF only gave us two baggage cars instead of three, as it had been agreed', and as a result they put some of the luggage in the cars with the passengers.[95] The Prefect from the Pyrénées-Orientales wrote that 'the cars being used were not only in a bad state, but they were very dirty when they arrived on the platform'.[96] The Prefect of the Saône-et-Loire directly criticised a cheminot for having sped through the

---

[90] Bachelier Report, 4.3.7.

[91] *Ibid.*, It is not known exactly where these orders first originated, although it is likely that they were enforced by the highest authorities in the French government.

[92] AN/F/7/15088: Letter (29 Jul. 1942) from Laval, stamped and signed by the Préfet Directeur Général Adjoint.

[93] Other stations on the border were also used, such as Moulins, Vierzon, L'Hommaize, Montpont, Langon and Orthez. Gérard Gobitz, *Les déportations de réfugiés de zone libre en 1942* (Paris: L'Harmattan, 1996) 281.

[94] AN/F/7/15088: Telegrams (30 Jul. 1942) from Police 2ème Bureau to Prefects of Bouches du Rhone and Saone-et-Loire.

[95] *Ibid.*, Letter (11 Aug. 1942) from Prefect of the Basses Pyrénées.

[96] *Ibid.*, Letter (17 Aug. 1942) from Prefect of the Pyrénées-Orientales.

Tournus station instead of stopping the train there – he accused the cheminot of having 'read his instructions wrong'.[97]

On the other hand, the railway company criticised the local authorities for the delays in the timetable. The Head of the Technical Delegation wrote a stern letter to the police authorities on 26 August 1942: 'on 24 August, the special IATP train ran in the most deplorable conditions. This was the result of the local service who (...) made mistakes and oversights'. 'I cannot emphasise enough' he declared, 'how the delays which this caused seriously disrupted the traffic. The train itself was completely off time, but, equally, all the other commercial trains were affected'.[98] The humanitarian organisations assisting Jews until the demarcation line were also a problem. In regards to the Jewish convoy leaving Nice on 31 August, 'there were too many representatives from charitable organisations, either before the train departure, or during the halts along the journey (...) Aside from the inconveniences that have just been cited, this has caused a delay which gradually worsened, and which caused great disruption on the entire traffic flow, forcing the SNCF to make severe remarks'. It was decided that humanitarian associations would get in touch with the SNCF beforehand: 'the SNCF can be warned far enough in advance in order to allow longer halts in the said stations'.[99]

With hindsight, these concerns with timetable delays seem petty, but from the perspective of the deportees, delays were insufferable. Life inside these transfer transports was very difficult. The journey was lengthy, mostly because the northbound train would make long stops in order to allow other trains from different internment camps to attach themselves.[100] Even though the deportees were supposed to get between 2 and 5 days' worth of food, the amounts were insufficient. Furthermore, the food distributed to them was often inappropriate: tomatoes and fruit caused severe cases of indigestion – a condition which was especially difficult to endure considering the huge lack of sanitation – or sardines and *saucisson* (French dried sausage) which were too salty and remained uneaten for fear that water supplies would run out.[101] Although

---

[97] *Ibid.*, Letter (14 Aug. 1942) from the Prefect of Saône-et-Loire.

[98] *Ibid.*, Letter (26 Aug. 1942) from the Délégation Technique de la SNCF.

[99] *Ibid.*, Note (19 Sept. 1942) for Directeur de la Police du Territoire et des Etrangers, 9ème Bureau.

[100] Cited in Anne Boitel, *Le camp de Rivesaltes 1941–1942: du centre d'hébergement au 'Drancy de la zone libre'* (Perpignan: Presse Universitaire de Perpignan: Mare Nostrum, 2001) 255.

[101] CDJC/CCXIX-31: Anonymous Jewish deportee, Deported 24 Jan. 1943 from Marseille.

humanitarian organisations lined up at various stations to distribute books, food, water and moral support, conditions were completely inadequate. Raymond Raoul Lambert was horrified by the events of August 1942: 'I have just witnessed the most tragic scenes of my entire life, since the last war. My country has dishonoured itself by conducting inhumane persecutions'.[102]

4   Controversies around deportation

Aside from the SNCF's involvement in the decision-making process, there are other controversies around French railways in the Holocaust. The first is the question of the payment. Those who have accused the SNCF of complicity in these deportations – Schaechter, Lipietz, Delpard – have all pointed towards a handful of documents whereby, even after the liberation of France, the SNCF was still requesting for payment vis-à-vis the Jewish transports it carried out during the Occupation. There seem to be two documents in particular: one letter, dated 29 May 1945, was from the Ministry of Interior who wrote that the SNCF had just sent them a bill for 166,618 francs for transporting Jews from Les Milles to Drancy in August 1942. The other was a bill from the SNCF's financial offices to, once again, the Ministry of Interior. It was dated 12 August 1944 and referred to the transfer of Jews 'from the Noé camp at the demand/expense of the prefecture of the Haute-Garonne'.[103] This would allegedly prove the SNCF's culpability in profiteering from a crime against humanity.

Bachelier and Ribeill have, however, closely examined the question of billing the Jewish convoys and come up with far more nuanced interpretations. First, Bachelier underlined that the SNCF was paid for *all* of its services, and in doing so it established a clear distinction between who ordered the transport, and who executed the transport. There were, however, some rare charitable gestures such as the delivery of POW parcels at Christmas time.[104] For Bachelier, this removes the moral question entirely: if the SNCF committed a moral crime it was that it had accepted to carry out these transports, not that it got paid for them. As Annette Wieviorka has stated, it would have been more controversial had the SNCF *not* been paid for these services, thereby implying some sort of agency and/or free will.[105]

---

[102] See Raymond-Raoul Lambert, *Carnet d'un témoin* (Paris: Fayard, 1985) 177–89.
[103] Ribeill, *Historail* (2008) 84.
[104] Bachelier Report: 4.3.13. Le règlement des transports de déportation.
[105] Wieviorka, 'La SNCF' (2007) 97–8.

Bachelier and Ribeill also emphasise the distinction between the deportation convoys from the Occupied Zone to the Reich on one hand, and the transfers between camps and zones within French territory on the other. The former were ordered, and paid for, by the Germans; the latter, however, were not deportations as such but rather transfers within French territory. The few documents relating to 1942 suggest that 'the French prefectures appear to be the main interlocutor with the SNCF'.[106] The French Ministry of Interior also appears to have been responsible for paying some of the transportation costs in the Occupied Zone. In a letter to the SNCF's Commercial Services regarding the transfer of Jews from Paris-Austerlitz to Pithiviers and Beaune-la-Rolande on 19 and 22 July 1942, the Director of Police asked that the bill for the transportation of the *French police escorts* who accompanied these convoys be addressed to the Ministry of Interior. He added in this letter that the cost of transporting the Jews in these convoys might also 'eventually' be billed to the Ministry of Interior. As Ribeill points out this 'eventually' highlights the lack of clarity and transparency about who, exactly, was paying for the transport of Jews requested by Germans. In a later correspondence regarding the final deportation of the Jews in Beaune-la-Rolande and Pithiviers to the camps, the division of costs for these transports becomes more apparent: 'Since these trains circulated on German demand, they will pay for them like they pay for those which depart from the Bourget-Drancy. That being said, the transport of the French escorts is charged to the French State, and will be billed to the Ministry of Interior . . .'[107]

Another major controversy is regarding the role of the SNCF's personnel, the cheminots. There is little information on cheminots' reactions to the deportations themselves, and the conclusions drawn from the archives are sometimes not much more than educated guesses. I have written extensively on this matter elsewhere, but certain issues deserve to be reiterated. Despite their involvement in the Shoah, men and women working for the SNCF did not necessarily know more about the Final Solution than the average French civilian. First, the proportion of Jewish transfers and deportation trains were a drop in the ocean of railway transports throughout the war, and since they tended to take the same trajectories only a handful of cheminots would have come into direct contact with them.[108] Second, few French people had any

---

[106] Bachelier Report, 4.3.13. Le règlement des transports de déportation; Ribeill reproduced this letter; see Ribeill, *Historail* (2008) 83.

[107] Ribeill reproduced this letter; see Ribeill, *Historail* (2008) 83.

[108] Broch, 'Professionalism in the Final Solution: French Railway Workers and the Jewish Deportations, 1942–1944', *Contemporary European History* 23.3 (2014) 359–81; Broch,

information about the targeted persecution of Jews. Unlike in Central and Eastern Europe where locals might have a clearer idea, it would seem that in France knowing bits of information and hearing rumours never equated to a full understanding of the extermination of Jews. Without a clear understanding of the consequences of deportation, protesting or intervening with the deportations did not necessarily seem worth the risk: 'Could we really stand up against something so mysterious?' asked the daughter of Henri Lang.[109]

But it is not the case that cheminots were blissfully unaware of the Jewish persecutions. Indeed, details of Jewish deportations were printed in the clandestine press, issues of which were regularly spread in railway sites.[110] The persecution of Jews was even mentioned in the cheminot underground press itself. However, Jewish persecution was assimilated with other sorts of repression in France at the time. The *Tribune des Cheminots*, wrote in 1942 that 'after the massive arrests of Jews, they've now arrested en masse the old trade union delegates and leaders who had remained the valiant defenders of their comrades [all this] in the hope of intimidating the mass of workers who they come to tear away from their homes'.[111] The specificity of the Jewish persecution or even deportations was never fully understood, not by the cheminots nor by much of the population. This in fact mirrors attitudes towards Jewish personnel in the SNCF who were considered to be persecuted colleagues more than persecuted Jews.

Finally, there is the question of railway sabotage: why were so many German military trains sabotaged, but never the Jewish convoys? As previously mentioned, cheminots' reluctance to sabotage trains carrying passengers meant that sabotaging Jewish convoys was not a natural reaction. It is vital to understand that cheminots never tampered with either Jewish or non-Jewish deportees after departure from the station. On a few occasions locals disrupted the STO convoys, but cheminots were never mentioned in the subsequent police reports.[112] Moreover, what would sabotaging a train of deportees do? If they did not come out of a sabotage dead or injured, where would these hundreds of men,

'French Railway Workers and the Question of Rescue in the Holocaust', *Diasporas* (Jun. 2015) forthcoming.

[109] AHICF: Catherine De Bechillon, interviewed for *Les Lois raciales*, documentary directed by Claude Binsse (Jun. 2000).

[110] See Broch, 'Rescue, Railways and the Righteous' (2015).

[111] SNCF/25/LM/258: 'Cheminots, opposez-vous aux départs en Allemagne', *La Tribune des cheminots*, Organe du Comité Populaire Central des Cheminots, dated Octobre 1942.

[112] Broch, 'Rescue, Railways and the Righteous' (2015).

women and children go? And what does one make of cheminots' gestures of support? After all, Germans were filing reports blaming cheminots for loosening floor planks and slowing down trains in order to make it easier for the internees to escape from the Jewish deportation convoys.[113] It is therefore by exploring these other gestures of support that one can better understand the link between cheminots and deportation trains – not by looking at the absence of sabotage.

Conclusion

Examining the involvement of the SNCF in the persecution and deportation of Jews offers insights into the Holocaust in France. First, it reveals the overlap between persecution and protection which certain French Jews received within their companies. The cases of Lang, Lévi and the other Jewish personnel are not unique in Vichy's history, and they contribute to a more complicated understanding of the relations between the French, the state and the Jews. Second, it confirms that the SNCF was a cog in the wheel of the Final Solution, and that it had no active decision-making role within the Holocaust. The German and French states held the reigns of this murderous operation, and the controversies around the SNCF are clouded by hindsight, emotion and judgement.

The study of both the SNCF's Jewish personnel and the deportations ultimately reinforces the importance of bureaucracy, professionalism and logistics throughout the SNCF personnel. It also shows levels of emotion and horror vis-à-vis the Jews who were excluded from French society and arrested by Germans and French alike. However, as has been argued, the archives indicate that this emotion had more to do with the fact that *colleagues* were being affected, rather than Jews. The specificity of Jewish antisemitic laws and later of Jewish convoys was never fully understood at the time. These events were considered part of a broader persecution across France, a persecution which cheminots were also victim to. Cheminots were neither philo- nor antisemites, nor were they necessarily indifferent to the fate of the Jews. Rather, they did their jobs, and at times we can see that they were trying to support colleagues and other victims of persecution, if and when they could.

[113] *Ibid.*

8   Liberation

On 25 August 1944, after four long years of occupation, Paris was finally liberated. Images of the events of that summer remain somewhat enshrined in local and national memory. Its legacy is inherently linked to the Resistance, showing the strength of France and its ultimate victory over Germans and fascism. The cheminots have their place in this history: they sabotaged the railway lines, paralysing transport and communications altogether, and they led the August insurrection. But these historic moments were not just about liberating France from the Germans – this was also about the liberation of workers who had newfound hope for their futures, their roles, their rights. 'In the summer of 1944, euphoria spread to the working classes', wrote Vigna, 'because considering the significance of the Resistance in the Liberation, and the strength of the communist party within the CGT, they felt they were in a position of strength (. . .). Was this finally the right time ?'[1]

The war in Germany, the purges, the dealings with the Americans and the on-going struggles with supplies and rationing would complicate this watershed moment. If the national elections in 1946 saw the rise of a unified left-wing block in government – a tri-party system combining the Socialist Party (SFIO), the *Mouvement Républicain Populaire* (MRP) and the French Communist Party which proved that there really was a certain degree of unity in post-war France – the strikes which erupted in 1947 challenged the idea that any real unity and change had been achieved. The veneer of patriotism and unity which had ensured the success of the 1944 strikes was dulled, and the old rancours and tensions had returned.

To what extent were the cheminots involved in the strikes of 1944? Were these bread strikes, or were they a popular insurrection? Did they buy into the atmosphere of unity and reconstruction which flavoured the post-liberation period? And after being so visibly absent from the strikes

[1] Vigna, *Histoire des ouvriers* (2012) 161.

in 1936, were they ready to join working-class protest in 1947? Understanding where the cheminots fit into the long story of French but also working-class liberation (1944–47) helps to further challenge myths of the *Bataille du Rail*, but also to understand the development of their professional and political identities between 1936 and 1947. In doing so, it is possible to draw certain conclusions in regards to the impact that Vichy had on this community.

1   Strikes and insurrection

The Liberation is a period often associated with the mass strikes of August 1944, but workers were already protesting earlier that Spring. On 21 March 1944, 6–8,000 metalworkers went on strike in Marseilles demanding more food supply and a salary increase.[2] The strike was aggressive and workers were not going to back down easily – that is, until the intervention of the *Kommandantur*. Indeed, the German authorities would not tolerate strikes[3], and the Prefect had to intervene: 'It is in these difficult conditions that [the prefect] decided to meet with delegations of workers and employers on the morning of the 22nd'.[4] On the afternoon of 22 March, 70% were back at work, and by the following morning no one was on strike anymore. The workers understood the risk they ran by not complying to his pleas to stop the strikes, and they also got assurance that their salaries would get raised to the same level as Parisian metalworkers.[5]

According to the Prefect, this had not been a communist political strike. 'In my region, the working-class milieu appears to place its hopes in M. Marcel DEAT', he wrote. And even if there had been some communist outcries, it was believed that the extremely difficult material conditions in Marseilles had been the major push behind the strikes.[6] The population had had no distribution of meat in February, there were no stocks of flour or cereal and the distributions of milk was grossly inadequate, 'provoking real anxieties about feeding children'. Not only that, but the Germans were doing massive seizures and evacuations of buildings in preparation for their military operations. These measures

---

[2] ADBR/76/W/218: Letter (26 Mar. 1944) from Prefet Régional de Marseille to Ministre du Travail.
[3] *Ibid.*, Letter (24 Apr. 1944) from Kommandantur Supérieure de Campagny to Préfets Régionaux à Marseille et Montpellier; Letter (19 Apr. 1944) from Arbeitseinsatzstab Marseille to the Inspecteur Divisionnaire du Travail.
[4] *Ibid.*, Letter (26 Mar. 1944) from Prefet Régional de Marseille to Ministre du Travail.
[5] *Ibid.*, Letter (31 Mar. 1944) from Sous-prefet d'Aix to Préfet Bouches-du-Rhône.
[6] *Ibid.*, Letter (26 Mar. 1944) from Prefet Régional de Marseille to Ministre du Travail.

may seem legitimate for the German military, the Prefect wrote, but the population had not been prepared for them at all.[7]

The conditions did not improve, however, and by May an acute shortage of bread was causing havoc. The prefecture sent an urgent message on 24 May: the 'serious situation in regards to flour provisions in the Marseille region' had led to some public manifestations. And if the situation did not improve immediately, they wrote, there was a serious risk that strikes and protests would erupt across the region.[8] This is exactly what happened. On 25 May, six bakers were arrested for selling bread and croissants on the black market when there was nothing to eat for anyone else.[9] At the same time, bread became the common slogan for the call to strike by the *Front National* and the CGT: '500 grams of bread', they cried, 'General strike for Bread'.[10] By the morning on 25 May, strikes had spread to a number of different industries, and there were approximately 12,000 workers on the streets, a third of whom were women.[11] On 27 May, arrested strikers were liberated, and certain workers were already heading back to work. But the Prefect believed it was in fact the bombing of Marseille that same day which changed things: the 'psychological shock' of the bombs had a real impact on the population in Marseille, and the workers had immediately gone back to work. The Prefect was nonetheless wary about the long-term effects: 'If the workers have understood what their duty called for at this tragic hour, there is reason to fear that the strike movement will re-surface if the bread ration is further reduced'.[12]

Cheminots were part of this upheaval, but they had not led it. The floors of *Gare Saint-Charles* were littered with tracts reading 'No Bread – No Work'. On 26 May, between 120 and 130 cheminots stopped work and gathered at the Honorat courtyard to hear their delegate report that the Prefect 'was maintaining the registration in the bakeries and supplementary tickets would be honoured'.[13] But before the delegate could continue, 'a German officer accompanied by armed men arrived and invited the cheminots to get back to work'. The reports of that afternoon suggest that cheminots returned to their work stations, but not all of

---

[7] *Ibid.*
[8] *Ibid.*, Telegram (24 May 1944) from Préfet Délégué Bouches-du-Rhône to Secrétaire Etat Intérieur.
[9] *Ibid.*, Communiqué de la Préfecture (25 May 1944).
[10] *Ibid.*, Tracts from Front National and CGT.
[11] *Ibid.*, Telegram (probably 25 May 1944) from Ministre Secrétaire Etat Ravitaillement to Laval and others.
[12] *Ibid.*, Letter (1 Jun. 1944) from Préfet Bouches-du-Rhône to Laval.
[13] *Ibid.*, Report (26 May 1944) on subject of strikes. This might, in fact, be rue Honnorat.

them went straight back to work. Eventually, at 15h50, 'machines started to come out of the depots', and ticket sales re-opened.

The decision to go on strike was not taken lightly. As Chevandier pointed out, miners and metalworkers repeatedly used strikes as tools during the Occupation, but cheminots did so less often. The *Service Fer* from the *Mouvements Unis de la Résistance* (MUR)[14] was itself wary about a general strike, warning cheminots over the BBC against taking any kind of disorganised action. They listed nine reasons as to why a general strike was a terrible idea, not least that 'if military operations ended up lasting for months on end, it would be impossible to hide 400,000 cheminots in the *maquis*', or that 'a strike would completely asphyxiate transports and cause famine in big [railway] centres'.[15] Instead, they preferred to encourage 'localised action', where consequences could be better monitored and controlled.

Cheminots did not always partake in local action and were, for example, absent from the workers' strikes in the Var region in July 1944.[16] However, this did not mean they were oblivious to the bread strikes. Along with other workers' delegations, they had approached the Prefect of the Var to try and obtain some form of assistance. The Prefect could only give them vague responses, although in some cases where workers were really desperate he allocated more wine.[17] Following these incidents, the Prefect warned the government that if flour did not arrive soon, and things did not improve, than they could only expect more protests.[18] In fact, protest was boiling over in other parts of France.

Cheminot strikes erupted in the Paris region in late July as they criedout for better working conditions. These strikes lasted longer than before: seven hours in the Villeneuve-Saint-Georges depot on 23 July, and an entire afternoon on 27 July in Noisy-le-Sec.[19] Before, strikes had lasted less than an hour, sometimes only one minute, and this increase in duration showed the boiling up of frustration and determination. Many other workers were also taking part in localised strikes. On the morning of 8 August, when there was no more bread available in the town, 88 women in La Ciotat did not show up to work at the *Maison GAMET* (leather goods).[20] Soon, the movement had spread to involve 2,400–2,800 locals – or

---

[14] Although Résistance-Fer did not exist as such, a small handful of resistance networks had a designated 'railway' section, such as MUR.

[15] Chevandier, *Cheminots en Grève* (2002) 207.

[16] ADBR/76/W/218: Letter (18 Jul. 1944) from Préfet du Var to Laval.   [17] *Ibid.*

[18] *Ibid.*

[19] Matthew Cobb, *Eleven Days in August: The Liberation of Paris in 1944* (London: Simon & Schuster, 2013) 20–1.

[20] ADBR/76/W/218: Report (8 August 1944) on strikes in La Ciotat.

'basically the whole population'.[21] The strike continued on the following day, and the *Kommandantur* in Marseille drove around the town with that afternoon, ordering factory workers to get back to work: if they did not follow these orders, then strikers would be arrested and 100 families would be immediately evacuated without luggage. Still, the strikers did not return to work, and the Germans carried out some arrests.[22]

Following from these local protests, a real insurrection began on 10 August when cheminots from Oullins and Paris started to go on strike. That morning, two men from outside of the SNCF arrived at the Noisy workshops in the Paris area and harangued the cheminots, sparking the very beginning of a strike. The movement was not completely spontaneous: the foreman, Mr Vallencien, had already known of this potential strike the evening before and had informed the police.[23] Moreover, the CGT was calling for a general strike, and workers were beginning to take part in an organised protest. Matthew Cobb gives a gripping detailed account of these railway strikes in mid-August, not least in Noisy: strikers downed tools, occupied their workplace, and threw hot coals onto the tracks. This was countered by immediate repression from the Germans, who arrested dozens of cheminots across the Paris region, using fear and force to calm the strikes.[24]

The strikes spread throughout the railway milieu over the next few weeks, peaking and dropping at different moments in different localities. By 14 August the movement was somewhat quelled, until it re-exploded through the call for general strikes from illegal syndicates on 18 August.[25] The works of Cobb, Chevandier and Bruno Carrière offer excellent insights into, and detailed analyses of, this month of August.[26] They reflect on the network of strikes across France, with different contexts and consequences in each town, each region. They also highlight the effervescence of violence in these last days of the Occupation. Indeed, these strikes were sometimes accompanied by considerable violence, such as in the Bobigny triage centre where explosions were set off and cattle cars were being set on fire.[27]

---

[21] *Ibid.*
[22] *Ibid.*, Communiqué du Commissaire de la Police de La Ciotat à 17h15 (9 Aug. 1944).
[23] ANMT/2004/040/009: Cessation de travail dans la région parisienne (undated).
[24] Cobb, *Eleven Days* (2013) 46–9.
[25] This date is sometimes said to be on 17, as Chevandier explains, but overall, Chevandier sees three key dates: 10 Aug.; 14 Aug.; 18 Aug. 1944.
[26] Cobb, *Eleven Days* (2013); Chevandier, *Cheminots en Grève* (2002); Bruno Carrière, 'Août 1944: Paris, les cheminots et la Libération', *La Vie du Rail*, n°2458 (28 August 1994) 20–6; See also Bruno Carrière, 'Le 6 juin 1944: Les Alliés débarquent, la batille du rail redouble', *La Vie du Rail*, n°2448 (1 Jun. 1994) 12–34.
[27] ANMT/2004/040/009: Rapport n°58 M.A. (28 Aug. 1944) de l'Entretien d'Ourcq.

The strikes caused a collapse of transports and communications. The writings of those who lived through the Liberation – not least of Paris – testify to the chaos caused by the workers on strike and the general disruption to all sorts of services: 'And then there was the general strike: no more electricity, gas, metro, nothing, not even undertakers. I witnessed a comical scene with two guys panting up the rue de Belleville, transporting a coffin in a wheelbarrow to Père Lachaise. We encourage them, we laugh, its cheerful'.[28] But the strikes also united the workers, and for several weeks workers joined together in a common cause. The unifying effect of war, resistance and strikes was palpable amongst the cheminots: starting late 1944, the railwaymen no longer referred to their old Companies – 'the *Midi* in Carcassonne or *PLM* in Valence' – but really began to speak of the SNCF.[29]

These strikes were not merely bread strikes regarding food, working conditions, salaries and rations; their insurrectional character and their usefulness for the liberation of France gave them a unique character. They are also key in the case of the cheminots, since for the first time in a long time railwaymen took an active role in a *general* strike. Still, they are not completely disassociated from strikes a few weeks and months earlier which were themselves tied to narratives of working conditions. The lead up of local bread strikes in Marseille and other areas would undoubtedly have helped in building up momentum. The cheminots had been part of those strikes, but it seems they only got the confidence to partake in a general strike that August. Since then, the 1944 strike has been crystallized in popular memory as a great unifying moment, and in many ways it was. But one should not lose sight of the hesitations and doubts which preceded these strikes, nor of the preceding bread strikes. Whilst the insurrection provided a unifying gloss over the railway but also working-class community in general, it would not be enough to dissipate the fears and frustrations which existed in parallel. By 1947, the tensions over working conditions would re-emerge with even more violence – but in the meantime, the country needed to be rebuilt.

2   The liberation

The cheminots also experienced the Liberation as a period of intense physical destruction. On Monday 21 August, everyone living in Romilly was told to lower the steel 'drapes' of their homes since Germans, retreating, would fire on anything and anyone. The following day, only part of the

[28] Guy Le Corre, *Un cheminot rennais dans la Résistance* (Paris: Editions Tirésias, 2003) 61.
[29] Chevandier, *Cheminots en Grève* (2002) 218.

cheminots turned up for work; at 13h30, Roger Thierry, the District Chief, recommended that all those living outside of Romilly itself go home to be safe. The German railway workers had all left by this stage. Indeed, the fear was so high that when agents returned from Troyes with the workers' salaries, they could not distribute them since all the workers had gone home. The following day, on 23 August, barricades were raised in Romilly; on 25–26 August they saw Germans evacuate, although not without first blowing up installations, munitions depot, factories and other infrastructure. However, all SNCF buildings in that town were untouched. By the afternoon 26 August, there were a few American formations.[30] The old mayor who had been removed in 1940 returned, and everyone was told to go back to work on 29 August. Almost immediately, three cheminots were arrested, two for being members of Marcel Déat's *Rassemblement National Populaire*[31] and one for being a denunciator.[32]

Whilst many towns were liberated in late August, other places such as Conflans and Longwy were liberated on 5 and 10 September, respectively.[33] In the Belfort territory, some SNCF establishments were liberated between late August and mid-September (Lérouville à Toul) and others in mid-to-late September (Jarménil à Docelles-Chéniméil).[34] In Charleville, in the Ardennes, the German troops evacuated a bit later, taking with them all the vehicles they could find, 'bicycles, motorcycles, cars and trucks'.[35] But overall, the depot itself had not suffered too heavily from bombings.[36] In contrast, the station in Epinal had been completely destroyed.[37] Worst still was when the American Army liberated St Dié on 25 November, after two thirds of the town had been set on fire. No cheminots were killed on this occasion, but three agents and their families were left homeless.[38] At the Avricourt, three agents were deported to Germany, and one lost his seven-year-old son.[39]

With liberation came destruction but also reconstruction. On 25 August, Ourcq was being bombed when cheminots raised the French

---

[30] ANMT/2004/040/009: Compte Rendu des Évènements qui se sont succédé à Romilly du 21 au 31 août avant et après la libération de la ville par les troupes alliées.
[31] For more information on the RNP, see Sweets, *Choices in Vichy France* (1986) 82.
[32] ANMT/2004/040/009: Compte Rendu des Évènements à Romilly (21–31 Aug. 1944).
[33] *Ibid.*, Report (7 Sept. 1944) of Mohon.
[34] Located near Belfort. SNCF/206/LM/9: Letter (23 Dec. 1944) from Wisdorff to *Chef du Service Matériel et Traction*.
[35] ANMT/2004/040/009: Report n°2.256 on 7 Sept. 1944 of 4th Arrondissement.
[36] *Ibid.*   [37] SNCF/206/LM/9: Report (4 Dec. 1944) by the *Chef d'Arrondissement*.
[38] *Ibid.*, Report (1 Dec. 1944) Premiers Renseignements obtenus après la libération de l'Entretien de Belfort et des Postes d'Avricourt et de St Dié.
[39] *Ibid.*, Renseignements (2 Oct. 1944) sur la circonscription de Belfort fournis le 22 Septembre à M. Garnier en tournée à Mirecourt.

Figure 8.1 Ceremony for the repair of the 100th locomotive since the Liberation. 28 January 1946, Lille Délivrance. *Notre Métier*, 52 (29 Mar. 1946). SNCF – Centre National des Archives Historiques.

flag in the workshop, and many went back to work on 28 August.[40] At Bobigny, they started with the easier repairs which needed few materials and men, like tearing out and removing broken glass.[41] By 1 September, everyone in Troyes was back at work and the cheminots were being complimented by Chauvigne, the chief engineer, for having done everything smoothly.[42] The 1945 summer issue of *Chemin de Fer* presented a 10-page summary of a conference on reconstruction which had taken place earlier that year, showing images and sharing details of the rebuilding of railway infrastructure. *Notre Métier* wrote a special report on the reconstruction in Orléans, explaining how the destruction opened up the possibility of turning this station, previously in a cul-de-sac, into a usable passage.[43] It mentioned the local celebration on 28 January in Lille-Délivrance when the 100th locomotive was repaired since the Liberation[44] (see Figure 8.1). The SNCF also featured at the Exhibition of Reconstruction in Nancy in March 1946, outlining its plans to seize the opportunity of 'reconstruction' and develop new technological plans.[45]

---

[40] ANMT/2004/040/009: Rapport n°58 M.A. (28 Aug. 1944) de l'Entretien d'Ourcq.
[41] *Ibid.*
[42] ANMT/2004/040/009: Compte Rendu des Évènements à Romilly (21–31 Aug. 1944).
[43] *Notre Métier* (1 Mar. 1946).   [44] *Notre Métier* (29 Mar. 1946).
[45] 'Une Exposition de la Reconstruction à Nancy', *Notre Métier*, (5 Apr. 1946).

Reconstruction came with its own set of problems. First, there were personnel problems. During the Liberation of Vesoul and Belfort alone, 20 agents were deported, 12 had not re-appeared and 5 had died.[46] In addition, there were all those POWs and deportees who had not yet returned, and all those who wanted to volunteer to fight for France in Germany. In Vesoul and Belfort, for instance, seven agents had joined the FFI ranks, two joined the French army. It was hoped that after a short stint during the Liberation, these cheminots would want to return to work. In Belfort, an official notice called out to SNCF agents who had fought for the FFI: following the liberation of Belfort, they had one month to come back to work. Most did, apart from two, who in December 1944 still refused to come back.[47] This was not a unique problem: already in early September 1944, Cambournac was regularly being informed that many cheminots were asking to leave their jobs and join the French armed forces. What to do? The initial reaction was to 'not oppose the departure of those agents when it is incompatible with the needs of the service'.[48] But what of those who were immediately needed for reconstruction? Or those who asked to be dismissed from the SNCF entirely? Indeed, some agents who wanted to join the army were asking for immediate dismissal.[49] By 6 December 1944, all recruitment of railway personnel by the military had been forbidden. In fact, those who had entered the army and planned on carrying out their contract risked losing their jobs at the SNCF. Even colonial soldiers temporarily working for the SNCF were banned from answering the call to re-join the troops.[50] According to the Minister of War, 'at a time when the SNCF must face heavy responsibilities and provide considerable efforts, it is important to make sure that it keeps the indispensable personnel'.[51]

Second, there were serious housing problems for the cheminots. The number of homeless men, women and children in January 1945 was still considerably high, about 122,134 in total, a quarter of whom were completely isolated.[52] Some regions were hit particularly hard, like the

---

[46] SNCF/206/LM/9: Report (12 Dec. 1944) from the Chef d'Arrondissement, discussing personnel in Vesoul and Belfort; see also *Chemin de Fer* (Revue de l'Association Française des Amis des Chemins de Fer, May–Jun. 1945) 45–55.

[47] SNCF/206/LM/5: Report 69 (12 Dec. 1945) de l'Entretien de Belfort.

[48] SNCF/73/LM/27: Letter (5 Sept. 1944) from Cambournac to many.

[49] SNCF/206/LM/5: Demande de Renseignements (9 Oct. 1944) from Chef d'Arrondissement de Traction à Vesoul to Chef de la Division de Traction.

[50] SNCF/73/LM/27: Letter (26 Jan. 1945) from Directeur, Chef de la Division Centrale de l'Administration du Personnel to many.

[51] *Ibid.*, Letter (10 Jan. 1945) from Minister of War to many Generals.

[52] SNCF/25/LM/1123: Situation des familles d'agents de la SNCF Sinistrées à la date du 1 Jan. 1945.

Indre-et-Loire (5,008), Seine-et-Oise (7,391), Calvados (8,320), Seine (9,248), Pas-de-Calais (9,662) and especially the Nord (14,679). These problems which cheminots and their families were now facing had been envisaged during the Occupation. In 1943, projects were already under way to solve the potential post-war housing crisis. There was a desire voiced to build, for the post-war period, cheminots blocks of flats, especially in the Paris region. But not everyone was enthusiastic. In 1943 the Head of the Department of Exploitation saw a risk in amassing people of a single profession – indeed, the days of Dautry's *cités cheminotes* were now gone and a high concentration of cheminot housing was probably considered a socio-cultural and political problem. Furthermore, the proposal was not very thorough, meaning that key cities which had suffered considerable damage had been completely forgotten.[53] Finally, there were problems other than housing. In St Quentin, life was tough for many agents. There was not enough food, difficult access to clothing and shoes, and all that with the ever increasing demands on the workers. 'These living conditions have been worst for younger agents starting their family life' commented one engineer.[54]

These daily hardships chipped away at the cheminots' morale. Just the fact that it took cheminots longer to get to work meant that they were growing more and more tired. Even in places such as Arras where there were fewer homeless people, rations were still insufficient, and there was a particularly high number of complaints about hygiene products accessible to agents.[55] Conditions were better in Boulogne, but generally they came to notice a substantial difference between those living in cities and in the countryside, those living in the former faced greater housing and rationing problems.[56] Workers were given extra rations to help overcome some of these difficulties. The distribution of daily food supplements varied across the railway hierarchy: certain agents got extra daily rations, although the quantity and variety of their rations varied according to the intensity of their job.[57] Others got extra monthly rations, and those who lived in devastated areas also got supplements.[58] Ultimately, life went on: the SNCF summer camps were still going ahead and 3,300 children went

[53] ANMT/202/AQ/245: Letter (winter 1943) from Dégardin, Chef du Service de l'Exploitation, to Chef de Service VB.
[54] SNCF/PNV/103919: Letter (1945) from Ingénieur de la Voie to Paradis, Chef de la subdivision du Secrétariat et du Personnel du service de la voie.
[55] *Ibid.*, Letter (20 Dec. 1945) from Chef d'Arrondissement VB to Paradis, Chef de la subdivision du Secrétariat et du Personnel du service de la voie.
[56] *Ibid.*, Letter (21 Dec. 1945) to Paradis.
[57] SNCF/25/LM/1123: Letter (18 Jan. 1945) from Ministère du Ravitaillement to Le Besnerais.
[58] *Ibid.*

on holiday; newly weds and young SNCF agents received interest free loans; library stocks continued to grow (153,000 books in libraries in 1943 to 176,000 books in 1944); the SNCF's *Oeuvre des Pupilles* for orphaned children doubled its intake between December 1943 (2,400) and December 1944 (5,600).[59]

3   'Purging' the SNCF

France had to be reconstructed physically, but also morally. In the months following the Liberation, there was serious reflection about attitudes, behaviour and experiences under Vichy. Who was to be rewarded, pardoned or purged? The problem swept over French society, and many historians have written extensively on it.[60] And yet, the story of the SNCF personnel does not tend to fit this pattern of bitter disputes and settling of scores which so frequently frames these narratives. Indeed, if this book has so far underlined the multiplicity of attitudes, behaviour and experiences within the SNCF, this is not the image the SNCF wanted to project at the Liberation. First, in order to rebuild the nation, it needed to mobilise its entire personnel around this single effort. Second, the company had not yet been nationalised for ten years, and it needed to seize this moment to legitimise the *famille cheminote* it claimed to be. In order to obtain these two goals, the SNCF needed to present a unified front, and it could not allow the personnel to be divided.

Despite appearing as a united front largely untouched by the post-Liberation purges, distinctions were made amongst the SNCF personnel. Indeed, there were many ways to punish workers whose actions were not considered honourable according to national but also professional terms. One of these ways was to refuse re-admission into the SNCF. Generally, everyone could come back after the Liberation – the railway company was, after all, desperate for personnel. But allocations and professional advancement depended on what had happened during the Occupation. Those agents who were dismissed or downgraded during the Occupation for 'reasons other than professional activity but who were neither arrested, deported or interned' were expected to return to their position as if they had never left.[61] If they had been expecting a

---

[59] *Ibid.*, Note on Social Services carried out by SNCF during year of 1944.
[60] Henry Rousso, 'L'Epuration en France: Une histoire inachevée', *Vingtième Siècle, Revue d'histoire*, n°33 (Jan.–Mar. 1992) 78–105; François Rouquet, *L'Épuration dans l'administration française: agents de l'État et collaboration ordinaire* (Paris: CNRS, 1993); Virgili, *Shorn Women* (2002).
[61] SNCF/201/LM/2: Letter (27 Mar. 1946) from Camboumac to Directeur de la Région Sud-Est.

promotion during their absence, their promotion would be happen immediately upon their return. The agents who were still interned in Germany as civilian prisoners for reasons other than professional error were also expected to be immediately reintegrated.[62] Similarly, those who had committed crimes against the state (communist propaganda, for example) were automatically re-integrated, whereas Jews and Free-masons were only re-integrated if they asked for it. It was different for personnel who had been dismissed for professional error; in those cases, the SNCF would only re-admit them if they requested it themselves, and after investigation of their dossier.[63]

Establishing whether these returning cheminots should receive a full salary for their absence was another issue. The SNCF's official policy was 'We have always maintained the principle that an agent who does not work cannot get paid'. But, since the Occupation was such a unique time, everything depended on individual cases.[64] The SNCF was not always sure that cheminots deserved to be given the full allocations they would have otherwise received had they not been absent from work, and it was especially difficult to know who was telling the truth – that is, they had fled to join the Resistance – or who had just decided to evade work. So, unless cheminots could show a certificate from a resistance move-ment, workers would not be paid for these absences. Those who stopped work to avoid forced labour in Germany – known as *réfractaires* – but did not join Resistance groups could claim financial aid for themselves and their families, but never a full reimbursement of their salaries.[65] In the case of those interned by Germans for crimes such as theft, they would be paid their salary only if it looked like an unfair judgement on part of German authorities. However, if the crime had been planned, then the SNCF saw no reason to pay their salary for a period when they were being justly punished. In regards to those interned for being communists, the SNCF began to consider giving them three-fourth of their salaries as a gesture of support and aid. Those interned by French authorities, however, were never paid their salary during the internment since they would have been entitled to family aid at the time.[66]

---

[62] *Ibid.*, Letter (5 Oct. 1944) from Cambournac to many.
[63] SNCF/25/LM/265: Report (undated) Situation des agents révoqués, licenciés ou déclarés démissionnaires (3 pages).
[64] *Ibid.*, Report (18 Sept. 1944) Situation des Agents incarcérérs par les autorités allemandes.
[65] *Ibid.*, Letters (9 Jan. 1947; 13 Feb. 1947) Application des dispositions du dernier alinée da la note du 15 Mar. 1945.
[66] *Ibid.*, Report (18 Sept. 1944) Situation des Agents incarcérérs par les autorités françaises sous le gouvernement de Vichy.

Indeed, there were a number of different ways to deal with returning personnel. Each case was carefully evaluated at the individual level, although what the archives suggest is a lengthy process which is not always easy to carry out. For example, there were two different kinds of treatment of those agents who just 'couldn't be found' at the time of the liberation and were delayed in coming back to work. Those who tried really hard to do whatever they could to get back/make themselves useful to any SNCF service would get full pay. However, those who 'passively waited for these events to unfold without making themselves available to the SNCF' could either use up their paid leave, or they were considered to have been on leave without pay.[67] There was obviously no perfect formula to distinguish between these attitudes.

Files about salaries, aid and pensions could be open for years, especially if there was no actual death certificate. These were especially difficult to obtain when there was no trace of a deportee. Information about those deported to Germany would trickle back to the SNCF in various ways – in one case, it was a cheminot returning from Buchenwald who informed his chief that three other cheminots had died in Buchenwald[68] – and sometimes they received no information at all. 'Georges Boudin, worker, Maintenance Bordeaux-Saint-Jean, arrested with his wife as Jew on 13.1.44 by the German authorities. Never gave any news'; 'Alfred Maly, worker, Maintenance Bordeaux-La-Bombe, Apparently died at the Dora camp'; 'René Herrera, unskilled worker, Bordeaux-St-Jean depot, Never gave any news. Was seen in Auschwitz by his sister who was deported and returned to France'.[69] Herrera was actually deported to Auschwitz from Drancy on convoy n°69, 7 March 1944, when he was twenty-five years old.[70]

Other individuals, however, suffered far greater consequences for their more controversial actions under Vichy. Indeed, many people in France considered that true victory could only be obtained by purging France of its 'corrupt' individuals: 'No Rations without Purges. No Victory without Purges'.[71] The process to purge French government, administrations, companies, institutions and society at large was already in motion before

[67] SNCF/206/LM/4: Letter (28 Oct. 1944) from Chef du Service Matériel et Traction (East) to many.
[68] SNCF/206/LM/9: Letter (31 Aug. 1945) from Chef d'Entretien to Roger Chagnot.
[69] SNCF/303/LM/10: Liste des agents prisonniers de guerre ou déportés non encore rentrés (5 Oct. 1945).
[70] Mémorial de la Shoah, CDJC: http://bdi.memorialdelashoah.org/internet/jsp/core/MmsRedirector.jsp?id=21463&type=VICTIM#
[71] AMA/6/H/67: Letter (undated) from the Comité d'Epuration de l'Arrondissement d'Aix to the Comité d'Epuration Locale.

the liberation.[72] The Order of 27 June 1944 dealt with *épuration adminis-trative*, or administrative purges, whereas the Order of 26 August 1944 (and then of 26 December 1944) dealt with *Indignité Nationale*, or National Indignity.[73] The SNCF personnel was affected by this first order which could see employees receive anything from a simple 'blâme' to a 'dismissal without pension'.[74] Seven Commissions were set up throughout the company: one for Central Services, one for each Region and one for former German-annexed Alsace-Lorraine. Each commission was composed of seven SNCF agents appointed by the Minister on the recommendations made by the local syndicates and railway resistance organisations.

By January 1946, 1,862 employees had received 'reprimands, demo-tions, displacements, etc.', 1604 people were temporarily suspended from the SNCF, 1,150 are still waiting to be solved, 1,037 dossiers were classi-fied 'shelved'. In regards to the second order on National Indignity, 449 cases were raised. In other words, 707 agents had been excluded from SNCF, and 1,900 had received a variety of other sanctions.[75] By August 1947, this total had increased: there were in all 6,950 files. The large majority of these were minor sanctions, with 3,000 sanctions equal or inferior to a relocation, and 2,150 labelled 'shelved'. Only two thirds of the remaining files – about 1,200 – consisted of actual exclusions from the SNCF. Over the next decade, these sentences and sanctions would be revisited. In 1,951, the sanction of 'dismissal without pension' was trans-formed to allow ex-cheminots to obtain their pension.[76] There was another amnesty law in 6 August 1953 which further widened the net.[77] Indeed, as time went by, the harsh conditions of the liberation began to dissipate.

Still, in the heat of the purges, the sanctions distributed within the SNCF were considered to be very lenient. Indeed, in a body of 400,000 workers, less than 2% of the personnel was affected by the process at all.[78] René Mayer was the Minister of Public Works at the time. A man of

---

[72] SNCF/274/LM/001: Ordonnance (27 Jun. 1944) relative à l'épuration administrative sur le terrotoire métropolitain.
[73] See Anne Simonon, *Le déshonneur dans la République: une histoire de l'indignité 1791–1958* (Paris: Grasset, 2008).
[74] SNCF/274/LM/001: Note (16 Jan. 1946) Epuration Administrative Historique.
[75] *Ibid.*
[76] *Ibid.*, Ministerial Decision (8 Feb. 1951) relative à l'attention des sanctions prononcées en application de l'Ordonnance du 27 juin 1944.
[77] *Ibid.*, Letter (30 Jul. 1954) from Bourrie, Directeur du Personnel, to many. See Sophie Wahnich, ed., *Une histoire politique d'amnistie: études d'histoire, d'anthropologie et de droit* (Paris: Presses universitaires de France, 2007).
[78] According to Chevandier, fewer than 0.3% of SNCF employees were affected by the purges. According to Paul Durand, 700 agents were affected, 198 of whom were fired, 467 cases of 'indignité nationale' and 36 were sent into early retirement. See Durand, *La SNCF* (1968) 630.

Jewish origin with ties to the Rothschild family, he was put in charge of the purges in the transport industry and was fully informed that the SNCF lacked compliance. At one meeting, it was stated that 'There is a great malaise within the SNCF, and it appears that the identification of some of its directors as being collaborators, anti-social and lacking in the moral attributes of a chief, is taboo. There is a kind of conspiracy going on, and friendships appear such that the men in question are saved, even though we are fully aware that they no longer deserve their place within the company, considering the current circumstances'.[79]

François Rouquet poses the question differently: was the SNCF less affected by the purges because of its strong ties to trade unions and to the high levels of resistance activities within its ranks? It is a possibility. There is also the fact that the SNCF was actually more concerned with rebuilding the railways (and thereby, the nation) than with purging its employees. This, Rouquet claims, seems to be backed up by the numerous documents emanating from the Ministry of Reconstruction and Urbanism.[80] In light of my own research, I would be inclined to agree with this argument: the needs of the railways always trumped every other consideration. Keeping the trains running was not a question, but a professional and even personal duty.

There has not been much work on the SNCF purges. Bachelier describes how the small committee of cheminots set up in Oullins took a very long time discussing each individual dossier. Thus three months after the Liberation, only 28 dossiers of potential collaborators had been examined (when there were over 4,000 workers in Oullins). Most of those who underwent investigation were generally released after having given explanations for their dubious behaviour. What is striking is that *any* excuse, from a marriage breakdown to a prolonged illness, was accepted to justify cheminot collaboration. Considering that Oullins, near Lyon, was a communist and Resistance stronghold, such leniency is surprising.[81] However, it is indicative of cheminots' collective identity and their immediate concern with rebuilding the railway after a period of sabotages and bombings than with the politics of revenge.

It took several months before the General Manager, Robert Le Besnerais, was ejected from his post. René Mayer, an ex-railway engineer who had been forced to flee France because of his Jewish origins, was

[79] AN/72/AJ/2296: Compte-Rendu de l'entrevue des membres des commissions d'épuration avec le représentant du Ministère des travaux publics (30 Sept. 1944).
[80] Rouquet, *L'Épuration* (1993) 118.
[81] Bachelier Report, 8.2.6. Les Epurations; Chevandier, *Cheminots en grève* (2002) 220–1. It is important to underline that exceptional incidents of violence occurred around Hirson.

reluctant to put Le Besnerais under examination. Indeed, both men had developed close relations when working for the North Company in 1936.[82] However, growing pressure from the communists meant that Mayer had no choice. Indeed, in early October 1944, L'Humanité published a letter from Le Besnerais, where he ordered the regional directors to take action against communists in their service. It is at this point that Mayer realised he could not do anything but release Le Besnerais.

Tuesday 3 October (...) Le Besnerais comes to see me at 16h. He says nothing, but his hands are shaking. After going over some technical points, I talk to him. I try to do this as best I can, although it troubles me deeply. He is dignified, and says he would rather not reject any actions he committed under Vichy. (...) I strongly reproached [Raymond] Tournemaine [a regional director] for having given his letter to L'Humanité instead of having brought it to me personally.[83]

Fournier, Chairman of the SNCF, was only replaced in August 1946.

That being said, the SNCF was not completely immune to the purge process. This is especially true of the those working in the Alsace-Lorraine region, but others were also affected.[84] In the Paris region, women, auxiliaries, handlers, a principal inspector, an assisting depot chief were all arrested by the French Police, the FFI or sometimes even by the Americans. The reasons for their arrests varied considerably.[85] Jean Agret, a skilled labourer in the Toulouse area, had been a member of the Milice and was condemned to twenty years of forced labour in 1945.[86] Raymond Stappers, an handler in Champigny, was arrested for having denounced the man who organised an attack against a Milicien. Georges Munier and Jean Goussiez, two turner at Epernay, were arrested for collaborating with the Germans.[87] Edouard Barthes was dismissed from the SNCF, condemned to forced labour, a 502 franc fine and was stripped of his civic rights for twenty years for having supplied Germans with information which threatened French military and diplomatic security.[88]

---

[82] Extract from René Mayer's journal-diary, cited in Bachelier Report, 8.2.4. Un nouveau Conseil d'administration de la SNCF.
[83] Ibid.   [84] Rouquet, L'Épuration (1993) 115.
[85] ANMT/2004/040/009: Agents de la Région parisienne incarcérés depuis la Libération pour motif politique et qui n'ont pas encore été jugés.
[86] SNCF/303/LM/15: Jean Agret, Letter (26 Mar. 1945) from Chef de la Division du Service Général to Chef des Services Administratifs.
[87] ANMT/2004/040/009: Agents arrêtés depuis la libération et actuellement incarcérés (Alsace-Lorraine).
[88] SNCF/274/LM/002: Edouard Barthes, Extrait des minutes du greffe de la Cour de Justice de Carcassonne (21 Dec. 1944); Letter (30 May 1946) from Directeur Région du Sud-Ouest to Directeur du Service Central du Personnel.

Some cheminots who were not brought before the courts were still subject to reprimand within the SNCF if their behaviour had been considered unacceptable.[89] Paul Eugène Weber had been a handler in the SNCF since 1929 and then became a train engineer in Mulhouse-Ville when, in July 1941, he voluntarily left the SNCF to work for the Reichsbahn. There, his political zeal was immediately commented upon, and after the Liberation the SNCF refused to hire him back.[90]

Other behaviours, however, were much more contested. The case of Pasquier is a particularly interesting example. This trade-union leader had originally left the CGTU for the CGT in 1936, and when the Vichy regime was erected he supported the *Charte* and was elected as a member of the Conseil National by Pétain. At the Liberation, Pasquier was dismissed from the SNCF and condemned with *Indignité Nationale*, but these decisions were much debated within the SNCF. Tournemaine and Sauvé, the two trade-union leaders, disagreed over the seriousness of Pasquier's actions: the former, a communist, found them intolerable, whilst the latter, a socialist, tried to nuance Pasquier's experience. Pasquier's sentences would eventually be lifted, but this does not belittle the vehemence of the dispute between Tournemaine and Sauvé. Tournemaine in fact wrote a letter to Sauvé, telling him how extraordinary he found it that all of the sudden he claimed to have moral scruples as a Frenchman and could not allow Pasquier to be judged by 'partisan justice', when he had been so absent from the battles of the Occupation: 'we heard nothing of Sauvé during the Occupation, when the Gestapo and Vichy were arresting cheminots, were torturing them and sending them to jail, or when the Vichy government and the *boches* were shooting the best militants of our Federation'.[91] There were other cases aside from Pasquier, such as the ex-trade unionist Alexis Ferrier who was ejected from the CGT but had no problems with the SNCF. Marcel Bidegaray, however, the ex-CGT and general secretary of the *Fédération*, was murdered in December 1944 for his 'collaborationist' activities.[92]

---

[89] Lists of the sanctions and decisions carried out within the SNCF can be found in the Archives du Monde du Travail, but a full study of these falls beyond the remit of this chapter. ANMT/2004/040/010: Sanctions infligeées aà des agents par le Ministre après comparution devant la Commission d'Epuration. There are 117 dossiers. ANMT/2004/040/012: Indignité Nationale des personnels (East) (May 1945–Feb. 1951). SNCF/274/LM/001: Epuration Administrative, Répertoire Alphabétique (1945–1947).

[90] ANMT/2004/040/009: Weber, Letter (18 Dec. 1944) from President de la Commission des Services Centraux to Directeur de l'Exploitation de la Région Est (Alsace Lorraine).

[91] Lettre de Tournemaine à Sauvé (11 Jul. 1945) cited in Le Crom, *Syndicats, nous voilà!* (1995) 370–1.

[92] Chevandier, *Cheminots en Grève* (2002) 223–4. Chenvadier cites the work of Peter Novick and Lucien Midol.

Nor was the railway milieu exempt from the bitter disputes over who had resisted or collaborated under the Occupation. On Friday 15 March 1946, around lunchtime, at the canteen during the rehearsal of the Workshop Fanfare, Emile Plat grabbed everyone's attention by reading out loud the announcement of a citation published in *Notre Métier* honouring the exploits of M. Callandreau, Principal Inspector in Paris, under the Occupation. Plat openly challenged the veracity of this citation, and called for a vote on the spot asking for its annulment. Plat assured his co-workers he would bring the results back to the Managing Director himself.[93]

Post-war tensions and disputes about how people had behaved in 1940–44 did not revolve solely around acts of resistance or collaboration; however, professional conduct under the Occupation was also a critical matter. When the chief engineer M. Biais arrived in the Epernay workshops in late October 1944, the workers rose in protest and went on strike. At the time, Biais was under investigation for two different affairs by the *Comité d'Epuration*, or Purge Committee, one of which apparently involved 'clumsiness' vis-à-vis the workers in Epernay. Biais was alleviated of any serious sanctions by the Committee, Louis Legros, the trade union representative of the East Region, who wrote a stern letter to the Minister of Public Works on 28 September 1945: 'we who are particularly familiar with the actions of this engineer from 1940 to 1943 believe your decision does not reflect the declarations made over the radio by the provisional Government in Alger saying you would crack down on anti-national and anti-social individuals, no matter how highly-ranked they were. Today, cheminots want to work in peace, Monsieur the Minister, with chiefs who are worthy of this name'.[94] At one point it was suggested that, to keep the peace, Biais be moved to another region. However, Biais' presence in Noisy, Chalons and Pantin had had no negative resonance, and so the Ministry concluded that the frustration in Epernay was probably an artificial one. Ultimately, it was decided that Biais would remain in his position.[95] A similar protest took place in the Mohon workshops, when cheminots went on a partial strike on 7 September 1944 to request that the chiefs and agents who had collaborated with the enemy be immediately summoned by the *Commission de Libération*.[96] They complained that for the past four years Detaint, an assisting chief,

[93] ANMT/2004/040/009: Compte-rendu (Mar. 1946) sur un incident produit à la cantine des ateliers de Noisy-le-Sec.
[94] *Ibid.*, Letter (28 Sept. 1945) from Louis Legros, representative of Union des Syndicats des chemins de fer de la Région Est, to Ministre des Travaux Publics.
[95] *Ibid.*, Letter (15 Oct. 1945) from Roger Narps to Directeur Général.
[96] *Ibid.*, Letter (12 Sept. 1944) from Detaint to Chef de la Division du Matériel.

had given the cheminots severe and unjustified punishments, and there were other disputes notably over the canteen and the local shop. Detaint did not seem too worried about this, though, and he believed that the announcement of a wide-ranging amnesty and a salary increase would appease the situation.

Judging behaviour was fraught with contradictory problems and information. Abd El Kader was officially considered an 'excellent Frenchman', who had served and fought for France, had been wounded on the battlefield, and had worked at the SNCF for a quarter of a century. He was originally in Strasbourg for twenty years where he learned German, and then had spent four years in Troyes. However, during the Occupation, Abd El Kader had had contact with the Germans, and after the Liberation he was beaten and his home ransacked. The accusations were that he had been seen chatting to Germans every morning, had declared he was leaving for Germany after the war, and had behaved badly with his French comrades. More seriously, he had allegedly denounced a cheminot to the Germans. The witnesses brought to his defence refuted the last fact, and it was argued that, if Abd El Kader had been 'tempted' by German offers, his past as a good Frenchman certainly counted for something.[97] In the end, Abd El Kader was dismissed of his duties.[98] It is unknown whether there was something more behind this story, perhaps even an issue of racial tensions. It may well be the case that he was readmitted afterwards since sanctions were often lifted in the late 1940s and early 1950s, and sentences revoked – but nothing more is known.[99]

The purges were indeed far from straightforward matters. Albert Franck, from Alsace-Lorraine, had gone back to work for the Reichsbahn during the Occupation, and for this he had been permanently dismissed from the SNCF, had been stripped of his civic duties and of his circulation rights. Devastated but not disheartened, he wrote directly to De Gaulle in the 1960s: 'Is it right to make me responsible for having submitted to the orders of the German railways and the sovereignty of the Reich ?' Franck was amnestied on 31 December 1968.[100] Indeed, the severity of certain sentences reflected the tensions of the time, rather than an objective assessment of the context of behaviour and attitudes under the Occupation. The way these sentences were carried was also a matter of debate, and even disgust. On 11 November 1944, the population of

---

[97] SNCF/274/LM/002: Abd el Kader, Report (22 Dec. 1944).
[98] *Ibid.*, Abd el Kader, Arrêté portant révocations, signed by René Mayer (20 Mar. 1945).
[99] ANMT/2004/040/013: Annulation des sanctions prononcées au titre de l'épuration administrative (1956).
[100] SNCF/274/LM/006: Letter (13 Feb. 1967) from Albert Franck to Charles de Gaulle.

214 Ordinary Workers, Vichy and the Holocaust

Aix was shocked when a '*collabo*' – the derogatory term for collaborators –
was hanged in full public view, right where the parade was supposed to go
down. A petition was sent a week later to the President of the Municipal
Delegation signed by 21 different institutions: 'The Germans hanged
patriots in Nice, in Nimes, and many other places ; they odiously
exposed their cadavers in public. Is it conceivable that French people
have taken up these inhumane methods?'[101]

The numbers alone show that only a small percentage of individuals
were dismissed or officially sanctioned in the SNCF. They were especially high in the Alsace-Lorraine region, although they were not limited
to that region alone.[102] The need to maintain a united front to rebuild
the nation was of the utmost importance, and there was no point in
dismissing skilled workers at a time when they were needed most. The
cheminot milieu was not, however, void of '*collabos*'. Moreover, if purges
as such did not exist, there were many local tensions about behaviour
under Occupation. This could include anything from familiarity with
Germans to harsh treatment of subordinate workers. Many of these
incidents would not have been recorded in official records of the Purge
Committee; and yet they are perhaps better reflections of the difficult
atmosphere of the post-war period, giving alternative insights which
challenge the idea of a homogenous group of workers eager to rebuild
the nation.

4   Strikes

Immediately after the Liberation, cheminots stopped their strikes. The
Bogy and Tampon comic strip showed two cartoon cheminots being
taken out of a dusty drawer and getting right back to work. Indeed,
cheminots were now embarking on a new 'battle': the 'battle of production' (see Figures 8.2 and 8.3). For three years, from 1944 to 1947, the
SNCF, the Communist Party and the trade unions would all agree that
production was the priority of the hour, and everything had to be done to
augment it. *Notre Métier* was littered with calls for cheminots to help fight
the battle for coal.[103] 'We must understand that there remains one urgent
duty to accomplish: (...) by any means (...) increase production', read

---

[101] AMA/6/H/67: Letter (18 Nov. 1944?) from Comité de Coordination des Activités
Chrétinnes to the Président de la Délégation Municipale.
[102] Rouquet, *L'Épuration* (1993) 115.
[103] See *Notre Métier* in 1946. See also Hanna Diamond, 'Miners, masculinity and the
'Bataille du Charbon' in France 1944–1948', *Modern and Contemporary France*, 19.1
(2011) 69–84; Nord, *France's New Deal* (2010).

Figure 8.2 Bogy and Tampon resurrect! 'Bogy and Tampon are snoring; Baths – Showers; Tailor. Bogy: 'That's better already!'; Tampon: 'And now ... let's roll up our sleeves for the SNCF!', *Notre Métier*, 1 (18 Jan. 1946). SNCF – Centre National des Archives Historiques.

the *Tribune des Cheminots*.[104] A new social agreement seemed to have been reached between trade-union leaders, its members, employers and the state. In fact, in order to enable production, trade unions had taken a radical anti-strike stance.[105]

Indeed, the atmosphere in French society and politics was one of unity. The motto of the new tri-partite government had been simple: *'produire d'abord, revediquer ensuite'* – 'produce first, demand later'. This was all to do with the battle for production which was animating the new leaders of the nation who were obsessed only with national reconstruction. Everything could wait, but not this. Maurice Thorez – the communist leader who had been in Russia during the war, had returned to the head of the PCF after the liberation and was now vice premier of France – was against a workers' revolution at that time. Indeed, France had to get back on her feet before ideological battles could fully play out.[106]

Yet there were still problems: the demands cheminots had made for better working conditions in 1943–44 had not been met in the wake of the Liberation, and despite some concessions – salaries and rations increased, and work hours were theoretically reduced to 48 hours[107] – shortages and hardships persisted. In light of these enduring conditions, the veneer of the common fight for coal, for productivity, for France soon

---

[104] *La Tribune des cheminots* (Oct.–Nov. 1944), cited in Chevandier, *Cheminots en Grève* (2002) 227.

[105] *Ibid.*, 236–7.

[106] Robert Mencherini, *Guerre froide, grèves rouges: parti communiste, stalinisme et lutes sociales en France: les grèves 'insurrectionnalles' de 1947–1948* (Paris: Syllepse, 1998) 13–5.

[107] Chevandier, *Cheminots en Grève* (2002) 219.

Figure 8.3 'The Railway will win the Battle of the Rebirth of France'. *Notre Métier*, 45 (1 Feb. 1946). SNCF – Centre National des Archives Historiques.

grew dull. But what to do? Small, scattered strikes erupted in 1945, but even these were organised in order to not disrupt production.[108] It would take about three years before the cheminots became fed up and, like they had done in 1944, began to trigger strikes from the bottom-up.

Bread strikes erupted in June 1947. On 2 June, a baker strike saw daily bread rations reduced to almost nothing.[109] In 1944, cheminots had learned the possibility for local mobilisation and violent protest, and many actions – like those in Marseille in May 1944 – had in fact been triggered precisely because of a lack of bread. Here, one finds the same pattern. The strikes began on 2 June 1947 by cheminots in the Paris area. The strikes spread in time and space, such that on 7–8 June almost all cheminots in the North region had stopped working and many in Paris were voting for a massive strike. The strike flared even more after that weekend until finally, in the early hours of Thursday 12 June, a negotiation was reached between all interested parties. The strikers, however,

[108] *Ibid.*, 238.   [109] *Ibid.*, 243.

had not been granted everything they had asked for, and Chevandier underlines that the best victory was by far in the name of the trade unions who had finally managed to regain control of the workers and get them back to work.[110] Marie-Renée Courty-Valentin concluded that, from her visit in the archives, the June strikes, triggered by the cheminots from below, were not ideological in nature.[111] Like the strikes of the occupation, they were a protest against bread rations and working conditions.

Not all cheminots agreed with such action: the *Comité d'Action Syndicaliste des Cheminots* (CAS) was born on 27 July 1947 to object these calls for strikes. Indeed, they did not believe that the *Fédération* was representing everyone's interests, or acting as a fair representative of all workers. Inaugurating this committee was not without its risks : 'it provokes, it will provoke, waves not only within cheminot ranks but within the broader French trade union movement. (...) Insults, slander, threats, even violence will not be spared against those who bravely take position. Incidents have already been signalled'. Indeed, they were ready for a fight in order to challenge the current trade union representation which revealed more about politics, and a 'party dictatorship' than a real representative body. 'The Unity restored at the Liberation has been emptied of its content', they declared.[112] It is not, however, that the CAS was not complaining. Led by Fernand Laurent, they too were angry with the bad conditions of the post-war period. '200 grams of food a day starting 1 September!' they shouted, 'There is no point in over-indulging this discussion: each worker can measure the consequences of this decision which adds to the thousands of difficulties of daily life'. But the solution was not to go on strike: rather, they suggested that trade unions come up with strong solutions and proposals which they should pitch to the government.[113]

By mid-1947, it was becoming clear that the unity exemplified by the tri-partite system formed in 1946 was slowly dissolving. At first, the trade unions had seemed on board with the politicians' call for unity, but before long the CGT was asking for a 25% salary increase.[114] In fact, the CGT did not want an all-out general strike – but growing pressure from workers across France meant they could not ignore the popular cry for better conditions. Likewise, although the PCF was obsessed with

[110] See Marie-Renée Courty-Valentin, 'Les grèves de 1947 en France: Recherche centrée sur le secteur public et nationalisé', unpublished thesis from the Institut d'Etudes Politiques de Paris (1981).
[111] Chevandier, *Cheminots en Grève* (2002) 248.
[112] 'Le Comité d'Action Syndicaliste est né!', *Le Rail Syndicaliste*, 1 (Jul. 1947) 1.
[113] Fernand Laurent, 'Le Pain', *Le Rail Syndicaliste*, 3 (Sept. 1947) 1.
[114] Mencherini, *Guerre froide, grèves rouges* (1998) 17.

productivity and unity, a growing international crisis was putting it in a difficult position. From the start of 1947, the increasing tensions between the United States and the Soviet Union meant that France had to choose sides. The government's growing entanglements with the Americans were thus problematic for the PCF. It is perhaps not so surprising, therefore, that when a strike broke out in April 1947 in Renault, the CGT as well as the PCF backed it up. The subsequent events were decisive: 'Despite the moderation of the PCF leadership who was concerned with maintaining a responsible discourse, the exclusion of the communists from the government helped to trigger a wave of strikes in June, strikes in the name of the constant shortages and the decrease of buying power'.[115]

By October, the situation had spiralled out of control as a number of social, political and military crises simultaneously overlapped. Indeed, Mencherini's study also reminds us of the growing tensions in the international arena, tensions which had real ramifications in France. The beginning of the Cold War only further exasperated the already growing tensions, whilst France's colonial problems in Indochina added considerable pressure to the situation. By the time November–December strikes happened, the divisions in French society were now in full view.

The strikes in November–December 1947 were different to those of that previous summer. First, they were led by workers other than the cheminots – indeed, workers in Marseille went on strike on 12 November but the cheminots only joined the movement on 20 December. Second, it was cheminots who stopped these strikes: by going back to work ten days later, they triggered the beginning of the dissolution of the strikes, and soon everyone was going back to work. Chevandier argues that the reasons for this is because the strike was ideological, rather than practical, but he underlines the huge difficulty in assessing how many cheminots exactly were involved in this process.[116]

Still, sections of the working class and cheminot communities were against these strikes. One tract published by the *Fédération des Syndicats Chrétiens des Cheminots de France et des Territoires d'Outre-Mer* warned cheminots to 'not let yourselves be fooled during CGT meetings where others will try to exploit your legitimate dissatisfaction. (...) Do not let yourselves get dragged into a political strike'.[117] Various trade unions including the CFTC and the CAS signed a petition denouncing the strikes. They argued that the legitimate concerns of the cheminots risked

[115] *Ibid.*, 19.   [116] Chevandier, *Cheminots en Grève* (2002) 252.
[117] ANMT/2004/040/016: Tract, Fédération des Syndicats Chrétiens des Cheminots de France et des Territoires d'Outre-Mer (around 12–13 Nov. 1947).

being compromised if they took such direct action, and denounced the monopoly that the CGT claimed to have over the railway workers. According to them, the political goals of the CGT were betraying the interests of the cheminots.[118] A poll was taken in certain establishments to get a better idea of who was for or against the strikes, and the result showed a majority of non-strikers.[119] The cheminot community was clearly divided. Roger Bodeau, an ex-CGT who had joined the CAS, published his letter of resignation on the edition November edition of *Le Rail Syndicaliste* : 'Please believe me when I say that, after fifteen years of activism within the CGT, it is with infinite sadness that I have made this decision (...) However, profound disagreements separate me from federal activism. (...) I am leaving an organisation where arguments are replaced by insults, where arbitrary attitudes, defamation, physical struggles against non-conformists and even cheap denunciations have become commonplace'.[120]

One of the major objections to the strike was the violence which accompanied it. The Sub-Prefect of Aix commented that, in November 1947, 'certain cheminots installed a revolutionary regime with particular brutality which led rise to several incidents'. He described one incident in particular, where the head of these 'agitators' forced 'several people to go down on their knees on a public square, to kiss the red flag, after which point the victims were extremely maltreated, and even spitting in their face'. This all in front of several hundred local inhabitants.[121] Another cheminot was severely beaten by a group of strikers right outside his home in early December 1947, an episode reminiscent of this wave of violence.[122]

Sabotage was another highly-contested method deployed during this strike. Derailing and small sabotages were committed all over the country, although it does not always seem that cheminots were not necessarily involved in these. *Résistance-Fer* violently objected to sabotage,[123] as did the CFTC, the CAS and other trade unions who denounced the use of violent methods.[124] Anti-sabotage sentiment became even stronger after

---

[118] *Ibid.*, Declaration 'Aux Cheminots' (26 Nov. 1947).

[119] It must be underlined that this only reflected some views; cheminots in the workshops in Romilly and Blainville, for example, refused to vote. ANMT/2004/040/016: Statistiques contre les grèves, Résultats connus au 28 Nov 1947 au soir.

[120] Letter from Roger Bodeau to the Secrétaire Général du syndicat des services centraux de la SNCF, *Le Rail Syndicaliste*, 6 (Nov. 1947) 1.

[121] ADBR/148/W/378: Lettre (2 Nov. 1948) from Richardot, Sous-Préfet d'Aix, to Prefect.

[122] Chevandier, *Cheminots en grève* (2002) 253.

[123] ANMT/2004/040/016: Grèves Nov.–Dec. 1947. Note by Resistance Fer Union des Cheminots Résistants (4 Dec. 1947).

[124] *Ibid.*, Declaration 'Aux Cheminots' (26 Nov. 1947).

220   Ordinary Workers, Vichy and the Holocaust

the tragedy in Arras that winter. A train doing the Paris-Tourcoing trip derailed near Arras in the early hours of 3 December, causing 16 deaths and 30–50 injuries. Waves of emotion and anger were immediately set off throughout the country, but even anti-strikers were quick to defend the cheminots: 'Cheminots are not assassins' headlined the *Union Nationale des Cadres et Techniciens des Chemins de Fer*, who could 'not believe, until more information has been released, that this sabotage was the doing of cheminots'.[125] The cheminot Edouard Deprez affirmed in his testimony that no cheminot in the area had been involved, although beyond his testimony there is no proof either way.[126]

The outcome of the November–December strikes was devastating in terms of the divisions it created within the cheminot milieu. On one hand, the CAS printed a scathing disapproval in its December edition, stating that if strikes were a 'sacred right', these current strikes were partisan, ideological, bullying and failed to really represent the body of cheminots and workers more broadly.[127] For such non-strikers, there was a real deep-seated fear that saying one was anti-strikes would generate bullying, and even physical violence. On the other hand, the strikers had seemed to set a new precedent. Indeed, cheminot strikers suffered less harsh consequences than their ancestors in 1910 and 1920. Over 1,000 sanctions were given, but only 65 agents were actually dismissed from the SNCF, half of whom were allowed to retain their pension.[128] Activism was perhaps not as risky as it had once seemed.

Conclusion

The long story of liberation, reconstruction and strikes tells us a number of things about the effect of Vichy on the cheminots. First, that there was, indeed, a unity amongst the workers. The insurgency of August 1944 showed a degree of grass-roots unity which had been absent for over two decades, and which promised a collegiate atmosphere in the months after the liberation. The upper-echelons of French society were particularly keen to see the workers unite against the Germans as it reinforced professional and personal ties which could only benefit the battle of reconstruction. Indeed, whether it was those at the top of the SNCF of those at the top of the trade unions, they all wanted to see

---

[125] *Ibid.*, Tract 'Les Cheminots ne sont pas des assassins !', Union Nationale des Cadres et Techniciens des Chemins de Fer Français et Coloniaux.
[126] Edouard Deprez, cited by Chevandier, *Cheminots en grève* (2002) 256.
[127] CAS bureau, 'Grèves et Sabotages', *Le Rail Syndicaliste*, 7 (Dec. 1947) 1.
[128] Chevandier, *Cheminots en grève* (2002) 258.

the workers work hard to rebuild the country. Ideology needed to be set aside for a while, and France needed to get back on its feet. There was also an important need for institutions to regain control over the population such that a new order could be established. But the patriotic fervour which had sprung up in the summer of 1944 could not be sustained, not least because of the continuity of personnel problems amidst the SNCF. Despite a wave of enthusiasm and unity in 1944, the reality of post-war shortages meant that material grievances had far from gone away after the liberation. The narrative of class struggle thus re-emerged with considerable force as many workers now blamed not the Germans but the French state and the company bosses for their dire conditions.

But following the 1947 strike, the illusions of working-class, national unity had been dispelled, leaving way for a re-emergence of fractures amongst left-wing parties and trade unions. The battle between communists and anti-communists would become more and more fierce with the outbreak of the Cold War, and to a large extent it would dictate working-class relations in the post-war era.

So had the unity of those last weeks of Occupation only been a temporal phenomenon? Almost certainly. More importantly, after the war we can see that cheminots' political culture had radically shifted, and a new code of conduct was emerging. After 1947, cheminots would be going on massive strikes approximately every 5–7 years – something which contrasts sharply to the pre-1945 years. But why this change? There is no doubt that the intense history and memory of the Vichy era – when class struggle was bubbling beneath the surface of anti-German and anti-Vichy resistance activities, as seen in Chapters 4, 5 and 6 – had a real part to play in the transformation of this community. Indeed, the hopes that many cheminots had placed in the French state in the late 1930s had been dispelled by the mid-1940s: in order to truly change their working conditions, they could only rely on themselves.

9   Epilogue
Memory

Although Vichy brought communities closer together in many ways, it would be incorrect to sweepingly claim that the workers – not least the cheminots – all unified together. Identifying common enemies helped to create an upsurge of enthusiasm and activity which had been absent for a long time, but the disparity of individual experiences cannot be overlooked. Beneath the veneer of unity, real problems continued, the eruption of these divisions in 1947 being a consequence of this.

Indeed, if the 'dark years' seemed to bring people together at one point, the realities of the post-war world were far too complex to maintain the image of unity for too long. The late 1930s had already been signalling difficult times for the railways as automobile and plane industries threatened to take over the transport market. And after the war, this is precisely what happened. Cars and planes completely transformed daily life, and trains now had to face the struggles of this new era. In fact, trains underwent massive modernisation through the electrification of the railways, a project which had been in the books for decades and was finally coming to fruition. The days of the steam engine were dying, and in this mixed atmosphere of excitement and nostalgia, of new technologies and old institutions, the centrality of railways to the nation's survival became more and more questionable.

The cheminots suddenly found themselves in a precarious situation. The modernisation of the railways reduced the body of railway workers by almost half: by 1982, there were approximately 252,000 men and women working for the SNCF.[1] This seriously altered the dynamics of the cheminot community. The ex-cheminots interviewed for this research talked with great nostalgia about the days of the war, not least because those were the days of the 'real cheminots', who had real physical skills and a real sense of community.

It is no surprise, therefore, that the post-war period saw cheminot communities clutch to the memory of the last glorious days – *the battle*

---

[1] Ribeill, *Les Cheminots* (1984) 5.

of the railways. How did this memory evolve? What does it look like now? And to what extent is the memory of cheminot resistance under Vichy tied more to the nostalgia of a lost era rather than a real belief in active, uniform resistance? The fact that cheminot memory has recently come under the public spotlight in France and beyond makes these questions even more relevant.

1   The resistance myth

It was René Clément's film *La Bataille du Rail* (1945) which propelled the image of the cheminot/SNCF resister into the social imagination. It did so through ecause of several technical and political tactics. By effect-ively combining documentary footage with a fictional storyline, it gave Clément's piece a feeling of authenticity which other resistance films seemed to lack.[2] The film makers went on site into railway stations and workshops and filmed the cheminots as they were, instead of hiring actors and decorating movie sets. Even in 2008, the ex-cheminot Fran-çois Crouzet still admired what he saw as the truthfulness of the images of the film,[3] and in June 2010, the French Institute in London described it as one of the most authentic films about the resistance.[4]

The powerful impact of René Clément's cinematographic masterpiece can also be largely explained by the history of its production. Before the Liberation, Clément was assigned to create a documentary on railway workers, *Ceux du Rail*. However, after France was freed from German Occupation, the *Comité de Libération du Cinéma Français* (CLCF) and the Military Commission of the *Conseil National de la Résistance* (CNR) asked Clément to change the topic of his film, such that it would focus on resistance in the railways.[5] The film, temporarily entitled *Résistance-Fer*, would tell the true stories of the members of the organisation. But when Clément showed his short film to the representatives of the three major cooperatives, the *Coopérative Général du Cinéma Français*, the *Comité Militaire Nationale* and the *Direction Générale du Cinema*, everything changed. The board of viewers was deeply impressed by the

---

[2] For list of films produced in this period, see appendix 2 in Rousso, *The Vichy Syndrome* (1991) 318.
[3] François Crouzet, 'Voyageurs sans billets' in *Les cheminots dans la guerre et l'Occupation: témoignages et récits*, 7 (Nov. 2004) 261.
[4] 'La Bataille du Rail', Ciné Lumière programme, Institute Français de Londres (Jun.–Jul. 2010).
[5] Martin O'Shaughnessy, '*La Bataille du Rail*: Unconventional Form, Conventional Image?' in H. R. Kedward and Nancy Wood, eds., *The Liberation of France: Image and Event* (Oxford: Berg, 1995) 15–27.

documentary, and they decided to invest hundreds of thousands of francs to turn it into a longer fictional movie.[6]

In March 1945, Gaullist and Communist associations, as well as the SNCF and Res-Fer, all joined forces to fund the filming of *La Bataille du Rail*. This collaboration was exceptional, for Gaullist and Communist resistance myths generally clashed in the post-war period.[7] According to Martin O'Shaughnessy, '[the film's] merging of left-wing collectivism and populist nationalism seemed so natural at the time that most critics felt no need to comment upon it'. In fact, the perfect merging of these opposing doctrines seems to suggest that the 'rival [Communist and Gaullist] myths of Resistance were far less radically separate immediately after the war than in later years'.[8] By combining their efforts and influences, the film satisfied all audiences. The Gaullists appreciated the constant references to national sentiment and patriotism, whilst the communists were pleased to see a hammer and sickle in the last scene of the movie. As for the railway company, it was the main character of the film. Indeed, the original prologue had been dedicated the film to the cheminots in *Résistance-Fer*, who had created a 'chain of solidarity' amongst themselves. However, by making such drastic changes to the prologue to include all railwaymen working for the SNCF, Sylvie Lindeperg underlines how 'the authors [showed] their desire to promote the corporation as a whole'.[9]

From the moment it was first projected in the Palais de Chaillot on 11 January 1946, *La Bataille du Rail* became a national phenomenon. De Gaulle presided over the screening, and *Résistance-Fer* organised a gala to follow that same night. Every time the film was released in a new town, Res-Fer set up a small exhibition in the town, showing the making of the film.[10] The acclaim was unanimous – Clément's piece had won the heart of the French people. A film critic reviewed the movie in *Combat:* '[the Resistance's story] has finally been told with the required dignity and talent'.[11] According to the historian Jean-Pierre Bertin-Maghit, 'almost half of the population of Bar-le-Duc went to see the film (...); in Lyon, it was the big hit of the season along with *La dernière chance*, another

---

[6] Sylvie Lindeperg, 'L'opération cinématographique: Équivoques idéologiques et ambivalences narratives dans La Bataille du Rail', *Annales* 51.4 (Jul.–Aug., 1996) 762.

[7] See Robert Gildea, *France since 1945* (Oxford: Oxford University Press, 2009, c1996) 68–71.

[8] O'Shaughnessy, *La Bataille du Rail* (1995) 25–6.

[9] Lindeperg, 'L'opération cinématographique' (1996) 767–8.

[10] Jean-Pierre Bertin-Maghit, '*La Bataille du Rail*: de l'authenticité à la chanson de geste', *Revue d'histoire moderne et contemporaine*, 33.2 (Apr.–Jun., 1986) 283.

[11] O'Shaughnessy, *La Bataille du Rail* (1995) 15.

Figure 9.1 Scenes from *La Bataille du Rail* were reproduced. *Notre Métier*, 52 (29 Mar. 1946). SNCF – Centre National des Archives Historiques.

Resistance film, (...); it was the most popular film in Strasbourg along with *Jericho, Les voyages de Gulliver* ...; in Nancy, the movie broke records'.[12] In 1946, *La Bataille du Rail* received the *Grand Prix du Jury* at the Cannes Film Festival. The SNCF readily embraced the film. Issues of *Notre Métier* included numerous photographs of scenes from the film, and it was repeatedly described as a must-see movie. In one issue, an iconic picture from the film was published next to the photos and letters of real cheminot victims[13] (see Figures 9.1 and 9.2).

[12] Bertin-Maghit, *La Bataille du Rail* (1986) 283.   [13] *Notre Métier* (8 Nov. 1946).

Figure 9.2 Our heroic deaths, in which an iconic picture of the Bataille du Rail is placed next to the photos and letters of real victims. *Notre Métier*, 79 (8 Nov. 1946). SNCF – Centre National des Archives Historiques.

A series of national commemorations of communist martyrs also helped impose a myth of resistance and martyrdom from above. On 12 March 1945, Pierre Semard was re-buried in Paris, in the Père-Lachaise cemetery, and a massive commemorative ceremony was organised in his honour. The railway trade unions also regularly honoured Semard's memory in meetings and rallies. Two other communists, Georges Wodli and Jean Catelas, were also integrated into the post-war communist myth of cheminot martyrs. Wodli had been arrested by the Gestapo on 30 October 1942 for his involvement in the resistance, and was sent to a high security camp in Germany where he died. 'At the ceremony for the third anniversary of the strikes of 10 August 1944, his portrait was placed next to Pierre Semard's'.[14] Catelas had been arrested and guillotined on orders from Vichy – probably for his involvement in communist activities – on 24 September 1941. Catelas achieved the same level of fame as Wodli, although neither would ever reach the legendary heights of Pierre Semard.[15]

At all hierarchical levels, and from all political backgrounds, individual cheminots were also honoured in local communities. In 1955, the ex-Chairman, Pierre Tissier, a Gaullist who had been part of De Gaulle's *État-Major* in London, received a grandiose inauguration at his funeral: 'his patriotism knew no limits. It is pointless to try and find out when he entered the Resistance. He is the Resistance'.[16] In a much smaller ceremony five years earlier, on a cold Sunday in late November, the mayor of St Quentin had inaugurated the *Place André Baudez* in memory of the local ex-cheminot: '[André Baudez] clearly saw that, amidst the spinelessness and cowardice which affected the majority of the citizens who lived under the Occupation, the SNCF stood on the front line of the resistance movement'.[17]

All 9,000 cheminots who died between 1939 and 1945 were uniformly honoured, with no distinctions between deportees, those who were shot and those killed in rail accidents during the Occupation.[18] This differed from typical French commemorative politics, where labelling one's wartime experience was key. Deportees alone were separated into different categories, such as racial deportees, political deportees and forced-labour workers. The last were banned from referring to themselves as

[14] Vincent Auzas, 'La Mémoire de la Résistance chez les cheminots: constructions et enjeux, septembre 1944–novembre 1948', Master's thesis in contemporary history, at the Université Paris 1, Panthéon-Sorbonne (2000) 38.
[15] *Ibid.*, 39.   [16] AN/72/AJ/2289: Pierre Tissier, '1903–1955'.
[17] AN/72/AJ/495: André Baudez.   [18] Chevandier, *Cheminots en grève* (2002) 232.

'deportees' in 1978, showing the deep tensions between these rival groups.[19] In contrast, the SNCF erected a monument dedicated 'Aux cheminots morts pour la France' in 1948. The inscription 'mort pour la France' was not uncommon. In 1915, it had been legally recognised as indicating anyone killed as a direct consequence of warfare.[20] However, in the case of the SNCF, commemorating *all* of the deceased cheminots reinforced the corporate myth of resistance and martyrdom.

On 10 May 1951, to honour its services from 1939 to 1945, the SNCF became the first company to receive the *Légion d'Honneur*.[21] As per tradition, the SNCF was thanked for all of its efforts in wartime; nonetheless, the gesture was automatically associated with the SNCF's resistance activities. Indeed, the SNCF's weekly paper, *La Vie du Rail*, announced that the railway company was awarded the *Légion d'Honneur* because '[it] had constituted the most efficient intelligence network for the Allies'.[22] A previous incident had already blurred the lines between military achievement and resistance to the occupier, when on 3 November 1945, in a town in Germany, General Koenig, a commander of the Free French, awarded the *croix de guerre* to *Résistance-Fer*.[23]

As previously mentioned, scholarly work in support of the SNCF myth helped legitimise its image as a body of resisters. Paul Durand, a well-ranked ex-cheminot, embarked on a research project in the 1950s and in over a decade had gathered 177 individual testimonies of ex-cheminots who had resisted. This initiative has produced valuable historical sources, yet Durand was mostly interested in showing a uniform SNCF resistance. The American historian James M. Laux criticised Durand's general approach: 'almost entirely descriptive, uncritical and rarely analytical, the book probably will be most appreciated by nostalgic French railway men'.[24] Durand's book was thus a product of its time, a symbol of the cheminot/SNCF resistance myth.

Not everyone shared Durand's point of view, however. Maurice Choury's publication of the communists' role in railway resistance in

---

[19] Patrice Arnaud, 'La longue défaite des 'requis' du STO', Tal Bruttmann, Hervé Joly and Annette Wieviorka, eds., *Qu'est-ce qu'un déporté? Histoire et mémoires des déportations de la Seconde Guerre mondiale* (Paris: CNRS, 2009) 368.

[20] Serge Barcellini and Annette Wieviorka, *Passant, souviens-toi! Les lieux du souvenir de la Seconde Guerre mondiale en France* (Paris: Plon, 1995) 11.

[21] Newsreal *Les Actualités Françaises* (10 May 1951).

[22] 'La proposition qui a valu à la SNCF la croix de la légion d'honneur', *La Vie du Rail* (1984) 2.

[23] AN/72/AJ/2289: Photograph (3 Nov. 1945) Remise de la croix de guerre avec palme par le Général Koenig au drapeau de Résistance-Fer, Spire, Allemagne.

[24] James M. Laux, Review of Paul Durand, *La SNCF pendant la guerre* (1968), *The American Historical Review*, 75.1 (Oct. 1969) 139–40.

Figure 9.3 Bogy and Tampon film stars: 'Tampon: "A marvelous film!"'; "Bogy: We can also become film stars..."; "I'm Tampon, this is Bogy, we are the brothers of the actors in *The Battle of the Rail*". Director: 'Ah! You want to be in cinema!'; Director: 'I don't need cheminots – but I'm doing a film about the convicts, and you've got the right look!!?'; Director: Let's re-take the head shaving scene...!', *Notre Métier*, 5 (18 May 1946). SNCF – Centre National des Archives Historiques.

1970 suggested that communist cheminots were dissatisfied with this dominant corporate myth. Furthermore, whilst Durand claimed that 'an army of resisters, from all different ranks, had emerged within those first hours [of the Occupation]',[25] most cheminots who had written to Durand in the 1950s doubted that they had been part of a vibrant group of resisters. 'I was only a very small resister', said the ex-cheminot Auguste Pineau.[26] 'My actions were very modest compared to those carried out by my comrades who were deported or killed', said L. Biette.[27] 'And according to Jean-Claude Huckendubler, cheminots were '10% resisters, 10% collaborators, and the other 80% were just people surviving the war'.[28]

Outside the railway milieu, the cheminot myth attracted some attention. The Americans made an adaptation of *La Bataille du Rail*, entitled *The Train* starring Burt Lancaster. Released in 1964, it was more 'Hollywood' than Clément's own docu-film, with far more explosions and special effects. The French were disappointed with this adaptation which failed, in their view, to capture the greatness of their resistance.[29] Even historians who repeatedly referred to cheminots' involvement in sabotages and strikes, especially at the Liberation, never delved into the subject more deeply. The realism of *La Bataille du Rail* had firmly established the corporate myth, and now the population was moving on to other topics. A comic strip published in *Notre Métier* in May 1946 was remarkably prescient in this regard (see Figure 9.3). The characters Bogy

[25] Durand, *La SNCF* (1968) 649.   [26] AN/72/AJ/497: Auguste Pineau.
[27] AN/72/AJ/495: L. Biette.   [28] AHICF: Huckendubler (1999)
[29] Ionascu, *Cheminots et cinéma* (2001) 62.

and Tampon approach a film director in hope that he will hire them to star in the next film on railways during the Occupation. However, the producer sends them away, because he is starting another project on convicts – the convicts, though, look a lot like camp inmates. As competing memories emerged in post-war France, the history of the SNCF was side-lined from mainstream historiographical debates.

2   Holocaust memory boom

Around 1970, the winds of change swept through France, making it possible to challenge the myths of 1940–44 for the first time.[30] In 1968, French students rebelled against the system in what Robert Gildea has called 'France's last great revolution'.[31] In 1969, Charles de Gaulle stepped down from office, and died the following year. In 1970, Marcel Ophuls released what was to become an iconic film, *The Sorrow and the Pity*, giving a very nuanced portrayal of life in a French town in the Puy-du-Dôme. In 1971, Charles d'Aragon published his memoirs under the title *La Résistance sans héroisme*, distancing himself from the heroic and glorious narratives often associated to stories of the Resistance.[32] In 1973, Louis Malle produced *Lacombe Lucien*, a film which blurs the lines between resistance and collaboration as it tells the story of a young boy who leaves home to join the maquis, but accidentally becomes a member of the French Milice. And finally, in 1972, Robert O. Paxton published *Vichy France: Old Guard, New Order*, an exceptional historical work which exposed the politics of collaboration in Vichy. Julian Jackson underlines how this work was not completely original, and that other historians had previously discussed the deeper issues of Franco-German collaboration in France. Yet Paxton's book appeared at the perfect time, when France was emerging from the myths in which it had been so tightly wrapped.[33] The Resistance myth did not disappear completely, of course, and many defended its legacy. Still, a drop in Resistance historiography after the 1970s shows the time had indeed come to challenge popular assumptions about Vichy.[34]

Holocaust history had seen a tremendous revival throughout the Western world from the 1960s onwards. Primo Levi published his memoirs, a

---

[30] See chapter 3 in Rousso, *The Vichy Syndrome* (1991).

[31] Gildea, *France since 1945* (2009) 1.

[32] Charles d'Aragon, *La Résistance sans héroisme* (Paris: Editions du Seuil, 1971).

[33] Julian Jackson underlines that Stanley Hoffmann published insightful works on the Vichy regime before Paxton's own book. Jackson, *France: The Dark Years* (2001) 11.

[34] Laurent Douzou, *La Résistance française: une histoire périlleuse: essai d'historiographie* (Paris: Seuil, 2005) 192–4; Jackson, *The Dark Years* (2002) 16–7.

cornerstone in Holocaust testimony, in 1958. Raul Hilberg's *The Destruction of the European Jews* was first published in 1961, and has been re-edited a number of times since. The trial of Adolph Eichmann, who coordinated the deportations of Jews to the extermination camps, took place in 1961–62. Hannah Arendt's book *Eichmann in Jerusalem: The Banality of Evil* became a worldwide seller in 1963, sparking fierce historiographical debates across Europe and America. The roundups of the *Vélodrome d'hiver* were commemorated for the first time in 1982. Claude Lanzmann's film *Shoah* in 1985 immediately became the most widely acclaimed film on the Holocaust. And the French president François Mittérrand officially attended the 16–17 July commemoration of the Vel d'Hiv in 1992, sparking a new tradition amongst French political figures, who thereafter presided over the ceremony every year.

But if Mittérand's attendance in 1992 confirmed that the Holocaust was a subject which could not be ignored, he was strongly criticised for refusing to apologise for France's involvement in the genocide, saying it was Vichy's fault and not the fault of the Republic. Three years later, the new French president Jacques Chirac broke this silence when at the Vel d'Hiv ceremony. In a ground-breaking move, he apologised for the crimes that France and the French had committed.[35] This ushered Holocaust history into high politics, and showed that national memory was being actively re-shaped.

It was during this recent explosion of 1990s Holocaust memory that the SNCF came under fire for its involvement in the Jewish deportations. Although the SNCF affair was part of a wider phenomenon of commemoration, it was mostly started by a single man: Kurt Werner Schaechter. Schaechter's parents, of Austrian origin, were deported from France and died in Auschwitz. In the early 1990s, he went to the archives in Toulouse and found hundreds of documents showing the financial and material involvement of the SNCF in the deportations. Schaechter illegally photocopied these documents (now housed at the Hoover Institute at Stanford University) and shared them with the press, above all the bills which allegedly proved the SNCF had financially benefitted from the Holocaust.

The first article on the subject of the SNCF's involvement in the deportations was released by the national paper *Le Point* on 23 May 1992.[36] The following year, when *Résistance Réalités* dragged up this story in autumn 1993, the SNCF was accused of wanting to hide its

---

[35] *Discours et messages de Jacques Chirac* (Paris: Fils et filles des déportés juifs de France, 2007) 23. See Tony Judt's remarks in his epilogue, Judt, *Postwar* (2005).

[36] 'Déportés: la SNCF avait les factures', *Le Point* (23 May 1992).

dark past.[37] The SNCF's weekly paper, *La Vie du Rail*, was also criticised for never having published anything on the subject of deportations, apart from a six-page article in May 1992 on the first Jewish convoys to leave France.[38]

André Frossard, the president of *Résistance-Fer*, was appalled by the attack. In a letter to Michel Slitinsky, the editor of *Résistance Réalités*, he asked 'which lobbies are trying to dirty the SNCF and the cheminots?'[39] An intensification of correspondence between Frossard, Slitinsky and Schaechter ensued. Frossard defended the memory of the cheminots who had been under German orders and tried, despite threat of retaliation, to help the deportees as best they could. On the other hand, Slitinsky and Schaechter wanted to raise the graver implications of the SNCF's actions, and thereby prove its participation in genocide. Slitinsky wanted to make clear that he was not accusing the cheminots directly, however. He reminded Frossard that in the same issue where he had published the information gathered by Schaechter, he had also published an article on cheminots' invaluable contribution to the Liberation with the *plan vert*.[40] Frossard was not convinced. On 10 March 1994, he wrote to Slitinsky: 'Your letter from 8 February proves that, no matter what explanations you are given, you continue to back up your lies regarding the activities of the SNCF and of the cheminots during the war – you continue to falsify history'.[41] That same day, Frossard wrote a second letter to Kurt Werner Schaechter: 'Your letter dated 12 February is a pack of lies and allegations proving that your "certain vision of the period" is nothing but that of those who falsify history, and that has nothing to do with reality'.[42] But Schaechter was not intimidated. In a subsequent letter, he accused 'the management of the SNCF as well as *Résistance-Fer* of being accomplices in crimes against humanity, and guilty of High Treason because they organised the last deportation trains headed to the horrific Nazi concentration camps'.[43]

The affair took a legal turn in 1998, when the SNCF was charged for crimes against humanity. In many ways this was part of a long lineage of

---

[37] 'Les Convois de déportés à travers ordres et factures de la SNCF', *Résistance Réalités*, 26 (Autumn 1993).

[38] '27 mars 1942, le premier convoi de déportés', *La Vie du Rail*, n°2346 (2 May 1992).

[39] AN/72/AJ/2288: Communiqué (2 Feb. 1944) from Frossard to Slitinsky. Frossard wanted him to print it in the upcoming issue of *Résistance Réalités* as a right of response.

[40] *Ibid.*, Letter (8 Feb. 1994) from Slitinsky to Frossard.

[41] *Ibid.*, Letter (10 Mar. 1994) from Frossard to Slitinsky.

[42] *Ibid.*, Letter (10 Mar. 1994) from Frossard to Schaechter.

[43] *Ibid.*, Letter (12 Mar. 1994) from Schaechter to Frossard. Schaechter also accused the Red Cross of crimes against humanity, as well as high treason, in 1994.

trials Jean Leguay was brought to trial in 1979; Klaus Barbie in 1987; René Bousquet in 1991; Paul Touvier in 1994; Maurice Papon in 1998. Outside the courtroom, the ex-president François Mittérand came under great scrutiny in the 1990s, as did ex-resisters Raymond and Lucie Aubrac. But bringing a company on trial in the civil courts was very different. The first claim in 1998, led by Jean-Jacques Fraenkel, went almost unnoticed. This is perhaps because Fraenkel lacked evidence to support his claim against the SNCF's behaviour in wartime, and his claim was swiftly rejected.[44] Schaechter's claim in 1999 was much better prepared, and he came armed with both the documents he had found in the Toulouse archives, and the Bachelier Report. Still, the judge decided that it was impossible to bring a case against a company in the French civil courts. As such, the case was dismissed.

One of the most extraordinary effects of the SNCF affair is its transnational dimension. In 2000 the French railways were accused of crimes against humanity in a district court in Brooklyn, New York. The claim was led by Harriet Tamen, a New York-based lawyer who had spent much of the 1990s gathering testimonies and claims against the SNCF. The SNCF never made it into the courtroom in New York, however, because of basic legal obstacles. Indeed, its status as a private company owned by the French state was a key problem. Tamen and her fellow lawyers needed to prove that there was the jurisdiction in America for foreign claimants (at the time the survivors had European nationalities) to accuse a foreign company or state (France and the SNCF) of a crime committed in a foreign country (France). The district court in Brooklyn decided in 2001 that, according to the Foreign Sovereign Immunities Act of 1976, the SNCF could not be tried in America.[45] The plaintiffs first appeal was rejected, but another appeal in 2004 was accepted.[46] Although they were still unsuccessful in obtaining jurisdiction, the court's final decision in 2004 expressed a clear moral judgement: '... the evil actions of the French national railroad's former private masters in knowingly transporting thousands to death camps during World War II are not susceptible to legal redress in federal court today (...). Nonetheless, the railroad's conduct at the time lives on in infamy'.[47] Although

[44] Ribeill, *Historail* (2008) 45.
[45] Abrams v. Société Nationale des Chemins de Fer Francais, 175 F.Supp.2d 423, 433 (E.D.N.Y.2001). Available at www.assetsearchblog.com/uploads/file/2ndCirSNCF(1).pdf.
[46] Abrams v. Société Nationale des Chemins de Fer Francais, 332 F.3d 173 (2d Cir.2003). Available at https://law.resource.org/pub/us/case/reporter/F3/332/332.F3d.173.01–9442.html.
[47] Abrams v. Société Natoinale des Chemins de Fer Français (2004) http://caselaw.findlaw.com/us-2nd-circuit/1228873.html.

there was no jurisdiction, the courtroom had issued a clear moral judgement.

Meanwhile, in France, the Lipietz family brought the SNCF to trial in 2006 for having deported George Lipietz from Toulouse to Drancy in unbearable conditions. George passed away before the trial began, and so it was his children, Alain and Hélène, who became the real forces behind the trial. Aside from the inhumane transport conditions, they accused both the state and the SNCF of financially benefitting from this illegal transport. On 6 June 2006, the Administrative Courts in Toulouse identified a wrongful attitude vis-à-vis the transfer transports. The SNCF was held responsible for its actions and had to pay 21,000 Euros to the plaintiffs.[48]However, the SNCF appealed this decision on the basis that it had disregarded key jurisdictional procedures, and an appeal which they won in Bordeaux on 21 March 2007.[49]

Within the academic milieu, there was almost always a general consensus that this affair misunderstood the realities of the Occupation. The writings of Ribeill, Wieviorka, Rousso, Margairaz and others all supported the argument that the SNCF had been a 'cog in the wheel' of the Final Solution, and had taken no initiatives. Michael Marrus also supported his French colleagues in their opposition to the SNCF trials.[50] His insight into the SNCF trials have been invaluable in showing the problems which surround delayed Holocaust justice. To sum up the situation in the words of Annette Wieviorka: 'the trial against the State and the SNCF in the Toulouse civil courts (was) a bad trial'.[51]

Despite academic attempts to nuance the SNCF's history, the SNCF came under more and more pressure to acknowledge its responsibility, commemorate the victims, and pay reparations to the survivors. By not complying, the SNCF risked losing billion-dollar contracts. Indeed, Tamen's goal had always been to receive money for her claimants, for the SNCF to pay up. However, it is the recent development of a high-speed train network in certain states which reveals the full extent of the SNCF affair's economic repercussions. As mentioned in the introduction, the SNCF role in the Holocaust was brought to the forefront of American plans to build high-speed trains in California, Florida, Maryland and New York since the 2000s. According to some leading democrats in the state of California, there were real ethical risks in hiring the SNCF to

---

[48] Lipietz et al v. Le préfet de Haute-Garonne et la SNCF (2001–06), available at www.haguejusticeportal.net/Docs/NLP/France/Lipietz_jugement_6-6-2006.pdf.
[49] See also Marrus, 'The Case of the French Railways' (2010), 245–64.   [50] Ibid.
[51] Wieviorka, 'La Shoah' (2007) 99.

build trains and train tracks in America. To think that 'there could be a train made by the very same company that took Jews to the camps' was unbearable to some.[52] A first law was passed in California in June 2010 to side-line the SNCF from this multi-million dollar project. Similar cases subsequently arose in other states, notably in Florida and Maryland. They pointed a finger at the SNCF for never acknowledging that it had taken part – and profited from – one of the most renowned crimes in all of history. Other companies were also affected, such as Japan's national railway which had deported American soldiers during the Second World War. Californian lawmakers were accused of American protectionism, for by claiming historical integrity they were in fact keeping the most competitive foreign firms at arm's lengths.[53]

These economic sanctions were very serious, and the SNCF risked losing out on billions of dollars. So whilst his predecessor Louis Gallois had been reluctant to publicly apologise for a crime which he felt the SNCF had not committed, Guillaume Pepy, the Chairman of the SNCF, saw things differently. In November 2010 he gave an apology speech in America publicly acknowledging the company's role in the Holocaust, followed by another speech in France in January 2011. The French speech took place at the Bobigny memorial, financed by the SNCF to commemorate the victims of deportation, and was a highly mediatised event which included personalities like Serge Klarsfeld and Simone Veil. Pepy expressed the SNCF's 'deep sadness and regret' for the its actions at the time. But if this mirrors Chirac's ground-breaking speech, Pepy also continued to uphold the memory of the resistance: 'I also want us at today's gathering to honour the 2,000 railway workers shot or dead in deportation, who paid with their lives for their insubordination, their resistance to the Nazi occupier and its Vichy collaborators'. Chirac had in fact done something very similar in his 1995 speech, where he contrasted the dark history of France's involvement in the Holocaust to the glowing light of its resistance activities.[54]

Neither Pepy's speech nor the various commemorative and research projects which the SNCF became involved in were enough to dissipate growing tensions in America, however. In fact, these repeated attempts to calm accusations were received quite negatively by some of the cheminot and French community: the SNCF seemed to be pandering to

---

[52] Julian Ryall and Nick Allen, 'California to force rail companies to come clean on Holocaust role', *Telegraph* (15 Aug. 2010).
[53] 'Rail firms' wartime records: What did you do in the war ?', *The Economist* (10 July 2010).
[54] Guillaume Pepy Bobigny Speech, 11 January 2011. See also *Discours et messages de Jacques Chirac*. Baruch, *Des lois indignes* (2013).

irrational and unfounded American demands. Online blogs and comment boxes were peppered with reactionary comments denouncing the SNCF's attempts to apologise for its past actions.[55]

The agreement between France and American in December 2014 seems to have been the only way to kill off the threat of economic (and legal) sanctions, but there is no doubt that the affair had left its mark on public memory. The international media had been seized by the drama of the SNCF affair for over a decade. French papers (*Le Monde*, *L'Express*, *Libération*, *Le Point*) commented on the SNCF's newfound role under Vichy, with emotional articles accompanied by harrowing photographs of the cattle cars. Some journalists also published books on this topic, shining an accusatory light on both the SNCF and the cheminots.[56] Journalists in the UK and the USA (*Daily Mail*, *Telegraph*, *New York Times*, *San Francisco Gate*, *The Economist*) also reported on the controversy, underlining the international resonance of the affair.[57]

3   The end of the resistance myth? The case of Leon Bronchart

In light of the SNCF affair, is the myth of cheminot resistance dead? Not quite. First, Pepy's speech, like Chirac's, underlined the on-going relevance of preserving the history and memory of the French resistance. Second, the online blogosphere confirms that cheminots and non-cheminots are quick to defend cheminot resistance activities of the period. And most important of all, the myth of cheminot resistance has not disappeared so much as it has been transformed. Indeed, the most heroised act of cheminot resistance is currently an act of rescue and defiance carried out by Léon Bronchart. Bronchart, an ex-cheminot, resister and deportee, has recently been acknowledged as the only railway worker to have acted 'morally' during the Holocaust. His story is praised in the press and online, but also in Yad Vashem, at the Shoah Memorial in Paris and at the Panthéon: indeed, Bronchart is the only cheminot recognised as a *Righteous Amongst the Nations* – or a *Juste de France*. And yet, Bronchart's story is not so straightforward. By exploring how

---

[55] See Broch, 'The SNCF Affair' (expected Nov. 2016).
[56] Delpard, *Les convois de la Honte* (2005); Laborde, *Ça va mieux* (2008) 95–6; Laborde, *Une histoire* (2011).
[57] 'La SNCF rattrapée par les fantômes d'Auschwitz', *Marianne* (23–29 August, 1999); Ralph Blumenthal, 'U.S. Suit says French Trains Took Victims To the Nazis', *The New York Times* (13 Jun. 2001); Fabrice Rousselet, 'Ce procès, je le dois à ma mère', *Libération* (24 Jun. 2003); Richard Lerchbaum and Olivier Nahum, 'La SNCF ne se souciait pas de ce qu'elle transportait', *Actualité Juive* (undated).

Bronchart went from being a cheminot under Vichy to a post-war hero of resistance and rescue, this case study sheds a very revealing light on contemporary memory politics and on the on-going desire to heroise the Vichy years.

When war broke out in September 1939, Bronchart – a fifty-year old train driver from Brive at the head of a large family who had fought and been imprisoned during the Great War – enrolled in the 7th section of the *chemins de fer de campagne*. After the fall of France in June 1940, Bronchart returned home a shattered man. In his memoirs he describes his inability to accept the fate of France, and he became one of the few to resist the German Occupation as early as the summer of 1940. He made contacts with other colleagues from Bordeaux, Toulouse, Nantes and Orléans, creating a small resistance network which transported letters and clandestine papers across the demarcation line. Independently of this group, Bronchart set up a tiny printing station in his basement where he could print illegal tracts, fliers and papers.

These 'anti-national' activities are not, however, what Bronchart is remembered for. On 31 October 1942, Bronchart was on the Montauban platform next to his locomotive, waiting for the cars to be attached which he would then drive into the Occupied Zone. However, when the convoy finally arrived Bronchart noticed that it was guarded by French police. Curious, he asked what was in the cars, and was told that the convoy was full of political prisoners. Bronchart immediately stopped the engine of his locomotive, and told the station master that he refused to drive these men anywhere. Another cheminot was ordered to replace him, and the train set off shortly afterwards.

Because the railway milieu was so insistent on obedience, Bronchart was immediately suspended from work and made to appear before a disciplinary court on 14 December. The head of the disciplinary council was apparently surprised to see Bronchart, who gave an emotional account justifying his action. He emphasised his loyalty to France, his love for his country and his experience as a prisoner of war in the First World War: 'Sirs, I would like to think (...) that you will allow me to believe in my conviction, that there are some duties which are superior to our professional obligations'.[58] The council was apparently very moved by Bronchart's speech. The head of the council, shaking his hand, assured him that he would have nothing to worry about. Bronchart's end of year bonus was cancelled, and he was sent back to work. A few weeks later, when Bronchart refused to drive a train of German troops to their destination, the event

---

[58] Léon Bronchart, *Ouvrier et Soldat, un français raconte sa vie* (Vaison-la-Romaine: H. Meffre, 1969) 107.

went completely unnoticed. But in January 1943, Bronchart was arrested by the Germans for having copies of the clandestine resistance paper *Combat* in his home. His son, Loulou, was also arrested that day, and both men were deported to the camps where they spent almost three years. After his release from Dora in 1945, Bronchart and his son were both physically and mentally scarred. According to Bronchart's daughter, Madeleine, family life was extremely difficult after the war.

Bronchart was awarded several medals and honours for his experiences of resistance and deportation during the war – however, it is his refusal to drive the train from Montauban which has projected him into public memory. Indeed, in the late 1990s he was made *Righteous Amongst the Nations* for having refused to drive a train of *Jewish* deportees.[59] The procedure to be nominated for such an award is quite rigorous. In 1994, Bronchart's old Jewish neighbour, Paulette Babiz-Rosenberg, spontaneously wrote a letter to Yad Vashem stating that '[Bronchart] was the only French railway worker, the only one, to have refused to drive a train of Jewish deportees who were heading to Drancy'.[60] She also described the assistance he had given her family, who went into hiding after November 1942, and to the Polish Jew Adolphe StrYkowsky who Bronchart had hid in his locomotive.[61] Babiz-Rosenberg's testimony was confirmed by her sister, Rose Rosenberg, and by Bronchart's daughter, Madeleine Bronchart. Following on from this, Léon Bronchart received the title of *Righteous Amongst the Nations* in 1998, and his name of is now carved into the *Mur des Justes* in Paris.

According to his own memoirs, the train Bronchart refused to drive had *political prisoners*, not Jews. The confusion pre-dated this award, however. Already in 1969, an ex-school teacher wrote to Bronchart, hailing him for his heroism and patriotism: 'You, the pioneer who embraced the morality of the cheminot and who acted when so many stayed quiet, trembling with fright . . . your battle against the occupier, your refusal to drive a train of

---

[59] This title was originally created in 1953 by Yad Vashem, the Holocaust Martyrs' and Heroes' Remembrance Authority, to honour the non-Jews who had helped rescue Jews from the Nazi persecution. Since 1989, the title has come to carry considerable weight. Under the presidency of Jacques Chirac in the late 1990s, France went so far as to appropriate the title, now commonly known as *Les Justes de France*. A *Mur des Justes* was then built at the *Mémorial de la Shoah* in the narrow streets of the 4th *arrondissement*, while the *Justes* entered the Pantheon in 2007. See Gensburger, *Les Justes* (2010); see also Sarah Gensburger, 'Le titre des Justes' in Jacques Sémelin, Sarah Gensburger and Claire Andrieu, eds., *La Résistances aux Génocides: de la pluralité des actes de sauvetage* (Paris: Presses de la Fondation nationale des sciences politiques, 2008) 39–52.

[60] YVA/Dossier n°6354: Léon Bronchart, letter (Jun. 1993) from Paulette Babiz-Rosenberg to Director of Yad Vashem in Jerusalem.

[61] *Ibid.*, Léon Bronchart.

Jewish deportees, your letter to Marshal Pétain . . .'[62] In 1993, the town of
Saint-Avertin renamed one of its streets after Léon Bronchart for having
refused to drive a train of Jewish deportees in October 1942.[63]

Since 1998, a myth has been built around this famous refusal. Alain
Lipietz has crowned Bronchart as 'the only cheminot who is a Righteous
Among the Nations, the only mechanic to have refused to drive a locomotive which led a train of deportees (. . .) Needless to say that the heads of the
SNCF were determined to keep this quiet'.[64] Another person commented
that 'The responsibility of the SNCF is one thing. Yet some of its agents
refused to participate in this collaboration (. . .). Thus 64 years ago, on
31 October 1942, Léon Bronchart, a train conductor, objected to and
protested against the convoy that he was requested to drive'.[65] Rappoport
further described him as 'the only railway worker who refused to drive a
convoy of deportees', and compared this to the attitude of the SNCF, who
not only 'sanctioned' Bronchart but also 'never objected to or protested
against these transports'.[66] His life and resistance activities are related in
Lucien Lazare's *Dictionnaire des Justes de France*, where he is further
praised for being 'the only known train driver to have the courage and
audacity to refuse to transport Jewish deportees'.[67]

The Holocaust Rail Coalition for Justice has also seized Bronchart's
story to further incriminate the SNCF and the cheminots – but how has
Bronchart's family reacted to this praise? I had great difficulties getting
an interview with Madeleine Bronchart, and was then insulted by her
brother. Indeed, the descendants of Léon Bronchart have been outraged
by the discussions in the press which glorify their father in order to
further demonise the railway company. In her interview, Madeleine
was extremely frustrated with the accusations against the SNCF for
crimes against humanity, and also the criticisms that it had not resisted
the deportation convoys. She was particularly enraged by those who were
using her father's memory against the SNCF.[68]

The story of Léon Bronchart is a strong reminder that there is still a
burning need to heroise, glamorise and ultimately simplify the actions of

[62] YVA/Dossier n°6354: Léon Bronchart, Letter (20 Sept. 1969) from anonymous sender.
[63] The inauguration took place in Saint-Avertin on 18 Apr. 1993, and the article in
question was published shortly after in the local newspaper. It was found amongst
other documents in Léon Bronchart's Dossier at the *Comité Français de Yad Vashem*.
[64] 'Léon Bronchart, juste, ouvrier et soldat' (22 Sept. 2007) available at Lipietz.net.
[65] Anthony Astaix, 'Le cheminot et le principe de désobéissance' (31 Oct. 2006) available
at www.Blogdalloz.
[66] Rappoport 'Les procès contre l'Etat et la SNCF, "une justice attendue depuis 60 ans"'
(3 Jul. 2007) available at in www.juif.org/blogs/1034,les-proces-contre-l-etat-et-la-sncf.php.
[67] Lucien Lazare, ed., *Dictionnaire des Justes de France* (Paris: Fayard, 2003) 125.
[68] Interview Madeleine Bronchart (30 May 2008).

ordinary people in the Occupation. On one hand, the cheminots continue to embrace the memory of Bronchart's resistance activities. Aside from his own family's ongoing concern with 'blaspheming the memory of cheminot resistance', an ex-cheminot in Montauban recently organised a commemoration in Bronchart's honour. On the other hand, this memory of Bronchart's involvement in cheminot resistance is overshadowed by his actions as a gentile rescuer. The fact that Léon Bronchart's story has been moralised and framed within a discourse of Holocaust history and memory shows that the myth of cheminot resistance no longer looks like *La Bataille du Rail* – but it still exists to a certain extent.

★★★

The history and memory of cheminot resistance is not dead. First, Léon Bronchart is an example that contemporary cheminot resistors exist in the guise of Holocaust heroes and rescuers. Second, there is more than a kernel of truth behind this myth. The various academic works which have been carried out, this book amongst them, show the realities of resistance in the cheminot milieu. But it would be a mistake to stop there – the aim is not to get a yes or no answer about whether or not cheminots resisted, but rather to understand how they lived under Vichy, and how those four years of occupation would impact their community in the long run. Holding on to the more glorious memories of the war is not, therefore, a misrepresentation of what happened. In fact, it could be argued that holding on to those memories is even more important at a time when the reputation of cheminots – criticised for their strike actions amongst other things – came under threat from the general public after the war (see Figure 9.4).

Beyond a history of cheminot resistance lies the story of a community simultaneously unique and ordinary. Acts of resistance, defiance and

Figure 9.4 Bogy and Tampon defend the railways: Passenger: 'The train is stopping again! You must be joking!!!'; Passenger: 'What an organisation! This SNCF!! It is shameful!!!'; Passenger: 'If there is a deficit in the railways, it's the fault of the cheminots . . .'; Passenger: '. . . in fact, all these cheminots are . . .', *Notre Métier*, 77 (25 Oct. 1946). SNCF – Centre National des Archives Historiques.

tactics play into this story at many levels, and in fact the cheminots are a fascinating prism to explore the many ways that individuals but also communities express their frustration under occupation. But the Vichy years also shed considerable light on the plurality of what appeared to be a uniform, tight-knit community. The relationship between the worker and the SNCF, the individual and the cheminot milieu, the French and the state, was constantly evolving and changing, not least because the circumstances of war and occupation put great strains on the French people. This evolving relationship helps to understand the re-adjustment of their own professional values and code of conduct during the occupation. In particular, it helps to understand why cheminots had been absent from the general strike in 1936 but been so present in the general strike of 1947. Indeed, it seems that the Vichy years allowed cheminots to redefine their relationship to their work, to the SNCF and to the state such that they would change their protest tactics in the post-war period.

This does not mean that conservatism and politics of negotiation were not still present in the post-war years; in fact, it was a major aim of this book to show the continuity of cheminot attitudes and behaviour from the late-nineteenth century to the post-Liberation period. Still in the 1980s, cheminots were objecting to railway sabotage for the very same reasons they had been objecting to them in the late 1800s: because it endangered the lives of travellers and cheminots alike, but also the lives of their machines.[69] There are many layers behind cheminots' relationship to sabotage and strikes, and some of these are clearly rooted in a long history of political and professional consciousness.

So rather than a picture of the 'cheminot resister' which is embodied in myth of resistance but also rescue, this book sought to show the history of the French railway workers as one of ordinary workers. Despite the undeniably unique traits of their community, their experiences under Vichy clearly show that the individuals who made up this community of over 400,000 workers were not isolated from the pains, pressures and struggles of the Occupation. In fact, their story highlights the economic pillaging of France in the Second World War, and the considerable strains of workers in Western Europe. Moreover, like all French people under Vichy, every day decisions were made through a combination of external factors, historic values, individual beliefs and opportunity. In addition, they felt particularly attached to deep-rooted professional values. Neither heroes nor bastards, the cheminots tell a fascinating and varied story of life under occupation.

---

[69] 'Lettre ouverte à tous ceux qui s'attaquent à l'outil ferroviaire', *Indépendant* (22 Feb. 1983), with special thanks to Andrew Smith for pointing this out.

Glossary of railway professions

French	English
aide-ouvrier	unskilled worker
aiguillage	switch
agent de triage	yardman
atelier	workshop
barons du rail	railway barons
cantonniers	roadmenders
chauffeur	train driver
chef de district	district chief
chef de gare	station master
chef de manœuvres	head of manoeuvres
chef de service	department head
chef de train	conductor
cheminot	railway worker
conducteur	locomotive engineer
contrôleurs	controllers
dépot	depot
directeur de la Région Nord	director of the North Region
directeur de la Région Sud-Est	regional director of the South-East Region
directeur général	managing director
directeur général adjoint	assisting managing director
directeur des installations fixes	director of fixed installations
directeur du département central MT	director of central department of Material and Traction
directeur du Personnel	Director of Personnel (Barth)
directeur Régional	regional director (Renard)
facteur au matériel	railway postman
fils de signaux	electric lines
garde-barrière	level-crossing keeper
garde-frein	brakeman

gardes des communications	guards communications
gare	station
homme d'équipe	handler
ingénieur	engineer
ingénieur des voies	track engineer
ingénieur en chef	chief engineer
inspecteur divisionnaire	divisional inspector
inspecteur en chef	chief inspector
inspecteur principal	principal inspector
manoeuvre	labourer
manœuvre specialisé	skilled labourer
mécanicien [de locomotive]	locomotive driver
ouvrier	worker
ouvrier-jardinier	worker-gardener
passage à niveaux	level crossing
poseur	track layer
Président	Chairman
sous-chef de depot	assisting depot chief
sous-directeur	assisting director
surveillant de ronde	supervisor of rounds
tourneur	turner
travailleur du rail	railway worker
triage	triage centre
wagons de marchandises	goods car

Bibliography

Primary sources

Centre d'Archives Historiques de la SNCF, Le Mans (SNCF)

25/LM/240
25/LM/256
25/LM/258
25/LM/265
25/LM/1123
25/LM/1933
25/LM/1934
25/LM/1940
206/LM/1
26/LM/018
26/LM/0020
26/LM/0022
26/LM/0036
26/LM/2
44/LM/149
73/LM/27
201/LM/1
201/LM/2
206/LM/1
206/LM/3
206/LM/4
206/LM/5
206/LM/6
206/LM/9
243/LM/10
274/LM/001

274/LM/002
274/LM/006
303/LM/1
303/LM/2
303/LM/7
303/LM/10
303/LM/11
303/LM/15
303/LM/22
303/LM/23
505/LM/105
505/LM/185
505/LM/257
PNV/103919

Archives Nationales de France, Paris (AN)

F/7/13493
F/7/14913
F/7/14881
F/7/14913
F/7/14919
F/7/15088
F/14/13698
F/14/16943
3/AG/2/234
3/AG/2/235
3/AG/2/236
72/AJ/47
72/AJ/414
72/AJ/415
72/AJ/473
72/AJ/474
72/AJ/477
72/AJ/478
72/AJ/495
72/AJ/496
72/AJ/497
72/AJ/1927
72/AJ/2280
72/AJ/2288
72/AJ/2289
72/AJ/2296

72/AJ/2297
307/AP/60

Archives Nationales du Monde du Travail, Roubaix (ANMT)

12/AQ/25
202/AQ/201
202/AQ/236
202/AQ/245
202/AQ/1191
202/AQ/1192
202/AQ/1193
202/AQ/1224
2002/026/023
2002/026/058
2002/026/087
2004/040/009
2004/040/010
2004/040/012
2004/040/013
2004/040/016
2042/W/10

Archives du Personnel SNCF, Béziers (APSNCF)

Robert Aron
Salomon Chich
Paul Ehrmann
Henri Lang
Robert Lévi
André Lévy
Elie Molina
Sabétaï Toross
Gabriel Touviès
Raymond Weil
Jean-Louis Wolkowitsch

Centre de Documentation Juive Contemporaine, Paris (CDJC)

XXVb-28
XXVb-86
XXVc-208
XXVc-208
CCXIX-31
CCXXXVI-62

DLXI-1
Alphonse Asch
Achille Lefschetz
Isaac Soudarski

Archives Départementales des Bouches-du-Rhône, Marseille (ADBR)

8/J/392
28/J/273
76/W/3
76/W/218
148/W/378

Archives Départementales de la Haute-Garonne, Toulouse (ADHG)

1831/W/98
2042/W/10
2060/W/82

Archives Départementales de l'Ariège, Foix (ADA)

25/W/13

Archives Départementales du Rhône (ADR)

45/W/35

Archives Municipales d'Aix-en-Provence (AMA)

6/H/67

Yad Vashem Archives (YVA)

Dossier n°6354: Léon Bronchart

Author's interviews

Gabriel Bonnin (22 Mar. 2008)
André Brosset (23 Feb. 2008)
Madeleine Bronchart (30 May 2008)
André Brussière (26 Feb. 2008)
Roger Charbonnier (24 Apr. 2008)
Monsieur Creusot (4 Mar. 2008)
Robert Lebrun (7 Feb. 2008)
Bernard Lévi (20 Nov. 2012)

Association pour l'Histoire des Chemins de fer Français (AHICF)

Interview transcripts:
Marcel Redempt (19 Oct. 1999)
Jean-Claude Huckendubler (19 Oct. 1999)

Bernard Le Chatelier (19 Nov. 1999)
Jacques Eisenmann (28 Apr. 2000)
Catherine de Béchillon (2 Jul. 1997)
Bernard Lévi (13 Apr. 2000)

Films and documentaries

Gare de la Douleur (1984), dir. Henri Jouf.
Je suis vivante et je vous aime (1998), dir. Roger Kahane.
L'inacceptable (2000), dir. Claude Binsse.
La Bataille du Rail (1945), dir. René Clément.

Newspapers

Actualités Juive
Chemin de Fer
Chicago Tribune
Courthouse News Services
Forward
France
Historail
Indépendant
L'Histoire
L'Union (Champagne, Ardenne, Picardie)
La Garonne
La Petite Gironde
La Vie du rail
Le Courier Picard
Le Midi
Le Point
Le Rail
Le Rail Snydicaliste
Libération
Marianne
Notre Métier
Paris-Soir
Paris Match
Renseignements Hébdomadaire
Résistance Réalités
Reuters
Spiegel
Telegraph
The Economist
The Guardian

The Independent
The Telegraph
The New York Times

Legal documents published online

Abrams *v.* Société Nationale des Chemins de Fer Francais, 175 F.Supp.2d 423, 433 (E.D.N.Y.2001). Available at www.assetsearchblog.com/uploads/file/ 2ndCirSNCF(1).pdf.
Abrams *v.* Société Nationale des Chemins de Fer Francais, 332 F.3d 173 (2d Cir.2003). Available at https://law.resource.org/pub/us/case/reporter/ F3/332/332.F3d.173.01-9442.html.
Abrams *v.* Société Natoinale des Chemins de Fer Français, (2004). Available at http://caselaw.findlaw.com/us-2nd-circuit/1228873.html.
Lipietz et al *v.* Le préfet de Haute-Garonne et la SNCF (2001–2006). Available at www.haguejusticeportal.net/Docs/NLP/France/Lipietz_jugement_6-6-2006.pdf.

Masters/doctoral theses

Vincent Auzas, 'La Mémoire de la Résistance chez les cheminots: constructions et enjeux, sep. 44–nov. 48', masters thesis in contemporary history, at the Université Paris 1, Panthéon-Sorbonne (2000).
Bruno Bachelot, 'La mise en place de la législation anti-communiste à la SNCF, sep. 39–nov. 42', masters thesis at the University of Maine (2002).
Thomas Beaumont, 'Communists and Cheminots: Industrial Relations and Ideological Conflict in the French Railway Industry, 1919–1939', doctoral thesis at the University of Exeter (2011).
Marie-Renée Courty-Valentin, 'Les grèves de 1947 en France: Recherche centrée sur le secteur public et nationalisé,' unpublished thesis from the Institut d'Etudes Politiques de Paris (1981).
Camille Warion, 'Quelques considérations sur l'hygiène des chemins de fer', doctoral thesis at the Faculté de Médecine de Paris, (Paris, Imprimeur de la Faculté de Médecine, 1872).

Bachelier report

Christian Bachelier, *La SNCF sous l'occupation allemande, 1940–1944, rapport documentaire*, 4 vols. (Paris: IHTP-CNRS, 1996). All references from the Bachelier report were accessed on the internet: www.ahicf.com/ww2/ rapport/av-propos.htm.

Published primary sources

Discours et messages de Jacques Chirac, maire de Paris, premier ministre, président de la Républisue, en hommage aux juifs de France victimes de la collaboration de l'Etat français de Vichy avec l'occupant allemand, en hommage au CRIF et aux justes de France et en mémoire de la Shoah (Paris: Fils et filles des déportés juifs de France, 2007).

Franco-German Armistice (1940) can be viewed at the Avalon Project, Yale University. Available at http://avalon.law.yale.edu/ wwii/frgearm.asp.

Great Western and Midland Joint Railways, *Rules and Regulations for the Guidance of the Officers and Men in the Service of the Great Western and Midland Railway Companies on their Joint Railways and at their Joint Stations*, (1 Jan. 1905).

The Holocaust Railway Coalition, see http://holocaustrailvictims.org/about-us/.

*Les Inconvénients de voyages sur les chemins de fer, par un ex-Chef de train (X***)* (Paris: 1862).

Livre-Mémorial des déportés de France arêtes par mesure de répression et dans certains cas par mesure de persécution 1940–1945, 4 vols. (Paris: Tirésias, 2004).

Mémoires d'ingénieurs, destins ferroviaires. Autobiographies professionnelles de Frédéric Surleau (1884–1972) et Robert Lévi (1895–1981), RHCF, Hors Série, n°8 (Mar. 2007).

Mémorial de la déportation des Juifs de France (Paris: Serge et Béate Klarsfeld, 1978).

The Life of a Railway Clerk. A Brief Description of the Main Conditions of Employment in the Offices of British Railway Companies, and a Statement of the Case for Higher Scales of Salary for all Grades of Railway Clerical Workers: Prepared by Three Experience Railwaymen, etc. (London: Railway Clerks' Association, 1911).

Charles d'Aragon, *La Résistance sans héroïsme* (Paris: Editions du Seuil, 1971).

Jean Berthelot, *Sur les rails du pouvoir: De Munich à Vichy* (Paris: Robert Laffont, 1967).

Pierre Blairet, *Cheminot* (Paris: Editions du Rocher, 1998).

Marcel Blanchard, Memoirs in *Les cheminots dans la guerre et l'Occupation, témoignages et récits*, Revue d'Histoire des Chemins de Fer, Hors Série, 7 (Mar. 2004).

Marc Bloch, *Strange Defeat, A Statement of Evidence Written in 1940*, translated by Gerard Hopkins (London: Oxford University Press, 1949, c1946).

Léon Bronchart, *Ouvrier et Soldat, un français raconte sa vie* (Vaison-la-Romaine: H. Meffre, 1969) 107.

Henri Castel, *Histoire ouvrière* (Vichy: Mouvement GLE, 1944).

Guy Le Corre, *Un cheminot rennais dans la Résistance* (Paris: Editions Tirésias, 2003).

François Crouzet, 'Voyageurs sans billets' in *Les cheminots dans la guerre et l'Occupation: témoignages et récits*, RHDC, Second Edition, n°7 (Nov. 2004).

Edouard-Adolphe Duchesne, *Des chemins de fer et de leur influence sur la santé des mécaniciens et des chauffeurs* (Paris: Mallet-Bachelier, 1857).

Jean Falaize and Henri Girod-Eymery, *A travers les Chemins de Fer, de l'origine à nos jours* (Paris: Denoël, 1948).

Louis Le François, *J'ai Faim … ! Journal d'un Français en France depuis l'Armistice* (Brentano's: New York, 1942).

Henri Frenay, *The Night Will End* (Sevenoaks: Coronet, 1976, c1973).

Jean Guéhenno, *Journal des années noires 1940–1944* (Paris: Gallimard, 2002, c1947).

James Lansdale Hodson, *Through the Dark Night, Being some Account of a War Correspondent's Journeys, Meetings and What Was Said to Him, in France, Britain and Flanders During 1939–1940* (London: Victor Gollancz Ltd., 1941).

Arthur Koestler, *Scum of the Earth* (London: Elan, 1991, c1941).
Raymond-Raoul Lambert, *Carnet d'un témoin* (Paris: Fayard, 1985).
Léon Malo, *La Sécurité dans les chemins de fer* (Paris: Dunod, 1882).
Jean Alcide Paroche, *Un Cheminot face aux technocrates à la SNCF* (Paris: La Pensée Universelle, 1976).
Emile Pouget, *Sabotage* (Chicago: Charles H. Kerr & Company, 1913).
C. E. R. Sherrington, *Raoul Dautry: An Appreciation* (Belmont, Surrey: The Author, 1950).

Secondary sources

Un Siècle en Train (Paris: Editions La Vie du rail, 2000).
Sébatsien Albertelli, *Les services secrets du général de Gaulle: le BCRA, 1940–1944* (Paris: Perrin, 2009).
Henri Amouroux, *La Grande Histoire des Français sous l'occupation*, vols. 1/2 (Paris: Laffont, 1976–1977).
Claire Andrieu, ed., *La perséceution des Juifs de France, 1940–1944, et le rétablissement de la légalité republicaine: Recueil des textes officiels, 1940–1999* (Paris: La Documentation Française, 2000).
Patrice Arnaud, *Les STO: Histoire des Français requis en Allemagne nazie, 1942–1945* (Paris: CNRS Editions, 2010).
Patrice Arnaud, 'La longue défaite des "requis" du STO', Tal Bruttmann, Hervé Joly and Annette Wieviorka, eds., *Qu'est-ce qu'un déporté? Histoire et mémoires des déportations de la Seconde Guerre mondiale* (Paris: CNRS, 2009).
Anthony Astaix, 'Le cheminot et le principe de désobéissance' (31 Oct. 2006) Available at www.Blogdalloz.
Jean-Pierre Azéma, *1940 l'année terrible* (Paris: Seuil, 1990).
Serge Barcellini and Annette Wieviorka, *Passant, souviens-toi! Les lieux du souvenir de la Seconde Guerre mondiale en France* (Paris: Plon, 1995).
Marc Olivier Baruch, *Servir l'Etat français: l'administration en France de 1940 à 1944* (Paris: Fayard, 1997).
Marc Olivier Baruch, *Des lois indignes ? les historiens, la politique et le droit* (Paris: Tallandier, 2013).
Rémi Baudouï, 'La cité-jardin de Tergnier de la Compagnie du Nord, 1921–1950: Elements d'analyse d'un modèle de société cheminote', *Les Chemins de fer, l'Espace et la Société en France*, Actes du Colloque, 18–19 May 1988 (Paris: AHICF, 1988).
Rémi Baudouï and Raoul Dautry, *1880–1951: la technocratie de la République* (Paris: Balland, 1992).
Jean-Pierre Bertin-Maghit, '*La Bataille du Rail*: de l'authenticité à la chanson de geste', *Revue d'histoire moderne et contemporaine*, 33.2 (Apr.–Jun. 1986).
Nathalie Bibas and Henri Lang, *1895–1942* (Paris: Editions LBM, 2012).
Pierre Birnbaum, 'Le rôle limité des juifs dans l'industrialisation de la société française', in Chantal Menoyoun, Alain Medam and Pierre-Jacques Rotjman *Les Juifs et l'économique: miroirs et mirages* (Toulouse: Presses universitaires du Mirail, 1992) 163–77.

Julien Blanc, *Au commencement de la Résistance: du côté du Musée de l'Homme 1940–1941* (Paris: Seuil, 2010).

Anne Boitel, *Le camp de Rivesaltes 1941–1942: du centre d'hébergement au 'Drancy de la zone libre'* (Perpignan: Presse Universitaire de Perpignan: Mare Nostrum, 2001).

Helga Elisabeth and Bories-Sawala, *Dans la gueule du loup: les Français requis du travail en Allemagne* (Villeneuve d'Ascq: Presses universitaires du Septentrion, 2010).

Laurence Bour, 'La réquisition des cheminots pour le travail en Allemagne: L'apport des archives de la SNCF' in Christian Chevandier and Jean-Claude Dumas, eds., *Travailler dans les entreprises françaises sous l'Occupation*, (Besançon, Presses universitaires de Franche-Comté, 2008) 131–5.

Jean-Yves Boursier, *La Résistance dans le Jovinien et le groupe Bayard: mémoire et engagement* (Joigny: Groupement Jovinien Bayard, 1993).

Florent Brayard, *La 'solution finale de la question juive': la technique, le temps et les catéfories de la décision* (Paris: Fayard, 2004).

Ludivine Broch, 'Martyred Towns at the Liberation: The Case of the Massacre d'Ascq' in Ludivine Broch and Alison Carrol, eds., *France in the Era Global Wars, 1914–1945: Occupation, Politics, Empire and Entanglements* (London: Palgrave Macmillan, 2014) 50–72.

Ludivine Broch 'Professionalism in the Final Solution: French Railway Workers and the Jewish Deportations 1942–1944,' *Contemporary European History* , 23.3 (2014) 359–81.

Ludivine Broch, 'Rescue, Railways and the Righteous: French Railway Workers and the Question of Rescue in the Holocaust', *Diasporas* (Jun. 2015).

Ludivine Broch, 'The SNCF Affair: Trains, the Holocaust and Divided Memories of Vichy France,' *Lessons and Legacies XII* (expected Nov. 2016).

Christopher Browning, *The Origins of the Final Solution : The Evoltuion of Nazi Jewish Policy, September 1939–March 1942* (Lincoln: University of Nebraska Press; Jerusalem: Yad Vashem, 2004).

Tal Bruttmann, *Au bureau des affaires juives: l'administration française et l'application de la législation antisémite, 1940–1944* (Paris: Le Découverte, 2006).

Tal Bruttmann, 'La Mise en œuvre du statut des Juifs du 3 octobre 1940', *Archives Juives*, 41.1 (2008) 11–24, Available at www.cairn.info/resume.php? ID_ARTICLE=AJ_411_0011.

Philippe Burrin, *Living with Defeat: France under the German Occupation* (London: Arnolf, 1996, c1995).

Luc Capdevila, 'The Quest for Masculinity in a Defeated France, 1940–1945', *Contemporary European History*, 10.3 (Nov. 2001) 423–45.

François Caron, *Histoire des chemins de fer en France*, vol.1, 1740–1883 (Paris: Fayard, 1997).

François Caron, *Histoire des chemins de fer en France*, vol.2, 1883–1937 (Paris: Fayard, 2005).

Peter Carrier, *Holocaust Monuments and National Memory Cultures in France and Germany Since 1989: The Origins and Political Functions of the Vel d'Hiv in Paris and the Holocaust Monument in Berlin* (New York; Oxford: Berghahn, 2005).

Bruno Carrière, 'Les rails de l'Exode' in *La Vie du Rail* (7 Jun. 1990)

Bruno Carrière, 'Le 6 juin 1944: Les Alliés débarquent, la batille du rail redouble', *La Vie du Rail*, n°2448 (1 Jun. 1994) 12–34.

Bruno Carrière, 'Août 1944: Paris, les cheminots et la Libération', *La Vie du Rail*, n°2458 (28 Aug. 1994) 20–6.

Larry S. Ceplair, 'La théorie de la grève générale et du syndicalisme: Eugène Guérard et les cheminots français dans les années 1890', *Le Mouvement Social*, 116 (Jul.–Sep. 1981) 21–46.

Michel de Certeau, Frederic Jameson and Carl Lovitt, 'On The Oppositional Practices of Everyday Life', *Social Text* n°3 (Autumn 1980) 3–43.

Herrick Chapman, *State Capitalism and Working-Class Radicalism in the French Aircraft Industry* (Oxford: University of California Press, 1991).

Christian Chevandier, 'La résistance des cheminots: primat de la fonctionnalité plus qu'une réelle spécificité', *Le Mouvement social*, 180 (Jul.–Sep. 1997) 147–58.

Christian Chevandier, *Cheminots en grève, ou la construction d'une identité (1848–2001)*, (Paris: Maisonneive & Larose, 2002).

Christian Chevandier and Jean-Claude Dumas, eds., *Travailler dans les entreprises françaises sous l'Occupation*, (Besançon, Presses universitaires de Franche-Comté, 2008).

Christian Chevandier, 'La Répression des Syndicats en France, avant, pendant et après les *"années noires"*', Congreso Historia Ferroviara, Palma (14–16 Oct. 2009). Available at www.docutren.com/HistoriaFerroviaria/PalmaMallorca2009/pdf/030108_Chevandier.pdf.

Christian Chevandier, 'Les Cités PLM dans l'agglomération lyonnaise au cours des années 1930 : las cas de Vanissieux et d'Oullins', *Les Chemins de fer, l'Espace et la Société en France*, Actes du Colloque, 18–19 May 1988 (Paris: AHICF, 1988).

Maurice Choury, *Les cheminots dans la bataille du rail* (Paris: Librairie académique Perrin, 1970).

Jackie Clarke, *France in the Age of Organization: Factory, Home and the Nation from the 1920s to Vichy* (New York: Berghan Books, 2011).

Rebecca Clifford, *Commemorating the Holocaust: The Dilemmas of Remembrance in France and Italy* (Oxford: Oxford University Press, 2013).

Richard Cobb, *French and Germans, Germans and French: A Personal Interpretation of France Under Two Occupations 1914–1918/1940–1944* (Hanover, New Hampshire: University Press of New England, 1983).

Matthew Cobb, *The Resistance: The French Fight Against the Nazis* (London: Simon & Schuster, 2009).

Matthew Cobb, *Eleven Days in August: The Liberation of Paris in 1944* (London: Simon & Schuster, 2013).

François Cochet, *Les soldats de la drôle de guerre: septembre 1939–mai 1940* (Paris: Hachette, 2004).

Robin Cohen, 'Resistance and Hidden Forms of Consciousness Amongst African Workers', *Review of African Political Economy*, 19 (Winter 1980) 8–22.

Terry Coleman, *The Railway Navvies: A History of the Men Who Made the Railways* (London: Penguin, c1968, 1981).

David L. Collinson, '"Engineering Humour': Masculinity, Joking and Conflict in Shop-floor Relations', *Organization Studies*, 9.2 (1988) 181–99.

Michel Cotte, *Le choix de la révolution industrielle: Les entreprises de Marc Séguin et ses frères (1815–1835)* (Rennes: Presse Universitaires de Rennes, 2007).

Martine Courbin, 'Les cheminots et leur famille dans le quartier de la gare Saint-Jean 1856–1905', *Les Chemins de fer, l'Espace et la Société en France*, Actes du Colloque, 18–19 mai 1988, (Paris: AHICF, 1988).

Jean-Louis Crémieux-Brilhac, *Les Français de l'an 40*, vols. 1&2 (Paris: Gallimard, 1990).

Jean-Pierre Le Crom, *Syndicats, nous voilà!: Vichy et le corporatisme* (Paris: Editions de l'Atelier, 1995).

Emmanuelle Cronier, 'Les permissionnaires du front face aux cheminots pendant la Première Guerre Mondiale', *Images de Cheminots, Entre représentations et Identités*, Revue d'histoire des chemins de fer (Paris: AHICF, 2007) 91–105.

Jacques Delarue, *Trafics et Crimes sous l'Occupation* (Paris: Fayard, 1968).

Raphaël Delpard, *Les convois de la honte: enquête sur la SNCF et la déportation (1941–1945)* (Neuilly-sur-Seine: Michel Lafon, c2005).

Rémy Desquesnes, 'L'organisation todt en France 1940–1944', *Histoire, Economie et Société*, 3ème trimestre (1992).

Hanna Diamond, *Women and the Second World War in France, 1939–1948: Choices and Constraints* (Harlow: Longman, 1999).

Hanna Diamond, *Fleeing Hitler: France 1940* (Oxford: Oxford University Press, 2007).

Hanna Diamond, 'Miners, Masculinity and the 'Bataille du Charbon' in France 1944–1948', *Modern and Contemporary France*, 19.1 (2011) 69–84.

Lindsey Dodd, '"Relieving Sorrow and Misfortune"? State Charity, Ideology and Aid in Bombed-out France, 1940–1944', in Claudia Baldoli, Andrew Knapp and Richard Overy, eds., *Bombing, States and Peoples in Western Europe 1940–1945* (London: Continuum, 2011) 75–97.

Laurent Douzou, *La Résistance française: une histoire périlleuse: essai d'historiographie* (Paris: Seuil, 2005).

Laurent Douzou, 'La résistance des cheminots, un champ ouvert à la recherche' in Polino, ed., *Une entreprise pendant la guerre* (2001).

Jean-Marc Dreyfus and Sarah Gensburger, *Nazi Labour Camps in Paris: Austerlitz, Lévitan, Bassano, July 1943–August 1944* (New York: Berghahn Books, 2011).

Jean-Marc Dreyfus, *Pillages sur ordonnances: aryanisation et restitution des banques en France, 1940–1953* (Paris: Fayard, 2003).

Paul Durand, *La SNCF pendant la guerre: Sa résistance à l'occupant* (Paris: Presses universitaires de France, 1968).

Rémy Desquesnes, 'L'organisation todt en France 1940–1944', *Histoire, Economie et Société*, 11.3 (1992) 535–50.

Phillippe Fabre, *Le Conseil d'Etat et Vichy: le contentieux de l'antisémitisme* (Paris: Publications de la Sorbonne, 2001).

Shannon Fogg, *The Politics of Everyday Life in Vichy France: Foreigners, Undesirables and Strangers* (Cambridge: Cambridge University Press, 2009).

Bernard de Fontgalland, *Cheminot sans frontières: 50 ans de carnets de voyages à travers le monder* (I.A. Diffusion, 1988).

Michael R. D. Foot, *SOE in France: An Account of the Work of the British Special Operations Executive in France 1940–1944* (London: Frank Cass, 2004).

Martin Francis, 'The Domestication of the Male? Recent Research on Nineteenth- and Twentieth-century British Masculinity', *The Historical Journal*, 45.3 (2002) 637–52.

Patrick Fridenson, 'Le Conflit Social' in Ebdré Burguière and Jacques Revel, eds., *Histoire de la France: les conflits* (Paris: Seuil, 1990).

Elie Fruit, *Les syndicates dans les chemins de fer en France, 1890–1910* (Paris: Les Editions Ouvrières, 1976).

Roland Gaucher, *Histoire secrète du Parti communiste français, 1920–1974* (Paris: Albin-Michel, 1974).

Sarah Gensburger, *Les Justes de France: politiques publiques de a mémoire* (Paris: Presses de la Fondation nationale des sciences politiques, 2010).

Sarah Gensburger, 'Le titre des Justes' in Jacques Sémelin, Sarah Gensburger and Claire Andrieu, eds., *La Résistances aux Génocides: de la pluralité des actes de sauvetage* (Paris: Presses de la Fondation nationale des sciences politiques, 2008) 39–52.

Robert Gildea, *Marianne in Chains: In Search of the German Occupation of France 1940–1945* (London: Pan Books Macmillan, 2003, c2002).

Robert Gildea, *France since 1945* (Oxford: Oxford University Press, 2009, c1996).

Robert Gildea, *Fighters in the Shadows: A New History of the French Resistance* (Harvard University Press, expected 2015).

Gérard Gobitz, *Les déportations de réfugiés de zone libre en 1942* (Paris: L'Harmattan, 1996).

Barry Godfrey, 'Law, Factory Discipline and "Theft": The Impact of the Factory on Workplace Appropriation in Mid to Late Nineteenth-Century Yorkshire', *British Journal of Criminology*, 39.1 (1999) 56–71.

Marie-Louise Goergen, ed., *Cheminots et militants: un siècle de syndicalisme ferroviaire* (Paris: Editions de l'Atelier, 2003).

Alfred Gottwaldt, 'Les cheminots allemands pendant l'Occupation en France de 1940 à 1944' in Polino, ed.,*Une entreprise pendant la guerre* (2001).

Roger Gould, *Insurgent Identities: Class, Community and Protest in Paris from 1848 to the Commune* (Chicago; London: University of Chicago Press, 1995).

Fabrice Grenard, 'Les implications politiques du ravitaillement en France sous l'Ocupation', *Vingtième Siècle. Revue d'histoire*, 94 (2007) 199–215.

Anne Grynberg, *Les camps de la honte: les internés juifs des camps étrangers français 1939–1944* (Paris: Editions La Découverte, 1998).

Jochen Guckes, 'Le rôle des chemins de fer dans la déportation des Juifs de France' in *Revue d'histoire de la Shoah, Le Monde Juif*, 165, (Jan.–Apr. 1999) 29–110.

Jean-Pierre Harbulot, *Le Service du Travail Obligatoire: La région de Nancy face aux exigences allemandes* (Nancy: Presses Universitaires de Nancy, 2003).

Ulrich Herbert, 'Good Times, Bad Times' in Richard Bessel, ed., *Life in the Third Reich* (Oxford: Oxford University Press, 1987).

Ulrich Herbert, 'Labour and Extermination: Economic Interest and the Primacy of Weltanschauung in National Socialism', *Past and Present*, 138.1 (1993) 144–95.

Ulrich Herbert, *Hitler's Foreign Workers: Enforced Foreign Labor in Germany under the Third Reich* (Cambridge: Cambridge University Press, 1997).

Raul Hilberg, 'German Railroads/Jewish Souls', *Society*, vol. 35, n°2 (1998) 162–74

Raul Hilberg, *The Destruction of the European Jews*, vol 2. (London: Yale University Press, 2003, c1961).

Eric Hobsbawm, *Labouring Men: Studies in the History of Labour* (London: Weidenfeld and Nicolson, 1986).

Cécile Hochard and Bruno Leroux, *La Lettre de la Fondation de la Résistance: Les cheminots dans la Résistance* (Fondation de la Résistance, 2005).

Stanley Hoffmann, *Decline or Renewal? France Since the 1930s* (New York: Viking Press, 1974).

Richard C. Hollinger and John P. Clark, *Theft by Employees* (Lexington, Mass: Lexington Books, 1983).

Edward Homze, *Foreign Labour in Nazi Germany* (Princeton: Princeton University Press, 1967).

Jean-Marie d'Hoop, 'La main d'oeuvre française au service de l'allemagne' *Revue d'histoire de la deuxième guerre mondiale*, 81 (Jan. 1971) 73–88.

John Horne and Alan Kramer, *German Atrocities, 1914: A History of Denial* (London: Yale University Press, 2001).

Roger Hutter, 'Les ingénieurs, anciens élèves des Mines de Paris, créateurs de chemins de fer en France et en Europe (à partir de 1824)', *Bulletin de l'association des anciens élèves de l'Ecole des mines de Paris* (1964).

Talbot Imlay, *The Politics of Industrial Collaboration during World War II : Ford France, Vichy and Nazi Germany* (Cambridge: Cambridge University Press, 2014).

Coralie Immelé, 'Le regard des historiens de la Résistance sur l'engagement des cheminots (1944–1997),' in *Les cheminots dans la Résistance, une histoire en évolution, Revue d'Histoire des Chemins de Fer*, n°34 (Spring, 2006).

Michel Ionascu, *Cheminots et cinéma: le représentation d'un groupe social dans le cinéma et l'audiovisuel français* (Paris: L'Harmattan, c2001).

R. W. Ireland, '"An Increasing Mass of Heathens in the Bosom of a Christian land": The Railway and Crime in the Nineteenth Century', *Continuity and Change*, vol.12, 1 (May 1997) 57–78.

Julian Jackson, *The Popular Front in France: Defending Democracy, 1934–38* (Cambridge: Cambridge University Press, 1988).

Julian Jackson, *France: The Dark Years 1940–1944* (Oxford: Oxford University Press, 2002).

Peter Jenkins, ed., *Railway Workers' Wages and Hours of Duty on the Prussian State Railways, 1890* (Pulborough: Dragonwheel, 1994).

Martin Johnes, 'Pigeon Racing and Working-class Culture in Britain, c. 1870–1950', *Cultural and Social History*, 4.3 (2007) 361–83.

Laurent Joly, *Vichy dans la 'Solution Finale': histoire du commissariat général aux questions juives* (Paris: Grasset, 2006).

Tony Judt, *Postwar: A History of Europe since 1945* (London: William Heinemann, 2005).

Jacques Julliard, *Fernand Pelloutier et les origines du syndicalisme d'action directe* (Paris: Editions du Seuil, 1971).

H. R. Kedward, *La Vie en Bleu: France and the French since 1900* (Penguin, 2006).

H. R. Kedward, 'Patriots and Patriotism in Vichy France', *Transactions of the Royal Historical Society*, vol. 32 (1982).

H. R. Kedward, *In Search of the Maquis Rural Resistance in Southern France, 1942–1944* (Oxford: Clarendon Press, 2003, c1993).

Robin D.G. Kelley, '"We Are Not What We Seem": Rethinking Black Working-Class Opposition in the Jim Crow South', *The Journal of American History*, 80.1 (Jun. 1993) 75–112.

Simon Kitson, 'Criminals or Liberators? French Public Opinion and the Allied Bombing of France, 1940–1945' in Claudia Baldoli, Andrew Knapp and Richard Overy, eds., *Bombing, States and Peoples in Western Europe 1940–1945* (London: Continuum, 2011).

Simon Kitson, 'The Police and the Deportation of Jews from the Bouches-du-Rhône in August and September 1942', *Modern and Contemporary France*, vol. 5, n° 3, Aug. 1997, 309–19.

Serge Klarsfeld, *Vichy-Auschwitz: La 'solution finale' de la question juive en France* (Paris: Fayard, 2001, c1993).

Annie Kriegel, *Réflexion sur les questions juives* (Paris: Hachette, 1984).

Annie Kriegel, *La grève des cheminots, 1920* (Paris: Armand Colin, 1988).

Françoise Laborde, *Ca va mieux en le disant* (Paris: J'ai lu, 2008).

Françoise Laborde, *Une histoire qui fait du bruit* (Paris: Fayard, 2011).

Pierre Laborie, *L'opinion Française sous Vichy* (Paris: Seuil, 1990).

Valérie Laisney Lauynay, *L'Exode des populations Bas-Normandes au cours de l'été 1944* (Caen: Centre de Recherche Histoire Quantitative, 2005).

Jochen von Lang, ed. *Eichmann Interrogated, Transcripts from the Archives of the Israeli Police* (London: The Botley Head Ltd, 1983).

Henri Lartilleux, *Le Réseau National des chemins de fer français: Histoire et Organisation* (1948).

James M. Laux, Review of Paul Durand, *La SNCF pendant la guerre* (1968), *The American Historical Review*, 75.1 (Oct. 1969) 139–40.

T. B. Lawrence and S. L. Robinson, 'Ain't Misbehavin: Workplace Deviance as Organizational Resistance', *Journal of Management*, 33 (Jun. 2007) 378–94.

Lucien Lazare, ed., *Dictionnaire des Justes de France* (Paris: Fayard, 2003).

Daniel Lee, *Pétain's Jewish Children: French Jewish Youth and the Vichy Regime, 1940–1942* (Oxford: Oxford University Press, 2014).

Pol-Jean Lefevre and Georges Cerbelaud, *Les Chemins de fer des origines à 1890* (Paris: Europe Editions, 1969).

James Lequeux, *François Arago, un savant généreux: physique et astronomie au XIXè siècle* (Paris: Observatoire de Paris, 2008).

Sylvie Lindeperg, 'L'opération cinématographique: Équivoques idéologiques et ambivalences narratives dans La Bataille du Rail', *Annales*, 51.4 (Jul.–Aug. 1996).

Alain Lipietz, *La SNCF et la Shoah: le procès G. Lipietz contre État et SNCF* (Paris: les Petits Matins, 2011).

Alain Lipietz, 'Léon Bronchart, juste, ouvrier et soldat' (22 Sep. 2007). Available at Lipietz.net.

Peter Longerich, *Holocaust: The Nazi Persecution and Murder of the Jews* (Oxford: Oxford University Press, 2010).

Yves Machefert-Tassin, 'Le bilan des bombardements aériens des installations ferroviaires en France, leurs conséquences stratégiques et humaines: tactiques incohérentes, résultats discutables, victimes civiles exorbitantes et destructions à long terme inutiles ?' in Polino, ed.,*Une entreprise pendant la guerre* (2001).

A. Marchand, *Les chemins de fer de l'Est et la guerre de 1914–1918*, (Paris: Berger-Levrault, 1924).

François Marcot, ed., *La Résistance et les Français, lutte armée et maquis* (Annales littéraires de l'Université de Franche-Comté, 1996).

François Marcot, 'Pour une sociologie de la Résistance: intentionnalité et fonctionnalité' in Antoine Prost, ed., *La Résistance, une histoire sociale* (Paris: les Editions de l'Atelier-Edition ouvrières, 1997).

François Marcot, Bruno Leroux and Christine Levisse-Touzé, eds., *Dictionnaire Historique de la Résistance* (Paris: Robert Laffont, 2006).

Michel Margairaz, 'La SNCF, l'Etat français, l'occupant et les livraisons de matériel: la collaboration ferroviaire d'Etat en perspective' in Polino, ed.,*Une entreprise pendant la guerre* (2001).

Michel Margairaz, *L'État, les finances et l'économie: histoire d'une conversion 1932–1952* (Paris: Comité pour l'histoire économique et financière, 1991).

Michael Marrus and Robert Paxton, *Vichy France and the Jews* (Stanford: Stanford University Press, 1995, c1981).

Michael Marrus, 'The Case of the French Railways and the Deportation of Jews in 1944,' David Bankier and Dan Michman, eds., *Holocaust and Justice: Representation and Historiography of the Holocaust in Post-War Trials* (Yad Vashem and Berghahn Books: Jerusalem, 2010), 245–64.

André Martel, 'Armées et chemins de fer en France de 1830 à 1918: pensée stratégique et emploi des forces armées' in *Armées et chemins de fer en France, Revue d'Histoire des Chemins de Fer*, 15 (Autumns, 1996).

Jean-Pierre Masseret, 'Ouverture du colloque' in Polino, ed., *Une entreprise pendant la guerre* (2001).

Tim Mason, *Nazism, Fascism and the Working Class* (Cambridge: Cambridge University Press, 1995).

Alfred Mierzejeski, *The Most Valuable Asset of the Reich: A History of the German National Railway, vol.2 , 1933–1945* (Chapel Hill: University of North Carolina Press, 2000).

Mark Mazower, *Hitler's Empire : How the Nazis Ruled Europe* (London: Allen Lane, 2008).

Robert Mencherini, *Guerre froide, grèves rouges: parti communiste, stalinisme et lutes sociales en France: les grèves 'insurrectionnalles' de 1947–1948* (Paris: Syllepse, 1998).

Alfred Mierzejeski, 'A Public Enterprise in the Service of Mass Murder: The Deutsche Reichsbahn and the Holocaust', *Holocaust Genocide Studies*, vol.15, n°1 (2001) 33–46.

Pierre Miquel, *L'exode: 10 mai–20 juin 1940* (Paris: Plon, 2003).

Alan Milward, *The New Order and the French Economy* (Oxford: Clarendon Press, 1970).

Philip Nord, *France's New Deal: From the Thirties to the Postwar Era* (Princeton; Woodstock: Princeton University Press, 2010).

Martin O'Shaughnessy, '*La Bataille du Rail*: Unconventional Form, Conventional Image?' in H. R. Kedward and Nancy Wood, eds., *The Liberation of France: Image and Event* (Oxford: Berg, 1995)15–27.

Sandra Ott, 'Duplicity, Indulgence and Ambiguity in Franco-German Relations, 1940–1946', *History and Anthropology*, 20.1 (2009) 57–77.

Sandra Ott, 'The Informer, the Lover and the Gift Giver: Female Collaborators in Pau 1940–1946', *French History*, 22.1 (2008) 94–114.

Richard Overy, *War and Economy in the Third Reich* (Oxford: Clarendon Press, 1994).

Richard Overy, *The Bombing War: Europe 1939–1945* (Allen Lane, 2013).

Mona Ozouf, 'Le Panthéon' in Pierre Nora, ed., *Les lieux de Mémoire*, vol.1 (Paris: Gallimard, 1984).

Jean Alcide Paroche, *Un Cheminot face aux technocrates à la SNCF* (Paris: La Pensée Universelle, 1976).

Robert O. Paxton, *Vichy France: Old Guard, New Order* (Toronto: Norton Library, 1975, c1972).

Denis Peschanski, *La France des camps: L'internement, 1938–1946* (Paris: Gallimard, 2002) 332–4.

Detlev Peukert, *Inside Nazi Germany: Conformity and Opposition in Everyday Life* (London: Batsford, 1987).

Jean-Paul Picaper, *Le crime d'aimer, les enfants du STO* (Paris: Syrtes, 2005).

Alessandro Portelli, 'What Makes Oral History Different' in Robert Perks and Alistair Thomson, eds., *The Oral History Reader* (London: Routledge, 1998) 63–74.

Marie-Noëlle Polino, John Barzman and Hervé Joly, eds., *Transports dans la France en guerre* (Mont-Saint-Aignan: Publications des Universités de Rouen et du Havre, 2007).

Marie-Noëlle Polino, ed., *Une entreprise pendant la guerre: la SNCF 1939–1945* (Paris: Presses Universitaires Françaises, 2001) all papers available at www.ahicf.com/ww2/actes.htm.

Marie-Noëlle Polino, 'La réquisition des cheminots pour le travail en Allemagne. Une étude de cas' in Chevandier and Dumas, eds., *Les entreprises françaises sous l'occupation* (2007) 155–74.

Renée Poznanski, *Les Juifs en France pendant la Seconde Guerre mondiale* (Paris: Hachette Littératures, 1997, c1994).

Renée Poznanski, *Propagandes et Persécutions: la Résistance et le 'problème juif', 1940–1944* (Paris: Fayard, 2008).

Antoine Prost, ed., *La Résistance, une histoire sociale* (Paris: les Editions de l'Atelier-Edition ouvrières, 1997).

Antoine Prost, Rémi Skoutelsky and Sonia Etienne, eds., *Aryanisation économique et restitutions* (Paris: Documentation française, 2000).

Rappoport 'Les procès contre l'Etat et la SNCF, "une justice attendue depuis 60 ans"' (3 Jul. 2007). Available at www.anciencombattant.com/article.cfm?id= 105196.

Georges Ribeill, 'L'accommodation sociale de la SNCF avec ses tutelles vichyssoise et allemande: résistance et/ou compromissions ?' in Polino, ed., *Une entreprise pendant la guerre* (2001).

Georges Ribeill, *Les Cheminots* (Paris: Editions La Découverte,1984).

Georges Ribeill, 'Les chantiers de la collaboration sociale des Fédérations légales des cheminots (1939–1944)', in Jean-Louis Robert, ed., 'Le Syndicalisme sous Vichy', *Le Mouvement Social*, n°158 (1992) 87–116.

Georges Ribeill, '*Résistance-Fer*, du "réseau" à l'association: une dynamique corporative intéressée?', *Revue d'histoire des chemins de fer*, 34 (2006). Available at http://rhcf.revues.org/534.

Georges Ribeill, 'Les cheminots reflétés aux miroirs de la pub', Actes du séminaire, *Les cheminots, images et représentations croisées* (2002–2005). Available at http://rhcf.revues.org/109#ftn11.

Georges Ribeill, 'Les Cheminots face à la lutte armée: les différenciations sociologiques de l'engagement résistant' in François Marcot, ed., *La Résistance et les Français, lutte armée et maquis* (Annales littéraires de l'Université de Franche-Comté, 1996) 71–81.

Georges Ribeill, 'Trafic sous contraintes et performances exceptionnelles des chemins de fer français: un bilan ambigü' in Marie-Noëlle Polino, John Barzman and Hervé Joly, eds., *Transports dans la France en guerre* (Mont-Saint-Aignan: Publications des Universités de Rouen et du Havre, 2007) 153–74.

Georges Ribeill, 'A propos du wagon couvert K, dit "wagon à bestiaux": de la réglementation militaires à ses détournements', *Historail*, n°4 (2008).

Georges Ribeill, 'SNCF et Déportations', *Historail*, 4 (Jan. 2008).

Jean-Pierre Richardot, *SNCF. Héros et salauds pendant l'Occupation* (Cherche Midi, 2012).

Jean-Louis Robert, ed., 'Le Syndicalisme sous Vichy', *Le Mouvement Social*, n°158 (1992).

François Rouquet, *L'Épuration dans l'administration française: agents de l'État et collaboration ordinaire* (Paris: CNRS, 1993).

Henry Rousso, 'L'Epuration en France: Une histoire inachevée', *Vingtième Siècle, Revue d'histoire*, n°33 (Jan.–Mar. 1992) 78–105.

Henry Rousso, *The Vichy Syndrome, History and Memory in France since 1944* (Cambridge, Mass: Harvard University Press, 1991, c1987).

Henry Rousso, *La hantise du passé* (Paris: Textuel, 1998).

Henry Rousso, 'Juger Le Passé', Florent Bayard, ed., *Le Génocide des Juifs entre Procès et Histoire (1943–2000)* (Bruxelles: Editions Complexe, 2000) 277.

Henry Rousso, 'Bilans et Perspectives' in Polino, ed., *Une entreprise pendant la guerre* (2001).

Guy Sabin, *Jean Bichelonne 1904–1944* (Paris: France-Empire, 1991).

James C. Scott, *Weapons of the Weak: Everyday Forms of Peasant Resistance* (New Haven, London: Yale University Press, 1985).

Michael Seidman, *Workers Against Work: Labor in Paris and Barcelona During the Popular Fronts* (Oxford: University of California Press, 1991).

Lowell S. Selling, 'Specific War Crimes', *The Journal of Criminal Law and Criminology*, 34.5 (1944) article 2.

Jacques Sémelin, *Unarmed Against Hitler, Civilian Resistance in Europe, 1939–1943*, (Westport, CT: Praeger Publisher, 1993, c1989).

Anne Simonon, *Le déshonneur dans la République: une histoire de l'indignité 1791–1958* (Paris: Grasset, 2008).

Timothy Snyder, *Bloodlands: Europe Between Hitler and Stalin* (London: Bodley Head, 2010).

Joe Starkey, 'The Silent Minority: Working Class Conservatism in Interwar France' in Ludivine Broch and Alison Carrol, eds., *France in the Era Global Wars, 1914–1945: Occupation, Politics, Empire and Entanglements* (London: Palgrave Macmillan, 2014) 111–32.

John F. Sweets, *Choices in Vichy France: The French Under Nazi Occupation* (Oxford: Oxford University Press, 1986).

Paul Michel Taillon, '"What We Want is Good, Sober Men": Masculinity, Respectability and Temperance in the Railroad Brotherhoods, c.1870–1910', *Journal of Social History*, 36.2 (2002) 319–38.

Lynne Taylor, *Between Resistance and Collaboration: Popular Protest in Northern France, 1940–45* (Basingstoke: Macmillan, 2000).

Lynne Taylor, 'The Black Market in Occupied Northern France, 1949–1944', *Journal of Contemporary history* , (1997) 153–76.

Pierre Thomas, *Des trains contre les Panzers: septembre* 1939–mai *1940* (La Voix du nord, 1999).

E.P. Thompson, *The Making of the English Working Class* (London: Gollancz, 1980).

Guy Thuillier, 'La pétition des mécaniciens et des chauffeurs des chemins de fer en 1871' *Le Mouvement Social*, 66 (Jan.–Mar. 1969) 65–88.

Selina Todd, *Young Women, Work and Family in England, 1918–1950* (Oxford: Oxford University Press, 2005).

Joan Tumblety, *Remaking the Male Body: Masculinity and the Uses of Physical Culture in Interwar and Vichy France* (Oxford: Oxford University Press, 2012).

Jean Vidalenc, *L'Exode de Mai–Juin 1940* (Paris: Presses Universitaires de France, 1957).

Xavier Vigna, *Histoire des ouvriers en France au XXe siècle* (Paris: Perrin, 2012).

Xavier Vigna, 'La mémoire de Pierre Sémard' in Serge Wolikow, *Pierre Semard: engagements, discipline et fidélité* (Paris: Cherche Midi, 2007) 261–84.

Fabrice Virgili, *Shorn Women: Gender and Punishment in Liberation France* (Oxford: Berg, 2002, c2000).

Fabrice Virgili, *Naître ennemi: les enfants de couples franco-allemands nés pendant la Seconde Guerre mondiale* (Paris: Payot, 2009).

Jean-Pierre Vittori, *Eux, Les STO* (Paris: Messidor/Temps Actuels, 1982).

Sophie Wahnich, ed., *Une histoire politique d'amnistie: études d'histoire, d'anthropologie et de droit* (Paris: Presses universitaires de France, 2007).

Lois A. West, 'Negotiating Masculinities in American Drinking Subcultures', *The Journal of Men's Studies*, 9.3 (2001) 371–92.

Annette Wieviorka, 'La Shoah, la SNCF et le juge', *L'Histoire*, 316 (Jan. 2007).

Michael Wildt, 'Generation of the Unbound: The Leadership Corps of the Reich Security Main Office', Paper presented at a lecture at the International Institute for Holocaust Research at Yad Vashem on 23 January 2002 (Jerusalem, Yad Vashem, 2002).

Serge Wolikow, ed., *Pierre Semard: engagements, discipline et fidélité* (Paris: Cherche Midi, 2007).

Serge Wolikow, 'Syndicalistes cheminots et images de la Résistance' Polino, ed., *Une entreprise pendant la guerre* (2001).

Limore Yagil, *L'Homme Nouveau et la Révolution Nationales de Vichy (1940–1944)* (Presses Universitaires de Septentrion, 1997).

Claire Zalc and Nicolas Mariot, *Face à la persecution: 991 Juifs dans la guerre* (Paris: Odile Jacob: Fondation pour la mémoire de la Shoah, 2010).

Theodor Zeldin, *France 1848–1945: Politics and Anger* (Oxford: Oxford University Press, 1979).

Index

Klarsfeld, Serge: 165, 171, 175, 184, 235
Knochen, Helmut: 183–184
Koenig, General: 228
Kohl Agreement: 160
Kommandantur: 74, 195, 199
Kornwestheim: 89
Kriegel, Annie: 3

Laborie, Pierre: 125
Labour Charter: *see* Charte du Travail
labour
   forced: 60–61, 112, 210
   laws: *see Forced Labour Service*
   mouvement: *see trade unions*
Lacombe, René: 150
Lagerhausen, Dr.: 78
Lambert, Raymond Raoul: 191
Lancaster, Burt: 229
landings: *see Allies*
Lang, Henri: 162n, 168–172, 174–175,
   178, 193, 194
Lanzmann, Claude: 231
Laon: 47
Laon-Soissons: 151
Latouche, Mr.: 163
Laude, Mr.: 90
Laurent, Fernand: 217
Laux, James M.: 228
Laval, Pierre:
   and aerial bombings: 151
   and cheminots/SNCF: 118, 161
   denunciation of: 129–130, 134–136
   government in interwar period: 33
   and Jewish deportations: 174, 184–185,
      189, 197n, 198n
   return to power: 80
Lawrence, T.B.: 111–112
Lazare, Lucien: 239
Lebrun, Robert: 77–78, 143, 155
Lee, Daniel: 10
Leeds: 29
Légion des volontaires français contre le
   Bolshévisme (LVF): 60
Légion d'Honneur: 168, 228
Legros, Louis: 212
Lemaire, Mr.: 163, 169
Lens: 47
Léon, Jean: 171
Lérouville: 201
Levallois: 176
Levi, Primo: 230
Lévi, Robert: 168–173, 175, 194
Lévy, Jean: 168–169
Lévy, Pierre: 169, 171
Lévy, Sadia: 176

Liaud, Roger: 64–66, 135
Libération: 236
Libération-Nord: 65
Lievin: 47, 153
Lille: 16, 41, 45, 47, 78, 113, 152, 202
Lille-Délivrance: 152, 202
Limoges: 189
Lindeperg, Sylvie: 224
Lipietz (family): 1, 191, 234, 239
Lipp, Bernard: 90
Livry: 128
locomotive: 18, 21, 28, 83, 85, 89, 124,
   130, 145, 155, 158, 183–184, 202,
   237–238
   locomotive driver/engineer: 20, 24, 28,
      84–85, 108, 143, 154, 163, 175
   handler: 55n, 107–108, 210–211
   train driver: 17, 25–26, 28, 81, 84, 107,
      154, 158, 237, 239
   auxiliary: 108–109, 210
London: 123, 148, 151, 223, 227
Longwy: 201
luggage: 48, 51, 103, 118, 189, 199
Luxemburg: 44
Lyautey, Hubert: 54
Lyon: 16, 23, 96, 128n, 173, 176, 189,
   209, 224
Lyon-Marseille: 172

Machefert-Tassin, Yves: 156
Maginot Line: 41
Maillé: 147
Maison Gamet: 198
Maly, Alfred: 207
Le Mans: 6
maquis: 107, 130, 153, 158, 198, 230 *see*
   also theft
masculinity: 13, 65, 105–106 *see also*
   German; patriarchy; theft
Marchendeau law: 167
Marcot, François: 124–125
Marcot, Nicolas: 10
Margairaz, Michel: 70, 234
Marrus, Michael: 3, 5, 10, 234
Marseille: 7, 23–25, 35, 79, 126, 128,
   133, 151, 158, 173n, 188, 196–197,
   199–200, 216, 218
Maryland: 1, 234–235
Masseret, Jean-Pierre: 70
martyr(dom): 2, 112, 130, 140 *see also*
   cheminots; communists
Maury, Mr.: 60
Mayer, René: 208–210, 213n
Mazower, Mark: 146
memorial: *see Shoah*

Union Nationale des Cadres Techniciens des
  Chemins de Fer: 220
Union Nationale des Syndicats Autonomes
  (UNSA): 4
United States: see America
United States Strategic Bombing Survey:
  91

Valence: 200
Valenciennes: 41, 47
Vallat, Xavier: 183, 185
Vallencien, Mr.: 199
Valmy: 131
Van Cleef, Roger: 89, 92
Var: 198
Varennes: 159
Veil, Simone: 235
Vénissieux: 188
Vény: 149
Vercors: 69
Verdun (battle of): 27, 45, 168
Le Vernet: 188–189
Verneuil: 61
Vesoul: 203
Veynes: 127
Vidalenc, Jean: 47–48, 186
La Vie du Rail: 228, 232
La Vie Ouvrière: 127, 129, 137, 140
Viel, Adolphe: 48
Vigna, Xavier: 54, 195
Villeneuve: 176
Villeneuve Saint Georges: 126, 198
Villerupt: 47
La Villette: 133
Violette, Jean: 89
Vitry: 127, 147
Voix du Nord: 149
La Voix du Peuple: 138
Les voyages de Gulliver (1944): 225

Wagner, Gauletier: 187
Wasier, Rémi: 56, 58
Warsaw: 41
Weber, Paul Eugène: 211
Weingand: 89–90
Werth, Léon: 68
Wiesbaden: see Armistice 1940
Wieviorka, Annette: 191, 234
wine: see alcohol
Wodli, Georges: 137, 140, 227
Wolikow, Serge: 120
Wolkowitsch, Jean-Louis: 176
women: see also Deutsche Reichsbahn; trade
  unions
  in Germany: 87, 91

as wives: 31–32, 42, 55, 93–94, 143,
  177–178
working class: 49, 100, 128, 197–198
working in railways: 13, 25, 42, 49–50,
  82, 133, 210
workers (types): see also Belgium; Deustche
  Reichsbahn; German; Germany;
  industrial; Italy; North Africa; Paris;
  Soviet Union; women
agricultural: 17, 64
aerial: 50, 99n
artisans: 22, 24
automobile: 24, 50, 54
bakers: 22, 197, 216
British navvies: 17
cloth merhcants: 23
factory: 24, 42, 150, 199
farmers/farmhands: 17, 106
foreign: 17, 79, 161n, 166n
industrial workers: 17, 31
merchants: 106
metal workers: 17, 64, 128n, 134, 196,
  198
milliners: 23
miners: 19, 24, 28n, 43, 150, 198
postmen: 18, 24, 48, 113
printers: 23
retailers: 106
sailors: 19
stationers: 23
tailors: 22
typesetters: 24
wholesalers: 106
wine merchant: 118
worker-gardener: 31
working class/workers: see also deportation;
  Forced Labour Service; Germany;
  grievances: moral; Occupation; Paris;
  Pétain; salary; strike; theft; working hours
archives: 6–7
attempts to control: 113
betraying: 130
cheminots distinct from: 14–15, 24, 26,
  28, 38, 141, 163
cities: 30
and clandestine press/tracts: 126–134,
  138
complaints/dissatisfaction of: 19, 35, 41,
  101, 105
conditions: 18–24, 33, 66, 91, 94, 133,
  198, 200, 215, 217, 221
conservatism: 9
criticism of: 43
historiography of: 11–12
interwar period: 33, 35, 40